The Uí Chellaig lords of Uí Maine and Tír Maine

For my wife Danielle,
son Patrick, and daughter Grace

Dedicated to the memory
of Phyllis Judge (née Hayes)

The Uí Chellaig lords of Uí Maine and Tír Maine

An archaeological and landscape exploration of a later medieval inland Gaelic lordship

Daniel Patrick Curley

FOUR COURTS PRESS

Typeset in 10.5pt on 13.5pt AdobeGaramondPro by
Carrigboy Typesetting Services for
FOUR COURTS PRESS LTD
7 Malpas Street, Dublin 8, Ireland
www.fourcourtspress.ie
and in North America for
FOUR COURTS PRESS
c/o IPG, 814 N Franklin St., Chicago, IL 60610.

© the author and Four Courts Press 2024

A catalogue record for this title is available from the British Library.

ISBN 978-1-80151-091-2

All rights reserved. Without limiting the rights under copyright reserved alone, no part of this publication may be reproduced, stored in or introduced into a retrieval system, or transmitted, in any form or by any means (electronic, mechanical, photocopying, recording or otherwise), without the prior written permission of both the copyright owner and the publisher of this book.

SPECIAL ACKNOWLEDGMENT

This publication has been supported financially by Galway County Council Heritage Office, Kelly Clans Association, National Monuments Service, Roscommon County Council Heritage Office.

Printed in Poland
by L&C Printing Group, Krakow.

Contents

LIST OF ILLUSTRATIONS		vii
LIST OF ABBREVIATIONS		xiii
ACKNOWLEDGMENTS		xv

1 *Introduction*   1
   Landscape setting   1
   Archaeological methods and techniques   5
   Historical sources   6
   Archaeological and historical work on Uí Maine   8
   Conclusions   9

2 *Historical background*   10
   The early medieval origins of the Uí Chellaig   11
   The Uí Chellaig and the lordship of Tír Maine, *c.*1100–1235   16
   The arrival of the Anglo-Normans to Connacht until the death of the Brown Earl, 1235–1333   21
   The late medieval Uí Maine lordship: the height of Ó Cellaig power   30
   The slow decline of the Ó Cellaig lordship   33
   Conclusions   38

3 *The landscape and economy of Uí Maine*   40
   The physical landscape   40
   Communication routes through the lordship   50
   Focal points of assembly and gatherings   54
   The economy of the lordship   56
   Resources derived from the natural environment   66
   Wealth and its expression   68
   Conclusions   76

4 *Settlement archaeology*   77
   High medieval castles in Uí Maine   77
   Ringforts and cashels   88
   High-cairn *crannóga*   91
   The *bódhún*   93

	Gaelic moated sites	94
	The *pailís* sites of later medieval Uí Maine	100
	Tower house castles	104
	Conclusions	106
5	*Lakeland elite settlement in later medieval Uí Maine*	108
	Lough Croan, Co. Roscommon	108
	Callow Lough, Co. Galway	129
	Ballaghdacker Lough, Co. Galway	153
	Conclusions	164
6	*Riverine elite settlement in later medieval Uí Maine*	165
	An Ó Cellaig *cenn áit* at Athlone	165
	Galey, Co. Roscommon	167
	Athleague, Co. Roscommon	193
	Conclusions	203
7	*Elite settlement sited on major roadways in later medieval Uí Maine*	205
	Aughrim, Co. Galway	205
	The fifteenth- and sixteenth-century elite settlement sites of the wider Ó Cellaig lordship	216
	A late medieval routeway-sited Ó Cellaig castle elsewhere in the lordship	232
	Conclusions	232
8	*Understanding medieval Gaelic Ireland through the lens of the Ó Cellaig lordship*	234
	The high medieval elite settlement forms of the Uí Chellaig	235
	The late medieval settlement landscape	256
	The landscape and economy of the later medieval Ó Cellaig lordship	263
BIBLIOGRAPHY		269
INDEX		291

Illustrations

PLATES

2.1	Temple Kelly, Clonmacnoise.	17
3.1	Woods of *Bruigheol*.	48
3.2	Lisseenamanragh townland, Co. Roscommon.	59
3.3	A wall painting: Gaelic lord on horseback, from Clare Island Cistercian Abbey, Co. Mayo.	63
3.4	Iron fish hook from Loughbown I.	68
3.5	Medieval coin, Gortnacrannagh, Co. Roscommon.	69
4.1	Galey Castle, Co. Roscommon.	87
4.2	Cuilleenirwan moated site, Co. Roscommon.	96
4.3	Cuilleenirwan moated site, detail.	97
5.1	Punch-dressed stones, Turrock House, Co. Roscommon.	112
5.2	Aerial photograph, Lough Croan, Co. Roscommon.	119
5.3	'Fair Hill': Taghboy, Co. Roscommon.	126
5.4	The high-cairn *crannóg*, Callow Lough, Co. Galway.	136
5.5	(a) Large stones around the Callow Lough *crannóg*; (b) Noost or jetty features.	136
5.6	Interior view of the much modified castle wall at Callow Castle.	143
5.7	Punch-dressed stones incorporated into the modern farm buildings on the site of Callow Castle.	143
5.8	Aerial photographs of Kilconnell Friary and infields.	149
5.9	Fourteenth- or fifteenth-century canopied tomb in the chancel at Kilconnell Friary.	150
5.10	Stony Island, Ballaghdacker Lough, Co. Galway.	158
5.11	Sally Island, Ballaghdacker Lough.	161
6.1	Athlone Castle.	166
6.2	Galey Bay, Co. Roscommon.	168
6.3	Details in the earthwork remains at Galey Bay.	173
6.4	Ground image of the internal remains in Galey tower house.	181
6.5	The medieval church remains in Portrunny townland, Co. Roscommon.	189
6.6	View over Portrunny Bay.	190
6.7	Fortified house at Athleague Castle, Co. Roscommon.	197
6.8	Vertical aerial image of the fortified house now known as Athleague Castle.	198
6.9	One example of the punch-dressed stone from within the fortified house of Athleague Castle.	199

6.10	The silted up and filled in remnants of the flanking defensive section of the *bódhún* ditch at Athleague Castle.	201
7.1	Aughrim Castle, Co. Galway.	209
7.2	Outer enclosure ditch surrounding Aughrim Castle.	211
7.3	Presumed entrance into the inner ward of Aughrim Castle.	213
7.4	The early fifteenth-century tomb in the presbytery of the Cistercian Monastery of Abbeyknockmoy, Co. Galway.	220
7.5	Depiction of the 'Three Living and Three Dead Kings', Abbeyknockmoy, Co. Galway.	221
7.6	Barnaderg Castle, Co. Galway, sixteenth-century tower house of the Uí Chellaig.	223
7.7	Monivea Castle, Co. Galway.	224
7.8	The remains of Garbally tower house, Co. Galway.	226
7.9	Original pointed doorway of Garbally Castle, Co. Galway.	227
7.10	The two light ogee-headed window at Garbally tower house.	227
7.11	Site of Gallagh Castle.	229

FIGURES

1.1	Baronies, rivers, lakes and elevations which comprise the Uí Maine study area, as per its extents in the fifteenth century.	2
2.1	Map of Hy Many, with some of the adjacent territories in the counties of Galway and Roscommon. Taken from *The tribes and customs of Hy Many*.	11
2.2	Approximate territorial extents of the sept families related to Uí Maine, *c*.800.	13
2.3	Territorial extents of Tír Maine, Soghan/Uí Maine and Machaire Connacht, *c*.1100.	16
2.4	Dioceses and archdioceses of Ireland.	20
2.5	The territorial extents of the King's Cantreds.	22
2.6	The parishes in the King's Cantreds in which land was granted to English (Anglo-Norman) tenants.	25
2.7	Reconstructed extents of Uí Maine and Tír Maine during the high medieval period, with principal locations mentioned in the text indicated.	29
2.8	Reconstructed extents of the Ó Cellaig lordship of Uí Maine by the beginning of the fifteenth century, with principal locations mentioned in the text indicated.	33
2.9	Composite map outlining the widest extents of the Ó Cellaig lordship of Uí Maine in the fifteenth century, in contrast with the conflated boundaries of Uí Maine, as illustrated by O'Donovan in 1843.	39

Illustrations

3.1	Griffith's Bogs Commission map, north-west and north-east of Ballinasloe, Co. Galway at the beginning of the nineteenth century.	41
3.2	Soil association map derived from Teagasc soil classifications, with National Monuments Service data plotted on top.	42
3.3	Section of Browne's *Map of the province of Connaught* (1591) indicating the *Feadha* of Athlone, at the beginning of the seventeenth century.	44
3.4	A graphical representation of the townland names that denote woodland and difficult land in Tír Maine, consistent with the historical and cartographic attestations to the wooded and treacherous *Feadha* of Athlone, woods of Athleague and *Bruigheol*.	45
3.5	Map of the study area and beyond, Boazio's *Irlandiæ accvrata descriptio* (1606).	47
3.6	Map of the study area, Speed's *The theatre of the empire of Great Britaine …* (1611).	47
3.7	The reconstructed woodlands of Uí Maine, based on the late medieval/early modern cartographic sources, and the surviving toponymy.	49
3.8	Medieval routeways through high medieval Uí Maine and Tír Maine, with the principal settlements from the text indicated.	51
3.9	Location of the assembly and inauguration landscapes.	55
3.10	Location of cattle-related townland names in relation to Ó Cellaig lordly centres.	61
3.11	Art Mór Mac Murchadha Caomhánach riding to meet the earl of Gloucester, Jean Creton's *Histoire du roy d'Angleterre Richard II*.	64
3.12	Reconstruction illustration of the Hospital of the Crutched Friars at Rindoon, *c.*1500, after its rebuilding under Ó Cellaig patronage.	73
4.1	The locations of the *caistél* fortifications constructed by Toirrdelbach Ó Conchobair during his twelfth-century reign as king of Connacht.	79
4.2	1st edition Ordnance Survey map illustrating the number of islets that made up the fording place of *Áth Nadsluaigh*.	81
4.3	Reconstruction of former course of the River Suck at Ballinasloe in the mid-nineteenth century, as well as the proposed location of *caistél Dún Leodha*.	82
4.4	LiDAR visualization of the earthwork remains at Dundonnell Castle, Co. Roscommon.	84
4.5	The Anglo-Norman baronial settler and royal castles in the study area.	85
4.6	LiDAR visualization of Cuilleenirwan moated site, and its proximity to 'Fair Hill'.	95
4.7	Topographical plan and cross-section of Cuilleenirwan moated site, Co. Roscommon.	95
4.8	Moated sites within the study area.	99

4.9	Location of the *pailís* sites in Tír Maine and Uí Maine.	101
4.10	Bogs Commission map of the district around Pallas townland and Clonbrock Demesne, Co. Galway.	102
4.11	Location of Cornapallis townland, Co. Roscommon.	103
4.12	Distribution map of the surviving tower house castles located within the Ó Cellaig lordship study area in *c*.1534.	105
5.1	Location of Lough Croan turlough within Tír Maine.	109
5.2	Lisnagavragh Fort.	110
5.3	Contoured topographical plan and cross-section of Lisnagavragh Fort.	111
5.4	Contoured topographical plan and cross-section of Liswilliam Fort.	113
5.5	The townland names of the Lough Croan *cenn áit*.	114
5.6	Extents of a digitally reflooded Lough Croan turlough, with the water level raised to 69m OD, recreating the former lake.	118
5.7	Contoured topographical plan and cross-section of the target location of Illaunamona, derived from LiDAR data.	120
5.8	Earth Resistance survey conducted in 10m x 10m grids.	121
5.9	Magnetic Susceptibility survey conducted in 10m x 10m grids.	122
5.10	Summary interpretation of the combination of topographical data and remote sensing investigations undertaken at the island on Lough Croan.	123
5.11	LiDAR DTM of the Tullyneeny landscape, indicating the substantial, but unrecorded bivallate *ráth* in the western part of Tullyneeny townland.	127
5.12	Summary of the Lough Croan case study, with principal locations outlined.	128
5.13	Location of Callow Lough within the *oireacht* of Tuahacalla – *Túath Caladh*, in the medieval *trícha cét* of Uí Maine in modern east Galway.	129
5.14	Section of Browne's *Map of the province of Connaught*, noting Callow Lough (1591).	132
5.15	Boazio's *Irlandiæ accvrata descriptio* noting 'Loughkelli' (1606); Speed's *The theatre of the empire of Great Britaine: presenting an exact geography of the kingdom of England, Scotland, Ireland* … (1611) noting 'Lough Kelly'.	132
5.16	Orthographic image of Callow Lough and environs, Co. Galway.	133
5.17	Contoured topographical plan and cross-section of Lisnagry Fort.	134
5.18	Plan of Callow Lough *crannóg*.	137
5.19	Flood mapping of Callow Lough, Co. Galway, based on survey work undertaken by the Office of Public Works.	138
5.20	Cross-section of the wet ditch across the promontory at Callow Lough, and the location of the cross-section.	139
5.21	Composite orthophotograph and DEM image of the southern shore of Callow Lough.	140

Illustrations　　　　　　　　　　　　　　　　　　　　　　　　　　　　　　　xi

5.22	Plan of the extents of Callow Castle as they survive today.	142
5.23	Lisfineel Fort.	146
5.24	Some of the principal townland names surrounding Kilconnell and Callow Lough, Co. Galway, and an interpretation based upon available source material.	147
5.25	Summary of the Callow Lough and Kilconnell case study.	151
5.26	Location of Ballaghdacker Lough in the *oireacht* of *Túath Átha Liaig*, close to the northern boundary of Tír Maine.	154
5.27	Orthophotograph of Ballaghdacker Lough and its environs, Co. Galway.	156
5.28	Contoured topographical plan and cross-section of Cornacask ringfort.	156
5.29	The probable moated site on the eastern shore of Ballaghdacker Lough.	157
5.30	Plan of Stony Island *crannóg* and levelled probable moated site, both located within the limits of Ballaghdacker townland.	159
5.31	Plan of Sally Island *crannóg*, with a potential dry-land service site evident 320m to the north-east.	160
5.32	Summary of the Athleague and Ballaghdacker Lough case study, with principal locations outlined, including Cornapallis *pailís* site.	163
6.1	The principal locations to be discussed in the Galey Bay case study, located in the *oireacht* of 'the Heyny' within the *trícha cét* of Tír Maine.	169
6.2	Plan of the promontory fort at Galey Bay.	175
6.3	Summary plan of the identified archaeological remains at the Ó Cellaig *cenn áit* of Galey Bay.	177
6.4	Reconstruction drawing of the Galey Bay *cenn áit* of the Uí Chellaig, conjecturally as it would have appeared in the mid-fourteenth century.	178
6.5	Topographical plan, Topographic profile, and Electrical Resistivity Tomography survey results at Galey.	179
6.6	Reconstruction drawing of the tower house castle at Galey Bay, Co. Roscommon.	182
6.7	Reconstruction drawing of the Galey Bay *cenn áit* of the Uí Chellaig, conjecturally as it would have appeared in the late medieval period.	183
6.8	Map of the merged OSi and TII LiDAR topographical datasets, highlighting the distribution of the unrecorded earthwork sites visible on the DTM.	184
6.9	Boazio's *Irlandiæ accvrata descriptio* (1606) highlights a settlement near the western shore of Lough Ree as 'B. Gally' – *Baile na Gáile*.	185
6.10	The former approach to Galey, and associated low relief features.	187
6.11	Summary of the Galey Bay case study, with the principal locations outlined.	192
6.12	Location of Athleague in the *oireacht* of *Túath Átha Liaig*, close to the northern boundary of Tír Maine.	193

6.13	Image of Athleague Castle in its wider landscape setting, taken from the Strafford Survey map *c.*1636.	200
6.14	Bog Commission map of the district of Athleague and Ballaghdacker Lough.	200
6.15	The wet ditch which surrounded the site of Athleague Castle, as per the Cassini 6-inch (a) and Historic 25-inch (b) maps.	201
6.16	*Bódhún* of Athleague, as indicated from the OS Historic 25-inch map.	202
6.17	Summary of the Athleague and Ballaghdacker Lough case studies, with principal locations outlined.	203
7.1	The location of Aughrim within the *oireacht* of Tuahavriana, within the *trícha cét* of Uí Maine.	206
7.2	Section of Browne's *Map of the province of Connaught* (1591).	207
7.3	Site of Aughrim Castle in the wider east Galway landscape.	208
7.4	Contoured topographical plan and cross-section of the site of Aughrim Castle.	210
7.5	Schematic plan of Aughrim Castle, derived from LiDAR data, and an interpretation of the elevation data.	212
7.6	Sketch of the Battle of Aughrim, illustrated by Jacob Richards, *c.*1691.	213
7.7	Magnetic Gradiometry survey at Aughrim Castle.	214
7.8	Summary interpretation of the remains at Aughrim Castle, Co. Galway.	215
7.9	Aerial image and cross-section of the largest enclosure recorded for Tiaquin Demesne townland, the most likely candidate for the 1401-attested *longphort* of Maolsechlainn Ó Cellaig at Tiaquin.	219
7.10	Contoured topographical plan of the area immediately surrounding Garbally Castle, Co. Galway.	225
7.11	Plan of the surviving elements of the ground and first floors of Garbally Castle tower house.	225
7.12	Contoured topographical plan and cross-section of the earthwork remains of Gallagh Castle.	228
7.13	Section of Browne's *Map of the province of Connaught* (1591) for the barony of Tiaquin.	228
7.14	Summary of the Tiaquin and Abbeyknockmoy case study area, with the principal locations outlined.	230

Abbreviations

AC	*Annála Connacht: the annals of Connacht, AD 1224–1544*, Freeman, A.D. (ed.) 1944. Dublin
Acallam	*Tales of the elders of Ireland*. Dooley, A., and Roe, H. (trans.) 1999. Oxford's World Classics, Oxford: Oxford University Press
ACl.	*Annals of Clonmacnoise*, Ó Muraíle, N. (ed.) 2022. Dublin
Acts Privy Council	*Acts of the privy council of England*, Vol. I–XXXII. Dasent, J.R. (ed.) 1890–1907. London
AFM	*Annala rioghachta Eireann: Annals of the kingdom of Ireland, by the Four Masters, from the earliest period to the year 1616.* O'Donovan, J. (ed.) 1856. Dublin
ALC	*The annals of Lough Cé*, 2 vols. Hennessy, W.M. (ed.) 1871. London
AT	'The annals of Tigernach', Stokes, W. (ed. and trans.), *Revue Celtique*, 16 (1895), 374–419
AU	*Annála Uladh, Annals of Ulster*, 4 vols. Hennessy, W.M. and MacCarthy, B. (eds) 1887–1901. Dublin
AU MacN	*The annals of Ulster*, Mac Airt, S. and Mac Niocaill, G. (eds) 1983. Dublin
Cal. Just. Rolls Ire.	*Calendar of the justiciary rolls or proceedings in the court of the justiciar of Ireland, preserved in the Public Record Office of Ireland*, 3 vols. Mills, J., and Griffiths, M.C. (eds) 1905–14. Dublin
Cal. Ormond Deeds	*Calendar of Ormond deeds*, 6 vols. Curtis, E. (ed.) 1932–43. Dublin
CDI	*Calendar of documents relating to Ireland*, Sweetman, H.S. (ed.) 5 vols, 1875–86. London
CIRCLE	*A calendar of Irish chancery letters, c.1244–1509*. Crooks, P. (ed.) 2012. Dublin: Trinity College
Clonfert	*A calendar of papal registers relating to Clonfert diocese*. Larkin, P. (ed.) 2016. Lettertec
Compossicion	*The compossicion booke of Conought*. Freeman, A.D. (ed.) 1936. Dublin
CSPI	*Calendar of the state papers relating to Ireland, of the reigns of Henry VIII, Edward VI, Mary and Elizabeth*, 5 vols (1509–96). Hamilton, H.C. (ed.) 1860–90. London
	Calendar of the state papers relating to Ireland, of the reigns of Henry VIII, Edward VI, Mary, and Elizabeth, 5 vols (1596–1601). Atkinson, E.G. (ed.) 1893–1905. London

FÉGH	'Filidh Éreann Go Haointeach: William Ó Ceallaigh's Christmas feast to the poets of Ireland, A.D. 1351.' Knott, E. (ed. and trans.) *Ériu*, 5 (1911), 50–69
Fiants	*Irish fiants of the Tudor sovereigns 1521–1603*, 4 vols. Nicholls, K.W. (ed.) 1994. Dublin
Foedera	*Rymer's Foedera*, vol. 1. Rymer, T. (ed.) 1739. London
Genealogies	'Genealogical tables'. In Moody T.W., Martin, F.X., and Byrne, F.J. (eds) *A new history of Ireland IX: maps, genealogies, lists – A companion to Irish history, Part II*, 121–76. Oxford: Oxford University Press
Haliday Privy Council	*The manuscripts of Charles Haliday, Esq., of Dublin: acts of the privy council of Ireland, 1556–1571*. Haliday, C., Ussher, W., Gilbert, J.T., (eds) 1897. London
La Geste	*The deeds of the Normans in Ireland: La geste des Engleis en Yrlande.* Mullally, E. (ed.) 2019. Dublin: Four Courts Press
MIA	*Miscellaneous Irish annals*, AD *1114–1437*, Ó hInnse, S. (ed.) 1947. Dublin
Nósa	'Nósa Ua Maine: "The customs of the Uí Mhaine."' Russell, P. (ed.) 2000. In Charles Edwards, T.M., Owen, M.E., and Russell, P. (eds) *The Welsh king and his court*, 527–51. Cardiff
Ó CGF i and ii	'The Ó Ceallaigh rulers of Uí Mhaine – a genealogical fragment, c.1400: Part I.' Ó Muraíle, N. (ed.) 2008. *Journal of the Galway Archaeological and Historical Society*, 60, 32–77
	'The Ó Ceallaigh rulers of Uí Mhaine – a genealogical fragment, c.1400: Part II.' Ó Muraíle, N. (ed.) 2010. *Journal of the Galway Archaeological and Historical Society*, 62, 51–77.
OS Letters, Galway	*Ordnance Survey letters Galway: edited with an introduction by Michael Herity MRIA*. Herity, M. (ed.) 2009. Dublin
OS Letters, Rosc.	*Ordnance Survey letters Roscommon: edited with an introduction by Michael Herity MRIA*. Herity, M. (ed.) 2010. Dublin
pers. comm.	personal communication
Reg. Clon.	'The Registry of Clonmacnoise; with notes and introductory remarks'. O'Donovan, J. (ed.) 1857. *Journal of the Kilkenny and South-East of Ireland Archaeological Society*, new series, 1:2, 444–460.
s.a.	*sub anno*
Táth aoinfhir	'Táth aoinfhir ar iath Maineach' in Hoyne, M. forthcoming. 'Uilliam Ó Ceallaigh, Gairm na Nollag 1351 agus stair eacnamaíoch fhilíocht na scol.'
Tribes	*The tribes and customs of Hy-Many, commonly Called O'Kelly's Country, now first published from the Book of Lecan, a manuscript in the library of the Royal Irish Academy*. O'Donovan, J. (ed.) 1843. Dublin

Acknowledgments

I would first like to thank my PhD supervisor, Dr Kieran O'Conor, for his great interest, knowledge and enthuasiam for my research, and of his willingness to bring me along this journey with patience, insight, mentorship and friendship. It was a real pleasure to be able to explore this topic with your encouragement behind me. I am very grateful to Dr Carleton Jones, as Head of Department for his encouragement, and his willingness to be my academic reader. I would also like to thank the rest of the faculty in the Department of Archaeology, for their help and advice, particularly, Conor Newman, Joe Fenwick, Dr Stefan Bergh, Professor Elizabeth FitzPatrick and Dr Maggie Ronayne.

I would like to thank my fellow postgraduate colleagues for their assistance, discussions and friendship throughout the course of my doctoral research, particularly Frank 'Jay' Hall, Chelsea Ryan, Kylie Crowder, Marcus Byrne, Enda O'Flaherty and Dr Peter Casby. Your help and collegiality will not be forgotten, and it was great to share this journey with you all.

I would like to acknowledge all of the people who assisted me in achieving my goal. Firstly, I must extend my gratitude to Mike McCarthy, Elaine Conroy, Kevin Barton of Landscape and Geophysical Services (LGS), Martin A. Timoney, Mary B. Timoney, Dr Christy Cunniffe, Dr Nollaig Ó Muraíle, Dr Katharine Simms, Kenneth Nicholls, an tOllamh Máirín Ní Dhonnchadha, Colmán Ó Raghallaigh, Dr Mícheál Hoyne and Dr Rory Sherlock for their time, for sharing their work and knowledge, and for their willingness to discuss my developing research.

I would like to thank all of those in the communities throughout the study area, who gave their time, facilitated access, and shared local knowledge. These include Noel Hoare (who also shared a wealth of information provided by Tom Kelly RIP), Mike Gacquin, Dean and Pauline Kelly, Paddy Naughton and Fr Gerard Geraghty PP, Brendan and Bernard Naughton, Joe Callahan, and Denis and Joshua Judge, the Naughton, McDermott, and Crofton families, Mary and Eugene Dwyer, James Moran and Sean Treacy, and Carl Bryer.

I am also very grateful to those who generously funded the research and this publication, including the Irish Research Council, the National Monuments Service, the Royal Irish Academy, Nollaig Feeney (Roscommon County Council), Marie Mannion (Galway County Council) and Joe Kelly (Kelly Clan Association).

Finally, I would like to express my deepest gratitude to my family, without whose support and patience, this work would not have been possible. To my wonderful wife Danielle, our amazing boy Patrick, and our sweet baby daughter Grace, thank you for always being there as I juggled home with work and research, always with a smile on your faces and love in your eyes. To my parents, Danny and Josephine, and my siblings, Aishling and Niall, thank you for your constant kind words and quiet encouragement. None of this would have been achieved without my family by my side.

CHAPTER ONE

Introduction

Many Irish archaeologists, historians and historical geographers have some knowledge of the Gaelic-Irish Ó Cellaig (O'Kelly) lordship of Uí Maine as either a subject or a territorial unit. This limited familiarity is at least partly due to the fact that John O'Donovan's mid-nineteenth-century translation and edition of *The tribes and customs of Hy-Many, commonly called O'Kelly's Country*, collated and published much information on the lordship (O'Donovan (trans. and ed.) 1843). This detailed early work seems to have caused many scholars erroneously to believe that a lot was known about the Uí Chellaig lordship of Uí Maine and, hence, the whole subject needed little in the way of further focused study. That no in-depth modern study has ever been published on the later medieval lordship of Uí Maine has led to many flawed conclusions and statements about the Uí Chellaig and their territory in eastern Connacht. The boundaries of Uí Maine at any stage in its history have never been truly defined, other than a vague understanding by scholars that the lordship covered a wide expanse of east Galway and south Roscommon. There seems to be a lack of understanding, too, that these boundaries did not remain static during the later medieval period and changed through time due to shifting circumstances. Despite the excellent preservation of archaeological monuments today in this region, little is known about the settlement sites associated with the Uí Chellaig and their sub-lords, or the lifestyle and economy of the people who lived in them.

LANDSCAPE SETTING

The study area is routinely defined, rather ambiguously, as south Roscommon and much of east Galway. The precise extents of the lordship will be discussed more fully later, but for the moment 'O'Kelly Country' is broadly consistent, at its greatest extent in the fifteenth century, with the baronies of Athlone and Moycarn, Co. Roscommon, and Clonmacnowen, Kilconnell, Killian and Tiaquin, Co. Galway (Fig. 1.1). The combined area of these six baronies is *c.*1,705.9km².

The landscape character of this region is mixed, with substantial zones of peatland throughout, between which are located tracts of riverine pastures, grazing land, low hills and generally undulating grassland. The underlying bedrock is primarily Carboniferous limestones. As a result, the soil composition of the agriculturally suitable areas are made up of a range of limestone tills, a soil type that contains an abundance in soil nutrients very complementary to high-quality livestock production

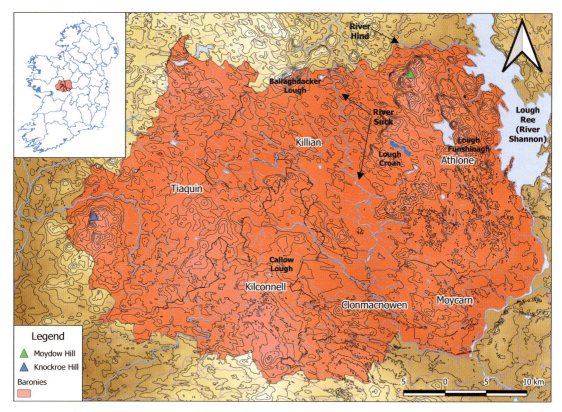

Figure 1.1 Baronies, rivers, lakes and elevations that comprise the territory known as Uí Maine, as per its extents in the fifteenth century, when the later medieval Ó Cellaig lordship was at its most powerful.

(Collins 2016, 2; O'Conor 2018, xxviii–xxix). This is borne out in the region's traditional agricultural practices, which centre on cattle and sheep production. The best farmland is in south Co. Roscommon, in the district north of the villages of Dysart and Brideswell, up to the banks of the River Hind, south of Roscommon town. By contrast, the most marginal land exists in pockets in the very far south of Roscommon, as well as considerable sections west of the River Suck in Co. Galway. Large tracts of peatland dominate, particularly in Killian, Clonmacnowen and Tiaquin baronies, resulting today in smaller farm sizes and meandering communication routes in places.

This region is predominantly flat and gentle in topography, served only by the occasional elevation. The highest point on the Roscommon side is Moydow Hill, which measures 137m OD (*Ordnance Datum*), while the highest prominence in the Galway part of the study area is Knockroe, which stands at 157m OD. Rather than elevated locations serving as the region's most prominent physical features, instead it

Introduction

is the rivers and lakes that define it. The eastern limits are bounded by the River Shannon and the western shore of Lough Ree, with a surface area of 105km². The value of Lough Ree and the River Shannon as economic resources and communication routes is well-attested in the historical sources and is discussed later. As it continues south beyond Athlone, the Shannon forms the eastern and some of the southern extents of the study area, until it meets with its major tributary, the River Suck, near Shannonbridge and then proceeds further south on its course.

The other major river is the River Suck, which serves today over much of its course as the administrative boundary between Co. Galway and Co. Roscommon. Interestingly, in the period under investigation, this was not the case and the lordship straddled both sides of the river, particularly in the late medieval period. Nevertheless, the River Suck was a key resource, and was utilized in a number of places and for a number of purposes. The Shannon and the Suck regularly flood their banks in winter but the stretches of low land beside these rivers, known as the Callows, provide excellent seasonal grazing land in summer (Meehan and Parkes 2014, 50–1). A number of smaller tributaries feed these two major rivers. The Suck is fed primarily by the Shiven, Castlegar, Cloonlyon and Bunowen/Ahascragh Rivers, which contribute to the more waterlogged conditions and peaty soils that dominate sections of east Galway. Conversely, there is only one noteworthy regional tributary to the River Shannon, apart from the River Suck itself. The River Hind runs broadly west to east across the middle section of Co. Roscommon, before emptying into Lough Ree. The river serves as the border between the baronies of Athlone and Ballintober South, the boundary between the medieval *trícha céta* of Machaire Connacht and Tír Maine.

A number of lakes also dot the study area. In Roscommon, Lough Funshinagh is the most substantial of these bodies of water, with a surface area measuring 3.8km². Two further lakes, Ballaghdacker or Hollygrove Lake near Athleague and Callow Lough or Lough Acalla, near Kilconnell, both Co. Galway, are much smaller in surface area, measuring 0.208km² and 0.141km² respectively. A former lake, now a turlough, known as Lough Croan, is located in the parishes of Dysart, Taghboy and Tisrara, Co. Roscommon. The surface area of Lough Croan measures approximately 1.440km².

The main settlements can be broken down into three categories: towns, villages and 'hamlets'. Two towns, Athlone, Co. Westmeath (population 2016, 21,351) and Ballinasloe, Co. Galway (population 2016, 6,662), function as the modern local centres of administration, employment and retail, and both serve a large hinterland. These towns occupy longstanding fording places over the Shannon and Suck, and are key locations along the main east–west transport and communication artery linking Dublin to Galway city. The villages, in certain cases, have also developed close to the regional waterways. Athleague, Ballyforan and Ahascragh have all developed on river fords, while Lecarrow and Knockcroghery both originated as settlements connected to sheltered bays on Lough Ree. All of the above settlements were established at intersections between overland communication routes and river routes, while both Kilconnell and Aughrim also served as key locations on the overland communication routes leading west to Galway. A number of 'hamlets' also exist and these serve as focal points for the local, rural communities of their areas, with at least one found in each of the civil parishes. The development of settlements at specific points in the landscape has grown from the needs of what is a predominantly rural population. They correspond with former fording places for driving livestock and goods across the larger rivers, and occur along parts of the terrestrial route network across the region. As a result, these settlements, up until recent times, all retained a regular market and seasonal livestock fair, the vestiges of which are still apparent in places.

***

This book seeks to identify and reconstruct the physical appearance of the Ó Cellaig lordly centres (*cenn áiteanna*)[1] in their lordship from their emergence as one of the principal offshoots of the Uí Maine *c.*1100, to the demise of the lordship around the year 1600. This has been achieved by embracing a number of disciplines. Medieval archaeology, being a form of 'historical archaeology', is both interdisciplinary and multidisciplinary in nature (Anderson, Scholkmann and Kristiansen 2007, 25). There is much debate as to the place which archaeology holds in terms of its role in reconstructing the historic past. In some cases, a hierarchy exists in the use of sources, with the written word often given primacy. In these instances, archaeology is often relegated to the position of an auxiliary science, in service to the narrative provided by the study of medieval history (ibid., 28). However, I believe that the approach espoused by Moreland in *Archaeology and text* is much more laudable and I have attempted to apply it to this study. Coined as 'contextual archaeology', Moreland describes it as follows:

> Contextual archaeology demands a close and detailed engagement with data, and should result in the production of histories with affinities to the kind of thick description advocated by Clifford Geertz and the 'microhistories of recent historical scholarship' … Contextual archaeology also demands that we use *all* the data we have available from the past … (Moreland 2007, 83)

Taking this approach, textual sources become a part of the interpretive jigsaw, as opposed to being the dominant element. It is only through the application of this

---

[1] The term *cenn áit* (literally chief or head place) was one of a number of terms used in Irish historical sources to describe the fortified earthen enclosures used by the pre-tower house Gaelic elite. Here, the term will be used to reference the lordly centre and the immediate landscape attached to, and manipulated by, the lord within the wider *trícha cét*/lordship. I have adopted this term as an alternative to the Latin *caput*, when referring to these elite places.

research model, which views the archaeological evidence and the written sources as 'discursive contexts', to be analysed in an equal and complementary manner, that an overall understanding of the medieval world will be achieved (Anderson, Scholkmann and Kristiansen 2007, 28).

In this work, a theoretical framework has been built around the complementary concepts of 'landscape archaeology' and 'contextual archaeology', and a methodology followed that brings all available archaeological, historical, literary, place-name and cartographical evidence together in order to create as full a picture as possible. This multidisciplinary, synthetic methodology has been particularly suited to the reconstruction of the cultural landscape of later medieval Uí Maine and, more specifically, to fulfil the aim of this research. Issues relating to the study of later medieval Gaelic Ireland mean that it is critical to adopt this multidisciplinary approach. For instance, the fragmentary manner in which evidence survives for Gaelic Ireland necessitates taking evidence from a number of disciplines, in order to fully understand native society during the later medieval period (Finan 2010, 11). For example, the relative absence of detailed socio-economic documentation for Gaelic Ireland before the late sixteenth century – the equivalent of Anglo-Norman manorial extents and inquisitions post-mortem – has been something of an impediment to the study of native society during the later medieval period (O'Conor 1998, 73–4; Nicholls 2008, 398). Meaningful research into later medieval Gaelic Ireland, therefore, has to be conducted by drawing 'large conclusions from small, but very densely textured facts' (Geertz 1973, 28). In the absence of detailed administrative accounts, alongside the archaeological evidence, the underexploited literary evidence (Simms 2001; Finan and O'Conor 2002) and the even more underutilized toponymical data (Ó Muraíle 2001, 244; Ó hAisibéil 2018, 158, 161) become vital resources in helping to reconstruct the landscape, economy and society of later medieval Gaelic lordships. As a result, in any future study of Gaelic Ireland, arguably archaeology and archaeological methods of enquiry will have a major role, if not even the primary role, to play in understanding the later medieval Gaelic world (see O'Conor and Fredengren 2019, 80; O'Conor 2021). One scholar who has comprehensively and successfully combined archaeological research with historical, literary and toponymical source material is Elizabeth FitzPatrick, creating what could be described as 'micro-histories' in Gaelic lordly landscapes and delving deep into the social organization of later medieval Gaelic Ireland (FitzPatrick 2004; 2012; 2015; 2016; 2018; 2023).

ARCHAEOLOGICAL METHODS AND TECHNIQUES

Archaeological fieldwork
The fieldwork methodologies in this study were preceded by an extensive desk-based assessment, in order to identify targets for field survey. This was necessitated by the

previous lack of identified Ó Cellaig sites apparent in existing research. A number of fieldwork methods and techniques were then applied to the chosen sites, based on their applicability to individual contexts. This included the analysis of modern and archive aerial photography, the use of Airborne Light Detection and Ranging (LiDAR) data as well as unmanned aerial vehicle surveys. Where deemed to be of most benefit, a number of ground-based remote sensing techniques were applied to target locations.

Geophysical survey
The techniques utilized as part of this methodology are as follows: Earth Resistance, Magnetic Susceptibility, Magnetic Gradiometry, and Electrical Resistivity Tomography. Utilizing a multi-method approach to the application of these non-invasive surveys can, in favourable conditions, yield important insights into the morphology and complexity of below-surface archaeological remains.

HISTORICAL SOURCES

The historical sources are a vital resource for the medieval archaeologist to be able to inspect (Barry 1987, 3–10). They can provide information on the location and form of monuments that no longer retain above ground remains and they can also inform us on additional features of a landscape that no longer survive. Historical sources can also be used alongside archaeological and architectural remains to throw light on the development and role of a historically attested monument through time. This approach can be seen with the research conducted on Rindoon Castle, Co. Roscommon, where the analysis of the standing remains, coupled with a close reading of the surviving references, provided valuable insights on the development of the castle and town through time (O'Conor, Naessens and Sherlock 2015). Outside of this, written sources can also provide key insights into the political, social and economic aspects of life in the medieval period.

With so few detailed socio-economic and administrative sources surviving from later medieval Gaelic Ireland, other types of written sources have been mined with a view to reconstructing later medieval Gaelic lordships and, in the present context, identifying settlement sites within them. The principal Gaelic written resources consulted were the medieval annalistic records, prose narratives such as the early-to-mid-fourteenth-century *Caithréim Thoirdhealbhaigh,* the Ó Cellaig genealogies, and legal rights tracts such as *Lebor na Cert* and particularly the *Nósa Ua Maine. The tribes and customs of Hy-Many* was also consulted as it is a valuable compendium of edited source material on the Uí Chellaig. While some of the conclusions drawn by O'Donovan are outdated, this source has served as a routine first port-of-call when researching the lordship and identifying the main later medieval Ó Cellaig settlement sites.

Alongside this, saga material, particularly the late twelfth- or early thirteenth-century prose narrative *Acallam na Senórach*, the most important of the Fenian Cycle tales, was unexpectedly useful. The final Gaelic source consulted for this study was praise poetry, a different class of historical source to those discussed above, in that it was usually addressed to the lay nobility, was designed to be publicly recited, and dealt primarily with the patron's present political ambitions, as opposed to anything ancient in character. These attributes make praise poetry the most valuable source material to the historical researcher of later medieval Gaelic Ireland (Simms 2009, 57) and their importance extends to the discipline of archaeology also. A particular motif within the praise poetry corpus is the 'house poems', verses which were either wholly or partially concerned with describing a nobleman's house (Simms 2001). Such poems can help locate later medieval Gaelic elite residences in the landscape and provide information about their physical appearance when in use (Finan and O'Conor 2002; FitzPatrick 2018, 179–87).

There is a wide range of Anglo-Norman and later English sources available to the researcher of medieval Ireland and some of these are of benefit in our attempts to reconstruct the medieval Ó Cellaig lordship and to recognize the main Uí Chellaig settlement sites within. These can be separated into two sections: the records created by the Dublin government and the English crown, and the historical sources produced by the great landowning families of Anglo-Norman Ireland (Barry 1987, 2–10; Connolly 2002). They will be encountered throughout this study. It is important to note, however, that references to the study area in the records emanating from the administration in Dublin become relatively rare from the early fourteenth century onwards into the later sixteenth century. This is clearly linked to the effects of the Gaelic Resurgence in Uí Maine, when Anglo-Norman control over parts of it waned and then collapsed totally, with the Uí Chellaig regaining complete control of their old lands and then expanding their territories in the late medieval period. This gap in references in documentary sources compiled by administrators working for central government ends in the later sixteenth century, and the increase is linked to the gradual reconquest of Gaelic and Gaelicized Ireland, including Uí Maine, and the re-establishment of English control during Tudor and Stuart times.

Alongside these sources, I consulted a range of ecclesiastical records as they relate to the study area, as well as the early modern and modern cartographic sources, the earliest being John Browne the Younger's 1591 Map of the Province of Connaught [TCD, MS1209/68], through to the 1st Edition Ordnance Survey maps of the mid-nineteenth century. Finally, one of the best preserved, yet underused, primary sources available to the Irish archaeological and landscape researcher is the toponymical record. The survival of townland names and the names of local features is an invaluable key to the former organization of the later medieval landscape and their societies (Mac Shamhráin 1991; Bhreathnach 2014, 19). A considerable amount of information can be gleaned from analysis of the toponymy, particularly townland names, as they are one of the primary forms of recording and remembering landscape (Kilfeather 2010, 167), a use that is often overlooked. Although evidence for the origins of the townland system is difficult to confirm, it is in place by at least the twelfth century, as townlands are referred to in documentary sources of that date (Ó hAisibéil 2018, 169). The divisions, and in many cases names, can be presumed to be of considerable antiquity, with possible origins for the townland system in the early medieval period or even earlier (McErlean 1983, 335; Nicholls 2008, 138–9). Careful consideration of these place-names can help to identify otherwise unknown places of importance in the landscape of the later medieval Ó Cellaig lordship and, indeed, throw some light on their function during this period.

ARCHAEOLOGICAL AND HISTORICAL WORK ON UÍ MAINE

Historical work on Uí Maine

There are a number of publications examining or partly throwing light on the history and emergence of Uí Maine and the ancestors of the Uí Chellaig during the early medieval period (Walsh 1936–7; 1940–1; Kelleher 1971; Byrne 2004, 92–3, 230–53; Mannion 2006; 2014; Ó Cróinín 2013; Devane 2013). Yet, in reality, little detailed research has been published on the early medieval history of the study area. Moving into the later medieval period, a similar dearth of research is evident, with a few notable exceptions. First, prominent mention must be given to an, as yet, unpublished manuscript written by K.W. Nicholls for the Irish Manuscripts Commission which is entitled 'Survey of Irish lordships: I Uí Maine and Síl Anmchadha' (Nicholls 1969). This document, which includes a series of hand-drawn maps of individual sub-lordships, has proved to be of major benefit in understanding the Ó Cellaig lordship, its geography and archaeology between the twelfth and late sixteenth century. Aside from this, a small number of papers relating to specific aspects of the later medieval history of the study area have been published, and these will be highlighted where they arise. A very welcome recent addition to this subject has been Joseph Mannion's book on the fortunes of the Ó Cellaig elites during the sixteenth century, in the face of ever-increasing interest in Connacht on the part of the Tudor monarchy (Mannion 2024).

Archaeological work on and within the territory of Uí Maine

A considerable amount of archaeological research has been carried out in north Roscommon on what were the Gaelic Irish Ó Conchobhair and Mac Diarmada lordships of Machaire Chonnacht and Maigh Luirg (see, for instance, Brady and Gibson 2005; Finan (ed.) 2010; Finan 2018; 2020; Finan and O'Conor 2002; FitzPatrick 2018; McNeary and Shanahan 2008; O'Conor 2001; O'Conor and Finan 2018; Shanahan 2008). Unfortunately, this has not been the case to date in modern south Roscommon and east Galway. Archaeological research on the later medieval period in the study area is virtually non-existent, and when it is published, the focus is primarily on the Anglo-Norman material remains extant in the region (Graham 1988a; Holland 1987–8; 1997; O'Keeffe 1998; Dempsey 2014; O'Conor, Naessens and Sherlock 2015; O'Conor and Naessens 2016a; O'Conor and Shanahan 2018). Moreover, little has been published on the archaeology of the Uí Chellaig lords and their vassal clans.

The study area during the early medieval period is somewhat better understood, suggesting a quite open, relatively rich agricultural landscape *c.*1100, at the beginning of the later medieval period. This picture is primarily gathered from the National Roads Authority excavations along the route of the M6 road project, which links Athlone to Galway, bypassing Ballinasloe. Key publications include *The mill at Kilbegly: an archaeological investigation on the route of the M6 Ballinasloe to Athlone National Road Scheme* (Jackman, Moore and Rynne 2013) and *The quiet landscape: archaeological investigations on the M6 Galway to Ballinasloe National Road Scheme* (McKeon and O'Sullivan (eds) 2014). A number of articles within the latter book are of particular relevance to the present research.

Aside from these major pieces of research, the later medieval archaeology of Uí Maine has been largely studied in a piecemeal fashion to date, with noteworthy investigations undertaken at the Augustinian Priory of St Mary at Clontuskert, Co. Galway (Fanning 1976; see, also, Barry 1987, 151–3) and the Hospital of the Crutched Friars at Rindoon, Co. Roscommon (O'Conor and Shanahan 2018, 40–1). More fleeting discussions are to be found elsewhere (Kerrigan 1996; FitzPatrick 2016, 204; Loeber 2001, 310). I have addressed some of these *lacunae* (Curley 2011; 2016; 2018; 2021; 2022).

***

In contrast to north Roscommon and other areas, little detailed archaeological and, for that matter, historical research has been published on the later medieval Ó Cellaig lordship of Uí Maine. This is despite the fact that its archaeology is very well preserved and, also, that good edited later medieval primary historical and literary sources survive for Uí Maine, in comparison to other parts of Gaelic Ireland. In all, this lack of focused research and the existence of good primary data, be it archaeological, historical, literary or toponymical, suggests that a study that attempts to understand aspects of the Ó Cellaig lordship of Uí Maine will be a significant contribution to furthering our knowledge of settlement and society in later medieval Gaelic Ireland.

CHAPTER TWO

Historical background

The medieval period in the study area has only received marginal interest from historians. To date, interpretations of the early and later medieval history of Uí Maine, and with it, the territorial area controlled by this group, and their principal offshoot, the Uí Chellaig, has depended on the 1843 map and description provided by O'Donovan (Fig. 2.1; *Tribes*, 5–6). A substantial quantity of published and privately published material since then has readily accepted O'Donovan's boundaries of Uí Maine. O'Donovan's depiction of the geographical extent of Uí Maine is based on the late fourteenth- to early fifteenth-century poetic source *Triallam timcheall na Fodla*, composed by Seán Mór Ó Dubhagáin, *saoi sheancadha ocus ollam* to the Uí Maine during his lifetime, and finished by Giolla-Na-Naomh Ó Huidhrín (*Tribes*, 4–6; see Carney (ed.) 1943. For continued use, see McGettigan 2016, 37, Map 1).

However, this source must not be accepted without interrogation, and Nicholls outlines the level of scrutiny that must be applied to later medieval sources such as *Triallam timcheall na Fodla*:

> A striking example of the techniques employed by politically-motivated antiquarianism is shown in the account of the boundaries of Uí Maine printed by O'Donovan (O'Donovan 1843, 4–6), which represents a conflation of the maximum extent of the Uí Maine of the pre-invasion period with the furthest limits of the conquests – or, indeed, in some cases the ambition – of the contemporary O'Kellys. (Nicholls 1982, 392)

Therefore, prior to progressing to a more detailed inspection of the lordly centres of the later medieval Ó Cellaig lordship, it is necessary to construct a historical background, by focussing on the surviving primary source material. This will be prefaced by a brief summary of the origins of Uí Maine to 1100 in order to understand how the Uí Chellaig emerged to control this territory in the later medieval period. This approach will do three things. First, it will help to locate the Uí Chellaig elites within the landscape, an outcome which has never been systematically undertaken before now. Second, it will provide for the first time a coherent chronological narrative for the Uí Chellaig lords, adding to our understanding of the later medieval history of this lordship, and the political and military machinations of later medieval Gaelic Ireland more generally. Finally, it will test O'Donovan's view of the boundaries of Uí Maine against the historical reality of the early and later medieval periods and in doing so evaluate the usefulness of his map to historians and archaeologists going forward.

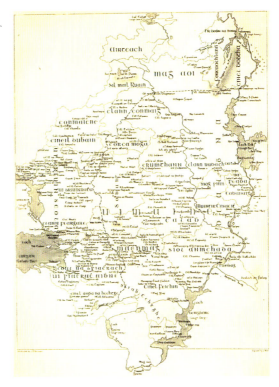

Figure 2.1 A map of Hy Many, taken from the *Tribes and customs of Hy Many*. Note the hashered line, indicating that the territory east and south of this, as far as the River Shannon boundary, is regarded as being O'Kelly Country.

THE EARLY MEDIEVAL ORIGINS OF THE UÍ CHELLAIG

The term Uí Maine has been used thus far as the name of the lordship over which the later medieval Uí Chellaig presided. However, there is much confusion as to what Uí Maine represents exactly. It has routinely been used in three linked ways: to describe an early medieval tribal grouping; to name a territorial unit, known as a *trícha cét*,[1] from roughly the beginning of the later medieval period; and to refer to the wider Ó Cellaig lordship throughout the later medieval period, no matter what its geographical extent. Another term, Tír Maine, 'the land of Maine', will be used throughout this study, denoting another *trícha cét* that is referred to extensively in historical sources, and which was under the authority of the Uí Maine at different points during the medieval period as a whole.

The Uí Chellaig are one of a number of septs originating from this common tribal grouping. The principal lordly septs that descended from the Uí Maine are the Ó Madadháin (O'Madden) sept of Síl Anmchadha and the Uí Chellaig themselves. Both held lands in eastern Connacht throughout the later medieval period (Jaski 2013b, 10; Ó hAisibéil 2018, 163). The Uí Maine believed that their genesis was tied to an

[1] *trícha cét* – literally thirty hundreds, a unit of landholding in the latter part of the early medieval period.

ancestor figure, Maine Mór mac Eochaidh Ferdaghiall, reputed descendant of the three Collas, founders of the Ulster kingdom of Airgíalla (Ó Muraíle 2008, 49; Jaski 2013a, 296; 2013b, 10). Ancestral claim from a real or mythical figure is a common motif in early Irish elite culture, as a means of strengthening an identity and legacy attached to a territory (FitzPatrick 2004, 66–8; McCarthy and Curley 2018, 58–61). Maine Mór is a reputed fourth-century personage who migrated from Ulster with his people, in order to settle in *Magh Seincheineoil* (the plain of the ancient kin). His arrival and settlement in Connacht is recorded in the Life of St Grellan, the patron saint of Uí Maine (*Tribes*, 8–14). Maine Mór migrated from *Clochar Mac Daimhin* (Clogher, Co. Tyrone) to *Druim Clasaigh* in Tír Maine (ibid., 10). *Druim Clasaigh* is identifiable today as a ridge, 60m to 90m high, which crosses the parishes of Drum and Taughmaconnell in south Roscommon (Devane 2013, 97).

The first annalistic entry to record the territory and tribe of Uí Maine occurs in 538 in relation to the battle of Claenloch (*AT*; *AFM*; Kelleher 1971, 64). After this battle, Uí Maine was incorporated into the Connacht over-kingdom, under the authority of the Uí Fiachrach kings of Connacht (Byrne 2004, 92). The position of Uí Maine as a sub-kingdom of Connacht would have corresponded with a levying of tribute by the greater power onto the minor kingdom, in return for certain rights and privileges. It is possible that this was organized along similar lines to that described in the later *Lebor na Cert* (49, 53, 57, 59, 145).

By the eighth century, Uí Maine authority was encroached upon by the expansion of the Uí Briúin. The Uí Briúin were a dynasty who originated in the central plain of Connacht, known as Magh nAí or Machaire Connacht, with its prehistoric landscape of Rathcroghan, in mid-Roscommon. It was from this dynasty that the Uí Briúin Aí emerged, and who claimed control over the latter region (Byrne 2004, 245–6). The expansion of the Uí Briúin Aí in the eighth century is seen particularly in the reign of Indrechtach mac Muiredaig (707–23), whose father was the originator of the dominant Síl Muiredaig sept of the Uí Briúin Aí. The Síl Muiredaig then produced the dynasty that monopolized the kingship of Connacht in the later medieval period, the Uí Chonchobair. Records from the eighth century indicate that three rival ruling lines within the Uí Maine tribal group had emerged for control of Uí Maine. There was the Clann Crimthann, who resided in an area broadly consistent with the later barony of Killian, Co. Galway, plus presumably some lands east of the River Suck, in Co. Roscommon. Then there was the Clann Chommáin of *trícha Máenmaige*, the later barony of Loughrea, Co. Galway, and finally the Cénel Coirpre Chruim, who came to reside in the *trícha cét* of Tír Maine (MacCotter 2014, 208, 141).

Between *trícha Máenmaige* and the Uí Maine lands east of the River Suck lay a territory known in the early medieval period as *Soghan*, named after the dynasty who resided there (Fig. 2.2). This *trícha* was absorbed into the wider Uí Maine lordship at some point in the early historic period, however, the Soghain retained a level of

Historical background 13

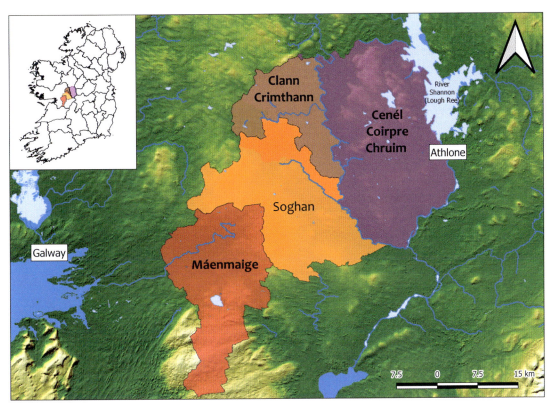

Figure 2.2 Approximate territorial extents of the sept families related to Uí Maine, *c.*800. Extents reproduced based broadly on MacCotter 2014, following Nicholls 1969. It is presumed that this is the territory over which the dominant king of Uí Maine claimed control in *c.*800, with the annals recording Uí Maine kings from each of these lines.

independence within Uí Maine, to the extent that they continued to elect their own chiefs until at least the twelfth century (Mannion 2006, 168).

By the middle of the tenth century, the Clann Crimthann and Clann Chommáin had furnished their last kings, meaning that from this point onwards, the kingship belonged nearly exclusively to the Cenél Coirpre Chruim (Kelleher 1971, 79). A period of relative stability seems to have played out in the annalistic record for Uí Maine throughout the majority of the tenth century as a result.

These other two suppliers of candidates to the kingship fell into relative obscurity after this time. The Clann Crimthann became overrun by an Uí Briúin Aí-related sept, the Muintir Máelruanaid, who were installed as kings in the late tenth century in order to effectively annex this territory for the Síl Muiredaig kings of Connacht (MacCotter 2014, 208). *Nósa Ua Maine* later records three vassal kings of Síl Crimtaind Cáeil, two of the Clann Crimthann themselves: the Uí Mhugróin (O'Moran?) and the Uí Chathail (Cahill), and the Uí Máelruanaid (*Nósa*, 537; *Tribes*, 73). It is interesting to note that the 'Rights of Mac Diarmada' seem to consciously echo the privileges accorded to the Uí Maine in *Nósa Ua Maine* (Ní Shéaghdha 1963, 156).

The Clann Chommáin also produced two vassal lineages in their later history. The Uí Nechtain (O'Naughton) and the Uí Máelalaid (O'Mullally) are recorded in *Nósa Ua Maine* as chiefs of Máenmaige (MacCotter 2014, 141). However, both groupings were forced from this area at some point in the twelfth century, possibly due to Ó Conchobair pressure (Egan and Costello 1958, 59, note 32). The Uí Nechtain came to reside thereafter in the area known as the *Feadha* of Athlone, where tradition placed them at *Carraig Uí Neachtain* [Ballycreggan] and *Lissadillure* [Lisdillure] (*OS Letters, Rosc.*, 19), and by the late sixteenth century, the Uí Máelalaid were settled at Tolendal [Tullinadaly/*Tulach na dála* – hill of assemblies], the modern townland of Castletown, Tuam civil parish, Co. Galway (*Tribes*, 70–1, notes a–b; Ó hAodha 2017, 18). The Uí Máelalaid held prominent ecclesiastical positions in Uí Maine in the later medieval period (*Clonfert*, 303–4) while a member of the kindred served in a learned capacity to the Uí Maine in the late fifteenth century (*AFM, s.a.* 1487).

One of the most noteworthy tenth-century Uí Maine entries in the annals occurs in 962, with the record of an attack undertaken by one Murchad Ó Cellaig, king of Uí Maine (*AFM*; Kelleher, 1971, 80). Murchad is the first Uí Maine king to have adopted the Ó Cellaig surname. *Ua/Ó*, anglicized to 'O', translates most specifically to 'grandson', and Murchad's grandfather was Ceallach mac Finnachta, the namer for the sept. This is a phenomenon unique to Ireland, in that most royal and noble surnames are derived from a tenth-century ancestor (Ó Murchadha 1999, 33–5; Byrne 2004, xxxiv; Hammond 2019, 101). Byrne suggests that this adoption may have occurred in order to fulfil the function of denoting eligibility to kingship within the agnatic *derbfhine* – the four-generational kin group from which eligible candidates could be chosen for the role (Byrne 2004, xli). This approach effectively narrowed the number of potential contenders, introducing a level of control and exclusivity over the position going forward.

A small number of episodes are recorded in the annals from this point through to 1014, primarily concerned with the deaths of members of the Uí Maine. The only noteworthy incident prior to the Battle of Clontarf occurs in 1004, with a battle fought between Tadg Mór Ó Cellaig, assisted by Máel Sechlainn Mór, king of Mide, against the Uí Fhiachrach Aidne. It seems that this battle was fought for control of *trícha Máenmaige*, with the Uí Maine leaving the battlefield victorious (*AFM*; Kelleher 1971, 82–3). Tadg Mór Ó Cellaig placed himself centrally within the politics of the island as a whole at the beginning of the eleventh century, owing to his alliance with Brian Boru. He gained the Uí Maine kingship in 1002, and with this, he attached himself to the Dál Cais high-king. As a result, Tadg Mór was closely allied, and acted as an advisor, to Brian Boru (Duffy 2014, 202), and his troops must have accompanied the Dál Cais on several military excursions, gaining the nickname – *lucht tige Taidg na taisteal* (the household troops of Tadg of the journeys), recorded in a contemporary praise poem *Beannacht, a Bruin, ar Brigit, fuil am thig rim nach anait* [A blessing, Bruin, on Brigit, who is in the house with me (and) who is not displeasing] (Ó Raghallaigh, C., pers. comm.; Meyer 1912, 226; Mannion 2014, 8). This alliance was beneficial to Uí Maine interests also, as evidenced by the elevated status which Tadg Mór possessed when he could call upon Máel Sechlainn Mór as an ally in the battle against the Uí Fhiachrach Aidne (Mannion 2014, 8).

Brian Boru's army at Clontarf in 1014 was made up primarily of his Munster forces as well as the support of Máel Sechlainn Mór, while only two Connacht kings were among his host: Tadg Mór, and the king of Uí Fiachrach Aidne, Máel Ruanaid Ó hEidin (Duffy 2014, 186). The Uí Maine and Uí Fiachrach Aidne are described in *Cogadh Gaedheal re Gallaibh* as taking on the Norse of Dublin, and by the end of the day, Tadg Mór was dead. His death assumed a mythical dimension in later times when tales were recounted about a mysterious dog-like animal appearing out of the sea to protect the dead warrior's body from the 'Danes' (Mannion 2014, 9).

Tadg Mór Ó Cellaig's legacy loomed large over his kin and descendants in later centuries, and his connection with Brian Boru was highlighted. This is seen with a possible contemporary or near contemporary praise poem *Samhoin so, sodham go Tadg* [This Samhain, I go to Tadg] (Ó Raghallaigh, C., pers. comm.; Meyer 1912, 222–3). It is also seen in the Ó Cellaig genealogies, where Tadg is consistently referred to as 'Tadg of the battle of Brian' (Ó *CGF* i, 49; ii, 53, 55). Moreover, in *Caithréim Thoirdhealbhaigh*, the military assistance provided by the Uí Chellaig to the Clann Toirdelbaig was partially predicated on the links established between both dynasties by their eleventh-century ancestors (*Caithréim Thoirdhealbhaigh*, 56–7). Finally, the prevalence of the personal name Tadg among the Uí Maine elite after this time may have been inspired by Tadg Mór Ó Cellaig and his career.

As the end of the eleventh century approached, and with it the close of the early medieval period, the bulk of Uí Maine-related annalistic entries were associated with conflicts at neighbouring religious establishments, such as Clonmacnoise (1038, 1065) and Clonfert (1045, 1065) (*AFM*). Kelleher equates this with the successful Ó Conchobair attempts to keep their Uí Maine vassal lords weakened, and the corresponding Uí Maine attempts to retain a foothold in the politics of Connacht (Kelleher 1971, 90–1). The Ó Cellaig position in the wider region was heavily dependent on their relations with their ambitious neighbours in mid-Roscommon. At this time, the core of their territory likely corresponded with the region under the authority of the dominant Uí Maine sept, the Uí Chellaig lords of the Cenél Coirpre Chruim line. MacCotter reconstructed the Ó Cellaig territory at *c.*1100 as corresponding with the *trícha cét* of Tír Maine (Fig. 2.3). The extents of the lordship at this point included the former Clann Crimthann lands constituted by Killian barony and the bulk of Athlone barony. However, excluded from the territory was the

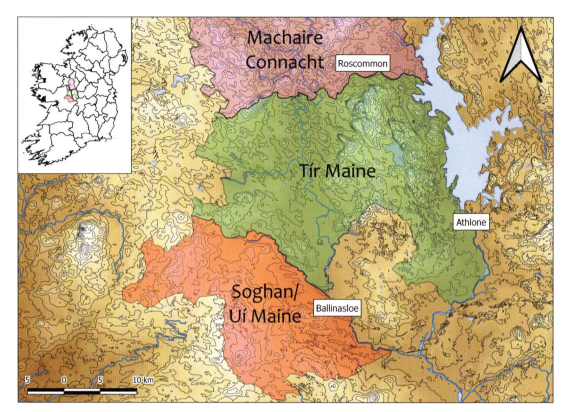

Figure 2.3 Territorial extents of Tír Maine, Soghan/Uí Maine and Machaire Connacht, *c.*1100, as reconstructed by MacCotter, 2014. Tír Maine represented the core territory controlled by the Uí Chellaig, *c.*1100.

túath of Magh Finn, consistent with the later civil parish of Taughmaconnell and the barony of Moycarn, which MacCotter deduces had been taken into the control of the Uí Mhadadháin of Síl Anmchadha (MacCotter 2014, 208, 147–8). It is possible that the Uí Chellaig also retained real or imagined claims over *trícha Máenmaige*, but their main preoccupation must have been to retain Tír Maine in the face of growing Ó Conchobair pressure.

THE UÍ CHELLAIG AND THE LORDSHIP OF TÍR MAINE, *c.*1100–1225

The late eleventh- and early twelfth-century sources indicate that the now established Ó Cellaig sept was based at this time within their patrimonial *trícha cét* lands of Tír Maine, in what is now largely south Roscommon (see Fig. 2.3). Donnchad Ó Cellaig, king of Uí Maine, died in 1074 on *Inis Locha Caoláin* (*AT*; *ACl.*; *AFM*). This may have been a *crannóg* residence located on the double lakes of Cuilleenirwan Lough and Coolagarry Lough, just to the south-east of Lough Croan in Tír Maine (Kelleher 1971,

Historical background 17

Plate 2.1 Foundational remains of Temple Kelly, Clonmacnoise (author's photograph).

92). No *crannóga* have been recognized on these connected lakes but three small natural islands (all *c.*25m in diameter) can be seen today on Coolagarry Lough. It has been noted that some small natural islands were used as defended residences in the same way as artificial *crannóga* (O'Conor 1998, 82–3; 2001, 336–7). It is possible that one of these islands was in use as an Ó Cellaig residence and *cenn áit* in the late eleventh century, something that can only be answered through archaeological excavation.

Thereafter, the sources are basically silent on the Uí Chellaig for sixty years, until 1134 and the death of Áed Ó Cellaig, king of Uí Maine (*AT*), who was interred in Clonmacnoise, just beyond the southern limits of Tír Maine across the Shannon in modern Co. Offaly (MacAlister 1909, 48). This suggests that Clonmacnoise continued to be used as the preferred location for interment of deceased kings from the Cenél Coirpre Chruim sept into the twelfth century. This arrangement is traditionally regarded to have originated with the sixth-century endowment by Cairpre Crom, king of Uí Maine, of the nascent monastery of Clonmacnoise with lands and other rights in Uí Maine (*Reg. Clon.*, 454–5). The later right of the Uí Maine, especially the Uí Chellaig, to burial at Clonmacnoise is linked to this supposed gift (*Tribes*, 80–1). The Uí Chellaig had a strong relationship with Clonmacnoise in later times. In 1167, Conchobhar Ó Cellaig, king of Uí Maine, had the masonry church known as Temple

Kelly (Pl. 2.1) built, and this may have replaced a timber oratory (*dearthach*) associated with the Uí Maine and their burial ceremonies (*AFM*; MacDonald 2003, 129–30). The annals also tell us a member of the sept was buried there in the late thirteenth century (*ACl.*, *s.a.* 1283).

On a wider scale, the political situation in early twelfth-century Connacht continued to be dominated by the expansionist policies of the Uí Chonchobair. This sept was to reach the zenith of its power in the first half of the century, under the kingship of Toirrdelbach Mór Ó Conchobair. Toirrdelbach ascended to the kingship of Connacht in 1106. He is considered to have been the most powerful king in Ireland by 1119 and in a long and impressive career that was to span five decades he placed the Uí Chonchobair at the centre of power in Irish politics. His career is also marked by predatory raids across Ireland, the construction of bridges and fortifications, the commissioning of high crosses, the Cross of Cong and much more (Ó Corráin 1972, 156; Lucas 1989, 144, 197–9; Manning 1997, 12; Murray 2014, 30–65; Moss 2015b, 480–1; Valante 2015, 51–2). Ó Conchobair's actions during his reign did much to shape the landscape and the course of the history of Connacht, including Tír Maine.

Some of Toirrdelbach's activities in eastern Connacht seem to have been attempted in order to directly subdue the Uí Chellaig, and restrict their power. One of the clearest manifestations of this is the manner in which related junior septs of the Síl Muiredaig dynasty came to be installed in new locales, outside of their traditional areas. This had already been seen with the insertion of the Uí Máelruanaid as vassal kings in what was Clann Crimthann territory in the tenth century. This tactic seems also to have been employed by Toirrdelbach in mid-twelfth-century Tír Maine. For example, the Clann Uadach are mentioned as being located at Druim Drestan in 1137, likely referring to the civil parish of Drum, south Roscommon (*AT*; Connon and Shanahan 2012, 165). This strongly implies that the Clann Uadach, and more particularly their chief family, the Uí Fhallamháin (O'Fallons), had been placed in Ó Cellaig territory by the end of the 1130s at least.

The Clann Uadach were originally located in Machaire Connacht either in the *trícha cét* of *Na Trí Túatha* (broadly the modern Strokestown area), particularly Tír Briúin na Sinna, or in Kilbride civil parish in the centre of modern Roscommon (Connon, A., pers. comm.). However, at some point in the early twelfth century, the Clann Uadach seem to have been transplanted away from their homeland, and their new territory was within Tír Maine, eventually coextensive with the parishes of Dysart and Cam, Co. Roscommon (MacCotter 2014, 208, 210). A reference in 1169 provides some certainty as to the motive for this movement of a cadet branch of the Síl Muiredaig into Tír Maine. It relates to the death of Ferchar Ó Fallamháin, chief of Clann Uadach. Ferchar is described as *maor Ua Maine* – the 'steward' of Uí Maine (*AFM*). In the twelfth-century, Irish kings gave the title of *máer* to their administrators in newly acquired territories. This suggests that the Uí Fhallamháin were installed as

Ó Conchobair's representatives in Tír Maine to control the area, and by extension, subdue their principal local residents – the Uí Chellaig (Byrne 2008, 871). The movement of the Clann Uadach is only one of a number of local twelfth-century relocations which seem to have been orchestrated by the Uí Chonchobair (Connon forthcoming, 2, 4–5), while other contemporaneous Irish provincial kings routinely placed related vassal clans into subject territories to suit political needs (Breen 2005, 65; MacCotter 2014, 169).

The battle of *Óenach Máenmaige* (located somewhere in *trícha Máenmaige*) took place in 1135 and was fought between competing Ó Conchobair factions. The losing side, led by Áed mac Domnaill Ó Conchobair, was supported by Conchobar Ó Cellaig, king of Uí Maine, who was slain in the battle (*AT*). The victors, led by Conchobar Ó Conchobair, Toirrdelbach's son, exacted punishment on the Uí Chellaig for taking the wrong side, by removing them from the Uí Maine kingship, with Ó Madadháin, the king of Síl Anmchadha, taking Ó Cellaig's place (*AFM*; Kelleher 1971, 95–6). It is possible that *trícha Máenmaige* was forfeited by the Uí Maine to the Uí Chonchobair at this time also, with the expulsion of the Uí Nechtain and the Uí Máelalaid in the process, with the former family settling in the *Feadha* of Athlone in Tír Maine. Later that year saw the swift reversal back to the normal order of Uí Maine kingship, with the death of this Ó Madadháin king, who was replaced by Tadg Ó Cellaig, son of the aforementioned Conchobar (*AFM*). From the 1130s onwards, the Uí Chellaig seemed to accept or at least acquiesce to Ó Conchobair overlordship. For example, in 1142 the Uí Maine accompanied Conchobar Ó Conchobair on a cattle raid to *Múscraige Tíre*, in what is now north Tipperary (*AFM*; Kelleher, 1971, 98–9).

Many of the historical entries over the next thirty years mention the Uí Maine forming part of the military hostings of Toirrdelbach, and then Ruaidrí Ó Conchobair, his son and successor (*AFM, s.a.* 1147; *AU, AT, AFM, s.a.* 1163; *AT, AFM, s.a.* 1170; *La Geste* 3240). These records are also interspersed with instances where any Ó Cellaig attempts of securing a level of autonomy from the Uí Chonchobair were put down, as in 1158 (*AFM*). The Uí Chellaig were now occupying a space where they served their Uí Chonchobair overlords, like many other regional kings or lords in Connacht at the time.

In attempting to reconstruct the twelfth-century territorial map of Connacht, two church synods provide insight. The synods of Rath Breasail (1111) and Kells (1152), in defining the medieval dioceses of Ireland, effectively also served as a political and territorial map of the island (Flanagan 2008, 915; Perros-Walton 2013, 288–91). Therefore, the diocese of Tuam at Rath Breasail, which was renamed and divided at Kells into the two dioceses of Tuam and Roscommon (later called Elphin) (Millett 1986, 8, 14), formed the area over which the dominant Uí Chonchobair exerted direct control. The diocese of Roscommon included the traditional Ó Cellaig lands of Tír Maine, signalling that the Uí Chonchobair held effective control over the region. The diocese of Clonfert broadly corresponded with the *trícha céta* of Soghan/Uí Maine and

Figure 2.4 Dioceses of Ireland from Mitchell 2009, 20, with the extents of Elphin (Roscommon) and Clonfert co-extensive with the territories over which the Uí Chonchobair and the Uí Cellaig/Uí Mhadadháin held direct authority respectively by the mid-twelfth century.

Síl Anmchadha. The former area became occupied more extensively by the Ó Cellaig elite as the century progressed (Fig. 2.4).

In terms of illustrating the shifting political situation between the Uí Chonchobair and the Uí Chellaig, relations warmed enough for a united defence of their territories from the incursions of Niall, the son of Muirchertach Mac Lochlainn, king of Ulster, in 1163 (*AFM*).

By contrast, 1180 saw the eruption of open conflict between the Uí Chellaig and a branch of the Uí Chonchobair, with the so-called 'Battle of the Conors'. This battle was contested between Conchobar Maenmaige Ó Conchobair and Conchobar Ó Cellaig, king of Uí Maine, occuring at *Mag Srúibe Gealáin* near *Daire na gCapall*. The Uí Maine were defeated, and Conchobar Ó Cellaig was slain (*ALC*; *AFM*). His son, Tadhg Tailltenn, died at *Cnoc Gail* – 'Hill of Bravery', apparently during the same campaign (*Ó CGF ii*, 63). Ó Muraíle has identified *Mag Srúibe Gealáin* (alias *Ruba Gealáin*) with Roo townland, Kilmore parish, Co. Roscommon, while also suggesting that Knockhall townland, Kilglass parish, Co. Roscommon may be the *Cnoc Gail* of the sources (Ó Muraíle 1989, 173). The location of the battle, well beyond Tír Maine, north-east of modern Strokestown, implies that Conchobar Ó Cellaig and the Uí Maine were the aggressors, perhaps signalling their desperation, railing against their marginalization by the Uí Chonchobair. Animosity between the two polities continued for a period thereafter, with tit-for-tat kidnapping and killings occurring in 1185 and 1186 (*ALC*; *AFM*).

Memory of these grievances continued into the thirteenth century, as in 1200 a dynastic dispute between two branches of the Uí Chonchobair afforded the opportunity for the 'grandsons of Tadg Ó Cellaig' to side with Cathal Crobhdearg against Cathal Carrach mac Conchobair Maenmaige (Kelleher 1971, 104). This was the continuation of a transgenerational grapple for authority between the Uí Chonchobair and Uí Chellaig, which can be traced back at least as far as the battle of *Óenach Máenmaige*.

After 1180, the annalistic entries relating to the Uí Maine become sparse, until 1224, and the death of Domnall Mór Ó Cellaig, king of Uí Maine (*AFM*; *ALC*). This entry is significant, highlighting the declining fortunes of the Ó Cellaig lordship by the early thirteenth century. Domnall is recorded in *Leabhar Ua Maine* as having died 'in his own bed' at *Eachdruim*, modern day Aughrim, Co. Galway (Nicholls 1969, 41). This is the first reference to Aughrim as a place of residence for an Ó Cellaig king. Aughrim was located within Soghan, that semi-independent territory of Uí Maine in the early medieval period. However, by 1224, it had become known as the *trícha cét* of Uí Maine. This implies that at some time in the early-to-mid twelfth century, the Uí Chellaig elite migrated into this territory. This migration into what became Uí Maine must have been a direct response to the Ó Conchobair strategy of marginalization, to such a degree that they sought to retain some level of autonomy in Connacht by establishing direct control over what was previously a sub-lordship of their wider territory (MacCotter 2014, 207). This ultimately led to the displacement of the Soghain elite themselves, the principal dynasty of which were the Ó Mainnin. While these elite families were forced to migrate from their ancestral lands in order to retain control over their territory, it is important to remember that the bulk of these communities must have remained where they were, relatively unaffected by the machinations of the higher-ranking members of society.

By the close of this period, the ruling branch of the Ó Cellaig seem to have lost full sovereignty over their patrimonial lands of Tír Maine, and their power base had shifted into Uí Maine, albeit under Ó Conchobhair overlordship. In terms of the lineage of Uí Maine kingship into the thirteenth century and beyond, Domnall Mór Ó Cellaig and his descendants made up the central pillar of Ó Cellaig dynasts for the next number of centuries.

THE ARRIVAL OF THE ANGLO-NORMANS TO CONNACHT UNTIL THE DEATH OF THE BROWN EARL, 1225–1333

The early decades of the thirteenth century saw the entrance of a new power onto the Connacht stage. For much of this period, Cathal Crobhdearg Ó Conchobair, king of Connacht, sought to retain control over the province. His attempts included negotiating with the English king John, and his successor, Henry III, for the security

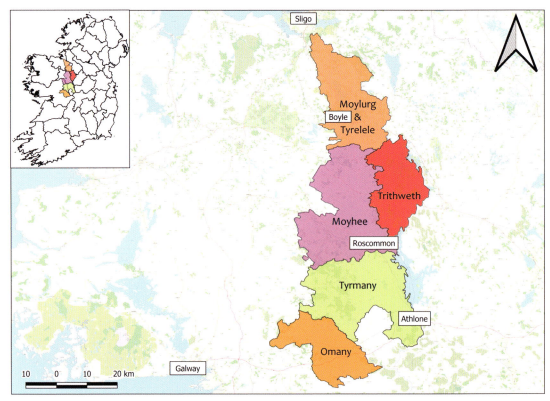

Figure 2.5 The territorial extents of the King's Cantreds, as reconstructed from MacCotter 2014.

of his title and lands, as well as making efforts to maintain these privileges for his son and chosen heir, Aedh (Lydon 2008a, 161). In 1215, Cathal Crobhdearg secured a charter at Athlone, granting him all of Connacht to be held directly of the king. However, on the same day, King John granted a similar charter of Connacht to the Anglo-Norman magnate Richard de Burgh (*CDI*, i, nos 653–4). This was an attempt by John to establish an insurance policy, based upon the likelihood of Cathal Crobhdearg reneging on the terms (Finan 2016, 43).

Upon the death of Cathal Crobhdearg in 1224, the kingship of Connacht passed to Aedh, and similar terms were provided to him as had been granted to his father. However, Aedh engaged in a number of violent acts as the newly inaugurated king, which led the Anglo-Norman administration to charge him with infidelity, culminating in the forfeiture of his lands. With this, Richard de Burgh's 1215 grant was enacted (ibid.). The terms of the grant to de Burgh were such that the king retained five cantreds,[2] named the 'King's Cantreds' for his own purposes (*CDI*, i, nos 1403, 1518, 1863, 1976). These were the five cantreds closest to the River Shannon,

---

[2] An Anglo-Norman land-unit, the general equivalent in Ireland to the earlier *trícha cét*.

Historical background

corresponding in large part to the modern extent of Co. Roscommon, and some adjoining areas (MacCotter 2014, 207–11; Finan 2016, 48–51). From north to south, these were *Moylurg and Tyrelele* (Maigh Luirg and Tír Ailello), *Moyhee* (Magh nAí), *Trithweth* (*Na Trí Túatha*), *Tyrmany* (Tír Maine) and *Omany* (Uí Maine) (Fig. 2.5).

The following years saw de Burgh exercise his grant through military action, backed by the crown in Ireland, and through alliances with compliant candidates for the Ó Conchobair kingship. De Burgh sought to secure his claim over the twenty-four cantreds which constituted his grant, while in the King's Cantreds, land was granted, and new settlements were established in the cantreds closest to the royal castle of Athlone, in Tír Maine and Uí Maine. After a turbulent time in the late 1220s and early 1230s, a period of stability set in during the reign of Feidlim mac Cathal Ó Conchobair as king of Connacht. Feidlim was granted the King's Cantreds in 1230, under the same terms of fee and good service as his predecessors were granted for Connacht as a whole, and this was twice reinstated after a break down in relations in 1233 and 1237 (Finan 2016, 45–6). The improved relations were such that Feidlim even supported Henry III in 1245 on campaign against the Welsh, during a period when he was in good favour with the English court (*AC*; Verstaten 2003, 22–3).

This growing Anglo-Norman presence in Uí Maine and Tír Maine was to directly affect Ó Cellaig fortunes also. In 1253, Richard de Rupella (de la Rochelle) was granted twenty librates[3] of land in Omany, and was approved of a grant to erect a gallows in his manor of *Haghedrium* – Aughrim, Co. Galway (*CDI*, ii, nos 223–4). It is apparent that 29 years after the death of Domnall Ó Cellaig, the Uí Chellaig had lost control of their demesne lands in the cantred of Omany. The precise year for this loss of control at Aughrim may be consistent with the details of provisioning an English army led by the then justiciar, John Fitz Geoffrey, in 1249, at *Athtruim in Connacht*, against chiefs who were disturbing the king's peace (*CIRCLE, Henry III*, 4). Having been removed from their *cenn áit* at Aughrim, the sons of Domnall Ó Cellaig seem to have dispersed in a number of directions. This was a low point in terms of Ó Cellaig power, however it is possible to piece together the origins of their later history from this point. Consultation of the place-name and locational evidence surviving in the Uí Maine genealogical tracts in *Leabhar Ua Maine* indicates that branches of the sept migrated west and east of Aughrim, while others remained within the immediate area.

Clonmacnowen migration
Dealing first with the third son of Domnall Ó Cellaig, Eoghan, he was the originator of a junior sept of the Uí Chellaig in his own right. The *Clannmhaicne Eoghain*, which survives in the later barony of the same name, inhabited the areas surrounding the ford of the River Suck at Ballinasloe, an important point on the communication route

---

[3] A librate is defined as a unit of land with an annual value of one pound, with an area of 4 oxgangs of 13 acres each.

linking Dublin to Galway (Geissel 2006, 93–5). The *Clannmhaicne Eoghain* chief residences are described as being *Áth Nadsluaigh* (Ballinasloe) and *Tuaim Sruthra* (*Ó CGF i*, 41). The former toponym indicates that this site served as an important fording place from an early period. Another fortification was also located in this area, known as *Caislen Suicin*, which was built in 1245 by the Anglo-Normans (*AFM*). The *Logainm* database equates *Tuaim Sruthra* with Ashford townland, immediately north-west of the Suck ford at Ballinasloe (https://www.logainm.ie/en/17581).

Migration beyond Uí Maine
Domnall's youngest recorded son, Lochlainn, and his kin, described variously as the *Sliocht Lochlainn* and *Síol Ceallaigh Cladaigh*, established strongholds across possibly scattered estates at *Cluain Cuill* (Clonquill, Co. Galway), *An Bhearna Dhearg* (Barnaderg, Co. Galway), *Cluain Buaráin* (Cloonburren, Co. Roscommon?) and *Dún na Mónadh* (*Reg. Clon.*, 456–7; *Ó CGF i*, 41). Interestingly, the *Registry of Clonmacnoise* records that Lochlainn and his kin were provided with lands granted by the then bishop of Clonmacnoise, and in return owed church rents and labour duties in perpetuity in respect of areas close to the latter monastery in south Roscommon and east Galway. Lochlainn and his descendants did not become players in the Ó Cellaig kingship succession.

Tír Maine migration
Domnall's second son, Tadhg Fionn, is recorded at *Magh Rúscach* (*Ó CGF i*, 65; also recorded in *Reg. Clon.* 456), which is Rooskagh in south Roscommon. As with the sons of Lochlainn, Tadhg Fionn's descendants were not notable in later historical entries. What is apparent is that some of the Ó Cellaig elite were residing alongside their Anglo-Norman counterparts in Tír Maine. Tyrmany is deemed to have been the most settled of the King's Cantreds by Anglo-Norman colonists (Fig. 2.5). Castlenaughton (possibly constructed in 1214 by Geoffrey de Constentin), Onagh (constructed as a 'stronghold against the men of Connacht' in 1235) and other potential sites present conceivable evidence of Anglo-Norman fortifications being constructed in Tyrmany with settlement in mind. New settlements, in the form of land grants, were designed to reward favourites of the Anglo-Norman court, while also serving to solve the problem of having a substantial Gaelic population to pacify (Fig. 2.6; Walton 1980, 217–18).

The fortunes of Conchobhair Ó Cellaig and his successors
The most telling indication of the position of the Uí Chellaig within thirteenth-century Connacht is seen with the career of Domnall Ó Cellaig's eldest son Conchobhair, who became king of Uí Maine in 1224. Conchobhair's reign lasted at least three but possibly four decades (*Ó CGF ii*, 64), during which time the Uí Chellaig assisted the Uí Chonchobair in military encounters against Anglo-Norman

Historical background

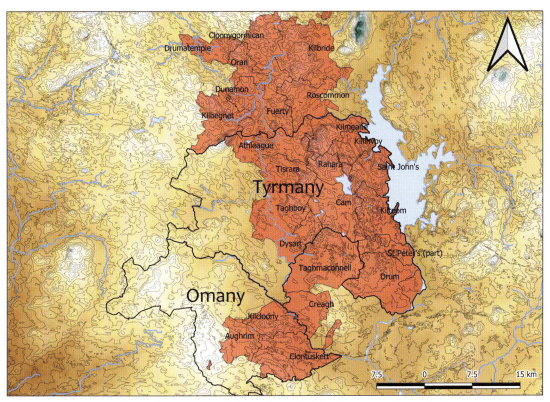

Figure 2.6 The parishes in the King's Cantreds in which land was granted to Anglo-Norman tenants (from Walton 1980, 568, Map IX).

lords, such as at the First Battle of Athenry in 1249, and against the de Burghs in 1256 (*AC*). Before this, Conchobhair Ó Cellaig was included in a list of the Irish kings summoned by Henry III in 1244 on his expedition against Scotland. Conchobhair was recorded as *Macthulaner O'Kellie de Ochonyl* – 'Mac Domnall Mhór Ó Cellaig of Kilconnell' (*Foedera*, 150). In the sixteenth century, this list was copied and expanded upon in order to refer to 'Mac Domnall Mhór' as *Okealy de Imayne* – 'Ó Cellaig of Uí Maine' (*CSPI*, ii, part iii, 1). This implies that the Ó Cellaig chief still resided in Uí Maine at this time, at a presumed *cenn áit* at or near Kilconnell. Given that this is prior to the 1253 land grant to Richard de la Rochelle, the entry is the last instance we have of the Uí Chellaig holding a position of authority in the *trícha cét* during the thirteenth century. We next hear of Conchobhair in 1260, when his *longphort* (stronghold), location unknown, was destroyed by Áed mac Feidlim Ó Conchobair's followers (*AC*). Feidlim Ó Conchobair was king of Connacht at the time. Judging by the evidence to be outlined below, it is likely that Conchobhair's *longphort* was located within Tír Maine.

In terms of locating the late thirteenth-century Uí Chellaig on the landscape, one place-name in the genealogies is informative. Recorded as *Gráinseach Chairn Bhuaileadh* (*Ó CGF ii*, 64), it is referenced as the place of death in 1268 of Maine mac Conchobhair, a king of Uí Maine who reigned just half a year. This name translates as 'Grange/granary of the cairn of the booley/cattle-enclosure' (Ó Muraíle, N., pers. comm.). The modern 'Grange' townland names in the study area provide one candidate in Athlone barony, Co. Roscommon, and two others in Roscommon more generally. Due to the speculative nature of this theory, a variety of other townlands, containing both the *Gráinseach* and the *Chairn Bhuaileadh* elements were considered as alternatives. One alternative is the *Carnebooley* referred to in 1608 (*Cal. Patent Letters*, 1800, Pat 6, 126), also referred to as *Grange-Mulconry* in both the aforementioned source, and in the Dissolution extents of 1569 (Stout 2015, 41). This is now Grange townland, Kiltrustan parish, and contains a mill, but no evidence of cairns or burial mounds are suggested in the place-name. The other alternative is *Cornebole* (ibid., 41), now Curraghnaboley townland, Kilronan parish, which was also listed on the Dissolution extents.

However, Grange (*An Gráinseach*) contains five burial mounds of various classes, including a substantial bowl barrow, which may be the physical manifestation of the toponym. To the south of this barrow is a large univallate ringfort with substantial earthworks. Its size suggests it may have served as residence and place of death for Maine Ó Cellaig. Grange is located immediately to the north of Lough Croan turlough, increasing the likelihood that the seat of Ó Cellaig kingship had now returned to a much-changed Tír Maine. Therefore, while there are a number of candidates for *Gráinseach Chairn Bhuaileadh*, Grange townland beside Lough Croan is, for a variety of reasons, the most likely candidate.

Further evidence corroborates a return of the senior Uí Chellaig to Tír Maine in the thirteenth century. An entry for 1255 reads, 'Godfrey de Lezignan … granted to him in fee the cantred of Tyrmany in Connaught (where the Oscalli dwell) …' (*CDI*, ii, no. 478). The term 'Oscalli' in this instance is a mutation of Uí Chellaig. Throughout this period, Ó Cellaig power had diminished significantly. They were living within a region that was now effectively granted to Anglo-Norman lords. These Gaelic lords continued to live within these landscapes, possibly still at a remove from the manorial or encastellated centres, but they did likely pay rent, tribute, and contributed military service to the Anglo-Norman overlords that managed to exercise their claim locally. Certainly, the Uí Chellaig were summoned to fight for Henry III on his 1244 campaign in Scotland, however, this expedition never materialized (Lydon 2003, 87; Verstraten 2003, 22). Although it isn't elicited in the historical sources, it is quite possible that the main branch of the Uí Chellaig required permission from the Uí Chonchobair and the Anglo-Norman powers in the region to be allowed to return to their ancestral lands and might be why we see them appearing in familiar parts of Tír Maine by 1268.

Historical background

The second half of the thirteenth century saw the beginning of a general change in mindset on the parts of some Gaelic lords. These chiefs capitalized on a combination of factors, including a situation where a host of Anglo-Norman lordships were without male heirs or their heirs were in minority (Lydon 2008b, 247). This ushered in a period of growing self-confidence among the Gaelic elite, who began expressing themselves in ways designed to enhance their dynasties ancestral prestige and underpin their territorial claims. Simms indicates that this self-confidence was certainly apparent by the mid-fourteenth century (Simms 2018a, 273), but I would argue that it was visible earlier. One of the early exemplars of this political recovery was Áed 'na nGall' mac Feidlim Ó Conchobair. Whereas his father practiced diplomacy repeatedly when engaging with the Anglo-Normans, Áed sought to use the sword. Even prior to his ascent to the Ó Conchobair kingship, he harassed and raided the colonists (Lydon 2008b, 248–9). The volatile career of Áed Ó Conchobair, which ended with his death in 1274, started the decline of centralized Anglo-Norman power in Connacht.

Returning to the Uí Chellaig, in 1268, the kingship passed upon the death of Maine to another son of Conchobar Ó Cellaig, Domnall. We know that Domnall Ó Cellaig marched with John de Sandford, justiciar for Ireland, in 1289, against the 'Irish of Meath' (*ACl.*). Aside from this, his reign was not noteworthy, dying in 1295 at the Cistercian Monastery of Abbeyknockmoy, Co. Galway (*AC*). Interestingly, directly after this entry, the next one records: 'Conn Mac Branain, chieftain of Corca Athclann, was killed by O Cellaig's sons as he was tracking his horses, which had been stolen from him.' (*AC*). Mac Branain was chieftain of *Corcu Achlann*, one of the *túath* which made up the *trícha cét* of *Na Trí Túatha* (cantred of *Trithweth*) (Fig. 2.5). Domnall Ó Cellaig's successor was his brother Donnchad Muimnech Ó Cellaig, and this entry may provide evidence for the practice of a *creach ríogh* or king's raid for the newly inaugurated Donnchad Muimnech, often the first expected duty of a newly elected chief in later medieval Gaelic Ireland (Lucas 1989, 146; FitzPatrick 2004, 6, 11).

The sources remain silent on the Uí Chellaig once more until 1307, the year of Donnchad Muimnech's death. In this year, the Ó Cellaig settlement of *Áth Eascrach Cuan* – Ahascragh, Co. Galway, within Tír Maine – was burned by Edmund Butler (*AC*). Edmund was the second son of Theobald Butler, one of the most prominent Anglo-Norman magnates in thirteenth-century Ireland. By 1282, the Butler lordship extended to include the former de la Rochelle estates of nearby Aughrim, and Edmund claimed the Butler lordship in 1299 (*Cal. Ormond Deeds*, i, 122). In retaliation for the burning of Ahascragh, Donnchad Muimnech defeated a great force of the 'English of Roscommon' (*AFM*). This attack itself may have been retaliation on the part of the Butlers, for in 1307 it was also recorded that 'Aughrim was burned by some of the Ui Maine, its own princes' (*AC*).

Donnchad Muimnech was succeeded to the kingship in 1307 by his nephew Gilbert. Progressing into the 1310s, Gilbert Ó Cellaig and his brother Tadg were in competition for the kingship, and in doing so, became embroiled in the wider political disputes of the Uí Chonchobair relating to which branch held the Connacht kingship. Gilbert sided with Fedlimid Ó Conchobair, who was inaugurated in 1310 (*AC*). Tadg supported the claim of Ruaidrí Ó Conchobair, a rival from the Clan Murtagh line. By 1315, Tadg had deposed Gilbert from the kingship of Uí Maine with the assistance of Ruaidrí. Moreover, the reputation of Gilbert and his ally Fedlimid were tainted among the Gaels of Connacht due to their seeking refuge with the 'Red Earl', Richard de Burgh, lord of Connacht and earl of Ulster (Simms 2018a, 287). Tadg used the opportunity provided by his alliance to use Ó Conchobair troops to burn the Butler manor and demolish the castle at Aughrim, and to plunder and burn the cantred of Máenmaige (*AC*).

Tadg's actions brought the Uí Chellaig into the wider political picture in early fourteenth-century Connacht, and the continuation of a steady decline of centralized Anglo-Norman influence in the region. Outside forces, such as Edward Bruce's campaign from 1315, led to the defeat of the once powerful 'Red Earl'. Prior to this, in 1298, a bitter struggle between the de Burghs and the Geraldines saw the disappearance of the latter lords from Connacht entirely (Simms 2018a, 286–7). In 1316 Tadg changed sides, joining Fedlimid Ó Conchobair when he regained the kingship of Connacht, at the expense of a murdered Ruaidrí. Tadg's military prowess may have been part of the reason why he was able to retain his status as king of Uí Maine after Ruaidrí's demise, as opposed to him being overthrown in favour of Gilbert. This military acumen was far-reaching and Tadg served one of the Uí Bhriain factions during their civil war in Thomond (*Caithréim Thoirdhealbhaigh*, 9, 56–8, 71). Also, one of the few surviving administrative accounts from the early fourteenth-century records Tadg leading a considerable cohort of light cavalry and infantry as part of a wider Connacht force into the Leinster Mountains under the ultimate command of the deputy justiciar, William *Liath* de Burgh, in late 1308 (Connolly 1982, 3). Plainly, Tadg was a prominent military figure in this period, and it is likely that his credentials as candidate king were reliant on this martial prowess.

Buoyed by his ascent, Fedlimid united the Gaelic chiefs of Connacht under his authority and turned his attention onto Anglo-Norman settlements. This culminated in the second Battle of Athenry, a disastrous defeat that saw Fedlimid and Tadg slain (Simms 2018a, 288), along with twenty-eight other Ó Cellaig nobles and countless others. However, much of the land recovered by this Gaelic uprising was not subsequently resettled by the Anglo-Normans, particularly in our study area, and the defeat at Athenry also played a role in the decline in power of the Uí Chonchobair into the late medieval period. Both occurrences came to be capitalized on by the Uí Chellaig (Nicholls 2003 170–1; Simms 2018a, 288). Upon Tadg's death, he was replaced by his brother Conchobar, who ruled until his death in a skirmish at Fossakilly, Co. Sligo, in 1318 (*AC*; *AFM*; *Ó CGF ii*, 65). This in turn paved the way

Historical background

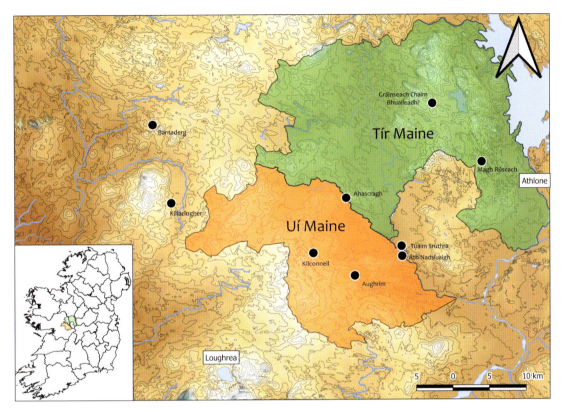

Figure 2.7 Reconstructed extents of the Ó Cellaig *trícha céta* of Uí Maine and Tír Maine during the high medieval period, with principal locations mentioned in the text indicated.

for Gilbert to return to the kingship, which he held until his death in 1322 (*AC; ALC*). The instability of the Uí Maine kingship continued after Gilbert's death, as he was succeeded by his cousin, Áed mac Donnchadh Muimhnigh. Áed was in turn succeeded to the kingship by Ruaidhrí mac Mathghamhna Ó Cellaig, the only member of the *Clannmaicne Eoghain* sept to attain the kingship. Ruaidhrí's reign ended in 1339 (*Ó CGF ii*, 65).

At this time, Connacht more generally was occupied by the growing divisions within the de Burgh family. Various claimants to the Ó Conchobair kingship became embroiled in this internecine struggle, culminating with the death in captivity of the lord of Mayo, Walter *Liath* de Burgh, in 1332. In 1333, in retaliation, the 'Brown Earl', William de Burgh, lord of Connacht and earl of Ulster, and grandson of Richard was murdered by his own kin. Thereafter, the de Burgh lands in Ulster were overrun and lost to Gaelic lords. In Connacht this turbulence ultimately led to the establishment of the two de Burgh lordships, the Mac Uilliam *Íochtar* (Mayo lordship), and the Mac Uilliam *Uachtar* (Galway or *Clann Ricaird*) (Nicholls 2003, 170–3;

Simms 2018a, 288–90). By the close of this period, the extents of Ó Cellaig lordship are likely to have remained largely within Tír Maine, again effectively under the authority of the Uí Chonchobair. However, the predations of Tadg Ó Cellaig in the early fourteenth century indicate that the Butler lordship of Omany was still viewed as Uí Maine territory and attempts to recover control over it may have begun in earnest at this time.

THE LATE MEDIEVAL UÍ MAINE LORDSHIP: THE HEIGHT OF Ó CELLAIG POWER

During the late 1320s and 1330s, a series of incidents took place between the Uí Chellaig and the Uí Chonchobair, probably as a result of the Ó Cellaig alliance with Walter *Liath* de Burgh, a chief rival to Ó Conchobair ambitions. Beginning in 1329, Cathal, brother of Toirrdelbach Ó Conchobair, king of Connacht, was 'forcibly expelled from the Faes and from Tir Maine by the Clann Cellaig and the Ui Maine, acting under the orders of Walter Burke' (*AC*). This action was retaliated upon in 1333, when Toirrdelbach took Donnchadh mac Áed Ó Cellaig prisoner (*AC*). In 1337, Toirrdelbach built a *foslongphort* or stronghold at Athleague, Co. Roscommon, for defence against Edmund de Burgh, most likely Edmund *Albanach* Burke, or Mac Uilliam Burke as he became known (*AC*; Simms 2018a, 290). However, later that year Toirrdelbach Ó Conchobair was taken prisoner by the Uí Chellaig (*AC*). This may have been in response to the construction at Athleague, which was located in what must have been a contested borderland between Tír Maine and Machaire Connacht. This indicates that the newly ascendant Ó Cellaig were willing to show their strength in re-establishing themselves as the principal lords in their ancestral lands.

Áed's successor, Ruaidhrí Ó Cellaig, met his end as a result of this conflict with Ó Conchobair in 1339, when he was 'treacherously killed by Cathal Ó Conchubhair in Cill Mhiadhan' (*Ó CGF ii*, 65). The annals record that Ruaidhrí was killed while going from Ó Conchobair's house to his own (*AC*). *Cill Mhiadhan* is identifiable with the parish of Kilmeane, Co. Roscommon. Kilmeane is bounded immediately to the north by the River Hind, which served as the northern limit of Tír Maine, indicating that Ruaidhrí must have resided at some location within the re-established lordship. Kilmeane continued to serve as a centre for cadet branches of the Ó Cellaig up until the sixteenth century (see Curley 2023). Ruaidhrí was succeeded by Tadhg Óg mac Taidg Ó Cellaig. He was the preferred and seemingly compliant candidate of Toirrdelbach Ó Conchobair (*AC*). Tadhg Óg identified his first cousin once removed, Uilliam Buide mac Donnchadha Muimhnigh Ó Cellaig, as his principal rival to the kingship and in 1340, attempted to remove this obstacle. Tadhg Óg banished Uilliam Buide from Tír Maine (*AFM*), again highlighting this *trícha cét* as the powerbase of these fourteenth-century Uí Chellaig lords. However, this act backfired on Tadhg Óg, with Uilliam Buide rounding on his rival, killing him (*AC*; *Ó CGF ii*, 66). Uilliam Buide did not directly succeed Tadhg Óg as lord of Uí Maine however. Tadhg Óg's successor was Diarmaid mac Gilbert Ó Cellaig, who reigned until *c.*1349. Diarmaid's most notable act was his hanging of Ó Mainnín, chief of Soghain, after which he seized the latter's 'castle' and estate of 'Clogher' (*Tribes*, 107). This is identifiable with Killaclogher, Co. Galway (Mannion 2004, 38), located beyond the traditional boundaries of Uí Maine. Ó Mainnín's residence may relate to the enclosure site in Killaclogher townland (Alcock, de hÓra and Gosling 1999, 199).

Uilliam Buide ascended to the kingship of Uí Maine in about 1349, and it is with his reign that we see the power of the Uí Chellaig reaching its zenith in the medieval period. The first annalistic reference to him as lord of Uí Maine was in 1351, with his hosting, along with his son Maolsechlainn, of a famous gathering known as 'Invitation Christmas' (*AC*; *ACl.*). This is described as a general invitation to all the poets in Ireland and the event is immortalized by a praise poem, entitled *Filidh Éreann Go Haointeach* [the poets of Ireland to one house], in tribute of the patron (Knott (ed. and trans.) 1911). The location of this great festivity is recorded as *Fionngháille* in the poem, arguably identifiable with Galey, Co. Roscommon. This event is often cited as an indicator of the efforts undertaken by Gaelic and Gaelicized elites to patronize the secular learned kindreds (Simms 2018b, 423), and Uilliam's actions can be viewed in this light. However, the political value of such an event cannot be understated either, as Uilliam sought to establish himself as a prominent figure in the politics of fourteenth-century Connacht (Simms 2020, 125).

In 1353, Uilliam Buide founded the Franciscan Friary of Kilconnell (*AFM*), as well as the 'bawn' of Callow (*Tribes*, 104, 171). The latter reference is identifiable with Callow, Kilconnell parish, Co. Galway. This patronage and expansion by Uilliam Buide was not without difficulty however, as continued Ó Conchobair interference in Ó Cellaig affairs nearly resulted in his death. Hostilities with the Uí Chonchobair were to re-emerge in 1356 and were the result of a personal dispute. Áed Ó Conchobair, king of Connacht, is recorded as having been killed at the behest of Uilliam Buide at Ballaghdacker by members of the Ó Cellaig dynasty and one of their vassal clans, the Clann an Baird (*AC*). Ballaghdacker is located in Athleague parish, on the Galway/Roscommon border, where there is a lake. Ballaghdacker Lough also seems to have been used in 1393 as a refuge by Maol Ruanaidh Mac Diarmada, newly installed lord of Maigh Luirg and an ally at this time to the Uí Chellaig (*ACl.*). These historical entries confirm that the Uí Chellaig lords had a residence here during the period, which was used by them as a safe house and as a prison for important prisoners, two key functions of defended elite residences throughout later medieval Europe (e.g. King 1988, 5). Furthermore, there is a record from 1424 in *Leabhar Ua Maine* which may describe the physical remains at Ballaghdacker Lough as a place-name – *Móinín na hAibhle Léithe ag Loch an Dúin* (*Ó CGF ii*, 68). This was the place of death of Donnchadh Ó Cellaig, lord of Uí Maine, and Ó Muraíle translates this as 'the little bogland of the grey/green spark, or thunderbolt, at the lake of the fortress' (Ó Muraíle, N., pers. comm.). Nicholls has identified the location as being near or on Ballaghdacker Lough (Nicholls 1969, 52). Donnchadh was murdered by his nephews, the sons of Uilliam Ruadh Ó Cellaig, while attempting to get them to submit to his chieftainship (*AFM*).

In the following years, Ó Cellaig became tightly allied to the Mac Uilliam *Íochtar*. This alliance was tested in 1366 when Uilliam Buide lined up alongside his Burke son-in-law Thomas as well as another Áed Ó Conchobair against the Clann Ricaird Burkes. After three months of engagements, the Mac Uilliam *Íochtar* brought the Clann Ricaird to submission (*AFM*). Two years later, in 1368, Uilliam Buide was imprisoned for a short period by his own vassal kinsmen, members of the *Clannmhaicne Eoghain* Uí Chellaig and Ó Madadháin (*AFM*). After this imprisonment, Uilliam Buide removed himself from the active rule in favour of his son Maolsechlainn. He didn't remove himself completely, however, and took the credit for the Ó Cellaig defeat of the de Berminghams or Clann Mac Feorais in 1372 (*AFM*). This clash may have resulted out of an Ó Cellaig territorial ambition to bring de Bermingham land to the east of Athenry under their control (Nicholls 1969, 47).

Uilliam Buide Ó Cellaig died in 1381, at which time he was remembered as a great patron of the learned classes (*AFM*) and, as seen above, a very ambitious and capable later medieval Gaelic lord. We do not have his place of death or burial, but it is possible that he was laid to rest in Kilconnell Friary, a likely repose as he was its founder. Uilliam Buide's successor, his son Maolsechlainn, reigned a further twenty years and, judging by his place of death, he actively sought to continue his father's ambitions. Maolsechlainn died in 1401 in his own stronghold at *Tigh Da-Choinne* (*Ó CGF ii*, 67). This is identifiable with Tiaquin, Co. Galway (Mannion 2004, 57), beyond the traditional western limits of Uí Maine. With his death, father and son had presided over the Ó Cellaig lordship for a combined fifty-two years, an unprecedented level of stability during the turbulent later medieval period.

The extent of the Ó Cellaig lordship at the beginning of the fifteenth century included the entire *trícha céta* lands of Tír Maine and Uí Maine. By this time, though, the Uí Chellaig seem to have extended their influence further to include much of the cantred of Clantayg, as evidenced by their taking control of first Killaclogher, and then Tiaquin, and with it influence over the Cistercian foundation of Abbeyknockmoy. The sixteenth-century 'Indenture of Hymany' in the *Compossicion Booke of Connought* records the division of Tír Maine, Uí Maine, and beyond, into a number of 'Eraghts', from the Irish *oireachtaí* – 'patrimony *or* territory' (*Compossicion*, 168, 172–3). These divisions possibly date to the fourteenth century, as some names refer back to thirteenth- and fourteenth-century Ó Cellaig dynasts, and their descendants. For instance, included is a division named 'O Murry & mcEdmonds Eraght called the Heyny', which indicates that the *oireacht* south of the River Hind was split between

Historical background

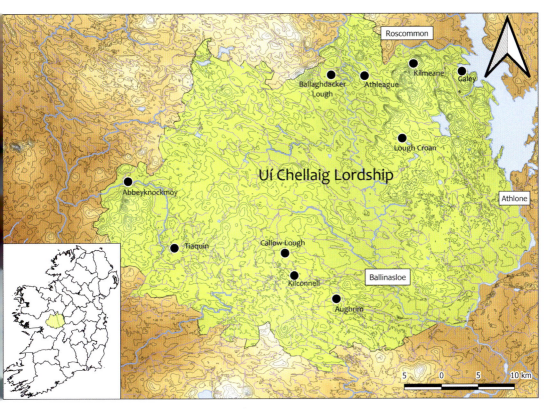

Figure 2.8 Reconstructed extents of the Ó Cellaig lordship of Uí Maine by the beginning of the fifteenth century, with principal locations mentioned in the text indicated. By this time, the Uí Chellaig had come to exercise power over a large expanse of eastern and central Connacht.

the MacEdmond branch of the Uí Chellaig and the Uí Muiredaig dynasty. Another example is seen with 'Sleight Gillebirt aka Eraight Huigh Toehaleage', which corresponds with the civil parishes of Athleague, Tisrara and Taghboy (Nicholls 1969, 265). The principal Ó Cellaig lordly centres discussed throughout this work primarily occupy Ó Cellaig *oireachtaí*, and these centres seem to have originated as *cenn áiteanna* of the senior Ó Cellaig sept, even if by the sixteenth century they are in the possession of related junior branches of the dynasty.

THE SLOW DECLINE OF THE Ó CELLAIG LORDSHIP

According to the historical sources, the early years of the fifteenth century did not see the continuation of this upward trajectory. In 1403, Conchobar Anabaidh mac Maolsechlainn Ó Cellaig, lord of Uí Maine, died at *Loch Cróine* (Lough Croan, Co. Roscommon) (*Ó CGF ii*, 67) and was buried at the Hospital of St John the Baptist at Rindoon (*ALC*). Conchobar was followed in comparatively quick succession by his brothers Tadhg Ruadh (died 1410 at Athleague) (ibid.), Uilliam (died 1420, and buried at Kilconnell Friary (*AC*)) and Donnchadh (died 1424, near Athleague) (Byrne 2011, 227).

While we have little information on either Tadhg Ruadh or Donnchadh, Uilliam Ó Cellaig possessed a similar ambitious streak as that of his father Maolsechlainn, and his grandfather and namesake, Uilliam Buide. 1413 saw Uilliam and the Uí Maine ally with the Ó Conchobair Ruadh to attack the Ó Conchobair Donn stronghold of Roscommon Castle. This was one of a series of assaults on Roscommon that took place over the next five years, culminating with Uilliam constructing what is described as a *caislen becc* or 'small castle' (*AC*), possibly a timber siege castle, beside Roscommon Castle. Ultimately, this alliance was unsuccessful in their efforts and later attempts by the combined force to impose themselves on another rival, the Clann Ricaird Burkes, in 1419, also ended in defeat (Cosgrove 2008, 578). Despite this, Uilliam Ó Cellaig's career serves as an illustration of Uí Maine ambitions into the early fifteenth century.

Uilliam died in 1420, and was buried at Kilconnell Friary, a religious house which he patronized extensively. His brother and successor, Donnchadh, is regarded by O'Donovan as having resided at Tiaquin (*Tribes*, 118), indicating a continued Ó Cellaig presence in this area. Donnchadh died in 1424 and his demise seems to have led to a period of over four decades of instability among the Uí Chellaig and their vassal clans. The evaluation of this period is exacerbated by a general lack of recording of Ó Cellaig events in the annals until 1464 (ibid., 109). During this period of uncertainty, a more junior branch of the dynasty took advantage of the instability and ascended to the Uí Maine lordship. This branch later became known as the Uí Chellaig of Athleague (ibid., 108–11).

It is at around this time, and slightly earlier, that we first see the Ó Cellaig utilizing the services of galloglass kindreds in their military encounters. Principal among these were an offshoot of the Scottish Clann Somhairle dynasty, the Clann Dubhghaill (MacDowell) kindred. The Clann Dubhghaill were one of a number of early Scottish galloglass kindreds that migrated to Ulster in the thirteenth century (McInerney 2015, 25), many finding employment as mercenaries in the armies of the Connacht lordships initially. The Clann Dubhghaill were the hereditary captains of galloglass to the Uí Chellaig (*AC, s.a.* 1377; 1419; 1521; *ALC, s.a.* 1557; *CSPI*, v, 521; Nicholls 1969, 68; 2007, 102). These professional heavy infantry would have been a core part of late medieval Gaelic musters, and the Ó Cellaig are reported in a late fifteenth-century military report as being able to call upon two 'battles of galloglass' (effectively between 120 and 160 fighting men) at that time (Price 1932, 204). The *Mac Duill* are recorded in possession of 'castles' at *Beallagalde* and *Cornegihy* in 1573 (Nicholls (transcribed) 1573, 2019). The possession at Ballygalda corresponds with the degraded remains of a castle of likely tower house form in the adjacent Derrineel townland. This may be the reason why the townland (*Béal átha gallda* – mouth of the foreigners ford) is named as such, indicating that the Mac Dubhghaill were positioned here effectively to act as sentries over a communication route through the northern borderlands of the Ó Cellaig lordship. The only visible archaeological remains in Cornageeha (*Cornegihy*) are that of a ringfort and a well-preserved cashel. It is possible that the cashel, or a no longer extant structure which once stood within the cashel, may be the physical manifestation of this 'castle' from the State Paper list.

In total, eight descendants of Brian mac Maolsechlainn Ó Cellaig (the originator of the Athleague Uí Chellaig line) became chiefs of the Uí Maine from the mid-fifteenth century through to the end of the sixteenth century. The first of these was Aodh mac Brian Ó Cellaig (r. 1424–67) (*Tribes*, 108–9) and it is with his reign that the fragmentation of the Ó Cellaig lordship and the decline in their fortunes is adjudged to have begun. This decline is typified by the recording of a number of periods during the late fifteenth century, and into the sixteenth century, when the lordship was divided between two distant and opposing familial branches. The River Suck served as the dividing line between these two halves of Uí Maine (*AFM, s.a.* 1472; 1486; 1487; 1499, Mannion 2024, 30) and resulted in a number of recordings of a chief being appointed for *Iarthair* (west) and *Airthir* (east) Uí Maine. This internal strife in the later fifteenth and sixteenth century is perceived to have sent the dynasty into an inevitable decline in power that they never recovered from (Nicholls 2003, 177).

One of the more noteworthy series of events during this period spans the last years of the fifteenth century, culminating in 1504 with the Battle of Knockdoe. The episode seems to have begun in 1487:

> An army was led by Mac William of Clanrickard (Ulick, the son of Ulick of the Wine) into Hy-Many, by which he destroyed the bawn of Athliag Maenagan, and destroyed much corn and many towns throughout Hy-Many … (*AFM*).

The lord of Clann Ricaird was Ulick Fionn Burke (r. 1485–1509), who was a notably aggressive warlord, while the Uí Maine lord in 1487 was Maolsechlainn mac Aodh Ó Cellaig. It is likely that Burke's attack was on Maolsechlainn's own residence. Burke returned to Athleague in 1499 to further meddle in the title of chief of Uí Maine. Burke's strength was such that he was able to imprison the lord of *Airthir* Uí Maine, Conchobhar Óg, hand the castle of Athleague to the sons of William Ó Cellaig, Maolsechlainn's brother, and instal another Maolsechlainn, son of Tadhg mac Donnchadh Ó Cellaig (died 1424), as a presumably compliant lord of Uí Maine (*AFM*). This obedience on the part of Maolsechlainn mac Tadhg was not to last, owing to Ulick Burke's own territorial ambitions over Connacht. These ambitions included wider Uí Maine as well as the territory of his now distant kin, the Mac Uilliam *Íochtar*, as seen by his military actions in 1503 (*AFM*). This hostile front was to continue on the part of Ulick Fionn Burke into 1504, when he attacked and defeated the Mac Uilliam *Íochtar* and their Ó Cellaig allies at *Bél Átha na nGarbhán* (*AFM*), after which he turned his attention directly on the Uí Chellaig. Burke demolished three of Maolsechlainn's castles, at Garbally (*Garbh dhoire*), Monivea (*Muine an mheadha*) and

Gallagh (*Gallach*), Co. Galway (*AFM*). Due to this potentially debilitating attack, Maolsechlainn approached the lord justice of Ireland, Gearóid Mór Fitzgerald, eighth earl of Kildare, for assistance, which led to the military encounter on 19 August 1504, the Battle of Knockdoe. Fitzgerald's army won the day, and celebrated the victory by marching on Galway and Athenry to exercise his control over these two wealthy towns (Hayes-McCoy 1969, 65), in the face of Clann Ricaird's erstwhile ambitions in the region.

Ultimately, as the sixteenth century progressed, the power of the Ó Cellaig lords in the wider Connacht landscape began to stagnate and decline. Indications of this loss of authority can be seen with the destruction visited on the Ó Cellaig *cenn áit* of Turrock Castle by a group of Connacht families on the southern shore of Lough Croan in 1536 (*AC*). In this instance, the lord of Uí Maine, Donnchadh Ó Cellaig, placed himself as a hostage as a means of ensuring that the Ó Cellaig lands were not destroyed, illustrating the nadir in the fortunes of these eastern Connacht lords. This was not absolute, however, as the reputation of Donnchadh Ó Cellaig was sufficiently strong to defiantly refuse to submit to the then lord deputy of Ireland, Leonard Grey, and the English crown at Aughrim in 1538, to which he received no direct retaliation. Grey and his company chose to avoid Ó Cellaig country on the journey eastwards from Galway, travelling back to Dublin through Síl Anmchadha instead (Mannion 2024 59).

The distance through which the Ó Cellaig title was now travelling is noted by the fact that Donnchadh's predecessor was his second cousin once removed, Domhnall mac Aodh *na gCailleach*, while his direct successor was his third cousin, Ceallach mac Domhnall (Genealogies 2011, 161).

Donnchadh's son, Aodh, reigned as the last of the unbroken line of Ó Cellaig lords, attaining the title in 1580, and possessing it until his death in 1590. An English state paper list of 1573 records Aodh Ó Cellaig's residence as *Lysdallon* – Lisdaulan, Co. Roscommon (Nicholls 2008, 406, 3). He was laid to rest at the nearby parish church of Killinvoy (*ALC*), rather fittingly within the region that his ancestors claimed as their sovereignty throughout the later medieval period, Tír Maine.

At this time, the political landscape of Connacht was beginning to change, as English Elizabethan rule began to be imposed. Galway, Mayo, Sligo and Roscommon were shired into counties in 1569, the first step towards the establishment of English common law as the legal reality in the province (Mannion 2012, 64). Branches of the Uí Chellaig became active adherents to, and indeed promotors of, the growing English influence on Irish affairs from at least the mid-1570s. The Ó Cellaig seem to have furnished the only Gaelic presence on an expedition of the Queen's forces under the Lord President of Connacht, Edward Fitton, to capture Shrule Castle in 1570 (Mannion 2024, 136). Indeed, Galway's first Gaelic sheriff was Tadhg mac William Ó Cellaig of Mullaghmore. This closeness to English affairs had its benefits for these Uí Chellaig septs, as both Tadhg and his kinsman, Maolsechlainn 'mac an Abba', were granted the offices of seneschals for life of Tiaquin and Kilconnell baronies respectively

Historical background 37

in 1578 (Mannion 2012, 71, see also 2024, 136–37). This exemplifies the transition of members of the Uí Chellaig lordly families from chiefs of their communities, towards adopting the role of English-style landlords.

While this was to provide short-term benefits for the septs involved, when it came to retaining or being permitted to re-establish the title of lord of Uí Maine at the end of the sixteenth century the English administration was less generous. The last holder of the title was Aodh of Lisdaulan. Upon his death, the title was abolished by the English as part of the terms of the *Compossicion of Conought*. The *Compossicion* was a series of indentures, usually divided into five sections, between the deputy and the landowners of the Connacht lordships, including Uí Maine. These comprised surveys of the estates in question, the agreement of rent to the Crown, and the abolition of Gaelic titles, customary divisions and elections (Ellis 1998, 322–5; Lennon 2005, 251–3). Therefore, when Tadhg Ó Cellaig of Mullaghmore led a petition to challenge for the title for himself in 1590, it led to a collective incarceration of all family connections with Tadhg, in order to mitigate against the Uí Chellaig going into rebellion for their now defunct title (Mannion 2012, 78–9).

A further claimant to the title came a year earlier, in 1589, in the form of Feardorcha Ó Cellaig of Aughrim. Feardorcha also vainly petitioned at the English court for the lawful inheritance of the name of Ó Cellaig (*Acts Privy Council*, xvii, 233–5). In the same year, Feardorcha was forced to seek a lease from the earl of Ormond for thirty-one years for his lands in the barony of Kilconnell (Curtis 1932/3, 125), with Ormond the re-established landowner in the area since 1541 based on the Butler claim to estates in Omany from the late thirteenth and early fourteenth centuries (Mannion 2024, 62–5). In 1595, Feardorcha supported Red Hugh O'Donnell, who in turn appointed him with the title of 'lord of Uí Maine' (*AFM*). The following year, he was deemed to have broken the conditions of the lease to Ormond and the lands were then leased to the earl of Thomond (Curtis 1932/3, 126). However, Feardorcha used the Nine Years War (1593–1603) to lay waste to his former lands. In 1607, his lease was restored, upon agreeing to pay reparations to Thomond (Egan 1960–1, 78). Upon his death post-1611, Feardorcha was effectively a landlord presiding over the barony of Kilconnell, under the greater authority of the earl of Ormond and the English administration.

While Feardorcha Ó Cellaig offered some resistance to the advancement of English interests in the 1590s, other branches of the family, such as Conor *na gCearrbhach* of Gallagh, and the sons of Shane *na Maighe* of Clonmacnowen, were described as loyal crown subjects (Mannion 2012, 79). This uneven pattern of submission and resistance was seen throughout the various branches of the family in the late sixteenth and early seventeenth centuries, beginning with the aforementioned Aodh of Lisdaulan, who in 1585 accepted his territory as a life-interest only, in return for rents and services (*Compossicion*, 169). This is also seen with the contrasting approaches taken by Brian

Óg mac Maolsechlainn Ó Cellaig of *Cluain na gCloidhe*, later Mount Talbot, and Colla O'Kelly of nearby Skrine, Co. Roscommon. Brian Óg marched to Kinsale with Red Hugh O'Donnell, while his kinsman Colla, whose father, Roger O'Kelly of Aghrane, served as sheriff of Roscommon in 1590, joined with Elizabeth I's army as a captain of foot under the lord of Clann Ricaird for the same conflict (Connolly 2014, 15). After Kinsale, Brian Óg travelled to Spain along with other members of the Gaelic nobility in search of military assistance, while Colla was granted 9,450 acres in south Roscommon and east Galway, in return for his loyalty in the Nine Years War (Cronin 1977, 176; Connolly 2014, 16; Lenihan 2018, 263).

***

Based on the historical background, a number of Ó Cellaig lordly centres have now been identified. These were the elite residences of Uí Chellaig for at least part of the later medieval period and are consistent with discrete archaeological complexes in south Roscommon and east Galway. Over the course of the following chapters, these *cenn áiteanna*, and their cultural landscape settings, will be inspected in order to reconstruct these past environments and thus build a picture of elite society in later medieval Uí Maine. As can be seen from the historical background, this later medieval lordship is a geographical entity that has been difficult to successfully identify, as it changed through time. Through analysis of the primary source material, it has become apparent that the extents of Ó Cellaig authority were by no means fixed through the period. The growth and decline in power of these eastern Connacht lords from the period of 1100 through to the commissioning of the late sixteenth-century *Compossicion Booke of Conought* is reflected in the geographical extents of their lordship at any given time.

The first part of the later medieval period shows that the dominant Uí Maine offshoot, the Uí Chellaig, were residing in their patrimonial lands of Tír Maine. By the early decades of the thirteenth century, their power in Tír Maine had declined in the face of Uí Chonchobair dominance in the region at large. This resulted in a migration of at least some of the Ó Cellaig elite into what was previously a sub-kingdom of their overall territory, once known as Soghan, and now broadly the *trícha cét* of Uí Maine. The mid-thirteenth century witnessed the arrival of a sustained Anglo-Norman presence in the region, which led to the multiplicity of movements of the sons of Domnall Mór Ó Cellaig, during which time they operated within a political landscape dominated by Anglo-Norman lords and the Uí Chonchobair. The early decades of the fourteenth century coincided with a re-emergence of Ó Cellaig authority in Tír Maine, and this served as the starting point for a period of growth, which was to see the greatest extents of the lordship realized in the historical sources by the late fourteenth and early fifteenth centuries. However, from the mid-fifteenth century onwards, first internal instability, and later Tudor ambitions in Connacht more generally, are

Historical background

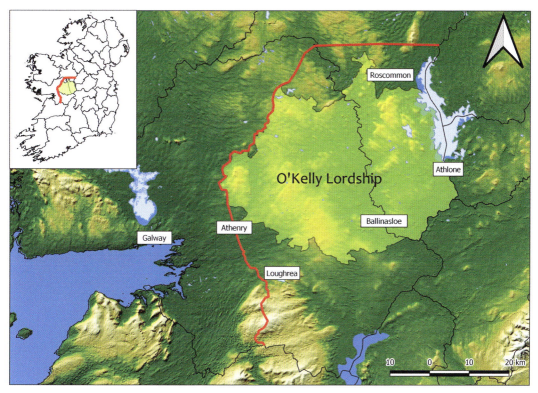

Figure 2.9 Composite map outlining the widest extents of the Ó Cellaig lordship of Uí Maine in the fifteenth century, in contrast with the conflated boundaries of Uí Maine, marked by the red line, as illustrated by O'Donovan in 1843.

perceived by historians as the major factors in the gradual decline of the Ó Cellaig lordship, such that by the late sixteenth century, the Ó Cellaig title had been abolished, and compliant branches of the wider kin group transitioned from Gaelic chiefs presiding over their communities towards English-style landlords within a Tudor administration.

The identification of Ó Cellaig lordly centres in this chapter has effectively shown that O'Donovan's 1843 map (Fig. 2.1), which is based on the late fourteenth-century Ó Dubhagáin poem, is incorrect. There are two main points of criticism concerning this map and its source. The territorial extent of Uí Maine was not fixed in time, rather it expanded and contracted with the fortunes of each individual Ó Cellaig lord. Even at its most extensive in the late fourteenth and early fifteenth century (Fig. 2.8), the territory was clearly far smaller than was suggested by O'Donovan (Fig. 2.9). It is clear, therefore, that the original Ó Dubhagáin poem reflected the ultimate territorial ambitions of the Uí Chellaig in the late fourteenth century, rather than reality. It seems that O'Donovan accepted the contents of the poem at face value in 1843 and failed to see that much of its content was propaganda.

CHAPTER THREE

The landscape and economy of Uí Maine

This chapter brings together the available source material in order to reconstruct aspects of the medieval landscape within which the Ó Cellaig lords operated. Understanding the physical landscape and the ways in which society interacted with and manipulated the natural environment are critical to understanding where and why elite locations were chosen and developed within the wider territory. Here I will focus on the physical landscape, communication routes, assembly places and the economic circumstances which dominated in this region in the later medieval period, as well as how these factors may have underpinned the prosperity of the Ó Cellaig lords.

THE PHYSICAL LANDSCAPE

A general account of the present-day physical landscape in what is south Roscommon and east Galway has been treated above. What is apparent from the sources is that this region is much changed today from how it would have appeared in the later medieval period and certain parts of this landscape were more and less suitable to settlement and economic activities. In the study area, the physical features which dictated where and why society developed are soil, bogland, woodland, rivers and lakes.

Soils and bogland
The types of soils that were conducive to settlement and agricultural activity in later medieval Uí Maine are soil associations defined primarily by fine or coarse loamy drift, underserved by limestones. A soil association is a group of soils forming a pattern of soil types characteristic of a geographical region. Teagasc categorizations of soil types[1] are used here to indicate the relative soil quality and grade the agricultural viability of zones within the region. The most productive soil in the territory is an Elton soil association – a fine loamy drift, with good calcium content. Modern land use would describe it as improved grassland, but it may have been suitable for arable in the past. This is characteristic of a large expanse of south Roscommon and a substantial zone located south of Ballinasloe. Coarse loamy drifts such as Mullabane, Rathowen and Baggotstown soils occur adjacent to these areas and would be regarded as being of similar productivity. In contrast to the agricultural high yields that could be generated on the latter lands, large zones are dominated by bog or peatland, as well as what today would appear as improved and drained, but nonetheless, peaty soils,

---
[1] http://gis.teagasc.ie/soils/soilguide.php. Accessed 13/11/2023.

The landscape and economy of Uí Maine

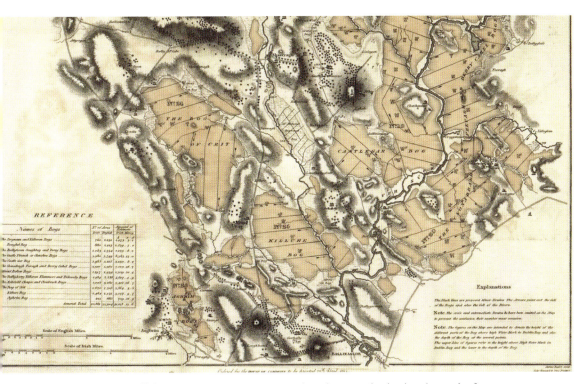

Figure 3.1 Griffith's Bogs Commission map, recording the extant bogland to the north of Ballinasloe, Co. Galway, at the beginning of the nineteenth century.

created out of what was originally bogland. The modern land improvement works sometimes disguise the true nature of this landscape, but Griffith's early nineteenth-century Bogs Commission map records, prior to improvement, what appears to be the extent of bogland as they would have occurred during later medieval times (Fig. 3.1). Some of these bogs are not extant today.

Plotting the distribution of ringforts and cashels on a regional soils map shows, not surprisingly, that settlement distribution conforms very strictly with soil quality. The Elton soil association sees the greatest density of archaeology, with the coarse loamy soil associations showing a slightly more dispersed distribution. Peatland is nearly devoid of settlement. As a result, the substantial zones of peatland in the very south of Roscommon, discrete bogland areas in the generally fertile landscape of central south Roscommon, and large pockets of bog both immediately west and east of the River Suck, were not permanently occupied in the medieval period (Fig. 3.2). Similarly, communication routes would have generally avoided peatland, or at least developed specific routes through it, with a view to safe transition through what would have been a naturally treacherous landscape. Therefore, soil quality and the presence of bogland played a major role in dictating where settlement was located. Bog wasn't completely

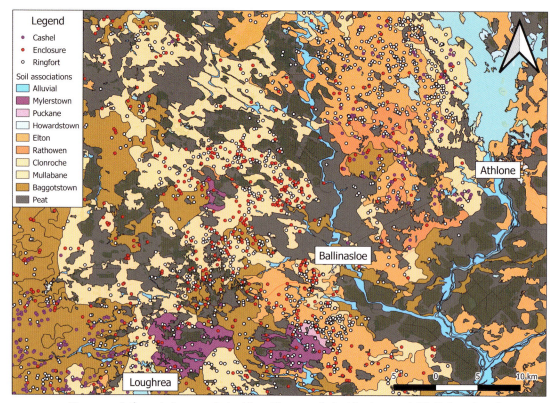

Figure 3.2 Soil association map derived from Teagasc soil classifications, with NMS data plotted on top (soils data courtesy of Teagasc).

devoid of use, however, and turf was cut to serve as a fuel for cooking and heating in Northern Europe and the British Isles from at least as early as the Iron Age (Giles 2020, 102–6). By at least the late thirteenth and fourteenth century, harvesting peat was a specified labour duty among manorial tenants on Anglo-Norman manors and the fuel was used throughout all levels of society (Lucas 1970; Glasscock 2008, 210; *AFM, s.a.* 1488).

Woodland
Woodland and forest were important components of the later medieval physical landscape. Native woodland has nearly disappeared from the region today, having been cut down since the early seventeenth century; however, in the later medieval period, woodland was much more extensive. These were not primordial forests; they were likely managed for their resources and their extents did not remain fixed through time (Hall and Bunting 2001, 208; Nicholls 2001, 181–2). The rates of medieval woodland cover in Ireland are difficult to estimate, but it is calculated that about 12% of the island was still wooded in 1600. This is a drop from a conservative estimate of 20% in

the twelfth century. By the beginning of the fourteenth century, Glasscock deduces that about 15% of the island was still afforested (Glasscock 2008, 209; see Nicholls 2001). These forests would have looked very different from today, and would have been largely composed of deciduous trees, such as oak, hazel, ash and birch, devoid of conifers (with the exception of Scots Pine), or the more recent deciduous introductions.

The historical decline of woodland cover for the island at large is representative of the situation in this region. This is borne out by the data collected from the, admittedly few, pollen analyses conducted locally by the Paleoenvironmental Research Unit at the University of Galway. The pollen profile from Ballinphuill bog, Co. Galway, on the western fringes of Uí Maine, indicates that for the period AD 400–600, agriculture began to expand in the area, but was initially extensive rather than intensive in character, identified through an increase in hazel pollen. Pastoral and arable farming increased substantially between AD 600 and AD 800, with hazel clearance, and the demise of yew and Scots Pine, while in the later medieval period (1250–1500), ash and elm became largely extinct, and oak and hazel were greatly reduced in numbers, a result of intensive farming with a strong cereal-growing component (Molloy, Feeser and O'Connell 2014, 117).

By comparison, a series of pollen profiles were established around the watermill at Kilbegly, Co. Roscommon, which lay within the territory of the Cenél Coirpre Chruim during its main period of use. The mid-profile values (AD 820–960) of one of the pollen cores indicates that there was a strong pastoral farming economy in the area, with hazel becoming less important and yew probably becoming extinct at the time. Higher in the profile (AD 960–1120), farming seems to have gone into decline, seen with an accompanying regeneration of oak. The end of the profile indicates a strong increase in farming once more, with woodland clearance resuming *c.*AD 1150 (Overland and O'Connell 2013, 69–71). It is clear that certain zones within the study area saw a steady reduction of woodland cover through time from the early medieval period onwards, and these cleared areas were then managed for both pastoral and arable farming in the later medieval period (ibid.). The fact that these cleared woods lay in the vicinity of medieval routeways may have facilitated their degradation and transition into farmland.

However, historical accounts strongly indicate that this region continued to be occupied by a number of major expanses of woodland during the later medieval period, the most prominent being the *Feadha* (woods) of Athlone, the woods surrounding Athleague, and the woods of *Bruigheol*. The Fews, Faes or *Feadha* of Athlone are referred to in *Cormac's Glossary*, dated to the ninth century (Stokes (ed. and trans.) 1862, 109). The level of afforestation in this area changed throughout the whole period, but an interesting calculation of the area of ploughable land available in Kilbegly totalled only *c.*60 acres in the fourteenth century from an overall area of 393

Figure 3.3 Section of Browne's *Map of the province of Connaught* (1591) indicating the extent of woodland, known as the *Feadha* of Athlone, at the beginning of the seventeenth century. The extent of bogland outlined in Fig. 3.2, coupled with the quantities of woodland indicated in Fig. 3.3, suggests that very little pre-modern settlement was located in the very south of Roscommon (TCD, MS 1209/68. Copyright 2011, courtesy of the Board of Trinity College Dublin).

acres in the townland (*Reg. Clon.*, 454). The availability of this relatively small area of agricultural land at Kilbegly may indicate that the wider environment and surrounding countryside here was not only pasture but contained substantial amounts of forest and bog (Devane 2013, 109).

The *Feadha*, also known in the early thirteenth-century sources as the cantred of *Tirieghrachbothe* or *Tír Fhiachrach bhfeadh*, was an extensive area of woodland that existed to the north-west and south-west of Athlone throughout the later medieval period (*CDI*, i, no. 137; Walton 1980, 34). These woods are depicted on late sixteenth-

The landscape and economy of Uí Maine

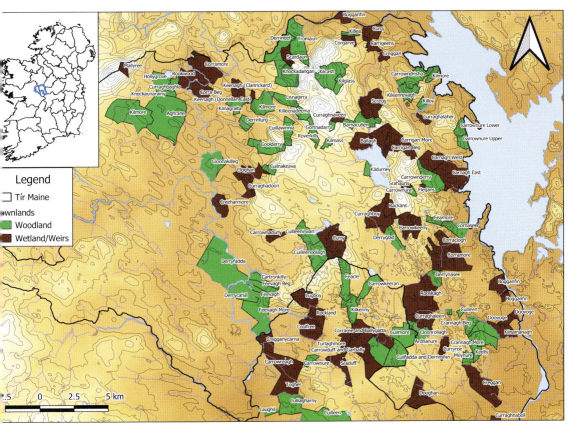

Figure 3.4 A graphical representation of the townland names which denote woodland and difficult land in Tír Maine, consistent with the historical and cartographic attestations to the wooded and treacherous *Feadha* of Athlone, woods of Athleague and *Bruigheol*.

and early seventeenth-century maps, taking up a considerable portion of the south-eastern part of Uí Maine (Figs. 3.3; 3.4). The Civil Survey of 1654–6 records that in its entirety, Roscommon possessed 6% woodland cover at that time and the district to the west of Lough Ree (the *Feadha*) made up a considerable portion of this (Doran 2004, 60). The woods are described in the early nineteenth century as still being extant, mostly comprised of oaks, with some hazel (Lewis 1837, 522; McCracken 1959, 278).

The townland names that survive for this part of south-east Roscommon provide important information when attempting to reconstruct the geographical extents of the *Feadha*. A predominance of names in the area relate to woodland. Moving north from Athlone we encounter Cornaseer – *Cor na soar* (round hill of the carpenters), Feamore – *Feádh mór* (great wood), Carrownderry – *Ceathramhadh an doire* (quarter of the derry or oak wood), Kilmore – *Coill mór* (great wood), Barnacullen – *Bearnaidh chuillinn* (holly-oak) and Kilglass – *Coill glas* (green wood), among others. Similar place-names exist to the south-west and west of Athlone. Coupling these with place-names relating to rough ground or weirs providing access through difficult or wet terrain indicates a landscape of restriction in terms of communication, transport and agriculture. Examples, among many, include Bogganfin – *Bogán fionn* (white bog), Corramore – *Corra mhór* (big weir), Corraclogh – *Corra chloch* (stony weir), Carnagh – *An Charnach* (abounding in heaps or cairns), Curraghalaher – *Currach a' leathair* (moor of the leather), Scregg – *Screag* (rocky land), Curry – *Curraidh* (a moor), and Corgarve – *Cor garbh* (rough hill) (Fig. 3.4).

The historical sources indicate that the *Feadha* was a natural obstacle to overland journeys between Athlone and Roscommon. Evidence of the nature of this obstacle is seen in 1273–4 when a pass was cut through the *Feadha* for security reasons, providing access between the Anglo-Norman castles of Athlone and Rindoon (Anon. 1904, 41). This was one of a series of infrastructural projects commissioned at this time by the justiciar of Ireland, Geoffrey de Geneville (Walton 1980, 256). Annalistic references to the *Feadha* further corroborate the afforested nature of the area and the difficulties that individuals and armies endured as they attempted to navigate these woods (*AFM*, s.a. 1268, 1535; *AU*, s.a. 1225; *AC*, s.a. 1268). Gaelic military tactics throughout the period utilized the natural landscape as a weapon of war and territorial defence (Ó Domhnaill 1946, 41–2; O'Conor 1998, 98–100; Nicholls 2001, 187). The *Feadha* was presumably an ideal location within which the Ó Cellaig could mount a resistance to Gaelic, Anglo-Norman, and later, English advances through their territory. Furthermore, during times of war, livestock and non-combatants could be hidden away in this large wood, and protected from attack (O'Conor 1998, 98–100). This impediment remained into the late medieval period, as the mid-sixteenth-century English state papers refer to the need to recruit large numbers of men to cut the woodland passes beyond the River Shannon near Athlone, as well as conferring the Ó Cellaig chief with the title 'Governor of the Great Pass beyond the water' (*CSPI*, i, 88–90).

The second historically and cartographically attested stand of native woodland in later medieval Uí Maine are the woods surrounding Athleague (see Figs. 3.5; 3.6). Contemporary records tell us that these woods were of mature oak, but also included species such as crabtree, hawthorn and hazel, suggesting that these woods were quite difficult to traverse (Nicholls 2001, 189).

The townland name survivals for this area again place a strong emphasis on describing the wooded environment. Taking just the parish of Athleague, which straddles Galway and Roscommon, there are a series of names that record wooded and wetland locations. These include, but are not limited to, Derrineel – *Doire an aoil* (oakwood of the limestones), Kilmore – *Coill mór* (great wood), Lisnagirra – *Lios na giorra* (fort of the scrub), Knockaunarainy – *Cnocán na Raithní* (the hillock of the bracken) and Bellagad – *Béal Átha Gad* (the mouth of the ford of the withes/wattles)

The landscape and economy of Uí Maine

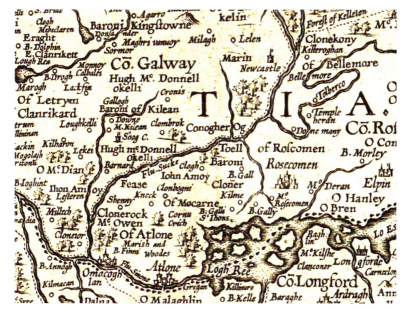

Figure 3.5 Extract from Boazio's *Irlandiæ accvrata descriptio* (1606). This map is oriented with north to the right. Note the area of woodland south of Athleague on the eastern bank of the River Suck, west of 'Clogh'. Note the *Feadha*, north and south of Athlone (Library of Congress Geography and Map Division Washington, DC 20540-4650 US).

Figure 3.6 Extract from Speed's *The theatre of the empire of Great Britaine …* (1611). Speed illustrates a stand of woodland to the east of the River Suck, surrounding and west of 'C. Clogh', which matches with what was recorded in Boazio's map (Atlas.2.61.1, Cambridge University Library).

Plate 3.1 Unimproved rough pasture in the midst of scattered boulder karst, Breeole townland, Co. Roscommon. This represents a small section of the degraded remains of the once extensive woods of *Bruigheol* (author's photograph).

(Fig. 3.4). It is possible to speculate that Knockadangan – *Cnoc a dainginn*, recorded by O'Donovan as the 'hill of the fastness', may have been a place where the wooded landscape was used for defence in the Athleague area in the medieval past (see *ALC*, s.a. 1557).

The final extensive stands of historically attested woodland in the region were the woods of *Bruigheol* (Pl. 3.1; see *AFM*, s.a. 1490; *ALC*, s.a. 1558). These were located on an east–west ridge in the south of Athlone barony, between the *túath* of Magh Finn and the lands further north, broadly represented today by the parish boundary between Taughmaconnell and Dysart, Co. Roscommon. This wood was deemed to have still been extensive in the sixteenth and seventeenth centuries and seems to be broadly co-extensive with a discrete area of scattered boulder karst, known now as the Killeglan Karst Landscape, which may have assisted in the preservation of the woods of *Bruigheol* to such a late date (Nicholls 2001, 193; Parkes, Meehan and Préteseille 2012, 47–9; Meehan and Parkes 2014, 14). Four townlands, among many, named Feevagh, Feevagh Beg and Feevagh More – *Fiodhbhach* (woody place) and Derryfadda – *Doire Fada* (the long oak-wood) highlight the former presence of the woods of *Bruigheol*. Other toponymical survivals for these woods are evident in Figure 3.4.

The landscape and economy of Uí Maine

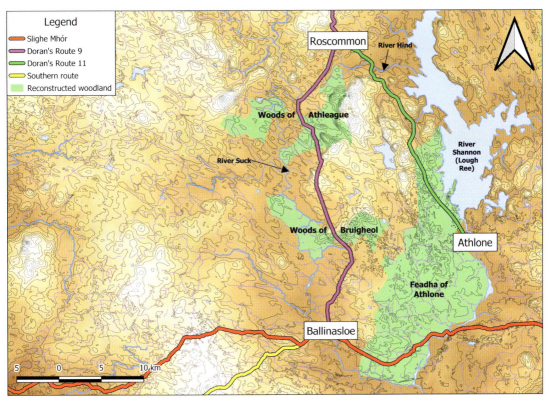

Figure 3.7 The reconstructed woodlands of Uí Maine, based upon late medieval/early modern cartographic sources, and the surviving toponymy. Rivers and lakes to be discussed below and some of the principal overland routes are overlaid on the physical landscape.

East Galway is more difficult to reconstruct in this respect and one of the few sources to survive for the period indicates that for the most part, the area between the rivers Suck and Clare possessed little woodland by *c.*1600, so little that O'Sullivan Beare lamented the lack of cover or areas to retreat into in the hinterland around Aughrim in 1602. Instead the region was composed largely of open ground, leaving him and his people prone to attack (McCracken 1971, 41) during their famous march from southern Munster to Leitrim. Overall, woodland in the region would have limited development and communication and been viewed with fear by outsiders (Finan 2016, 58), but by contrast to the limitations provided by bogland environments, it did not result in the general avoidance of these zones. Combining these woodland areas with bogland, however, indicates that large parts of the study area, particularly its south-eastern quadrant, were either uninhabited or lightly settled.

Rivers, lakes and turloughs
The riverine network of eastern Connacht provides some of the most characteristic features of Uí Maine and the district is drained by two substantial regional waterways,

the River Shannon, including Lough Ree, and the River Suck. The historical background gave some indication of the role of these rivers as boundaries and yet, as both were and are still navigable, they were a vital economic and communication resource also (O'Conor and Naessens 2016a). A third river, the Hind, also played an important role, and served in a general way as the physical boundary between the *tricha cét* of Tír Maine and the Ó Chonchobair heartland of Machaire Connacht. This river runs eastwards from its source near Athleague, and empties into Lough Ree near Galey Bay. Apart from Lough Ree, the lakes of the study area are characteristically small in size. They include Callow Lough and Ballaghdacker Lough in east Galway and the former lake of Lough Croan and Lough Funshinagh in Co. Roscommon. Along with these relatively small bodies of water, the region presents with a phenomenon known as the turlough – a low-lying area on limestone that becomes flooded in wet weather, particularly in winter, through the welling-up of groundwater from the bedrock. There are a number of turloughs located in the area, particularly to the east of the River Suck (Meehan and Parkes 2014, 21–7).

COMMUNICATION ROUTES THROUGH THE LORDSHIP

Medium-to-long-distance overland communication was provided primarily by a small number of regional routeways. Travel through the landscape was not limited to these routeways and a matrix of minor routes must have snaked through the lordship. However, information on these subsidiary routes is generally lacking. Academic research into the pre-modern, medieval and perhaps prehistoric road systems of this part of the island is limited (Ó Lochlainn 1940; O'Keeffe 2001; Doran 2004). The principal routeway through the territory was the *Slighe Mhór* or *Eiscir Riada*, a road linking the east of the island through to Galway Bay (Ó Lochlainn 1940, 470). Eskers and drumlin belts provided a natural, dry linear platform giving easier access through a region characterized by much wetland and river floodplains, that would have been naturally treacherous or impassable at certain times of the year (Meehan and Parkes 2014, 28–34). This route linked large parts of Connacht with the lands further to the east, across the Suck and Shannon rivers, with their broad and treacherous callow wetlands. Geissel plotted the most likely course of the *Slighe Mhór*, an important reference point when attempting to understand where and why settlement developed in Uí Maine (Geissel 2006) (Fig. 3.8).

Major natural fords and bridges existed along the *Slighe Mhór* across the Suck at Ballinasloe and across the Shannon at Athlone. Reconstructing the more regional routes, Doran highlights the presence of two secondary roads connecting south Roscommon with the other major east-west route through Connacht, the *Slighe Assail*. The first, which she termed 'Route 9', left the *Slighe Mhór* at Ballinasloe heading north, via *Tochar-choille-an-chairn* (Togher and Culliagharny townlands,

The landscape and economy of Uí Maine

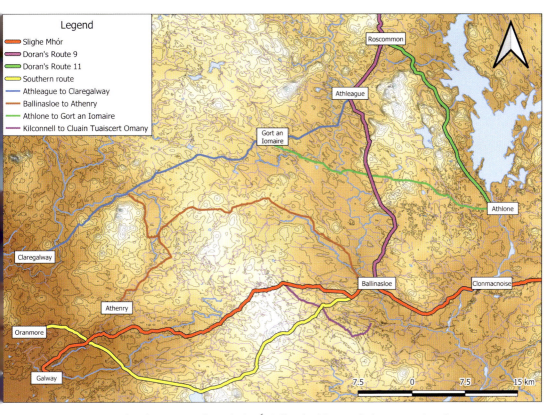

Figure 3.8 Medieval routeways through the Ó Cellaig lordship, with the principal settlements from the text indicated.

Taughmaconnell and Creagh parishes respectively), through the woods of *Bruigheol*, past Lough Croan, on to Athleague, then Roscommon, and connecting with the *Slighe Assail* at Tulsk (Doran 2004, 72). The townland names surrounding Athleague support the presence of a long-established communication route through woodland and bog, as seen in the cases of Derrinlurg – *Doire an loirg* (derry or wood of the track) and Tibarny – *Toigh beárna* (house of/in the gap), two adjacent townlands near Athleague. Doran's 'Route 11' left Athlone, went north through the *Feadha* of Athlone, passed through the historically attested settlement of *Baile na Gáile*, present-day Knockcroghery, before connecting up with Route 9 at Roscommon (ibid.). It is presumably this route which Geoffrey de Geneville had a pass cut through in 1273–4. Plainly, sections all along these routeways, especially parts which went through bog and wood, required constant maintenance and, in some cases, the construction of wooden causeways – *tóchair* – in order to traverse bogland. A number of *tóchair* are recorded in the annalistic records as having been required in order to cross bogland along the River Suck corridor during the later medieval period (Lucas 1985, 50).

The manner in which access along these roads was restricted or even blocked is also demonstrable in numerous later medieval annalistic entries (O'Conor 1998, 98–100). One example of this is seen near Athleague in 1425 and 1560 [*Áth gallda*], showing how a combination of physical features, namely bogland, river and narrow communication routes, and their manipulation, could be used to devastating effect in military encounters (*AC*; *ALC*). The references indicate that there was a ford over a modified River Hind on Route 9, between Athleague and Roscommon. Another entry, in 1489, records a skirmish between the Uí Chonchobair and Uí Chellaig, at the pass of Cluainin – *bealach an Cluainin* (*AFM*) – Clooneen townland, which lies directly to the north of Athleague, the townland split by the modern N63, the continuation of the medieval routeway. There is a bog at Clooneen today and the word *bealach* may suggest a *tóchar* through a relatively substantial marshy area in this period. Given the vulnerable nature of such a communication route, access could have been restricted, or closed entirely, under certain circumstances. This reference could also be an inference to the tactic of 'plashing', the bending and interweaving of branches and twigs to form defensive thick, hedge-like obstacles across a line of march (Ó Domhnaill 1946, 41; Cronin 1980, 116; O'Conor 1998, 98–100; Everett 2015, 20).

This intersection of river, woodland, bog and routeway would have been a bottleneck to travel north-south on Route 9 that dated to much earlier than the fifteenth century. Route 9 would have crossed over Toirrdelbach Ó Conchobair's 1139 engineering works, which by joining the River Hind with the turloughs of Correal and Ballinturly, and then digging a ditch between the latter lakes and the River Suck, created a barrier that defended his ancestral lands from attack from the south. It also created a boundary between Tír Maine and Machaire Connacht. It is highly likely that the three late medieval skirmishes mentioned above took place at crossing points across this canal-like feature (*AT*; Ó Corráin 1972, 151; Barry 2007, 38; Valante 2015, 51, 60–1). This waterway, which included much of the natural River Hind, must have been used by boats, particularly cots, to travel for either military or trade reasons, from Athleague on the Suck to Lough Ree on the Shannon. Its 13km-long course would have saved travellers a boat journey of about 70km down the Suck and then up the Shannon, into the latter lough (Curley and Timoney 2024). Another regional routeway branched off the *Slighe Mhór* and charted an alternative journey to Galway Bay than that of the latter road. Simply termed the 'Southern Route' in this book, it was broadly consistent with the modern R446 (formerly N6). Connecting Ballinasloe with Aughrim, Kilreekill, the later medieval town of Loughrea, Craughwell and on to Oranmore (Fig. 3.8), this road provided access through a diversity of landscapes between modern east Galway and the coast, thus facilitating trade, travel and martial activities for centuries (McKeon and O'Sullivan 2014, 6–7).

Minor roads through the area must have existed, but identifying them through the historical or archaeological disciplines is difficult. However, consideration of these

The landscape and economy of Uí Maine

sources allows us to theorize that some of the modern minor road network existed in the later medieval period. The basis for this relies on the siting of prominent archaeological sites close to these roads today, coupled with the fact that certain entries in the historical record relate to incidents which took place due to them seemingly being close to a known routeway. As a result, the following minor roads likely existed throughout the medieval period:

R363: Athlone to *Gort an Iomaire*/Cruffon, (modern Newbridge), Co. Galway, via Brideswell–Dysart–Ballyforan.

N63/R354: Athleague, Co. Roscommon to Claregalway, Co. Galway, via Mount Talbot–Ballygar–Newbridge–Abbeyknockmoy.

R358/R339/L3107: Ballinasloe to Athenry, via Ahascragh–Caltra–Castleblakeney–Menlough–Tiaquin, Co. Galway.

L3415/3413: Kilconnell to Cluain Tuaiscirt O Máine, via Aughrim–Callaghan's Loughs, Co. Galway.

Water-based travel during the period is more difficult to identify, since it is not as regularly attested to in the historical record. However, it is well understood that the entire course of the River Shannon, from Lough Allen, near its source in Bréifne, to where it meets the Atlantic Ocean near Limerick, was navigable, albeit potentially with some portage involved, and it was an important communication and transport artery throughout the entire period (O'Conor, Naessens and Sherlock 2015, 85). Waterborne traffic, both naval and trade, is attested to on Lough Ree in the surviving thirteenth- and fourteenth-century sources, while Garton has argued that the ready movement of influence and ideas, along with merchandise, was part of the routine navigation of the Shannon system during the high medieval period (Garton 1981, 36, 54; O'Conor and Naessens 2016a, 238–9). It is clear that the Shannon saw plenty of waterborne traffic during early medieval times and, probably, the prehistoric period (Murtagh 2015, 192–3; O'Conor and Naessens 2016a, 239). The survival of a later medieval slipway and dry-stone built jetty-features on Safe Harbour has been noted at Rindoon on Lough Ree (O'Conor, Naessens and Sherlock 2015, 86; O'Conor and Naessens 2016a). It might be added that, further south along the Shannon, the presence of quay and harbour features were noted at a series of late medieval castle sites on the shores of Lough Derg (Stark 2012, 54–6; Hall 2016, 75–6). The existence of these features at Rindoon and Lough Derg perhaps offers an indication of the high level of water traffic that must have occurred along the Shannon during this time.

Navigation on the River Suck is difficult to chart, but one of the indicators that this river was readily accessible in the later medieval past can be concluded from another episode in the career of Toirrdelbach Ó Conchobair, when his fleet of ships were burned on Lough Loung in 1146 (*AU MacN*; *AFM*). *Loch Long* – 'lake of the ships' –

is a small lake connected to the Suck between Ballymoe and Dunamon, 12km to the north-west of Athleague. Plainly, Toirrdelbach's fleet at Lough Loung was in place to facilitate military action and the transfer of troops, operating up and down the River Suck corridor as required, indicating that this river was readily navigable to relatively large vessels throughout the later medieval period. Furthermore, this fleet could have easily accessed the 1139 canal-like waterway mentioned above.

What type of vessels and boats were used on the Shannon and Suck rivers? Clinker-built, oared galleys, which developed from early medieval Norse longships, were a feature of later medieval Gaelic Ireland, being used along coasts, rivers and lakes (Breen 2001, 429–35; Etchingham 2015, 79–87; Murtagh 2015, 194). Smaller vessels, such as logboats, known as cots, and coracles/currachs, built of wattle and hides, were seemingly a commonplace sight on Irish rivers from prehistory through the medieval period up until the recent past. Cots could be quite large if carved out of a substantial tree trunk, with seventeenth-century accounts describing 60-80 people routinely being transported on these vessels at that time (Dowdall 1932, 25). The mid-fourteenth-century praise poem *Táth aoinfhir ar iath Maineach* describes the use of galleys and coracles in the waterways of the lordship (Lanting and Brindley 1996; Murtagh 2015, 192–201; *Táth aoinfhir*, q7). There is also evidence along the Shannon for the use of plank-built wherrys – effectively a large rowing boat with perhaps one sail (O'Conor and Naessens 2016a, 239). There is even evidence for rushcraft being used on the River Suck near Dysart and Ballyforan, Co. Roscommon, in the last century, and their manufacture may be of considerable antiquity, suggesting their use on this and the other rivers of the study area during the late medieval period (Mac Philib 2000, 1). Overall, as can be seen, communication and travel through Uí Maine in the later medieval period would have taken many forms, but was dictated by both natural and man-made influences on the landscape. The area was well supplied with roads and it is clear that both the Suck and Shannon were navigable at this time. This would have facilitated the movement of people and merchandise.

FOCAL POINTS OF ASSEMBLY AND GATHERINGS

Settlement in the later medieval lordship was essentially rural and dispersed in character. As a result, society routinely operated around the premise of gathering for a particular purpose. The motive of the gatherings could be martial, however, by and large, these communal events were social, economic and administrative in nature and primarily came in the form of an assembly or seasonal fair (Ir. *óenach*). The *óenach* was an event that seems to have had origins in prehistory (MacNeill 2008, 68–9). This institution evolved through the centuries, but the concept of communal gatherings remained in later medieval times (MacNeill 2008, 106–39; FitzPatrick 2015a, 54–5). These assemblies performed a number of roles in Gaelic society, chief among them

The landscape and economy of Uí Maine

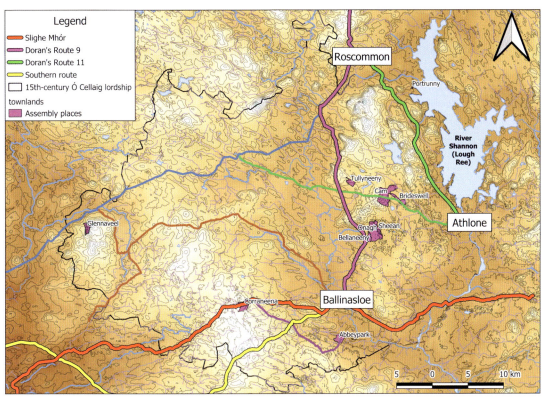

Figure 3.9 Location of the assembly and inauguration landscapes of Tír Maine and Uí Maine, some of which will be explored further below.

festivities, feasting, the racing of horses and chariots (Gleeson 2015, 104), as well as the payment of tax, the provision of tribute (*cís*), the settling of inter-territorial disputes, trade and market activity (FitzPatrick 2015a, 54; Simms 2020, 467–70). There is evidence to indicate that vestiges of these assemblies continued to be celebrated right up into the post-medieval period and beyond (Simms 2020, 464). The late medieval literary tale *Cetharnach Uí Dhomnaill*, set in sixteenth-century Ireland, includes a sequence where the protagonist attended an *óenach* convened by the historically attested Tadg Ó Cellaig at his residence, indirectly indicating that the Uí Chellaig elite continued to host these assemblies into that period at least (O'Grady (ed. and trans.) 1892, 320).

MacCotter advocates that each *trícha cét* possessed its own assembly site and this place remained fixed through time (MacCotter 2014, 50). Based on what has been uncovered over the course of this research, there seems to be a number of assembly sites in each *trícha cét*, possibly serving separate purposes or seasonal periods, or which fell in and out of use over the course of time. This conclusion is supported by the research conducted at three case study locations in the north of Ireland, which advocates that the late *túatha* or vassal lordships that constituted the *trícha cét* would also have had routine communal places of assembly (Logue and Ó Doibhlin 2020, 160). In attempting to identify the Uí Maine assembly landscapes, there is no hard-and-fast template one can use. The difficulty in trying to identify and interpret the archaeological character of assembly practice is marred by the transient nature of these events and the vagaries of their survival in the landscape (MacCotter 2012, 1). However, consultation of the toponymical, archaeological, topographical, historical, literary and folkloric sources collectively can yield information that helps in identifying an assembly place (Logue and Ó Doibhlin 2020, 172). These identifications provide insights into the way in which later medieval Gaelic society was ordered and organized (FitzPatrick 2004, 13). This approach has uncovered a number of assembly locations in the Ó Cellaig lordship. Identifying these sites is also beneficial in terms of understanding where the *cenn áiteanna* of the Ó Cellaig were located, what forms they took and how people may have interacted with these assembly locations through time. These sites will be considered in the following chapters.

THE ECONOMY OF THE LORDSHIP

When studying the economic situation in later medieval Gaelic Ireland, it is pertinent to quote Nicholls, who noted that, 'No other aspect of medieval Irish life and society is more scantily served by the surviving evidence than the economic basis of society, the cultivation of the land' (Nicholls 2003, 131). Thus, reconstructing the economy of later medieval Gaelic Ireland and of this inland lordship, in particular, is a difficult, but not impossible, task. While Gaelic Irish administrative documents are generally lacking, other sources can assist in informing our understanding of how wealth was generated and distributed at this time.

Pastoral agriculture
Pastoral farming served a very important function in later medieval Gaelic Ireland and a considerable part of this society depended on cattle and the resources derived from their herds. The main breeds herded in later medieval Ireland may have been the ancestors of the modern Kerry and Dexter breeds – short in stature, black or dark brown in colour, which, if their descendants' physical traits can be used as a comparison, had a relatively strong milk yield for the period, and a profitable carcass (Nicholls 2003, 137; Walsh 2017, 47). In the north-west of Ireland, the *Moiled* cattle were once a prominent native breed, and these may also have been found among the herds in eastern Connacht. *An Bhó Riabhach* was an equally prominent native type, a normal part of Irish herds up until recent times, particularly along the western seaboard (Walsh 2017, 29, 37). These dual-purpose animals were well suited to grazing and maximizing marginal, less profitable land, and their milk product was a vital

supplement to the medieval Irish diet. This milk was turned into butter, a variety of cheeses and associated *bánbidh* (white meats), buttermilk and sour curds, while the animal's blood was also collected, when required, in order to mix it with oatmeal to create a blood pudding for sustenance. Beef was obviously consumed, with more regularity by the aristocracy than the lower classes, while tallow was an important product for candle making (Lucas 1989, 200–22; Nicholls 2003, 137; Downey and Stuijts 2013, 112–16; Kelly 2016a, 47–8). From the early medieval period, there is strong evidence that cattle were regarded as one of the principal expressions of wealth and status in Ireland. As such, one of the more routine entries from the annalistic records indicates that cattle raiding, as a means of acquiring wealth, but also as a means by which to test the military skills of young men, to lessen the power of rival lords and thus increase your own status, was a regular activity for many medieval Gaelic elites (Lucas 1989, 125–99).

In the west of Ireland, particularly in the less productive lands, the farming of cattle involved a form of transhumance, called 'booleying', from *buaile* – cattle enclosure. This involved the cyclical movement of cattle from winter pasture, close to the settlement centres of the area, to summer pasture, whereby grazing was undertaken in upland, woodland and bogland environs, or in the areas vacated by the seasonal flooding in turloughs (Watt 2008, 331; O'Flaherty 2014; Costello 2020). Place-name survivals in the study area, such as Boleyduff, Cloonboley, Corboley, Boleymore, Knocknaboley and Shanboley may all be relics of this farming practice. It has been suggested that the cultivation of oats was often a complementary practice to transhumance, with the spring-sown oats occupying the spaces where the cattle had resided the previous winter (Watt 2008, 331).

Pastoralism is traditionally seen as the predominant form of agriculture practiced throughout the medieval period in Gaelic Ireland, with cattle management overwhelmingly seen as the primary activity, for dairy produce, meat and hides (McCormick 2008, 210–12; Bhreathnach 2014, 21–2; O'Sullivan, McCormick, Kerr and Harney 2014, 180). This did not remain fixed through time, however, and it has been demonstrated that farming practice evolved through the early medieval period, with crop cultivation playing an important role from an early date. The diversification of agricultural activities, the increase in importance of other species of livestock, and even the development of lordly centres in good arable areas is noted in the archaeological record from around the ninth century (O'Sullivan, McCormick, Kerr and Harney 2014, 180). In the study area, however, the prevalence of cattle-related place-names, coupled with contemporary documentary evidence and modern agricultural practice, would suggest that the economy of the region in the early medieval period depended to a considerable extent on cattle.

The data suggests that cattle production remained a primary economic driver in this region during the time under inspection. The primacy of cattle and their resources in later medieval Connacht is easy to illustrate. One of the terms of the Treaty of Windsor (1175) agreed between Ruaidrí Ó Conchobair and Henry II, king of England, indicates that Ruaidrí was granted his lands as long as he paid fealty to Henry II and gave tribute of one cattle hide for every ten cows he possessed (*Foedera*, 13–4). The economic value that bovine-derived products held in later medieval Ireland is illustrated with a record from 1290, where *c.*51,000 cattle hides were exported out of Ireland (Campbell 2008, 918). What is apparent from the historical record more generally is that one of the chief exports from Gaelic Ireland was cattle hides and tanned leather (O'Conor 2005, 216; Lennon 2005, 46; Nicholls 2008, 413–14; Simms 2015, 102–3).

The importance of cattle to this lordship is seen in our earliest account of Uilliam Buide Ó Cellaig's ascension to the Uí Maine lordship in *c.*1349, in *Táth aoinfhir ar iath Maineach*. One of the key motifs of the poem is cattle raiding, which served as an important indicator of Uilliam's martial eligibility for his new role. The poem recounts a series of successful cattle raids led by a young Uilliam to Athenry, *Maonmaigh* (later barony of Loughrea), the parishes of *Liathdruim* and Duniry, all Co. Galway, the islands of Lough Ree and *Breaghmhuine* (later barony of Brawney, Co. Westmeath) and supposedly on to Limerick and east Munster (*Táth aoinfhir*, q64–72). Although these raids were included in order to highlight his martial prowess, the fact that they are on identified locations and sought in every case to plunder cattle, would suggest that the raids themselves were not just a literary flourish.

The bone assemblages from two excavated ringforts in the region, Loughbown I and Mackney, Co. Galway, indicate that cattle made up the largest percentage of domestic bone. In the case of Loughbown I, the cattle were mainly kept to adulthood, primarily functioning as dairy animals and for draught (Bower 2014, 178). At Mackney, the majority of animal bone is attributed to the early medieval period, however, 22% of the assemblage came from later medieval contexts. Again cattle and sheep dominated this assemblage both in early medieval and later medieval times. The cattle bones belonged to animals of a relatively low physical stature, not unlike the Kerry and Dexter breeds. The peak of slaughter was in the second and third years, indicating that more of these animals may have been reared, primarily, for meat production, rather than dairy, perhaps indicating the high status of the ringfort occupiers (Delaney 2014, 195).

Toponymical evidence uncovers a series of townland names that point towards districts having been utilized extensively for cattle production and trade, and for the processing of the resources derived from livestock in the later medieval past. Inspecting the environment around Lough Croan, for instance, results in a list of names that point toward the organized production and routine trading of cattle in that area. Assembly or periodic livestock fairs are indicated by Tullyneeny – *Tulaigh an aonaigh* (hill of the cattle fair/assembly). To the east of Tullyneeny is Cornalee – *Corr na Lao*

The landscape and economy of Uí Maine

Plate 3.2 Lisseenamanragh townland. Recorded as ancient field system. Thomas Street, Roscommon, Ireland. CUCAP no.: BDO024, photo date: 1970-07-15 (image courtesy of Cambridge University Collection of Aerial Photography).

(the round hill of the calves). Immediately to the south are Lisseenamanragh and Carrowntarriff. Lisseenamanragh – *Lisín na mannrach* (little fort of the stalls or mangers) is a name which corresponds directly today with the, as yet, undated archaeological remains of a combination of masonry enclosures and field systems, designed to enclose livestock for darying (Pl. 3.2). Carrowntarriff – *Ceathramhadh an tairbh* (quarter of the bull) – is immediately to the south of Lisseenamanragh. This clustering of bovine-related place-names in such a discrete area cannot have been coincidental and the division of the landscape according to the age and purpose of the animal seems to indicate that this area was given over to the intensive production of, and trade in, cattle attached to the lord.

I would like to speculatively include a further townland name to the list: Grange. Grange townland bounds Lough Croan to the north. An elongated version of the name was posited above – *Gráinseach Chairn Bhuaileadh* (Grange/granary of the cairn of the booley/cattle-enclosure) (Ó Muraíle, N., pers. comm.). If this is the location theorized, it carries the confirmation that this district was used as a monastic farm (Stout 2015, 39–45). This form of farming was highly organized and may point to the seasonal movement of cattle into and out of this land unit, in unison with the growth and harvest of spring-sown cereals, which were then stored in the attested grange, an approach readily identifiable in other locations (Watt 2008, 331). The speculative inclusion of Grange brings the total number of cattle-related townland names in the Lough Croan environs to five.

At Galey, another Ó Cellaig elite centre, a continuation of this trend is apparent. The names of Cornamart – *Cor na mart* (round hill of the beeves/butchered cattle), Corboley – *Corbuaile* (possibly round hill of the dairy), Curraghalaher – *Currach a' leathair* (moor of the leather), as well as nearby Pollalaher – *Poll a leathair* (hole of the leather), all indicate a predominance in the practices of cattle rearing, dairying and livestock movement, as well as butchery and processing of the associated resources. In the latter cases, this process utilized the naturally occurring tannic acid from wetland contexts for tanning and leather production.

Equating townland names with activities in the past environment in this manner can be undertaken with a relatively high degree of certainty. A comparable example can be seen in the relics of the practice of blood-letting of cattle for sustenance, which are found recorded in townland names, micro-toponymy and through local information gathered from as late as early twentieth-century Ireland. Examples of this, usually undertaken in times of food shortage throughout the history of Ireland, can be seen with *Poll na Fola* (hollow of the blood), *Gleann na Fola* (glen of the blood), and Cornafulla (*Cor na Fola* – round hill of the blood) (Lucas 1989, 216–17; Nicholls 2003, 137). The latter townland lies within the study area.

The land units whose names describe a range of medieval cattle farming practices in Uí Maine strongly adhere to the high-yield soil associations outlined above. The underlying geology of this area, and indeed Co. Roscommon as a whole, is primarily one of Carboniferous Limestones (Parkes, Meehan and Prétesseille 2012, 18), while the chemical composition of soils in most of these limestone regions contains an abundance in soil nutrients which are very complementary to high-quality cattle production (Collins 2016, 2; O'Conor 2018, xxviii). These clusters of bovine-related names are also close to Ó Cellaig lordly centres, which cannot have been by chance, and instead indicates that the generation of wealth in this part of later medieval Gaelic Ireland was still tightly aligned to cattle and cattle farming. The link between cattle and wealth did not diminish in later medieval Gaelic Ireland and there are numerous instances in the historical sources where cattle were used as currency, gifts, in order to pay taxes and tribute, and as compensation for crimes under Irish law (Lennon 2005, 59; Watt 2008, 330. For use of cattle as tax payment by the Uí Chellaig to the Anglo-Normans in 1281–2, see Walton 1980, 469). A section of a legal treatise, written by Giolla na Naomh Mac Aodhagáin *c.*1300, is illuminating for a number of reasons, not least the amount of cattle involved. The section specifies that a fine of 210 cows was due in the case of the secret murder of a king's son (Kelly 2016a, 44). Indeed, evidence

The landscape and economy of Uí Maine

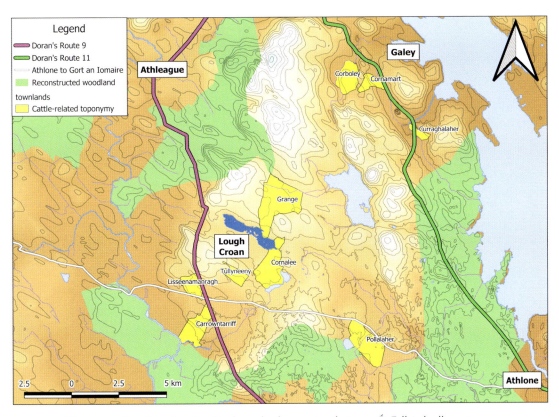

Figure 3.10 Location of cattle-related townland names in relation to Ó Cellaig lordly centres.

for the late medieval period indicates that, due to a number of factors, the average price for cattle increased, and a correlation between this and the increased engagement in pastoral activity is strong (Simms 2015, 104–8). Seventeenth-century sources indicate that it was not uncommon for members of the Gaelic elite to routinely be in possession of around 2,000 head of cattle, while earlier accounts record some Gaelic lords owning as many as 6,000–8,000 cattle at a given time (Nicholls 2003, 136; Curtis (ed.) 1924–7, 293; *ALC, s.a.* 1565). Aodh Ó Neill, then baron of Dungannon, was reported in 1571 as being in possession of 50,000 head of cattle (Logue 2018, 271).

Swift has provided persuasive evidence on how landscapes such as this may have been organized in a royal or lordly context when discussing the financial resources of the twelfth-century Leinster king, Diarmait Mac Murchada. The tribute owed to such rulers was provided primarily as food render or livestock and the seasonal assembly (*óenach*) gave the opportunity for this tribute to be levied. It also served as the venue at which tribute could be redistributed, in the form of food provision and a communal feast to the assembled host, a mark of the lord's hospitality. These assemblies also served as a focus for market and fair activity, enabling the lord to convert his livestock tribute into coin for his coffers (Swift 2015, 91–102) and a version of this economic model is likely to have persisted throughout the rest of the later medieval period in Gaelic Ireland.

Interpreting this cluster of cattle-related names surrounding Lough Croan would suggest that the lands, particularly to the south of the lake, served as the venue for a significant and long-standing livestock market attached to the convention of a regular assembly in the Ó Cellaig lordship and a key contributor to the lord's wealth in the process. In the case of the place-names that surround the sheltered bay and Ó Cellaig *cenn áit* at Galey, we are looking at the possibility of an extensive butchery and leather-producing complex, perhaps similar, but in a rural context, to the tanning complex uncovered south of the River Poddle in Dublin (Simpson 2004, 15–16, 32–4; Swift 2015, 100). These toponymical survivals may indicate that the excess livestock given in tribute to the Ó Cellaig lord at an assembly could have been processed here with a view to it being transported along the River Shannon for trade or sale further afield, again to enrich the lord's wealth.

Of course, cattle were not the only animal to have been intensively produced in this environment and modern agricultural practices in the region routinely incorporate large numbers of sheep also, with mixed livestock farming particularly commonplace in what was once Tír Maine (Soderberg and Immich 2010, 109–13). Whether this reflects anything of the later medieval past is debateable, but at Loughbown I and Mackney, the sheep bone assemblages correspond with the second-largest percentage of domesticated animal bone in each case, with pig placed third (Bower 2014, 178, 182; Delaney 2014, 195–6). Wool was plainly a key resource derived from sheep farming and would have been the primary raw material used for clothing by society at large. One of the most visible expressions of the use of wool in later medieval Ireland is seen with the production of the characteristic Irish 'mantle' or cloak, which from the fourteenth to sixteenth centuries had become a key export throughout Europe (Lennon 2005, 46; Nicholls 2008, 415; Simms 2020, 475). The trade in sheep, wool and wool products (sheep skins, woolfell, mantles) must have formed part of an organized trade commodity in later medieval Uí Maine, however, outside of the estates of religious houses, this is unfortunately undocumented. Sheep and pigs played a more subordinate role in Irish pastoralism in the later medieval period, particularly by comparison with Anglo-Norman areas (Nicholls 2008, 415).

Horse breeding and trade
Horse breeding, and the retention of large herds of horses, seems to have been a regular preserve of the Gaelic elite, and historical sources indicate that this was also the case in Uí Maine. A 1295 entry highlights how the Uí Chellaig raided a chieftain of *Corcu Achlann*, with the specific intention of stealing his horses (*AC*). In 1337, Toirrdelbach

The landscape and economy of Uí Maine

Plate 3.3 A probable fifteenth-century wall painting of an armoured Gaelic lord on horseback, riding in distinctive Irish fashion without a saddle, from Clare Island Cistercian Abbey, Co. Mayo (image source: agefotostock).

Ó Conchobair, king of Connacht, was defeated and taken prisoner by the Uí Chellaig, as well as having his horses and armour plundered, and many of his men killed (*AC*). In both cases, it was deemed noteworthy that the Uí Chellaig acquired their opponents' horses. Horses were bred for a multiplicity of purposes, for transport and travel, for farming endeavours, for war, for sport, and as gifts and *túarastla* between elites (Nicholls 2008, 416; Gleeson 2015, 35; Mannion 2024, 36). According to the literature, all Irish chiefs of any standing kept studs, and the horse-trade could be a considerable source of wealth (O'Neill 1987, 104; Watt 2008, 330).

For Uí Maine-specific information relating to the importance of the horse, we have some faint insights. *Nósa Ua Maine* anachronistically records the Cenél Áedha na hEchtghe as the kindred in charge of rearing Ó Cellaig's horses (*Nósa*, 545). In 1308, a considerable number of Ó Cellaig light horsemen, of the *hobelar* type, accompanied William *Liath* de Burgh on campaign (Connolly 1982, 3–5). An English military intelligence report on numbers of fighting men available to the Irish chiefs, dated *c*.1490, indicated that the Ó Cellaig chief could call upon two hundred horsemen at that time (Price 1932, 204; Breen and Raven 2017, 176). This number of horsemen seems still to be at the disposal of the Ó Cellaig lord into the 1530s at least (*CSPI*, ii, 252, see Mannion 2024, 49). The horses used in both cases were likely 'hobbies'. These were a small, nimble horse bred for scouting endeavours and for operating in rough terrain (Bolger 2017, 93–6; see Pl. 3.3; Fig. 3.11).

Figure 3.11 Art Mór Mac Murchadha Caomhánach riding to meet the earl of Gloucester, in an illustration to Jean Creton's *Histoire du roy d'Angleterre Richard II*. Note the small size of the horse used by Mac Murchadha Caomhánach, a likely depiction of the 'hobby' horse breed used by the later medieval Gaelic Irish (image permissions: British Library Harleian MS 1319).

Presumably the Uí Chellaig operated a number of studs throughout the lordship in order to breed such horses that operated effectively in the often wet lowland landscapes of the region. An entry for 1558 indicates that the Ó Fallamháin of Clann Uadach, by that time a vassal clan of the Uí Chellaig, maintained a horse stud on their lands (*ALC*), while a fiant from 1585 lists pardons granted to 'Hugh O Kelly of Lisdalone' and his company, a number of whom are described as 'horsemen' (*Fiants* II, 673 [4661]). The survival of the Ballinasloe Horse Fair as a significant regional annual horse fair from at least as early as the mid-eighteenth century, and arguably a lot earlier, suggests that horse breeding and trading may have been one of the normal economic practices underpinning the Ó Cellaig lordship in the later medieval period.

Arable farming
Evidence for arable farming in later medieval Gaelic Ireland is difficult to establish due to the relative lack of archaeological excavation and historical pollen analyses in these areas and the consequent reliance on surviving historical documentation. These sources indicate that pastoral products provided the larger portion of the Irish diet, however, it wasn't the exclusive source of food. The Gaelic Irish seem to have grown large quantities of oats, some barley and wheat, as well as considerable amounts of flax,

for the production of linen. Oats and oatcakes were a staple food, as attested to in Irish and overseas accounts (Nicholls 2008, 411; Downey and Stuijts 2013, 118). This farming practice was apparently undertaken on a relatively small-scale, and tephra-dated pollen evidence from Gaelic Ulster supports the argument for this regime (Hall and Bunting 2001, 220–2). This cereal production may have coincided with the transhumance cycle. There is suggestion of long-fallow cultivation occurring in these areas, in order to allow the soil to recover suitably for replanting (Nicholls 2008, 411).

The prominence of cereal production as a routine farming practice in later medieval Uí Maine is more difficult to demonstrate. The cereals processed at early medieval Kilbegly were not grown in the immediate area and the production or acquisition of this product was likely controlled by Clonmacnoise (Jackman and O'Keeffe 2013, 149–52). By contrast, the later medieval pollen profile collected in Ballinphuill bog indicates that its hinterland was intensively farmed and possessed a strong cereal growing component. Indeed, the excavations at nearby Loughbown I and Mackney ringforts both uncovered corn-drying kilns (Bower 2014, 177; Delaney 2014, 194–5). Two further candidates for horizontal watermills of likely medieval date from the study area include Liscam, Co. Roscommon, and Kilconnell, Co. Galway. So while there is little in the way of surviving historical documentation describing the level of arable cultivation in later medieval Uí Maine, the pollen and archaeological evidence, such as it is, is hinting that cereal cultivation was more prominent in this later medieval Gaelic lordship, at least, than historians such as Nicholls believe.

The late fourteenth-century Ó Cellaig praise poem *Fá urraidh labhras leac Theamhrach* is careful to highlight the bounty of the land provided by Maolsechlainn Ó Cellaig's reign, by describing the 'dark corn in the white fields' surrounding Athleague (*Fá urraidh labhras leac Theamhrach*, 14). The slightly earlier poem, *Filidh Éreann Go Haointeach*, also has an allusion to crop production in the vicinity of Galey in the mid-fourteenth century (*FÉGH*, 61). This indicates that by the late medieval period, cereal production was seen as an important resource to the people of the lordship. More concrete evidence of this development of cereal production is seen in two late fifteenth-century annalistic entries (1487 and 1489) near Athleague, which clearly indicate that corn was grown in the area at that time (*AFM*). The presence of a mill at both Athleague and Lisdaulan castles may assist in further understanding the economic character of these parts of the lordship. While the earliest record we have for a mill at Athleague comes from the mid-seventeenth-century Strafford Survey,[2] it is not beyond reason that milling at the site was a long-standing activity, while the OS 1st Edition 6-Inch map records a mill near Lisdaulan. Mills were commonly associated with tower house castles and their estates, and are indicative of economic growth and cereal production (McAlister 2019, 78–80).

Cereal production could also be theorized from toponymical information, as seen in the survival of 'grange' townlands in the lordship, which correspond with the

[2] http://downsurvey.tcd.ie/down-survey-maps.php#bm=Athlone&c=Roscommon. Accessed: 13/11/2023.

outfarm estates attached to, usually, a Cistercian foundation in the region. The grange was an economic unit designed to provide a food surplus for the use of the monastic order. In the south-eastern part of Ireland, in particular, they are synonymous with cultivation, cereal production and sheep farming (Stout 2015, 28–9, 66–7). Two 'grange' townlands attached to Boyle Abbey are located in Tír Maine, the aforementioned Grange, and the *Grange of O'Fallon*, which corresponds with Milltown townland (ibid., 45). Milltown, with the remains of a castle of unclassified form, the wall footings of a surrounding castle bawn, houses and field systems, was a late medieval *cenn áit* of the Uí Fhallamhain of Clann Uadach. The reference to milling in this place-name may corroborate the point that cereal production was far more common in the Ó Cellaig lordship than it initially seems.

RESOURCES DERIVED FROM THE NATURAL ENVIRONMENT

Woodland resources

Substantial zones of woodland were to be found throughout the region. These semi-natural stands of native woodland would have provided a variety of resources to later medieval society. Cattle and sheep were routinely grazed in woody pasture and the 'mast' (acorns and other nuts) harvest was a vital food source for keeping pigs (Nicholls 2008, 415; Finan 2016, 75). The bark of certain trees would have been used for tanning leather (Everett 2015, 17). Timber resources were a very valuable commodity and may provide a reason why the *Feadha* were briefly defined in early thirteenth-century Anglo-Normans grants as a named cantred. This timber would have provided the raw materials for the great majority of buildings constructed in the territory, as well as providing a ready source of firewood and building materials for both domestic and industrial purposes, while charcoal was another commodity that would have been derived from these areas, all suggesting managed woodland (Nicholls 2003, 198–202; Gardiner and O'Conor 2017, 150).

One arboreal-themed place-name illuminates the value that these woodlands possessed for construction purposes: Cornaseer – *Cor na soar* (round hill of the carpenters) is located on Route 11 between Athlone and Roscommon. It is interesting to note that William de Prene, the king's carpenter, was granted a manor at Moyvannon in 1286, the next townland directly to the north of Cornaseer (*CDI*, iii, no. 528). Perhaps the king's carpenter was granted this manor to be in a position to provide seasoned and worked timber from the *Feadha* for maintenance works on local royal castles, such as Roscommon, Rindoon or Athlone. It might also explain why de Prene was fined £20 for wasting timber in the same year (Stalley 1978, 38; Walton 1980, 282–3).

Although undocumented, it is likely that the region benefited from a trade in timber throughout the period under inspection. Certainly the river network would have assisted in the transportation of large quantities of timber out of the territory and further afield (Nicholls 2001, 198–200). Irish oak was prized for church construction in both England and France in the later medieval period and there was a steady export of Irish timber to England and Wales. This trade in timber was apparently largely managed by Gaelic lords (O'Neill 1987, 99–100).

Other resources could be derived from the wild animals that used these areas as their habitat. Deer would have been hunted for its meat and antlers, while there was a brisk trade between Ireland and England in animal pelts, both wild and domestic (ibid., 98). Attaching this hunting and trade specifically to Uí Maine is difficult, however, the toponymy does point to what were traditionally good loci for hunting within the lordship, examples such as Glennanea – *Gleann an fhiadh* (vale of the deer or stag), Feacle – *Fiadh-choill* (deer wood) and Skeanamuck – *Sgiatha na muc* (shrubbery of the wild pigs), all found within the *túath* of Magh Finn. The survival of Clonbrock – *Cluain Broc* (meadow of the badgers) may also directly reflect this area to be a former hunting environment. Early medieval sources regarded the badger as one of the three principal game-animals during the period and suggest that they were hunted for food (Kelly 2016b, 282). It is also likely that they were hunted for their pelts and for sport.

Freshwater fish
Documentation is again lacking in terms of the economic value that freshwater fish may have provided to the lordship, however, the number of viable fishing rivers and lakes in Uí Maine must have been utilized. The fish trade was important to the later medieval economy, particularly when considering the religious dietary restrictions imposed on the population (O'Neill 1987, 38). Organized harvesting of freshwater fish for the table would have been undertaken. Athlone Castle was recorded as operating a fishery in 1284 (*CDI*, ii, no. 2329). More than this, two fish weirs survive for the region. The 'Old Weir' on the River Suck at Mount Talbot was extant in 1837, while the second is located at the ford over the River Shannon at Raghra, modern-day Shannonbridge, and was historically attested to in 1620 (Mac Cuarta 1987, 178–9).

The principal fish sought were salmon, trout and eels, while an early seventeenth-century source refers also to bream and pike, which once caught were an important component of trade locally or were salted or pickled for longer-distance trade (McInerney (ed.) 2012, 36). Merchants from as far afield as Bristol routinely travelled to ports in the west of Ireland to acquire salmon, while fish merchants regularly brought eels from Athlone to Dublin, where they were a valuable foodstuff (O'Neill 1987, 38–43). Commercial or semi-commercial trout and eel fishing are attested to on Lough Ree in recent centuries, with the fishermen selling their produce in Athlone and at other local markets (O'Brien 2015, 225–6). This hints that the rich fisheries of Lough Ree, the Shannon, and the Suck were utilized in later medieval times. One indication of this is a later medieval iron fish hook (Pl. 3.4), found during the excavations at Loughbown I (Bower 2014, 179).

Plate 3.4 Iron fish hook from Loughbown I. Image from Archaeological Excavation Report E2442 – Loughbown 1, Co. Galway (Bower 2009, 69).

WEALTH AND ITS EXPRESSION

A considerable diversity of commodities were available to the populations living in later medieval Uí Maine. Historians would have us believe that these commodities were traded and utilized in a largely coinless economy (Watt 2008, 330–1). However, archaeological investigations, both within the study area and in its near vicinity, present a different picture. A hoard of about 50 fourteenth-century silver pennies were recovered from Ballyeighter townland, near Aughrim, in 1975–6, while another small find of early thirteenth-century halfpennies, with a findspot in the Ballinasloe area, demonstrate that coinage was circulating in high medieval Uí Maine (Kenny 1985; Dolley 1966, 135–6). Later medieval Anglo-Norman coinage has also been uncovered at both Loughbown I and Mackney ringforts, while a substantial early fourteenth-century coin hoard was uncovered in 1969 at the Ó Conchobair inauguration venue of Carnfree, Co. Roscommon, a focal point of their lordship. In 2019, excavation nearby on a previously unidentified ringfort in Gortnacrannagh townland, in advance of the N5 Bypass project, uncovered another Edward I or II silver penny (Dolley and Murphy 1970; Bower 2014, 179; Delaney 2014, 195; Channing, J., pers. comm.; Pl. 3.5). Excavations at Kilteasheen, Rockingham Demense, the Rock of Lough Cé and Trinity Island, all within the Mac Diarmada lordship of Maigh Luirg, Co. Roscommon, uncovered late thirteenth- and fourteenth-century coins in both burial

The landscape and economy of Uí Maine

Plate 3.5 Medieval coin, Gortnacrannagh 2, N5 Road Project, Co. Roscommon (photo John Channing, provided courtesy of AMS, TII and Roscommon County Council).

and settlement contexts (Clyne 2005, 57, 68–9; Read 2010, 58; Finan, T., pers. comm.). Furthermore, a substantial hoard of 234, primarily English minted, coins of mid-thirteenth-century date was uncovered at Drumercool, Co. Roscommon, in 1941, also within the limits of Maigh Luirg, which could have been deposited for safekeeping by either the local Irish or Anglo-Normans operating in the area (Kenny 1983, 171). This all indicates that coinage was commonplace throughout later medieval Gaelic Connacht. These findings are unsurprising, when considering the relative proximity of the study area to the Anglo-Norman towns of Athlone, Athenry, Loughrea, Rindoon, Roscommon and the port of Galway, along with the trade which undoubtedly occurred with these settlement hubs. This in turn created a wealth which ultimately benefited the Ó Cellaig lords, as it returned to them directly, or via tax, rents and tribute (Nicholls 2003, 34–40). However, prior to engaging in a discussion about how prosperous this likely made the Ó Cellaig, consideration must be given to those who generated the wealth.

Although we are primarily concerned with the archaeological manifestations of lordship in later medieval Uí Maine, it is apparent that beneath the elite were several strata of lower-status communities whose work and lives were responsible for creating the environment within which the lords could operate. These people are nearly invisible and thus easily forgotten. We have no accurate measurement of population numbers during the period, however, extrapolating from the numbers of available 'fighting men' in the late fifteenth-century military report entitled 'A description of the power of Irishmen', following Breen and Raven, can provide a loose population range for the late medieval lordship. Based on the aforementioned approach, it is possible to suggest that somewhere between 8,000 and 10,000 people lived across the territory at that time (Breen and Raven 2017, 176–7, using Price 1932, 204). Unfortunately, there has been little archaeological investigation of the settlements of these populations more generally to date (O'Conor 2002a; Gardiner and O'Conor 2017, 146–8). If, however, we use the evidence from the excavations at Ballyhanna, Co. Donegal, as proxy for understanding how rural communities in a Gaelic region lived and died, it creates a compelling image of the lives of the general population. This includes, among other things, the relatively high levels of young adult male mortality, the common instance of accidental death and how vulnerable these communities were to changes in the wider environment such as disease and famine (McKenzie and Murphy 2018, 106–14). This is in contrast with the Gaelic elite, whose obits indicate that, aside from death in battle or assassination in succession disputes, the lordly class routinely lived much longer. For example, Uilliam Buide Ó Cellaig was politically active by 1339, but his father died in 1307, while Uilliam himself didn't die until 1381, meaning that he was at least in his early seventies, if not much older, upon his death. His son Maolsechlainn first appeared in 1351 and did not die until 1401, meaning it is quite possible that he also lived into his early-to-mid-seventies. Maolsechlainn's great grandson and namesake, the builder of the castles at Garbally, Gallagh and Monivea, was at least seventy-one upon his death in 1511. Ultimately, their status and resources played a role in securing this longevity, with access to better quality and quantities of food, as well as their ability to call upon professional medical care. The landholdings of hereditary physician families can be identified in some instances close to the residence of a chieftain in later medieval Gaelic Ireland (FitzPatrick 2015b, 175; 2023, 30) and evidence for a family operating in this capacity for the Ó Cellaig lords will be outlined later.

It is from the lower-status communities that the lord's herders and farmers were derived, those who milked the vast dairy herds, made the butter, cheeses and curd, sheared and worked the wool into clothing, and tended the fields. These people slaughtered, skinned and butchered the livestock and game animals for the table and trade, and toiled in the processing of skins into hides and tanned leather. It is also from these strata of society that the tree-fellers, foresters and construction teams of the elite's buildings came from. We must not forget the groups who sought to generate a livelihood from hunting, fishing and fowling in the lord's territory. It is these people who underpinned the economy of the Ó Cellaig lordship and we must be aware of their stories as we piece together the lordly centres of this region. In the future, hopefully, excavation can answer questions relating to these communities.

The wealth derived from these economic activities is difficult to calculate. The lack of detailed socio-economic and administrative records for Gaelic Ireland makes it hard to get an accurate understanding of the prosperity of a region. One source that bucks this trend is the Ecclesiastical Taxation of Ireland, 1302–6. However, even this does little to accurately inform us of the wealth of Uí Maine at the beginning of the fourteenth century. Chevallier has argued against using the Ecclesiastical Taxation as an unbiased indicator of wealth in later medieval Ireland. He also argues that the accepted belief that the later medieval Gaelic Irish were economically disadvantaged is misplaced, rather that the economic organization of early fourteenth-century Gaelic lordships meant that they did not produce easily countable surpluses. He contends that the Gaelic economy is not readily identifiable in the taxation, owing to it being primarily a pastoral economy, with the transfer of earnings routinely occurring through the provision of gifts, the use of barter, the billeting of troops, as well as direct consumption, all of which are difficult to measure. These traits, along with the exclusion of unsold livestock and pastoral landholdings from assessment, have created a skewed impression of the wealth of later medieval Gaelic lordships. The absence of these surpluses meant that they did not contribute to the valuations of the parish churches in their respective dioceses to the same extent as was seen in other regions, rather than it being an indication that the Gaelic Irish were poorer than their Anglo-Norman counterparts (Chevallier 2019, 21).

In terms of the evidence of wealth in the lordship, it can be argued that the ability to put 'fighting men' in the field could be seen as a demonstration of prosperity. With that in mind, the aforementioned late fifteenth-century military report indicates that the Ó Cellaig of Uí Maine could bring greater combined numbers of galloglass (120-160), horsemen (200) and kern (400) to the field than any other contemporary Connacht lord (Price 1932, 204–5). More generally, however, in the absence of detailed written indications of wealth, information must be sought elsewhere. One of the most visible displays of lordly affluence in the region corresponds with the foundation and patronage granted to religious houses. Four of the principal religious houses associated with the Uí Chellaig are Kilconnell Franciscan Friary, the Augustinian priory of Cluain Tuaiscirt O Máine (Clontuskert, Co. Galway), the Cistercian Monastery of Abbeyknockmoy, all Co. Galway, and the Hospital of the Crutched Friars at Rindoon, Co. Roscommon.

The most heavily Ó Cellaig patronized of these four religious foundations was Kilconnell. The friary was founded by Uilliam Buide Ó Cellaig in 1353 (*AFM*), while historically attested patronage and remodelling works during the fifteenth century correspond with the majority of the surviving architectural remains. However, this has also led to the erroneous date for its foundation being ascribed to 1414 by some scholars (Gwynn and Hadcock 1970, 251; Harbison 2005, 58–9). Numerous highly decorative tombs are found within the friary and although the occupants of some are unidentified, some are likely to be members of the Ó Cellaig family, with one of them possibly holding the remains of Uilliam Buide himself. Ó Cellaig patronage at

Kilconnell also came in the form of more portable items. These include numerous chalices, illustrated books and other religious pieces. A number of the items retained inscriptions indicating that they were donated by Ó Cellaig lords in the fourteenth and fifteenth centuries (Jennings 1944). This patronage echoes the wider interest among the ascendant fourteenth- and fifteenth-century Ó Cellaig lords in showing off their prestige and surplus wealth to the world. This was also achieved through the patronage of poets and the commissioning of praise poetry, the convention of feasts, the recording of *Nósa Ua Maine*, the collating of *Leabhar Ua Maine*, among other endeavours. Historical evidence for the continued use of Kilconnell Friary as an Ó Cellaig place of burial can be seen into the fifteenth century, with the burial of another Uilliam, lord of Uí Maine. It is unsurprising that Uilliam was buried here, considering as he is remembered as a prominent patron of the site (Smith 2014b). The mid- and late fifteenth century (c.1450–75) saw a substantial programme of rebuilding as well as the introduction of Observant reform at Kilconnell, both commissioned by Maolsechlainn Ó Cellaig, an undertaking that contributed to the bulk of the surviving remains. The best surviving of these remains include the tower, nave, choir and south transept and aisle (ibid.).

A second religious foundation extensively patronized by the Ó Cellaig was Cluain Tuaiscirt O Máine, a house of the Augustinian Canons Regular, deemed to have been founded in the mid-to-late twelfth century (Gwynn and Hadcock 1970, 165; Fanning 1976, 97, 100). One of the first records of the sobriquet of Cluain Tuaiscirt 'O Máine' is found in a papal petition of 1379 (*Clonfert*, 283; Molloy 2009, 52), indicating that it was regarded as under Ó Cellaig patronage at this time. It was 'burned by lightning' in 1404 (*MIA*; *Clonfert*, 33–4), an unfortunate incident that most likely initiated the major programme of rebuilding seen at the priory throughout the fifteenth century, seemingly Ó Cellaig-sponsored and concluding with the erection of the western doorway in 1471 (Fanning 1976, 102; O'Mahoney 2014). The surviving remains, much of it fifteenth century in date, include the nave, chancel, rood screen, transepts, cloister arcade, chapter room, sacristy, cellars, and an oven. Elaborate decoration is also seen on the eastern traceried window and particularly on the carved stone panels of the western doorway, which was the main entrance for the lay congregation. This work is likely to have been produced by a prominent local sculptor known as Johannes. All of it shows the prosperity of the house under its Uí Chellaig patrons (Moss 2015a, 194). In this century, the wealth of the priory can be seen increasing thanks to the surviving papal letters, a growth that was matched by the development, and eventual supremacy, of Ó Cellaig patronage and monopoly over the priory (Fanning 1976, 102–3). The papal registers record a number of reported offences, nearly exclusively undertaken by Ó Cellaig priors. In 1445, prior Odo (Aodh) Ó Cellaig was accused of simony, while in 1473 prior Donatus Ó Cellaig was accused of keeping a concubine and of committing homicide (*Clonfert*, 80, 153–4). Judging from these historical entries from

The landscape and economy of Uí Maine

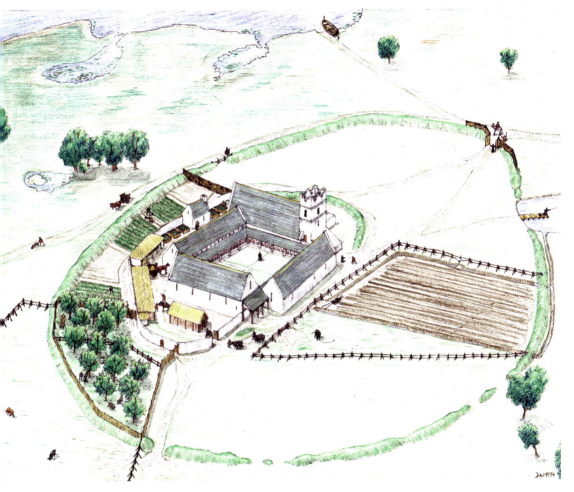

Figure 3.12 Reconstruction illustration of the Hospital of the Crutched Friars at Rindoon, *c.*1500, after its rebuilding under Ó Cellaig patronage (reconstruction drawing by Dan Tietzsch-Tyler, commissioned by Roscommon County Council).

the fourteenth century onwards, Cluain Tuaiscirt O Máine was effectively under Ó Cellaig control, presumably with some access to the wealth that this brought. The hillock immediately to the east of the priory is likely to have been a venue of Ó Cellaig inauguration (Curley 2021a, 464–76).

Abbeyknockmoy – *Mainistir Chnoc Muaidhe*, is a twelfth-century Cistercian foundation established by Cathal Crobhdearg Ó Conchobair (Gwynn and Hadcock 1970, 124; Stalley 1987, 133, 183, 188, 240; Moss 2015a, 203). Abbeyknockmoy was one of a number of foundations associated with a group of masons known as the 'School of the West' (Moss 2015b, 481). The majority of the buildings date from the early thirteenth century, with some building work in the late medieval period. By at least the mid-fourteenth and fifteenth centuries, the Uí Chellaig had overtaken the Uí Chonchobair as its principal patrons, however members of the senior Ó Cellaig line had used the religious house as a place of retirement and burial from at least as early as 1290 (*AC*; Moss 2015a, 204). From the late fourteenth century onwards, the lords of Uí Maine, as well as the younger Ó Cellaig sons who went into the religious orders, heavily patronized the foundation, as their territorial ambitions came to fruition at nearby Tiaquin (*Ó CGF ii*, 67; Smith 2014a). Displays of wealth can be seen with the early fifteenth-century tomb to Maolsechlainn Ó Cellaig and his wife Fionola and the wall paintings that once adorned both this area and other locations within the abbey (Morton 2004, 342–6; Moss 2015a, 204). With Abbeyknockmoy, the Uí Chellaig used their new position to exercise authority over what was another wealthy resource in their expanded lordship, with Mannion indicating it to be the wealthiest foundation in the archdiocese of Tuam at the time of the suppression of the monasteries (2024, 73).

The Hospital of the Crutched Friars at Rindoon, Co. Roscommon, was also patronized by the Uí Chellaig, particularly from the mid-fourteenth century onwards. This would coincide with the increased authority these lords held in Tír Maine from this period. The hospital was presumably founded by Henry III in the late 1220s, at the same time as the Anglo-Norman town was established, but it continued to be patronized by the local Gaelic elite after the desertion of the town in the early fourteenth century (O'Conor and Shanahan 2018, 19). All that remains of this foundation today is what has been interpreted as the hospital's infirmary, however, this would have been accompanied by a church and other friary buildings, which would have served a range of functions for the religious community and its dependants here (ibid., 21). Uí Chellaig involvement at the hospital is seen with the retirement and death of Seán Mór Ó Dubhagáin at Rindoon in 1372 (*AU*; *AFM*) and the burial of Conchobhar Anabaidh Ó Cellaig, lord of Uí Maine, at the religious house, on which he had bestowed many benefits in 1403 (*AC*; *ALC*). It is clear that the hospital was heavily rebuilt, under Ó Cellaig patronage, at some stage in the fifteenth century. This seems to have included the insertion of fine traceried windows, the re-building of the cloister arcade and the erection of a tower, among other things (Fig. 3.12; O'Conor and Shanahan 2018, 40–1)

It is clear from all of this that one of the ways in which wealth was both displayed and accrued by the Gaelic elite was through patronage and involvement in religious foundations. Plainly, this investment was beneficial to the Uí Chellaig also, in that it served as a suitable location to place younger sons and junior branches of the sept, but the wealth generated by these religious houses would also have been considerable, and may have entered the coffers of the lord, either directly or indirectly. There are indications more generally that by the beginning of the fifteenth century, monasteries and priories in Gaelic lordships were becoming increasingly controlled by the local secular elite. This was part of a nuanced evolution of the church in Gaelic Ireland during the whole later medieval period, whereby abbacies and priorships became quasi-hereditary to particular families and, as has been demonstrated here and elsewhere, there are examples where the lord's kin, or indeed the lord himself, profited from involvement in the church (Nicholls 2003, 123–5).

Public displays of wealth could also manifest in the construction of lordly residences and feasting halls. A noteworthy example of this is seen with the moated site of Cloonfree, Co. Roscommon, the historically attested residence of an early fourteenth-century king of Connacht. Two poems record the presence of a substantial and elaborate post-and-wattle-constructed feasting hall in the interior of the moated site, showing the level of detail in a building for the purpose of public display (Finan and O'Conor 2002, 83–6). While elsewhere in medieval Europe such constructions, and their settings, were seen as being out of fashion, building practice in Gaelic Ireland seems to have espoused the patronage of fine craftsmen, but in order to construct residences which were deliberately archaic looking.

In our study area, the residences of Uilliam Buide Ó Cellaig are similarly described. In *Filidh Éreann Go Haointeach*, the poet sets out the interior of Uilliam's residence at Galey as follows:

> The choice of stone and timber is the spacious court of the Spark of Cualu; the beams of his domed court are of oak, joined without splitting, There is much artistic ironwork upon the shining timber; on the smooth part of each brown oaken beam workmen are carving animal figures. (*FÉGH*, 61, 63)

Similarly, *Táth aoinfhir ar iath Maineach* records another of Uilliam's residences, the description of which implies an island or *crannóg* siting. Here the opulence of the interior is used to highlight the subject's wealth and prosperity (*Táth aoinfhir*, q14–21). While these locations cannot be regarded as impressive in a European sense, they likely result out of the practicalities of how Gaelic society operated at that time, and they were nonetheless to be experienced by a select cohort of guests, including other Gaelic lords, vassal chiefs, political rivals and local freeholders. Therefore, the appearance and decoration of these residences and feasting halls was designed to highlight the affluence and power of the patron. Certainly it seems that the creation of environments which retained a real or imagined antiquity and timelessness was a major preoccupation of later medieval Gaelic lords, presumably with the continued use of older elite settlement forms and the incorporation of deliberate anachronisms into these public theatres, a means by which the lord could demonstrate his long-standing legacy and legitimacy in the landscape (O'Conor 2018, 164–5; Fig. 6.4).

These are just some of a number of ways in which the Gaelic elite expressed the wealth and power that they derived primarily from the economic activities of their lordship. Other expressions included the convening of regular feasts and outdoor assemblies, the patronage of a retinue of learned professions, particularly poets, *brehons*, physicians and historians, but also musicians, the keeping of armed retainers and the ability to muster combatants, and the maintenance of large herds of cattle and horses, which all served as demonstrations of the wealth and aristocratic status of a lord of Uí Maine (O'Conor 2005, 219). Further evidence of these various attributes will be outlined in the coming chapters.

∗ ∗ ∗

This chapter has reconstructed many aspects of the physical landscape, society and economic activities which evolved in later medieval Uí Maine. The physical landscape played a major role in shaping society and how it sustained itself in this eastern Connacht lordship, as the attributes and limitations of the landscape dictated settlement and economic endeavours. Outlined above is the range of economic activities from which the Uí Chellaig lords would have profited, from farming regimes through to the exploitation of the resources of the natural environment. What is apparent from this chapter is that the Uí Chellaig lords became more prosperous and powerful from the early-to-mid-fourteenth century onwards, with an increase in the number and diversity of displays of wealth. These correspond with the historical narrative of earlier chapters, and indicate that the increase in authority over larger and more economically prosperous areas within the lordship resulted in a parallel increase in wealth. This affluence was then expressed through a range of lordly undertakings, some of which are still apparent in literary survivals, as well as in upstanding architectural and archaeological remains.

CHAPTER FOUR

Settlement archaeology

One of the key questions that this book seeks to address is our understanding of what settlement forms the Ó Cellaig elites constructed and occupied throughout the later medieval period. An attempt to start answering this question is initiated in this chapter and lays the foundations for the more detailed analyses of selected Ó Cellaig lordly centres provided in the following three chapters. Here the changes in settlement forms selected by the Uí Maine lords throughout the period will also be charted, between 1100 and 1600.

HIGH MEDIEVAL CASTLES IN UÍ MAINE

The origin of the castle in medieval Irish archaeology is a topic that creates much debate. The castle is traditionally regarded as having been introduced into Ireland with the arrival of the Anglo-Normans. However, some believe that the origins of castle-building predate 1170 and depend largely on historical references and morphological similarities in order to prove their point. These scholars are helped with a broad definition that could be applied to the castle. In its simplest terms, a castle has been defined as a systematically defended residence of someone of lordly status in medieval society (King 1988, 1–13; De Meulemeester and O'Conor 2008, 323–4). This definition incorporates a substantial diversity of castle types from a morphological point of view. This has led to the superficial and erroneous labelling of a number of high medieval Gaelic lordly sites as castles, when their morphology and setting indicates that they are, in fact, an evolution of a series of native site types and are more complex and nuanced than the label implies. An example that impacts upon our understanding of the Ó Cellaig lordship concerns the term *caistél*, which is found in a small number of historical entries, particularly from the twelfth century. Many of these fortifications were constructed by Toirrdelbach Mór Ó Conchobair, particularly in the early part of his reign (Ó Corráin 1972, 150–1). One of these occurred within the study area – the *caistél* of *Dún Leodha*.

The caistél *of* Dún Leodha
In 1124, Toirrdelbach constructed a *caistél* fortification at *Dún Leodha*, now Dunlo townland, Ballinasloe, Co. Galway (*AFM*). Previously a fortification on this site was described as a *dún* in 1114 (*AFM*). What form, or forms, these *caistél* took has been

the source of much debate, owing in large part to the lack of immediately identifiable examples in the Irish landscape today (Nicholls 1982, 389; Graham 1990, 233–5; O'Keeffe 1998, 187–9; Barry 2007; O'Conor, Brady, Connon and Fidalgo-Romo 2010, 34–40; Naessens and O'Conor 2012). As regards the morphology of *Dún Leodha* specifically, most studies cite Molyneux's *Journey to Connaught, April 1709*, which provides the following description of a monument located in Ballinasloe:

> Here is a Danes-mount, with a large trench round it: 'tis so flat one might almost take it for a fort: this, with one more, were the only mounts I saw on all ye road between Killeglan [townland in Taughmaconnell parish] and Gallway, tho' their forts were all along mighty frequent. (Smith 1846, 166)

According to O'Keeffe, Molyneux used the term 'Danesmount' when describing high, motte-like mounds (O'Keeffe 1998, 188; 2019, 122–3; 2021, 38–43), a description that has its own difficulties. In this respect, it has been suggested that the *caistél* built at *Dún Leodha* in 1124 was a motte castle. Furthermore, it has recently been suggested that all of these pre-Norman *caistéll/caislen* sites were also motte castles, being a type of fortification recently imported into Ireland with the ideology known as feudalism (O'Keeffe 2019). However, other research has concluded that at least some of these pre-Norman strongholds, while more imposing and utilizing mortar in their construction, were really a hybrid of the native ringfort, *crannóg* and cashel-building traditions (Naessens and O'Conor 2012, 266–7). Notable examples which incorporated aspects of the *crannóg* and cashel can be seen at Iniscremha Island and *Caislen na Circe* on Lough Corrib, Co. Galway, *Caislen na Caillighe* on Lough Mask, Co. Mayo, the Rock of Lough Cé and possibly *Loch Cairgín* (Ardakillin Lough), both Co. Roscommon (Shanahan 2008, 9; O'Conor, Brady, Connon and Fidalgo-Romo 2010, 21–40; Naessens and O'Conor 2012, 263–6; see Fig. 4.1).

Unlike these *'caistél' crannóga*, however, which have survived intact in some form to the present day, the physical manifestation of the 'dryland' *caistél* is more elusive. One noteworthy characteristic of these constructions is the pairing of the fortification with a bridge or ford, something that is seen at Athlone (1120), Dunmore (burned 1133), Collooney (1124), Killaloe (1170), and also, in the present context, *Dún Leodha* (1120) (*AFM*; Flanagan 1997, 63; Curley and Timoney, 2024). Therefore, as regards the complex of features that were constructed, the presence of a bridge or fortified river-crossing is telling. On the morphology of the 'dryland' *caistél*, however, there is further debate.

Many 'dryland' *caistél* are likely to have been constructed of a combination of stone, earth and timber, as evidenced by the annalistic records for them being burned on numerous occasions, with Athlone burned in 1131 and 1155 (Leask 1941, 6; Sherlock 2016, 5) and *Dún Leodha* burned by casual fire in 1131 (*ACl*). Considering then the earthen remains at *Dún Leodha*, as described by Molyneux, there is an issue. The site

Settlement archaeology

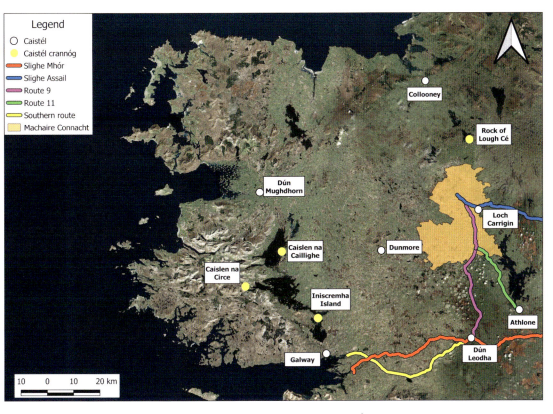

Figure 4.1 The *caistél* fortifications constructed by Toirrdelbach Ó Conchobair during his twelfth-century reign. The other *caistél crannóga* referred to in the text are also indicated.

of *Dún Leodha* does not survive above ground today and there is even confusion as to its location. As a result, other monuments must be considered as a means of providing a comparison. Candidates for this have been proposed in the past, such as the flat-topped mound and enclosure at Dunmore, Co. Galway, as well as a number of excavated raised ringforts, particularly in Co. Down. The excavated evidence indicates that they are multi-period in date (with some dating to as early as the later eighth and ninth century), with the later horizons consistent in broad chronology with the historically attested *caistél* of the twelfth century (O'Keeffe 2000, 27–9; O'Sullivan, McCormick, Kerr and Harney, 2014, 78–9). These sites provided better defence and a suitable level of elevation over the wider landscape than what could be deemed for 'flat' ringforts and it has accordingly been suggested that they indicate a pre-Norman adoption by the Gaelic elite of motte castles for defence and habitation in the twelfth century, following a wider European trend (Nicholls 1982, 389; Graham 1988b, 117; O'Keeffe 2000, 29; 2019). Other research, as noted, into these twelfth-century structures argues that the new fortifications, associated with the terms *caistél* and *caislen*, were inspired from a fusion of native traditions as opposed to influence from abroad, suggesting that they were an Irish development from their own building practices, possibly a result of changes in societal and military needs during the preceding centuries (Naessens and O'Conor 2012, 267).

In the absence of surviving archaeological remains for *Dún Leodha*, an interpretation of the site can only be attempted based upon its presumed location. Barry suggested that *Dún Leodha* may have stood where the later medieval masonry castle now stands, on the eastern bank of the River Suck (Barry 2007, 38). However, this ignores the fact that Dunlo townland is located entirely to the west of the river. More recently, O'Keeffe argued that the site of *Dún Leodha* is located beneath the nineteenth-century St John the Evangelist Church in Ballinasloe (O'Keeffe 2019, 122–3). This identification is suspect though. First, the latter church is not in Dunlo townland. More than this, John O'Donovan, writing in 1838, states, 'This name (Dunlo) it received from a fort which stood over the Suck where the present Roman Catholic chapel stands, but which is now just destroyed' (*OS Letters, Galway,* 127). The 'chapel' referred to in the letter is consistent with the 'R. C. Chapel' marked on the western side of the river in the 1st Edition OS 6-Inch map, now the site of St Michael's Catholic church, completed in 1858. Should O'Donovan's information be correct, then this, coupled with the place-name evidence, would tell us that *caistél Dún Leodha* was located on the western bank of the River Suck, on the boundary between Townparks to the north-west, and Dunlo to the south-east, previously a larger townland of the latter name (Wallace and Maguire 2021, 14).

In evaluating the likelihood of *Dún Leodha* being sited where St Michael's Church is now, we must interrogate the extent to which this landscape has changed over time. The modern course of the River Suck through Ballinasloe is modified from how it once flowed, even as late as the middle of the nineteenth century. The aforementioned map records a series of islets between the eastern and western banks of the river, which have since become consolidated as a single, much larger, island on the river in the twentieth century (Fig. 4.2). Judging from the cartographic source, the river once flowed in multiple courses through the settlement that built up around this ford. Two main courses are identifiable, with the more westerly and wider of the two original courses flowing beneath the late medieval stone bridge and right next to where St Michael's Church is located. Therefore, if the fortification of *Dún Leodha* was sited here, it would once have been strategically located and in effect be in the best position to control all riverine navigation up and down the River Suck and overland transportation across the ford at this point. Thereafter, one can only theorize that perhaps *caistél Dún Leodha* served as an impressive earthwork, which cast a shadow over the ford of *Áth Nadsluaigh* (Fig. 4.3), matching the combination of bridge and fortification at the Shannon ford of Athlone at this time. Molyneux's description of what may be *Dún Leodha* seems to be describing a monument that was

Settlement archaeology

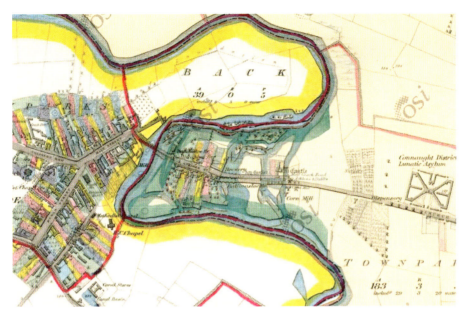

Figure 4.2 1st Edition OS map illustrating the number of islets that made up the fording place of *Áth Nadsluaigh*. The RC chapel is labelled, with the location of the late medieval stone bridge to its north (image courtesy of OSi).

morphologically somewhere between a mound and an ordinary ringfort – perhaps best described as a low mound. Was this a motte castle? Without excavation, this is at the very least uncertain. Arguably, it could have been an earthwork fortification in the tradition of the 'raised' *ráth* but even this is uncertain as another way of interpreting Molyneux's description is that the site was a flat 'ringfort' with a slightly raised interior. Nor were raised *ráthanna* just eleventh and twelfth century in date and examples of this form of ringfort had been in existence in the Irish landscape since the later eighth and ninth century (O'Conor, Brady, Connon and Fidalgo-Romo 2010, 37–9; O'Sullivan, McCormick, Kerr and Harney 2014, 65–6).

It has been shown that the things that made a raised *ráth* different in physical terms from a motte or, for that matter, a substantial ringfort from a ringwork castle, were the scale and complexities of defences and buildings seen on these sites when occupied. They may at times look similar to one another today but excavation and the historical sources from across Europe have shown that motte and ringwork castles carried much larger timber (and cob) buildings within them and had far more complex defences than what was seen on different forms of ringfort, even ones constructed by great princes (O'Conor 2002b, 175–80; De Meulemeester and O'Conor 2008, 323–31; O'Conor, Brady, Connon and Fidalgo-Romo 2010, 39–40; Higham and Barker 1992; 2000; Mittelstraß 2004). Higham and Barker (1992, 348–52) have argued that it was these complex defences and great wooden buildings that distinguished mottes and

Figure 4.3 Reconstruction of former, much more extensive, course of the River Suck at Ballinasloe in the mid-nineteenth century, as well as the proposed location of *caistél Dún Leodha* (base image: Bing Maps).

ringworks as castles, not their earthworks. So, arguably, mottes and ringworks looked physically very different when occupied to fortifications such as the different forms of ringforts (including contemporary ones), moated sites and *crannóga*. Therefore, O'Keeffe's (2019, 122–3; 2021, 38–43) decision to interpret Molyneux's rather vague early eighteenth-century description of the now-levelled earthwork at *Dún Leodha* as definitely being a motte is dangerous without excavation or, failing that, better evidence. Furthermore, O'Keeffe (2019, 119–20) seems to be of the view that any earthwork fortification built and occupied by the elite in Ireland during the hundred or so years prior to 1169 has to be a motte or ringwork castle, simply because Irish society had 'adopted' the hierarchical social structure known as feudalism. Leaving aside the fact that certain historians argue that 'feudalism' never existed (Brown 1974) or was very different to what is the accepted view of this construct by most historians (Reynolds 1994), it would appear that O'Keeffe is saying that pre-Norman Irish society had evolved in more-or-less the same way as contemporary Norman England and so had similar settlement forms, most notably the castle, as a form of elite residence. However, while Gaelic Ireland from even before 1100 down to *c.*1600 had many of the characteristics of contemporary European society and in certain ways developed along similar lines, native Irish society, which was a clan- or lineage-based society with a very distinct law code, was different in many respects to contemporary 'feudal' Anglo-Norman, English and Western European society (Nicholls 1972; 1987; 2003; Richter 1988, 189–93; O'Conor 1998, 74–5). In this respect, it would be hazardous to assume that the Gaelic Irish response to, for example, fortification was precisely the same as in the contemporary Norman and Angevin world, especially as there is now considerable evidence for the continued usage of *crannóga* and different forms of ringforts in Ireland during the later medieval period. Given the fact that it has been argued that at least some of the pre-1169 *caistéll/caislen* seem to have evolved from the cashel/*crannóg* tradition, one viable argument is that the 1124 *caistél* built at *Dún Leodha* was some form of well-defended ringfort that did not carry the same complexity of defences seen on contemporary Norman timber castles in Wales and England, such as Hen Domen on the present English-Welsh border.

Nonetheless, the strategic siting of this fortification would have resulted in *Dún Leodha* being a highly-prized location of elite residence into later periods, and it is likely to have served as a principal residence of a cadet branch of the Uí Chellaig, the *Clannmhaicne Eoghain*, into the thirteenth century and beyond, as they grappled for control of the important ford over the River Suck at *Áth Nadsluaigh*.

The Anglo-Norman baronial castles of Uí Maine
For much of the thirteenth century and the early decades of the fourteenth century, the King's Cantreds of Omany and Tyrmany saw manorial settlements develop as Anglo-Norman lords sought to benefit economically from their speculative grants in the region. As a result, a series of baronial settler castles are recorded in historical sources as having been constructed to serve as the administrative focal point of these manors. These references serve as an indication of the power now being exerted by Anglo-Norman barons west of the River Shannon in this area, resulting in a constriction in power of the traditional Uí Chellaig lords.

The year 1245 saw the construction of *Caislen Suicin* (AC). It is difficult to conclude from this single reference where *Caislen Suicin* was located, what form it took and who constructed it, however, a reference from 1300–1 indicates that the manors of both *Aththrym* (Aughrim) and *Suthkyn* (Suicin) were part of the landholdings of the Anglo-Norman Butler family by that time (*CDI*, iv, nos 765–7, 814; Walton, 1980, 472). Walton has suggested that *Caislen Suicin* was constructed in order to command the river-crossing at Ballinasloe (Walton 1980, 446), which would suggest that the fortification in question was located on the eastern bank of the River Suck, on the site of, or close to, the remains classified as an 'Anglo-Norman masonry castle' (Alcock, de hÓra and Gosling 1999, 418).

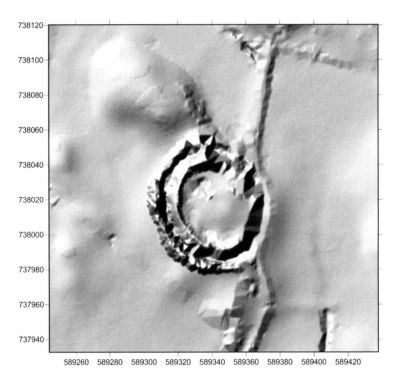

Figure 4.4 LiDAR visualization of the earthwork remains at Dundonnell Castle, Co. Roscommon (data source: OSi; visualization courtesy of LGS).

In 1258, Richard de la Rochelle was granted the entire cantred of Omany, and permitted to construct a castle at Aughrim, and to host 'markets, fairs and warrens' wherever in the cantred he saw fit (*Cal. Ormond Deeds*, I, 55–6). This was offered to de la Rochelle as a means of promoting settlement in the cantred (Walton 1980, 467) and provides the first mention of the intention to construct a castle at Aughrim. In 1282, these lands in Omany, including Aughrim and Suicin, were granted by Philip de la Rochelle, Richard's son, to his cousin, Theobald Butler (*Cal. Ormond Deeds*, I, 101–3; Curtis (ed.) 1932/3, 123; Walton 1980, 470). By the 1290s, there was a castle recorded at Aughrim, but what form it took is difficult to ascertain from the present remains. Walton states that Aughrim Castle is one of only three castles (aside from the royal castles of Athlone, Rindoon, Roscommon and presumably Onagh) recorded as being constructed by Anglo-Norman settlers in the King's Cantreds, with the other two constructed at Athleague and Dunamon, Co. Roscommon (Walton 1980, 404). To this list of colonial castles should be added the aforementioned *Caislen Suicin*.

In all cases, these thirteenth-century fortifications are no longer extant, however, it has been suggested that the construction at Dunamon was of an earthwork character, primarily due to the lack of above ground thirteenth-century remains. These settler

Settlement archaeology

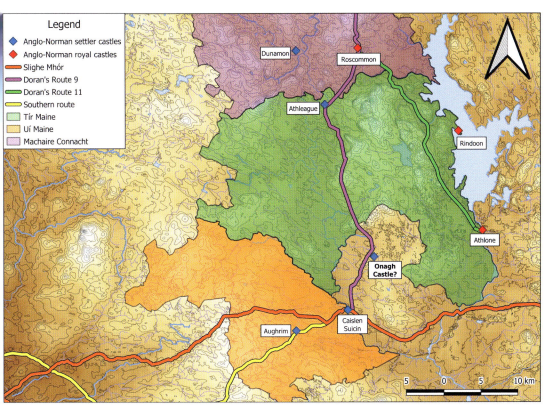

Figure 4.5 The Anglo-Norman baronial settler and royal castles in and near the study area. Note the strategic location of these castles in the vicinity of the major regional routeways.

castles, as distinct from the royal castles of Athlone, Rindoon and Roscommon, may not have been constructed initially in stone. A likely comparison to the morphology of these earthwork castles comes with the earthen remains that form part of the Dundonnell Castle complex, Co. Roscommon, which likely constitute the physical remains of the historically attested thirteenth-century Anglo-Norman fortification of 'Onagh Castle' (Curley 2018, 138–41). Arguably, Dundonnell may have been a ringwork castle modified out of an existing bivallate ringfort (Fig. 4.4; ibid., 149–50; Barry 1987, 52–3; Graham 1988a, 28–9; Sweetman 2000, 197–8). It is also clear that when taken altogether, most of these Anglo-Norman castles in the study area occur along major regional roads and often at fords on navigable rivers (Fig. 4.5).

The reason why these baronial castles are being considered as part of this chapter relates to their later history, and the evidence indicates that these sites were later occupied, re-occupied and remodelled by members of the Uí Chellaig and their vassal clans into the late medieval period.

The erroneous labelling of high medieval Gaelic lordly sites as 'Castles'
When investigating the evidence relating to the construction of high medieval castles by the Ó Cellaig elite, the researcher must be wary of issues in terminology, especially in the case of the translation of historical sources. There has been a commonplace practice among medieval Irish historians and linguists to insert the term 'castle' when translating literary and historical sources after the original Irish refers to the stronghold as *dún* (*Ir.* Fort), *ráth* (*Ir.* earthen rampart, ringfort), *longphort* (*Ir.* Stronghold; fortified residence)*, caiseal* (*Ir.* Stone fort), *cathair* (*Ir.* Circular dry-stone fort, dwelling place) or a similar term. Ringforts and dry-stone walled cashels would not be considered castles by either contemporaries or modern scholars. The moated sites at Rockingham and Cloonfree in Co. Roscommon, for example, are both referred to as *longphort* in the sources (Finan and O'Conor 2002; O'Conor and Finan 2018, 116–22). Again, moated sites would not be considered to be castles in a physical sense then or now (O'Conor 2015, 335–6). Another example of this is seen in the case of the Ó Cellaig *cenn áit* of Galey, Co. Roscommon.

While the location of Ó Cellaig's residence at Galey is in little doubt, the same cannot be said of the form this site took when originally described in the fourteenth century. One issue that must be addressed is the perceived form of the residence. A number of historians equate the surviving masonry remains, the remnants of a tower house, with Uilliam Buide Ó Cellaig's 1351 residence mentioned in a praise poem of that general date (Pl. 4.1; *FÉGH*, 57; Simms 1978, 91; Kerrigan 1996; C.M. O'Sullivan 2004, 221). However, there are a number of compelling reasons why the standing remains are best interpreted as later in date than the poem. The likely origins for this misidentification can be traced to Knott's 1911 translation of *Filidh Éreann Go Haointeach*, which repeatedly refers to Ó Cellaig's residence as a 'castle' (*FÉGH*, 57, 59, 61). However, the original Irish portrays a different picture. The original poem uses variations of the terms *brugh* (dwelling, mansion), *dún(adh)* and *cathair* (dry-stone walled fort or cashel) to describe the residence, but the translation mistakenly inserts the English word 'castle'. Thus this misidentification was born, a classification which, as we have seen, has been blindly adopted by a number of authors. Interestingly, Knott's preference in translating the latter words as 'castle' is seen in other poetic translations (Simms 2001, 247). It is always dangerous to equate a date that comes from an historical or literary reference with a standing building, such as a castle, without excavation and/or a detailed architectural survey. Very often, as sites are inhabited for centuries, the standing remains of any given structure were constructed at far later dates than the first historical reference to it (W. Meyer 2011, 234; O'Conor 2023, 181–3).

The mortared masonry remains of Galey Castle consist of a tower house of either fifteenth or sixteenth-century date (Pl. 4.1). This means that there is no evidence at Galey for what modern scholars or, indeed, contemporaries would classify as a castle

Plate 4.1 Earthworks and tower house castle remains at Galey, Co. Roscommon, viewed from the north (author's photograph).

in the mid-fourteenth century. In summary, both the historical and physical evidence suggests that most castles built in the study area between the twelfth century and late fourteenth century (when tower houses start to be built) were few in number and erected in some way by the Anglo-Normans. *Caistél Dún Leodha* may have been a pre-Norman 'castle' but other interpretations exist for the morphology of this site.

RINGFORTS AND CASHELS

The most readily identifiable archaeological evidence of secular settlement in early medieval Ireland comes in the form of ringforts, cashels and enclosures. The term 'ringfort' embraces a number of different types of enclosure, which differ from one another in size, morphology and construction material. The majority consist of a circular enclosure, *c.*30m in internal diameter on average (with smaller and larger examples), defined by an earthen bank and outer fosse. These are known as univallate ringforts and are sometimes referred to as *ráth* in the literature. Predominantly in rocky landscapes, with the enclosed area defined by a dry-stone wall, this form of ringfort is known as the cashel. These dry-stone enclosures tend to be slightly smaller in internal diameter to earthen univallate ringforts. Most ringforts and cashels are defined by one earthen bank or dry-stone wall. However, between 15% and 20% of *ráthanna* have two or more banks around them, being bivallate and trivallate enclosures. Some cashels also have a second or even third dry-stone wall around them (Edwards 1990, 6–33; Stout 1997, 15–18; O'Conor 2015, 332–3). It has been argued that this multivallation was a physical manifestation of societal hierarchy (Stout 1997, 17–18), an argument that is now generally accepted (O'Sullivan, McCormick, Kerr and Harney 2014, 82), with the more complex sites having been constructed and occupied by members of the local or regional elite.

Looking at the numbers of ringforts, cashels, and enclosures surviving in Tír Maine and Uí Maine provides a clear indication that this region was extensively settled throughout the medieval period. 76 cashels, 258 enclosures, which in many cases may actually be degraded ringforts, and 767 ringforts are located in the study area (Alcock, de hÓra and Gosling 1999, 32–257).[1] The highest densities of ringforts are evident in the parts of the landscape with the highest potential agricultural yield (Fig. 3.2). Ringforts and cashels are traditionally deemed to be the principal settlement forms of the early medieval period. The height of occupation of these monument types seems to occur between the seventh and ninth centuries and certainly the majority of the sites enumerated above were probably constructed, occupied and abandoned during that time (Stout 1997, 22–32). An evolved form of the site type, the more elevated platform or raised ringfort, seems to possess a later chronology, AD 750–950. This

---

[1] https://heritagedata.maps.arcgis.com/apps/webappviewer/index.html?id=0c9eb9575b544081b0d296436d8f60f 8.16/11/2023.

chronology for ringforts and cashels must be tempered by the fact that it is derived from a small, and probably not fully representative, sample size (O'Sullivan, McCormick, Kerr and Harney 2014, 65–6). However, there is growing evidence from throughout the island of Ireland, including that outlined in the later chapters of this book, that ringforts and cashels continued to be occupied and perhaps constructed, even by members of the minor elite, throughout the later medieval period and down to the seventeenth century (O'Conor 1998, 84–7, 89–94; FitzPatrick 2009).

O'Conor investigated the archaeological expression of the *longphort*, a term used regularly in *Caithreim Thoirdhealbaigh*, in order to describe the lordly residences of the elite of what is now Co. Clare. Using a range of historical and archaeological material uncovered in north-western Munster more generally, coupled with the references from *Caithreim Thoirdhealbaigh* itself, O'Conor demonstrated that these *longphort* regularly presented a physical manifestation as cashels and ringforts (O'Conor 2004, 246–50). Further evidence from Clare, in the form of the excavations at Caherconnell, are equally significant in that the dating evidence suggests that the site was occupied continuously from the tenth century through to the early seventeenth century (Comber and Hull 2010). Despite the considerable numbers of ringforts and cashels that survive in the study area, hardly any of these monuments have ever been subjected to archaeological investigation. Of the few to have been inspected in this manner, three sites excavated as part of the National Roads Authority (NRA) M6 road infrastructural project presented with later medieval dates: Loughbown I and II, and Mackney ringforts, Co. Galway. These are important to our understanding of the settlement forms in use in the later medieval Ó Cellaig lordship.

Loughbown and Mackney ringforts
Loughbown I was a large bivallate ringfort located 3.2km to the east of Aughrim. The maximum external diameter was *c.*60m, with two ditches, and presumably two banks, although neither survive. Dateable material from a variety of contexts throughout the site contributed a broad date range, from the fifth century through to the fifteenth century, suggesting that it had a very long period of habitation (Bower 2014, 175). Access to the site was granted via a causewayed south-eastern-facing entrance. Within the interior there was evidence of a souterrain, two structures and a number of corn-drying kilns. Evidence was also uncovered of what has been interpreted as 'occasional metalworking', which was concentrated between the two ditches and was conducted late in the use of the ringfort, occurring between the eleventh and thirteenth centuries (ibid., 175–7). The later medieval artefactual assemblage included a wooden comb, a bone weaving tool, a fish hook (Pl. 3.4), an iron knife and an iron pin. The only securely dated later medieval find was a silver Edward I coin, probably minted at Bristol in 1280 or 1281, though this was found in topsoil, slightly lessening its diagnostic value (ibid., 179). Loughbown II was a much smaller example, located

500m to the west. There is very little evidence that this ringfort was ever inhabited and the excavators have interpreted it as an animal stockyard. However, a knife blade of later medieval date was recovered, again highlighting the continuity of use of these monuments beyond the period accepted for ringfort construction and use (ibid., 180–3).

Mackney ringfort, located 2.5km to the south-west of Ballinasloe, was a very substantial univallate earthwork, with a maximum external diameter of *c*.61m, marked by a single ditch, measuring 5–6m in width and over 3m deep. The excavation suggests that the largely removed internal bank would have been an impressive barrier to intruders and presents evidence of having had an internal stone revetment (Delaney 2014, 188–90). The entrance was located to the east of the site. A total of nine possible buildings were uncovered within the interior, the most substantial being a 5.4m diameter round-house, which was sited centrally. An L-shaped, two chambered souterrain was uncovered to the west of this, and thus furthest away from the entrance, adding to the ringfort's complexity (ibid., 192–3). Dateable material from a variety of contexts contributed a date range from the eighth century through to the sixteenth century, with the later dates in particular coming primarily from corn-drying kilns, as well as hearths and a post-hole. There were also a number of later medieval artefacts uncovered, including a possible Henry III silver coin, dateable to between 1247 and 1272, a Henry VIII silver coin minted in 1546, and a socketed, iron 'bodkin' arrowhead, typically of tenth to thirteenth-century date (ibid., 194–5). Combining this information, Delaney concluded that Mackney ringfort was an impressive habitation site still in use well into the later medieval period (ibid., 199–200). Gardiner and O'Conor have noted that at least some of the NRA/TII-excavated ringforts throughout Ireland present clear evidence of continued occupation into the later medieval period and that the results of these excavations mirror the archaeological findings at Caherconnell. However, they also note that the excavators of these sites have tended to downplay the evidence for later medieval occupation within them, presumably because of the strong traditional and embedded narrative among professional archaeologists that ringforts and cashels were 'only' occupied during early medieval times (Gardiner and O'Conor 2017, 147–8).

The evidence from these two sites, which are not documented in the surviving historical sources, would indicate that the ringfort occupants are likely to have been relatively affluent members of later medieval society. The people from both sites may represent members of a prosperous farming community in later medieval Gaelic Uí Maine, who were still choosing to reside in ringforts and cashels. The value that these excavations have for this research relate to the fact that the historical research conducted here has uncovered a significant number of locations of residence for members of the Ó Cellaig elite, their service kindreds and vassal clans. Where these locations correspond with identifiable townland names, in most cases the only monument type to be found within is a ringfort or cashel. The information from the excavations of Loughbown and Mackney seem to suggest that the historically attested residences of these elites and minor elites correspond with the ringfort or cashel, although only excavation will confirm this. This strengthens the argument that these monuments were certainly still occupied and may have been constructed in the region during the later medieval period. Individual examples of this will be identified and discussed over the coming chapters. It is highly significant that Mackney, Loughbown I and Loughbown II were the only three ringforts excavated along the course of the M6 road that occur within the study area. Noticeably, all three turned up evidence for later medieval occupation and use, hinting that many of the other hundreds of ringforts within the Ó Cellaig lordship were also inhabited during later medieval times.

HIGH-CAIRN *CRANNÓGA*

Crannóga are mostly artificial or sometimes modified natural islands, constructed using stone, timber and soil and particularly found in the lakes and former lakes of the drumlin belt that runs from Mayo across northern Connacht, south Ulster, and the north Midlands to Co. Down. While small artificial islands were built close to certain lakeshores in the Mesolithic and Neolithic periods, *crannóga* proper, defined as being mainly artificial islands with an average living space of 20m to 25m in diameter and located out in lakes, first start to be built during the Late Bronze Age. However, the great majority seem to have been first built from the fifth and sixth centuries AD onwards during the early medieval period. The size, artefactual assemblages and complexity of some of these sites indicate that they operated as high-status and even royal residences at that time, offering a degree of protection, exclusivity and privacy (Edwards 1990, 34–41; O'Sullivan 1998, 103–47; Fredengren 2002; O'Sullivan, McCormick, Kerr and Harney 2014, 58–62; O'Conor 1998, 79–84; 2015, 333–4).

The evidence for *crannóga* in early medieval Uí Maine is limited, not least by the relative absence of the characteristic small lakes that these monuments are usually found on. However, where small lakes do occur, *crannóga* are to be found. As such, Callow Lough, in what was the early medieval *trícha cét* of Soghan, has a large *crannóg* constructed at its centre (Alcock, de hÓra and Gosling 1999, 30). Ballaghdacker Lough, in what was the *trícha cét* of Clann Crimthann, possesses two *crannóga* (ibid., 29, 31), which may have been focal points for elite settlement among that branch of the Uí Maine in the early medieval period. The Clann Chommáin branch of the Uí Maine, styled *rí Locha Riach*, implies that their centre was located on or near Loughrea Lake (MacCotter 2014, 141). The fortress of *Locha Riach* was destroyed in 802 (*AU*), and this may have been a *crannóg*. Indeed, thirteen *crannóga* are recorded on the lake today. Either one of Reed's Island or Island Mc Hugo may have been the site recorded in 802, based not least on their size and artefactual assemblage respectively (McDonald 2022, 10–15). In the territory of Cenél Coirpre Chruim, there are hints from the mid-eighth century that a pre-Uí Maine group known as the *Delbna Nuadat* may have had a centre among the *crannóga* on Lough Croan, before being supplanted by the latter sept, possibly with their *cenn áit* taken over also (*AT*; *AFM*; Kelleher 1971, 70–1; Ó Corráin 1972, 13; Byrne 2004, 92; Devane 2013, 101).

However, it is becoming increasingly apparent that the *crannóg* did not cease to be used as a settlement form of choice in the period post-1100 and there is mounting archaeological and historical evidence that *crannóga* were occupied, rebuilt and strengthened during the later medieval period as defended lordly residences (O'Sullivan 1998, 150–6; 2001, 401–13; O'Conor 1998, 79–84; 2014, 333–4; 2018; Brady and O'Conor 2005). A series of radiocarbon and dendrochronological dates from Fermanagh *crannóga* clearly indicate their widespread occupation during the whole later medieval period (Foley and Williams 2006), and the excavation of Drumclay *crannóg*, in this county, is a prime example. This *crannóg* was built in the eighth century, but was continuously occupied down to the late sixteenth or early seventeenth century (Bermingham, Moore, O'Keeffe, Gormley 2013; Bermingham 2014). Furthermore, a series of nine radiocarbon dates derived from eight *crannóga* in Co. Leitrim show clear evidence for later medieval occupation and activity on them. This information is supported by historical references in the annals, which likewise confirm *crannóg* occupation in the Leitrim area right down to 1600 (O'Conor and Fredengren 2019, 91). It might be added that there is also historical and excavated evidence for later medieval *crannóg* occupation in the *tricha céta* of Machaire Connacht, *Na Trí Túatha* and Maigh Luirg in north Roscommon (O'Conor and Finan 2018, 113–16).

A total of eleven *crannóga* are recorded for the study area, which is a small number by comparison with the quantities recorded in the rest of Co. Roscommon and further north. There are two forms of evidence which point to *crannóga* being occupied and possibly modified in later medieval Uí Maine. Firstly, a number of entries in the annalistic record, the Ó Cellaig genealogies and in the literary sources confirm that these lords were operating on and in the vicinity of the small lakes of the lordship, all of which possess *crannóga*. Secondly, the archaeological remains of these *crannóga*, in terms of their morphology, as well as the artefactual assemblage uncovered at two sites in particular, point to their construction or reconstruction in the later medieval period.

Chapter 5 discusses a particular type of *crannóg* in the lakeland setting. Known as a high-cairn *crannóg*, this monument type was coined by Fredengren while examining *crannóga* on Lough Gara in south Sligo/north Roscommon. These *crannóga* are generally quite large and are up to 2.5m high above the present water level, with a dense stone packing in the top layers. Some of these sites also present with jetties and small harbour features (Fredengren 2002, 83–6; Fredengren, Kilfeather and Stuijts 2010, 146–7). The evidence suggests that the uppermost stone dumps on these *crannóga* were put in place in the later medieval period, to act as occupation platforms

(Fredengren 2002, 100–2, 272–6), and these high-cairn *crannóga* seem to have been occupied by the later medieval Gaelic elite in any given area. For example, four *crannóga* identified by Brady and O'Conor as being of high-cairn construction seem to have been important lordly centres in their respective regions (Brady and O'Conor 2005, 129).

THE *BÓDHÚN*

The term *bódhún*, later anglicized as 'bawn', occurs in historical entries in relation to a number of elite sites within the Ó Cellaig lordship (*Tribes*, 74; *AFM*, s.a. 1487), and its physical manifestation is something that has not been satisfactorily dealt with previously. To begin with, the term 'bawn' is potentially problematic, in that a distinction must be made between the term used in the medieval historical and literary record, and the later archaeological monument referred to as such. The *bódhún*, from the medieval Irish *badhbhdhún/badhún* (Lat. *Bawona*), meaning 'cattle fort/cow-fortress', indicates the origin of the name and the root of its primary use. The supposed absence of the term from the early medieval law tracts and their commentaries suggests that the word, and thus presumably the construction itself, does not seem to have been pre-Norman in origin (Kelly, pers. comm.). Fergus Kelly helpfully describes the enclosure as being 'where the cows of the whole neighbourhood could be brought for protection from cattle-raiders' (Kelly 2016b, 366). The term is in use more generally in the twelfth and thirteenth centuries, with references to the '*bódhún* of *Ath*' (Athlone – 1199 AD), the '*bodhún* of *Luimnech*' (Limerick – AD 1200), the *bódhún* of *Áth Buide* (Ballyboy, Co. Offaly – AD 1214) and the *badún* of Rindoon (AD 1236) (*ALC*; *AC*).

Plainly these entries do not refer to the walled or defended courtyards, called bawns, surrounding the tower houses of the fifteenth and sixteenth centuries. Nicholls addresses this point, indicating that the *bódhún* was one of a number of terms, alongside the *cenn áit* (chief or head place) and the *garrdha* (gardens), which were originally used to describe the fortified earthen 'enclosures' occupied by the high medieval Gaelic elite. In some cases, these terms must have corresponded archaeologically with ringforts and cashels. The term *bódhún* was later appropriated to describe the defended courtyards around tower houses (Nicholls 2003, 141–2; 2008, 405). Some late medieval sources continue to specifically mention these larger defensible enclosures surrounding the lordly residence, using terms such as 'large yard' and 'great bawn' (Loeber 2001, 275-6), indicating that the *bódhún* didn't simply evolve into its later namesake, rather that in some cases the two structures must have coexisted adjacent to one another at the late medieval *cenn áit*. For instance, comparison by Simms of an early fifteenth-century ecclesiastical record and two praise poems connected to the residence of Rudhraighe Mac Mathghamhna, later chief of Oirghialla (modern Co. Armagh), encounter his *cenn áit* being described in one instance as his *bódhún*, and separately as a *lios* (Simms 2001, 253). This group of references is possibly actually informing us about different parts of the *cenn áit* complex, and we must also be aware that the terminology used in this period is very much fluid and interchangeable, depending on what the writer is attempting to achieve. Up until now, it has been uncertain what a *bódhún* looked like during the high medieval period. The physical examples of two of these *bódhún* from the study area will be discussed below.

GAELIC MOATED SITES

Moated sites mostly present as rectangular or wedge-shaped defended enclosures, defined by an external, often water-filled, ditch and an internal bank. These monuments were constructed in the late thirteenth and early fourteenth centuries by prosperous peasants and minor Anglo-Norman lords in the south-east of Ireland (Barry 1977; 1987, 84–93; O'Conor 1998, 41–3; 2014, 335–6; O'Keeffe, 2000, 75–6; Gardiner and O'Conor 2017, 138–9). However, it has been successfully demonstrated that the moated sites in what is now Co. Roscommon, particularly in the north of the county, were constructed by members of the Gaelic elite (O'Conor 1998, 87–9; 2000, 100–1; 2001, 338–40; Finan and O'Conor 2002; O'Conor and Finan 2018, 116–22).

The available evidence from Cloonfree moated site, including its recording in no less than three praise poems, with one of the poems even detailing its construction at the behest of Áed Ó Conchobair, king of Connacht, serves to clarify the case for these sites being adopted as a residence type of choice by lords of the highest rank (Finan and O'Conor 2002; McCarthy and Curley 2018, 53–5; FitzPatrick 2018, 179–87; O'Conor and Finan 2018, 119–21). What could be termed Gaelic-constructed moated sites are not limited to medieval Connacht either. Historical research and excavation conducted at Clontymullan moated site, Co. Fermanagh, has demonstrated it to be a lordly residence of the Maguire lords of that region and it continued to be occupied into the sixteenth century (Logue, Devine and Barkley 2020; Logue and Barkley 2022, 96–9). Furthermore, at least three moated sites were built and occupied by members of the Gaelic elite in west Bréifne during later medieval times (O'Conor and Fredengren 2019, 87–8).

Turning our attention to the moated sites of the study area, a total of eight are located across the two *trícha cét*. In Uí Maine, their distribution is dispersed. Two of the more prominent examples are at Cloonigny and Pallas, Co. Galway. Cloonigny (Alcock, de hÓra and Gosling 1999, 389) is a large and well-preserved example, within which is located the remains of a castle of unclassified form. This later fortification, inserted into the moated site, was owned by Shane *na Maighe* Ó Cellaig of Clonmacnowen in 1574 (Nolan 1900–1, 110). This may indicate that the

Settlement archaeology

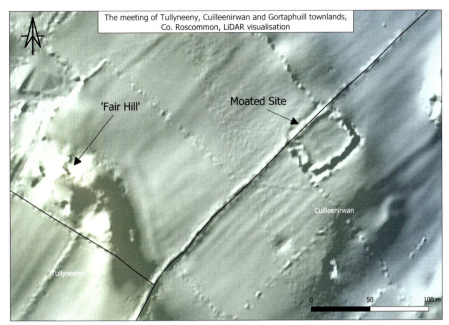

Figure 4.6 LiDAR visualization of Cuilleenirwan moated site, and its proximity to 'Fair Hill'. Note the subtle topographical features within the moated site platform, a possible sunken entranceway and hall-type building (data source: OSi, courtesy of the Royal Irish Academy).

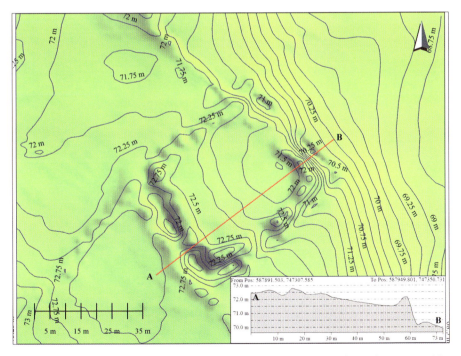

Figure 4.7 Topographical plan and cross-section of Cuilleenirwan moated site (data source: OSi, courtesy of the Royal Irish Academy).

Plate 4.2 Cuilleenirwan moated site, viewed from the north-east (author's photograph).

earthwork was also an Ó Cellaig construction. Pallas moated site (Alcock, de hÓra and Gosling 1999, 391) will be discussed below, but is also adjudged to have been used by the Ó Cellaig elite (FitzPatrick 2016, 204). While there was Anglo-Norman settlement within parts of the study area, as noted, it has been suggested that this was never very intensive (Graham 1988a, 36; Finan 2016, 164–6; O'Conor and Finan 2018, 107). This makes it more likely that the moated sites of this region were Gaelic-built.

There are three recorded moated sites within Tír Maine. All are located south of Lough Croan, in the adjacent parishes of Dysart and Cam, Co. Roscommon. These are Cuilleenirwan and Bredagh moated sites in Dysart and Coolnageer moated site in Cam. Located 212m east of Fair Hill (Fig. 4.6), Cuilleenirwan moated site is a well-preserved, slightly wedge-shaped example, with internal dimensions of *c.*42.4m north-east/south-west by *c.*39m north-west/south-east, and a causewayed entrance on its north-eastern side (Fig. 4.7; Pl. 4.2). The entrance breaks a flat-topped internal bank

Settlement archaeology

Plate 4.3 Bank height at corner of moated site, viewed from the north, Cuilleenirwan moated site (author's photograph).

and external ditch, surviving all around the site with an average external height of *c.*2.5m (Pl. 4.3). A number of ground-fast stones revet the outer edge of the enclosure bank, as well as three discrete zones of ground-fast stones located within the interior, possibly the remains of either stone-built or dwarf-walled wooden buildings. These are consistent with the series of raised features visible in the LiDAR visualization (Fig. 4.6), and bear resemblance to a rectangular feature (length *c.*16m, width *c.*10m), oriented NNW–SSE on its long axis, with a possible sunken entranceway aligned with the site entrance to the north-east. This may present the remains of a substantial rectangular house site or feasting hall. The dimensions and location within the moated site compare well with the possible *pailís* or hall-type building identified by FitzPatrick on the Mac Firbhisigh landholding at Lackan in Tír Fhiachrach, Co. Sligo (FitzPatrick 2015b, 187–8).

There is a clear inter-visibility between this moated site and Fair Hill, an important part of the Lough Croan *cenn áit* (Curley 2020, 207–10), and the visual relationship between both monuments may have been important to the builders of Cuilleenirwan moated site.

In light of this evidence, there may be merit in considering that Cuilleenirwan moated site was of possible Gaelic construction. A statistical analysis of the moated sites of Co. Roscommon, conducted by Finan, divided the monument type into five clusters, based on a series of distributional criteria. Key criteria included: location within a townland, proximity to transportation routes and proximity to *crannóga* specifically (Finan 2014, 178). Of the three moated sites close to Lough Croan, two [Cuilleenirwan and Bredagh] are classified as Cluster 1 moated sites, indicating that they were near to a townland boundary and were in close proximity to an identified medieval road and *crannóg* (ibid., 179, Fig. 1). This is also the cluster into which the moated sites of Machaire Connacht are categorized, sites which, in some cases at least, may be the physical manifestation of the term *longphort* used when describing the locations of elite Gaelic settlement in the same period (O'Conor 1998, 87–8; Finan 2014, 178).

Speculation on the builder of Cuilleenirwan moated site is helped by a series of thirteenth-century annalistic references. In 1260, a party of Aed Ó Conchobair's followers burned the *longphort* of Conchobar Ó Cellaig (*AC*). No location was recorded for this lordly *longphort*, but his son, Maine, seems to have died close by. Nearby, Lough Croan was a fixed Ó Cellaig *cenn áit* through much of the medieval period, allowing one to consider Cuilleenirwan in this light. With its location within the territory defined from the twelfth century as belonging to the Clann Uadach, it is also possible that this was one of a small number of moated sites constructed by the Uí Fhallamháin.

The other moated site in this area is in Bredagh townland, 2km south of Cuilleenirwan. The archaeological remains in Bredagh and Milltown in particular are of interest when attempting to understand the past environment of this part of Tír Maine. Bredagh contains the remains of two barrows, a possible prehistoric mound, one cashel, and a substantial univallate ringfort, in addition to the moated site, evidence of a long history of settlement in the area. To its south is Milltown, the late medieval *cenn áit* of the Uí Fhallamháin of Clann Uadach. Bredagh appears in the historical record in 1159, when Donnchad Ó Máel Sechlainn, king of Mide, raided into Tír Maine until they reached *in Breuadh agus Durudh Mainnin* (*AT*; Kelleher 1971, 100). The location is also mentioned on two occasions in *Nósa Ua Maine*. The second reference is the more informative: 'The Brétach[2] is responsible for his (the king of Uí Maine's) battle implements, the preserving of his treasure and the keeping of his hostages' (*Nósa*, 549).

2 The Brétach = Uí Máelbrigde vassal lords of Magh Finn [parishes of Taughmaconnell and Moycarn, Co. Roscommon] prior to the majority of the Ó Cellaig-related Meic Eochadha [Mac Keogh] sept as lords of the area.

Settlement archaeology

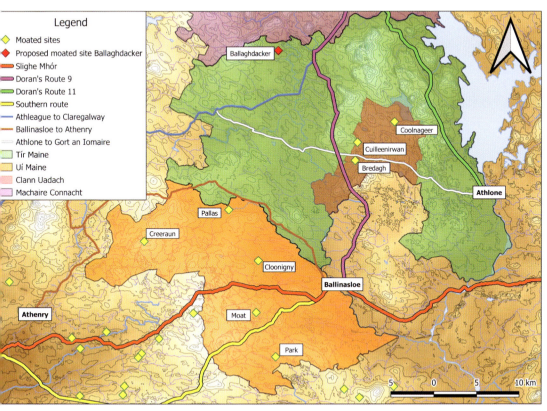

Figure 4.8 Moated sites within the study area. The sites in Uí Maine are of a dispersed distribution, while the three Tír Maine examples are located within Clann Uadach.

Bredagh is situated close to what was likely to have been an important medieval crossroads in the region, now marked by the village of Dysart. The location of Bredagh on a routeway may be at the heart of why it was raided by Ó Máel Sechlainn in 1159 and also why it is described as a central place for the Uí Maine in *Nósa Ua Maine*. Plainly, Bredagh retained an importance to the Uí Chellaig, and perhaps the Clann Uadach, from the twelfth century through to at least the fourteenth century, something that is reflected in the archaeological evidence. The substantial ringfort in the townland may have played a role in the above events, while the moated site indicates the continuation of elite settlement activity, possibly of Gaelic-construction, into the later medieval period.

The final recorded Tír Maine moated site is located in Coolnageer townland. In much the same way as Cloonigny moated site, Coolnageer too was occupied in the late medieval period by a member of the minor Ó Cellaig elite. In the north-eastern corner of what is a much degraded moated site is the remains of a castle of unclassified form, which was in the possession of 'Edmund mc Brene O'Kelly' in 1573, and owned by

'Egnaham McDonell O'Kelly' in 1617 (Nicholls (transcribed) 1573, 2019, 57; Moore 1978, 59). This later evidence linking an Ó Cellaig to the site may suggest that the primary moated site at Coolnageer was originally built by a member of this sept at some stage in the late thirteenth or early fourteenth century.

To add to the catalogue of moated sites in Tír Maine, the site of a previously unrecorded example was recognized close to Ballaghdacker Lough, Co. Galway, a lordly centre of the Uí Chellaig. Combining the information relating to the eight known moated sites from the region, particularly their location in relation to known Ó Cellaig centres and the lack of intensive Anglo-Norman settlement in the whole region, would therefore suggest that they were primarily of Gaelic construction (Fig. 4.8).

THE *PAILÍS* SITES OF LATER MEDIEVAL UÍ MAINE

Building on the information outlined above on the ringfort/cashel and moated site settlement forms, there is an historically attested elite Gaelic construction type that is amorphous in form. The *pailís*, anglicized as Pallas or Pallis, is conventionally translated as a palisade or stockade (eDIL, *s.v.* pailis). FitzPatrick has theorized that this translation may be oversimplified and argues that some of the surviving place-name examples may actually be a descriptor applied to an elaborate timber hall commissioned and used by Gaelic lords in the thirteenth and fourteenth centuries. These halls combined the roles of hunting lodge and feasting hall and were routinely located near territorial boundaries (FitzPatrick 2016, 202; 2018, 180). A place-name search of the study area detected three names with the *pailís* descriptor, Cornapallis – *Corr na Pailís* (the round hill of the *pailís*), Tisrara parish, Co. Roscommon, Caltrapallas – *Cealtrach na Pailíse* (the *pailís* of the old burial place), Killosolan parish and Pallas – *An Phailís*, Fohanagh parish, both Co. Galway (Fig. 4.9).

Of the three, Caltrapallas is the most difficult to interpret. A friary seems to have been founded here by the de Berminghams *c.*1320 (Gwynn and Hadcock 1970, 288). However, nothing survives in the archaeological record and there are no remains marked on the 1st Edition OS 6-Inch map. Consequently, two locations can be considered with the *pailís* theory in mind. Pallas, Co. Galway, is in an area taken up by a substantial zone of bogland, particularly on its western boundary, adjacent to Fohanagh townland. Two monuments, an enclosure and a moated site (Alcock, de hÓra and Gosling 1999, 391), are located on comparably good ground, close to the eastern townland boundary between Pallas and what is now Clonbrock Demesne. The most likely location for a timber hall which would fit the description of a *pailís* from among the two extant sites is, as has been argued, the moated site (FitzPatrick 2016, 204), labelled 'Lismore' in the nineteenth-century cartographic sources. FitzPatrick identifies this site as being the location of the famous fourteenth-century Christmas feast of Uilliam Buide Ó Cellaig, a point which will be discussed in Chapter 6. While

Settlement archaeology

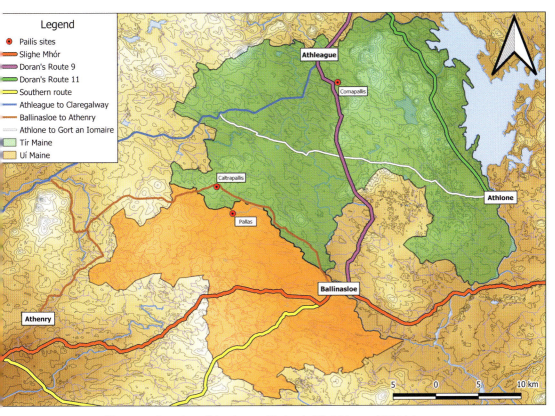

Figure 4.9 Location of the three *pailís* sites in Tír Maine and Uí Maine.

I argue that this feast was held elsewhere, it is highly likely that FitzPatrick's identification of Pallas moated site as an important Ó Chellaig *pailís* site is correct. Its peripheral location within the catchment area of the Callow Lough and Kilconnell *cenn áit* suggests that Pallas moated site was the location of a lordly feasting and hunting lodge used by the Ó Cellaig lords (FitzPatrick 2016, 210–11; Fig. 5.25). There are a number of factors that further suggest that Pallas is a potentially suitable location for elite gathering and feasting activity in later medieval Uí Maine. First, Pallas is located close to the *trícha cét* boundary of Uí Maine. The border of Ó Cellaig country lies 7km to the west of Pallas, where it meets with the eastern boundary of the *trícha cét* of Clann Taidg and Uí Diarmata. In the later medieval period, Clann Taidg and Uí Diarmata became the cantred of Clantayg and were held by the Anglo-Norman de Bermingham barons of Athenry (MacCotter 2014, 134–5). Having seen that *pailís* sites tend to be located in boundary zones between territories, FitzPatrick suggested that they may have been used as high-status indicators in the configuration or reaffirmation of Gaelic sept boundaries (FitzPatrick 2016, 205).

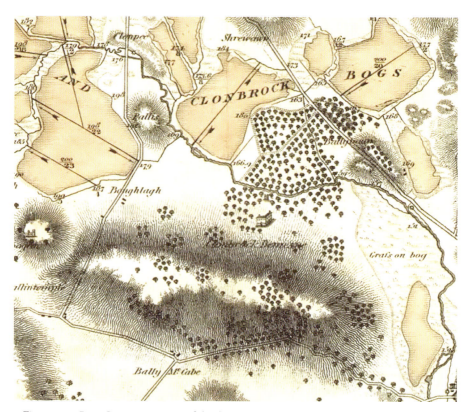

Figure 4.10 Bogs Commission map of the district around Pallas and Clonbrock Demesne, Co. Galway, highlighting the continued presence of woodland in the area into the nineteenth century (Griffiths 1809–14).

The physical environment that surrounds Pallas and Clonbrock Demesne contains relatively extensive bogland, wooded areas and streams, a landscape more of use to the production of game animals than agriculture. Griffith's Bog Commission map depicts the survival of substantial woodland within Clonbrock Demesne, showing the endurance of this sylvan landscape into the modern period (Fig. 4.10).

As a result, Pallas and its vicinity may have served as a suitable hunting district within reach of the lordly centre, as it is located 5.3km to the north of Callow Lough, and with the presence of a series of landholdings of Ó Cellaig-associated service kindreds close to the latter lake (Curley 2021b, 8–13), Pallas would be a likely location for a hunting lodge and feasting hall in the wilder and less cultivated Uí Maine border districts.

Cornapallis townland is located 4km to the south-east of Athleague, and no more than 5km to the south of the northern boundary of Tír Maine, represented by the River Hind. Served by Route 9, it is located between two historically attested Ó Cellaig lordly centres, Lough Croan and Athleague. It contains two ringforts, either of

Settlement archaeology

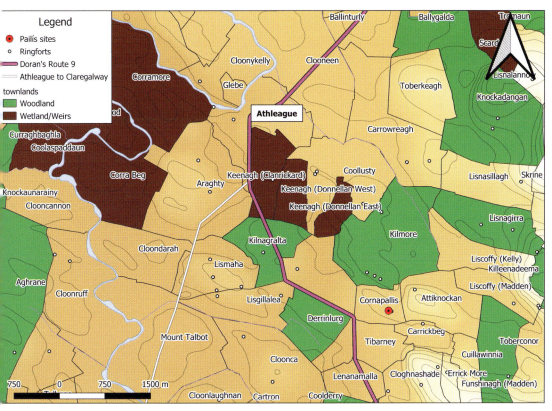

Figure 4.11 Location of Cornapallis townland in relation to Coolderry, Liscoffy, woodland toponymy, and the Ó Cellaig *cenn áit* of Athleague.

which could conceivably be the site of a *pailís*. The toponymy surrounding Cornapallis presents a case for the past environment being populated with extensive woodland, particularly to the north, named above as the Woods of Athleague. It can be argued that, once more, hunting was an activity that could have been routinely practiced here. Much like at Pallas, Cornapallis is situated adjacent to one of the major service kindreds of the Uí Chellaig, with the Ó Dubhagáin poet historians in residence at nearby *Culdaire* – Coolderry, where there is a large ringfort (*Reg. Clon.*, 456), less than 2km to the south.

A second learned kindred landholding may also be identifiable close to the Cornapallis *pailís* site. Two townlands named Liscoffy – *Lios Cobhthaigh*, 'Ó Cobhtaigh's fort', originally one larger townland, are located north-east of Cornapallis. The Uí Chobhtaigh were a prominent Gaelic poetic family and in the fifteenth and sixteenth centuries they were settled in Rathconrath barony, Co. Westmeath (Moore and Ó Cróinín 2004). However, a branch of this family was located in Uí Maine into the seventeenth century, at *Tuaim Cátraige*, today Kellysgrove, Co. Galway (Breatnach

1967, 82; *Tribes*, 39–40). The fourteenth-century praise poem *Táth aoinfhir ar iath Maineach* is said to have been composed by an Ó Cobhtaigh poet for Uilliam Buide Ó Cellaig (Breatnach 1967, 82; Hoyne 2023, 278). The setting of Uilliam's court in the poem is reminiscent of the elite settlement archaeology seen at nearby Lough Croan. Liscoffy (Madden) possesses two ringforts and one or both may have served as residences for the Ó Cobhtaigh in the fourteenth century (Fig. 4.11). The presence of these learned families, particularly those whose duties were tied into performance at feasting events, at both Pallas and Cornapallis adds to the argument for their consideration as *pailís* sites. The location of these sites within marginal landscapes but at a slight geographical remove from the lordly and settlement centres, with possible feasting and hunting associations, display traits that provide a convincing argument for them being focal points for lordly display.

TOWER HOUSE CASTLES

The final settlement form which can be identified as having been utilized by the Uí Chellaig is the tower house castle. The tower house is a monument type constructed across Ireland from potentially the later fourteenth century to the 1640s, with the vast majority, particularly the ones built by Gaelic lords, built in the fifteenth and sixteenth centuries (Cairns 1987, 9; Sherlock 2011, 131; 2013, 21–3). They are generally constructed of masonry, however historical sources indicate that timber versions were also built (Donnelly, Logue, O'Neill and O'Neill 2007; Logue 2018, 271–2). Usually rectangular in plan, with a ground floor entrance, they were built four to five storeys in height. The upper floors were generally more commodious. Despite this, they routinely possess little ornamentation, either internally or externally, but they were likely 'harled' and lime-washed upon construction and through their occupation. The castles were internally plastered, and there is some evidence for decoration with wall paintings (Morton 2002; 2004, 327; 2010). Quite a number of these sites would have possessed a defended courtyard, known as a 'bawn', whose walls were constructed of stone or, sometimes of more organic materials such as wood, although only twenty percent of tower houses have extant bawns or have evidence for one (Cairns 1987, 16–17; Leask 1941, 75–112; McNeill 1997, 222; Sweetman 2000, 158; McAlister 2019, 11–14, 22). Halls, along with administrative and agricultural buildings, lay within the bawn and these seem to have been mostly built of timber or cob (Barry 1987, 188–9; Cairns 1987, 24; O'Conor 1998, 33; McAlister 2019, 65–89).

Tower houses were constructed by both Anglo-Irish and Gaelic lords and their construction was one way of displaying wealth in late medieval Ireland. The distribution of tower houses is not uniform across the island and in some, particularly Gaelic, areas, such as west and south Ulster, they are notable by their scarcity

Settlement archaeology

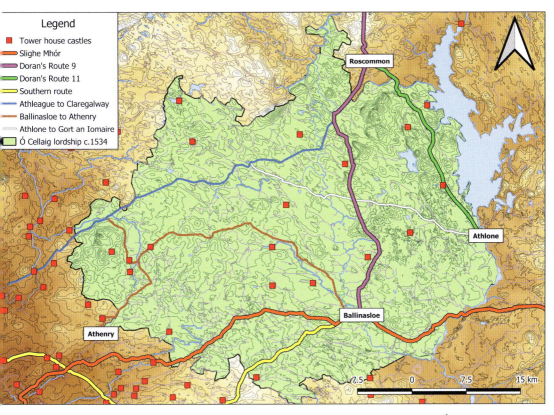

Figure 4.12 Distribution map of the surviving tower house castles located within the Ó Cellaig lordship study area in *c.*1534.

(O'Conor 1998, 102; Sherlock 2015, 354; McAlister 2019, 14). Nevertheless, tower houses do represent the first large-scale evidence for the Gaelic Irish building what English and European contemporaries then, and modern scholars now, would accept as masonry castles (O'Conor 1998, 102). Much has been written about the Gaelicization of families of Anglo-Norman descent during the fourteenth century. Yet the adoption of tower houses by the Gaelic elite from an Anglo-Norman milieu, especially from *c.*1380–1400 onwards, is an indication that this was a two-way process and that native lords were taking on elements of contemporary Anglo-Norman culture too, throughout the course of the fourteenth century and later (ibid., 103–4). This amalgamation of ideas arguably produced the very rich culture of Gaelic and Gaelicized Ireland seen throughout the fifteenth century and up to at least the mid-sixteenth century (Cairns 1987, 9; Simms 1987, 99–101).

Evidence for the construction and occupation of tower houses among the Uí Chellaig in the fifteenth and sixteenth centuries is difficult to quantify. The ASI database records twenty tower houses in the area defined as Ó Cellaig territory as it appeared *c*.1534 (Alcock, de hÓra and Gosling 1999, 393–418; Fig. 4.12).[3] The surviving tower house castles of the study area can, in most cases, be attributed to either the Ó Cellaig themselves, members of their vassal clans, such as the Meic Eochadha of Magh Finn and the Uí Mainnin of Soghain at Killaclogher, Co. Galway (ibid., 410), or prominent service kindreds. For instance, the degraded remains of two tower houses in the parish of Taughmaconnell, Co. Roscommon, at Cloonbigny and Castlesampson, were in the possession of the Meic Eochadha in the lists compiled of Galway and Roscommon castles and their owners in 1573–4 in advance of the *Compossicion of Conought* (Nolan 1900–1; Nicholls (transcribed) 1573, 2019), as is the partially extant Ó Cellaig tower house at Galey, referred to earlier. Tower houses also survive at a small number of historically attested Ó Cellaig *cenn áiteanna*, such as at Garbally and Monivea, Co. Galway (Alcock, de hÓra and Gosling 1999, 409, 415). These will be discussed at greater length in Chapter 8.

***

This chapter has outlined the variety of settlement forms which were constructed and occupied by the Uí Chellaig elite, their vassal clans and their service kindreds through the period from *c*.1100 to *c*.1600. This has been divided primarily between high medieval and late medieval settlement forms. It will be demonstrated, however, over the course of the coming chapters, that in many instances a continuity of settlement occurs at these *cenn áiteanna*. Two main issues relate to the high medieval settlement forms used by the Gaelic elite. The first concerns the construction of castles in the period prior to the advent of the tower house castle. In the study area, there is no definitive evidence for the construction of castles of earth and timber or masonry form by the high medieval Uí Chellaig. Some have suggested that the more powerful Ó Conchobair kings, who extended their overlordship over all of eastern Connacht in the early twelfth century, were the first to construct castles here, but the evidence for this is nowhere near as clear as has been argued for in the case of the *caistél* of *Dún Leodha* at least. The second issue relates to what settlement forms were advocated for by the Ó Cellaig elite, if they were not building what can be interpreted as castles. A series of site types, some of which are traditionally regarded as belonging to an earlier historical milieu – ringforts, cashels and *crannóga* – present with persuasive evidence for their continued use, and possible construction, during the later medieval period. Added to this is the adoption of the moated site as an elite settlement form among some of the Gaelic lords of eastern Connacht.

3 https://heritagedata.maps.arcgis.com/apps/webappviewer/index.html?id=0c9eb9575b544081b0d296436d8f60f8. Accessed 16/11/2023.

Settlement archaeology

Aside from this, two additional site types have been proposed, the *bódhún* and the *pailís*, and these will be discussed in greater detail in the coming chapters. Finally, the late medieval period witnesses the adoption of the tower house as one of the principal elite settlement forms of the Irish landscape and this will be explored further in the case of the Uí Chellaig. The successful identification of lordly centres and an understanding of how these manifested at a given point in time are crucial to understanding how the Uí Maine elite lived throughout the later medieval period. Understanding the evolution of elite settlement practice among the Gaelic Irish is also vital in determining where they were located, how they viewed themselves, and how they wished to be viewed. These insights can now be used to reconstruct something of the culture and social organization of later medieval lordly centres of the Ó Cellaig lordship. The coming chapters will thematically reflect the different settlement environments that developed as elite focal points in Uí Maine during the period under investigation.

CHAPTER FIVE

Lakeland elite settlement in later medieval Uí Maine

The first settlement environments to be considered are lordly centres and associated elite landscapes which have developed in lakeland settings. As indicated earlier, the study area is not naturally replete with lacustrine locations, but where they occur, settlement archaeology of a broad medieval date is also apparent. Moreover, where these small lakes occur, in each case, later medieval Ó Cellaig settlement has been identified, with evidence for its continuity through the period. This seems to indicate that in this area at least, lakes were highly prized as places of the Gaelic elite. It must be noted that settlement activity in the lakes of the study area is not limited to the medieval period and despite the relative lack of research into the *crannóga* sites of, for instance, Loughrea Lake in Co. Galway, which was part of early medieval Uí Maine, it is likely that these environments, when inspected thoroughly and critically, may turn up very broad chronologies. For the purposes of this study three elite landscapes have been identified which centre on either a current or former lake within the lordship: Lough Croan, Co. Roscommon, Callow Lough and Ballaghdacker Lough, Co. Galway.

LOUGH CROAN, CO. ROSCOMMON

My findings from Lough Croan, and, later, the Callow Lough, provide building blocks in terms of understanding how these lordly centres can be reconstructed, as well as outlining the range of shared attributes demonstrating the presence of a later medieval Gaelic lordly centre. Accordingly, an in-depth summary of the findings of both case studies will be provided here.

Lough Croan has emerged from the historical background as an important location for both the early medieval Uí Maine and later the Uí Chellaig. This former lake is located in what was once the *tricha cét* of Tír Maine. Lough Croan and its environs are shared by four parishes, Cam (east), Dysart (south), Tisrara (north-west) and Taghboy (north-east). This is the Tír Maine heartland, buffered sufficiently from the more northerly Machaire Connacht by a distance of over 12km, where the boundary of Tír Maine is located, consistent with the course of the River Hind. By the beginning of the fifteenth century, Lough Croan was split between the two *oireachtaí* of *Túath Átha Liaig* and Clann Uadach (Fig. 5.1). The turlough has an approximate area of 106.9ha

Lakeland elite settlement in later medieval Uí Maine

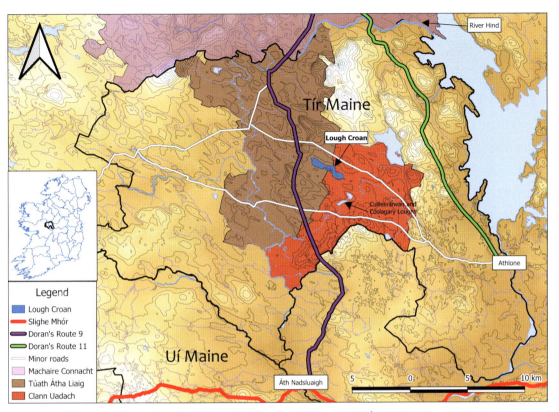

Figure 5.1 Location of Lough Croan turlough within Tír Maine, the Ó Cellaig patrimonial lands. Boundaries of these territories in *c*.1400, defined after Nicholls (1969) and MacCotter (2014).

(Goodwillie 1992, 148). It measures 3.4km in length at its furthest extents and 0.57km at its widest point. The underlying geology of the area is primarily one of Carboniferous Limestones, while the soil composition of the turlough bed is primarily peaty, with silt and an impure marl in places (Curley 2022, 202). In winter, the potential of Lough Croan as a hunting locale must be taken into account also, particularly for wildfowl. Communication through the landscape was provided primarily by its close proximity to Route 9. From a logistical point of view, the communities settling Lough Croan were centrally placed in terms of accessing trade and transport routes both to the south and to the north of them. This routeway was of vital importance, considering that substantial areas to the west and east of Lough Croan possessed zones of bog and woodland.

The toponymy, history and archaeology of the Lough Croan cenn áit
The townland toponymy of Lough Croan is very interesting, and can be explored thematically. Martial associations can be seen with Lisnagavragh – *Lios na gCabhrach*

Figure 5.2 Lisnagavragh Fort, satellite aerial image (left) courtesy of Bing Maps. DTM of fort (right), data courtesy of OSi.

(enclosure/fort of the embossed shields *or* huts) and Turrock – *An Turrac* [also *Caisleán an Turraic*] ([the castle] of the attack/onslaught). Lisnagavragh contains eight recorded monuments, four of which are ringforts. The most prominent of these, and presumably the one which provides the place-name, has an internal space of 52m diameter, a possible entrance to the ENE, and is surrounded by a well-preserved ditch and bank system at a combined width of *c.*8–10m (see Fig. 5.3). The LiDAR topographical plan (Fig. 5.2 right) records a faint circular feature attached to the east of the extant remains. This enclosure is of a comparable size to the extant monument, with an external diameter of 55m, possibly with an entrance to the south, consistent with a pair of bulbous terminals. This enclosure underlies and likely predates the upstanding remains. The interior contains the foundations of two rectangular stone house sites of indeterminate date, possibly evidence for continued habitation at this ringfort into the high or even late medieval period. Similar suggestions have been made in other Gaelic lordship research areas, not least for the later medieval Ó Súilleabháin Bhéara lordship in west Cork (Breen 2005, 54), an indication of where the pre-tower house elites may have lived in the area.

Turrock contains eleven monuments, with the settlement archaeology being split between 'Turrock Fort', a substantial ringfort with an external diameter of 50m, and a small cluster of monuments near Turrock House, with a building categorized as a seventeenth-century house serving as the focal point of the precinct.

Lakeland elite settlement in later medieval Uí Maine

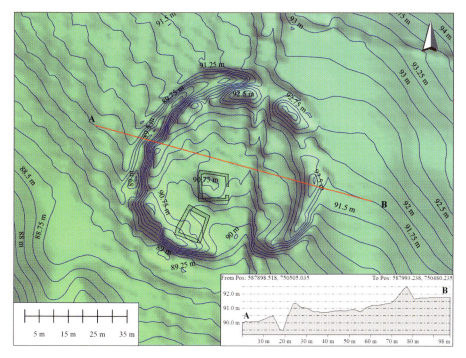

Figure 5.3 Contoured topographical plan and cross-section of Lisnagavragh Fort, including the foundational remains of the two houses (data source: OSi, courtesy of the Royal Irish Academy).

Turrock Castle is recorded in relation to Donnchadh Ó Cellaig, who was attacked at what is regarded as his residence here in 1536 (*AC*; *ALC*). The 'ornamented' door of the castle was so prized that it was stolen and brought to Sligo Castle by the aggressors (*AC*; *ALC*). O'Keeffe discussed the importance that doors and doorways may have had in the medieval mindset, particularly in relation to the acceptance of visitors into a tower house. The removal of the front door of Turrock by the Uí Chonchobair *Sligigh* would have been an embarrassment to the victims of this theft, hinting at the role such an object may have had beyond its physical form (O'Keeffe 2015, 97, n51). In 1545, an incident of Ó Cellaig internecine strife is recorded, with Turrock Castle again the setting (*ALC*). Later in the century, a number of individuals bearing the surname were residing in the townland, while it was also part of an estate leased by the Dublin government to the Ó Fallamháin, but it is unclear if this lease was acted upon (*Fiants* II, 174 [1361], 206 [1569], 464 [3382], 519 [3753]).

The government's list of castles and their owners in Co. Roscommon for 1573 records *Turuk* Castle in the possession of 'William & Connor O Kelly', the last such entry for Turrock being in Ó Cellaig ownership (Nicholls (transcribed) 1573, 2019). It is marked on the Strafford Survey map of *c.*1636, when it was most likely in the possession of Michael Pinnocke, who continued to hold it throughout the

Plate 5.1 Some examples of the range of punch-dressed stones (left) centre of image; (right) below modern concrete girder, which have been incorporated into the building fabric of an outbuilding attached to Turrock House (author's photographs).

Cromwellian period (Cronin 1980, 110). The site of Turrock Castle, presumably consistent with the remains of Turrock House, retains a number of punch-dressed stones, which are incorporated into the building fabric of the later seventeenth-century house, adjacent field walls and a substantial two-storey outbuilding, the latter possibly once functioning as a grain store or mill (Pl. 5.1). Punch-dressed stones are a feature of late medieval masonry buildings in Ireland, particularly friaries and tower houses (Leask 1941, 75–124; McAfee 1997, 28; McNeill 1997, 201–2; O'Conor 2008, 331–2; O'Keeffe 2015, 75–9; O'Conor and Williams 2015, 62). These traces of punch-dressed stone around the site indicate that a late medieval castle was likely once located here and seems to have taken the form of a tower house.

Assembly or fairs may be recorded in the place-name Tullyneeny – *Tulaigh an aonaigh*, and this location will be discussed more fully below. Liswilliam – *Lios Uilliam* (William's fort), west of Lough Croan, records a personal name and refers to a substantial oval-shaped ringfort with impressive external dimensions of 66m (Fig. 5.4). It is located in the north-western quadrant of the townland, and contains evidence for a souterrain.

The ringfort is the only such monument in the townland and the name is most likely to have referred to Uilliam Buide, who perhaps constructed or modified the ringfort at some point during his long reign. The Anglo-Norman personal name William seems to have been first adopted by the Ó Cellaig dynasts with the aforementioned Uilliam Buide (Curley 2022, 212) and serves as an indication of the cultural borrowing between the native Irish and the Anglo-Normans which took place over the course of the fourteenth century.

Lakeland elite settlement in later medieval Uí Maine

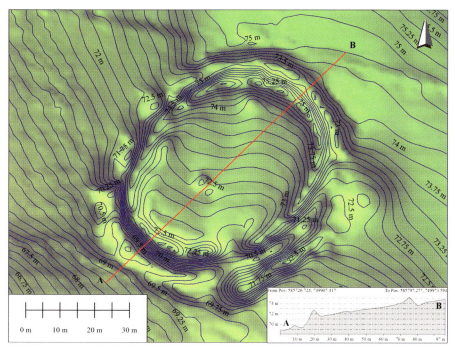

Figure 5.4 Contoured topographical plan and cross-section of Liswilliam Fort. The depression slightly west of centre represents the remains of the souterrain (data source: OSi, courtesy of the Royal Irish Academy).

Lough Croan contains a number of place-names relating to the natural and man-made islands located on the former lake. First, there is Garrynphort – *Garraí an Phoirt*, 'the garden/court of the bank/landing-place'. An alternative translation for the prefix *garraidh*, which MacCotter outlines is a colonial import (from the Norse *garth*), would be 'chief house' or 'chief enclosed residence' (MacCotter 2018, 86). This would give the translation as 'the chief house of the bank/landing place'. Located on the southern shore, two townlands bear this name, indicating that this area likely served as the routine location from which watercraft were launched in order to access the islands of the lake. O'Sullivan presents a convincing argument that *crannóga* and occupied natural islands would have been habitually approached from a specific location on the shoreline, a defined boat landing place or harbour, and in doing so allowed the island-dwellers to control access to the islands, as well as creating a social performance when people travelled out on to these sites (O'Sullivan 2009, 83–4). In this instance, and others to follow, the place-name survivals strongly corroborate this argument.

The site of a ringfort is located close to the shoreline of the lake here and although no visible surface remains survive it may have been the monument referred to in the place-name. This could be evidence of a dry-land service site associated with one or more of the *crannóga* on the former lake, operating as the administrative and

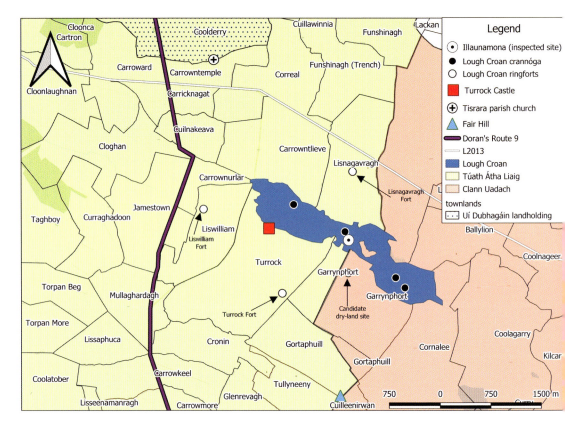

Figure 5.5 The townland names of the Lough Croan *cenn áit*, showing the pre-modern routeway through the landscape, as well as the principal monuments discussed.

agricultural centre for the occupants of the Lough Croan *crannóga* (see O'Conor 2000, 94, 100; 2001, 339; O'Conor, Brady, Connon and Fidalgo-Romo 2010, 31–2; O'Conor and Finan 2018, 118–19; Finan 2018, 145; O'Conor and Fredengren 2019, 95).

Turning to the islands themselves, all of their names are preserved on the 1st Edition OS 6-Inch map. From west to east, the first recorded is Edward's Island. This is identifiable with the site of a *crannóg*, one of five recorded on the ASI database for Lough Croan. It is unclear who is being referred to in the name, but it may relate to the father of a sixteenth-century Ó Cellaig lord of Uí Maine, Éamonn Ó Cellaig, whose son Donnchadh was attacked at Turrock Castle in 1536 (*AC*). As noted, Turrock House was likely constructed on the site of the now ruined Turrock Castle and situated less than 500m from the *crannóg* on what was once the lake shoreline. Irrespective of the connection between the place-names in this instance, there is a strong likelihood that Turrock Castle and Edward's Island were linked in terms of use. The tower house could have operated as the dry-land residence for the *crannóg* in the sixteenth-century, with the latter acting as a refuge, guest accommodation or location for feasting for the occupiers of the tower house, as well as a legitimizer of their antique origins in the area (see O'Conor 2018; Logue 2018). The advent of the tower house as the residence type of choice among the late medieval elite does not necessarily result in the wholesale abandonment of what was previously used and this may also be true of the pairing of Edward's Island and Turrock Castle.

Edward's Island *crannóg* survives as a circular grass-covered mound, measuring *c.*26m in diameter. Within this there is a raised area, *c.*16m in diameter and *c.*0.6m in height above the wider platform. It is divided today by a substantial drain, 5.5m wide at the top, which runs through the centre of the site and continues the length of the former lake, one which is partly responsible for the turning of the lake into a turlough. The upcast material from the excavated drain may have contributed to the height difference at the centre of the *crannóg* and has obscured much of the archaeology of the site as a result. Luckily, an artefactual assemblage survives for Edward's Island.

The next named island is Inchnaveague – *Inse na bhFia* (Deer Island), also categorized as a *crannóg*. The monument description records elements of a wooden palisade protruding through the sod around the perimeter on three sides. Located roughly at the centre of the turlough, Inchnaveague is in line of sight of Lisnagavragh ringfort. Located 200m to the east of Inchnaveague is Illaunnamona – *Oileán na Móna* (Turf Island). It is marked on the ASI database, but no longer deemed to be an archaeological site, instead a natural island, and is named for its physical appearance. There are two further named islands located in the south-east end of the turlough, Inchnagower – *Inse na nGabhar* (Goat Island), and Inchnagreeve – *Inse na gCraobh* (Bush/Branch Island). Local information states that bones were found at Inchnagower, while a 7.9m long dug-out canoe was discovered and kept in situ between Inchnagower and Inchnagreeve (NMI I.A./167/66), confirming that these two islands were likely in use at some point in the past.

Artefactual assemblage uncovered at Lough Croan
A significant artefactual assemblage survives in the care of the National Museum of Ireland (NMI) for the *crannóga* of Lough Croan. Twenty-four items form the collection, twenty-two of which are concentrated on two locations. The majority were found through illegal metal-detecting, with find-spots at Edward's Island and Illaunamona. The Edward's Island collection comprises ten items, including iron items in the form of a Jew's harp, a tool fragment and a knife, copper-alloy items such as a button, a possible gun fragment, an ingot, decorative mounts, trapezoidal buckles, and one decorative annular brooch-pin. One of the mounts (NMI 1991:14) is described by Murray as a twelfth-century 'clasp' with red and yellow *champlevé* enamel work and he has deduced that it was probably produced in the same Roscommon workshop that created the Cross of Cong (Murray 2014, 138–9). This hints at high-status occupation

of this *crannóg* during the twelfth century at least. The Illaunamona assemblage comprises eleven items, including a possible awl fragment, an iron hook, a small lead vessel with looped handles, a decorated vessel rim fragment, a decorated disc and a mount with floral design, with the majority of finds being of copper-alloy or bronze. Aside from these assemblages, there are two other items which complete the collection. One is a bone pin or needle (NMI 1977:2350) found in Garrynphort townland, in a location described as 'A Crannóg on Lough Croan'. The second is a carved stone head (NMI 1971:952), which was found in Coolnageer townland. Rynne published details of the carved stone head, identifying it as a king, and surmised it to be part of a king-bishop-queen unit, usually found in Gothic churches, meaning that it post-dates the very late twelfth century. It may have served as the right jamb of a window within a church. Rynne also suggested its place of origin may have been a burial ground and ecclesiastical enclosure in Coolnageer, known locally as Caltragh (Rynne 1966–71, 92–3) and located 2.2km east of Lough Croan. No church remains survive at Caltragh today for inspection.

While this assemblage is quite extensive for an unexcavated archaeological landscape in Co. Roscommon, it is difficult to interpret. The discoveries are primarily the result of metal-detecting and do not provide a representative sample selection of the material culture surviving in these locations. Another issue is the lack of a reliable find circumstance for any of these artefacts, despite the information on file. Taking into account these limitations, there are still conclusions to be drawn from the available evidence. If we accept that Edward's Island and Illaunamona Island are the genuine find locations, then it confirms that these two *crannóga* were inhabited in the later medieval period. Evaluating the material composition of the largest group of found items (copper-alloy/bronze, 14/24 – 58%), indicates that the character of these items portrays elite habitation, with the presence of a number of decorated copper alloy and bronze artefacts mixed in with the everyday tools. Comber highlights the significance of bronze as a high-status metal in later medieval contexts (Comber 2018, 100) and such a conclusion can also be advocated for here. The discovery of the possible gun fragment also points towards late medieval use of Edward's Island, considering as the introduction of firearms to Ireland seems to have occurred in the late fifteenth century, although gun ownership became much more common in the sixteenth century (Hayes-McCoy 1938, 47). The discovery of the enamelled clasp can date one phase of the *crannóg*'s occupation to at least as early as the twelfth century. Illaunamona is more difficult to interpret from its artefactual assemblage due to an uncertainty over its location. An inconsistency was encountered locally over Illaunamona's location, which seems now to have been resolved in favour of the local knowledge (Curley 2022). The items uncovered suggest settlement activity, as well as the working of material for making clothes and personal ornamentation. The presence of the vessel fragments point toward later medieval occupancy. More than this, the extant collection indicates that the ASI were wrong to de-list Illaunamona as an archaeological site. Natural islands can be used as *crannóga*, if they are about the same size and morphology (O'Conor 1998, 82–4; 2001, 336–7).

The territory of the Uí Fhallamháin of Clann Uadach
Lough Croan's geographical centrality, as well as its agricultural value, clearly made the lake and its immediate surroundings a much sought after territory in the later medieval period. It is therefore unsurprising that a number of polities competed for control in the area surrounding the lake. As outlined above, the Uí Fallamháin sept of the Síl Muiredaig were moved into the area consistent with the parishes of Dysart and Cam during the twelfth century as a means of limiting Uí Chellaig authority in the *trícha cét* and the Uí Fhallamháin remained in their new lands for the duration of the period under inspection and beyond. From the mid-fourteenth century onwards, the Uí Chellaig again came to exercise control over Tír Maine, an authority which, judging by the near absence of the Clann Uadach from the historical sources, must have included the area to the south and east of Lough Croan. It seems that the Uí Chellaig operated as the Uí Fhallamháin's overlords from at least this period until the end of the later medieval period (see Curley 2022, 205–6).

The focal point of the Lough Croan landscape
The diversity of toponymical and historical evidence confirmed that Lough Croan required further study. As outlined in a recently published article, a series of aerial and ground remote sensing techniques were applied in a phased approach in order to build up a more complete understanding of the former lake and its settlement archaeology (Curley 2022, 214–19). The acquisition of LiDAR data and the creation of a Digital Terrain Model (DTM) of the former lake and its immediate environs provided highly accurate dimensions of the turlough. This then enabled its digital re-flooding outlining the former lake shore and ascertained the true extent of the collection of *crannóga* that survive on the turlough, in terms of size, shape above the water level and inter-visibility (Fig. 5.6).

The digital modelling to raise the water levels to 69m OD revealed a natural island, appearing centrally on the former lake (ITM 587885; 749494). This island, with the faint impression of a circular enclosure on it, is also visible on a CUCAP photograph [APH034] (Pl. 5.2), along with other features, some of which can no longer be identified on the ground. This is the site known locally as 'Illaunamona'. Coupling this information with the artefactual assemblage bolsters the case for this place having been inhabited in the medieval past.

As regards the island, I noted that along with the elevation of the feature above the turlough bed, about 3m of a height difference, the perimeter of the summit of the island was marked by a substantial circle of boulders (avg. $0.5m^3 - 1m^3$), 25m in diameter (Pl. 5.2), with further, higher concentrations of stones in adjacent areas also.

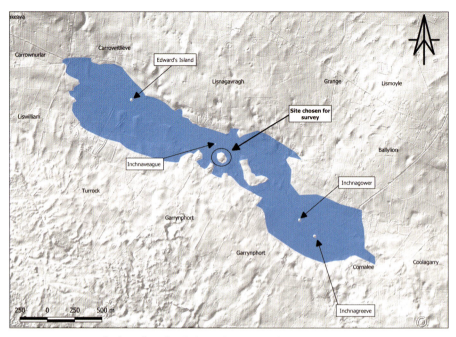

Figure 5.6 Extents of a digitally reflooded Lough Croan turlough, with the water level raised to 69m OD, recreating the lake. This is draped over the OSi-derived LiDAR DTM for the landscape. Illaunamona is the site marked by the black circle (data source: OSi, courtesy of the Royal Irish Academy).

This feature was then the subject of a multi-method remote sensing survey approach in order to identify any structural and superficial components on the mound which may confirm it to be a *crannóg*. Four techniques, a georeferencing of the ground-fast boulders with a Total Station, followed by an Electrical Resistivity Tomography (ERT), Earth Resistance and Magnetic Susceptibility surveys, were all focused on this site. The results, which were illuminating, can be summarized as follows:

The survey of the ground-fast stones (Fig. 5.7) confirmed the existence of a sub-circular arrangement of stones on the summit of the island, which had an internal diameter of 25m. The ERT survey recorded a relatively dense, compacted core of higher resistivity material over a large section of the island. This may indicate that an outcrop of limestone bedrock or a stony moraine located in the linear depression that forms the lake resulted in the formation of the island. The Earth Resistance survey uncovered a distinctive complex circular feature with a diameter of *c.*25m in the western half of the survey area. This is accompanied to the east by an alternate banding of high and then low resistance values running in a north-south direction towards the eastern end of the survey area. The low resistance band to the north-east may be evidence of a ditch surrounding the site.

Plate 5.2 Aerial photograph at Lough Croan. Looking west over Garrynphort and Turrock. CUCAP no.: APH034, photo date: 1966-07-17. The natural island is visible in the centre, with its circular enclosure (image courtesy of CUCAP).

Finally, the Magnetic Susceptibility survey was conducted over the same footprint as the Earth Resistance survey grids. This investigation revealed a pair of higher susceptibility zones, possible industrial activity or hearths, within the circular anomaly, potentially the remains of two dwellings located within the interior of the *crannóg*. Interpreting the results, this unrecorded feature carries the hallmarks of a settlement site (Fig. 5.10).

The investigations revealed a wealth of new information which is consistent with elite settlement and industrial activity in this part of Lough Croan. The exploration of what was a modified natural island near the southern shore of the former lake was informed by a number of independent sources of information. Its size and morphology

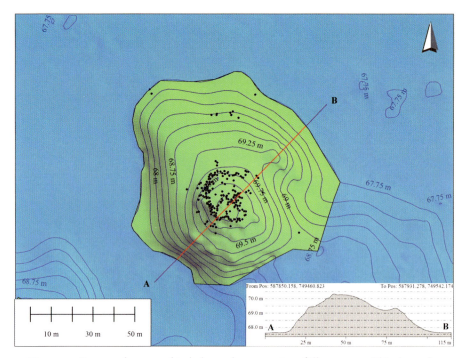

Figure 5.7 Contoured topographical plan and cross-section of Illaunamona. This shows the natural island, as well as a central circular-shaped platform on the island's summit. The surviving ground-fast stones were georeferenced (data source: OSi, courtesy of the Royal Irish Academy).

is consistent with *crannóg* settlement sites more generally. The presence of artificially-set boulders in the shape of a circular enclosure highlights the presence of archaeology on the summit of the island in the form of a degraded cashel. Local informants refer to this particular island as Illaunamona, which is also the place-name reported as the find spot for the previously discussed artefactual assemblage, indicating later medieval high-status habitation. More than this, an erroneously geo-referenced ASI record with a description which matches the physical remains at Illaunamona is located 107m distant to the west. The Garrynphort place-name implies a dry-land settlement site or landing place which was paired with the islands of the lake and the site of a ringfort may be the location referred to in the place-name. Historical sources confirm that Lough Croan was of particular importance to early medieval Uí Maine, a prominence that remained for the later medieval Uí Chellaig dynasts up until at least the middle of the sixteenth century. The picture that then emerges for this site is that it is recognisable as a high-cairn *crannóg*, which utilized the naturally formed high ground as a foundation upon which to build a cashel or cashel-like enclosure. The absence of substantial stone remains today may be explained by the abundance of dry-stone walls in the surrounding fields. Presumably most of the original stones in this enclosure were

Lakeland elite settlement in later medieval Uí Maine

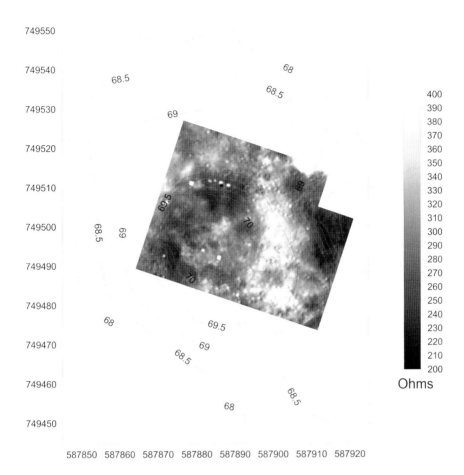

Figure 5.8 Earth Resistance survey conducted in 10m x 10m grids. The remains of a circular anomaly of low resistivity values are visible in the centre of the image (image courtesy of LGS).

removed in recent centuries to build these walls, while the surviving ground-fast boulders are the skeleton of the original cashel. This would tally with the growing evidence for the continued use of cashels, including cashels on *crannóga* and natural islands, in parts of Gaelic Ireland during the later medieval period (Brady and O'Conor 2005, 134; O'Conor, Brady, Connon and Fidalgo-Romo 2010; see, also, O'Conor and Naessens 2012; Comber 2018). Therefore, Illaunamona was probably a major site within later medieval Tír Maine, operating as a pre-tower house centre of the Uí Chellaig at Lough Croan, while potentially continuing to be occupied into the late medieval period.

It has been demonstrated that while this area has to date been overlooked from an academic perspective, it was, without doubt, of particular significance to the Uí Maine,

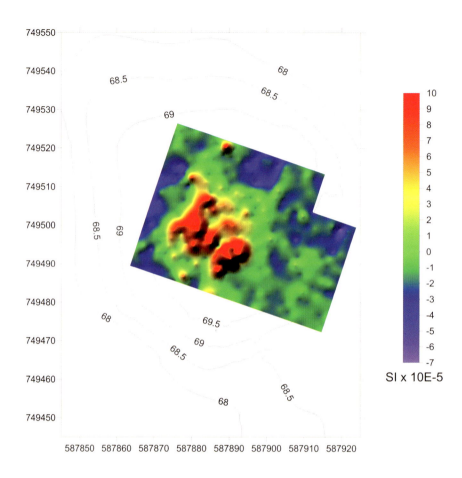

Figure 5.9 Magnetic Susceptibility survey conducted in 10m x 10m grids. The high susceptibility values are located within the circular anomaly from the Earth Resistance survey (image courtesy of LGS).

and later the Uí Chellaig, throughout the medieval period. While it is impossible to ascribe direct historical references to the site, there are a number of entries within the sources which may correspond with an Ó Cellaig *crannóg* residence at Lough Croan. For example, a reference in the mid-fourteenth-century poem *Táth aoinfhir ar iath Maineach* [One man has united the land of the Í Cheallaigh] suggests that one of Uilliam Buide Ó Cellaig's residences was surrounded by water and that the main building within it was constructed of post and wattle (*Táth aoinfhir*, q14–19; Simms 2020, 455). The description implies a *crannóg*, quite possibly the ones on Lough Croan, either Illaunamona or Edward's Island. Uilliam Buide's grandson, Conchobar Ó Cellaig, lord of Uí Maine, died in 1403 at or on Lough Croan in Clann Uadach (*Ó CGF ii*, 67). His death record in the annals describes him as dying after 'Unction and

Lakeland elite settlement in later medieval Uí Maine

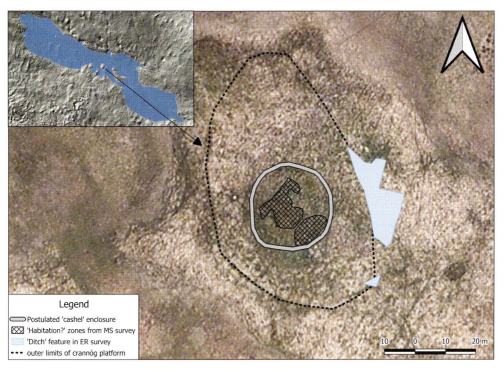

Figure 5.10 Summary interpretation of the combination of topographical data and remote sensing investigations undertaken at the island on Lough Croan.

Penance', indicating that he died at his residence as opposed to on a battlefield (*AC*). This implies a residence either on the lake or by the lakeshore of Lough Croan. The Illaunamona site, a natural island utilized in a *crannóg*-like fashion (Brady and O'Conor 2005; O'Conor, Brady, Connon and Fidalgo-Romo 2010) on the southern shoreline of the lake, may be the location referred to. The lake's artefactual assemblage corroborates the chronology outlined by these historical references. More than this, the mention of Clann Uadach may be directly referring to the island site, since it is located off the shore of the adjacent Garrynphort townlands, the parish boundary between Dysart and Taghboy, which is likely to have been the effective border between the Ó Cellaig *oireacht* of *Túath Átha Liaig* and the Ó Fallamháin *oireacht* of Clann Uadach during the later medieval period (Fig. 5.5).

The cultural landscape of the Lough Croan cenn áit
This substantial body of evidence demonstrates that Lough Croan was a place of considerable importance to the Uí Chellaig throughout the later medieval period. The inspection of the cultural landscape which surrounds the lake only serves to further demonstrate this place as a later medieval Gaelic lordly centre.

Churches associated with Lough Croan
A number of churches are located in the vicinity, the most notable of which is the medieval parish church of Cam or Camma, 9km to its south-east. The townlands of Cam and Brideswell possess strong associations with the cult of St Brigid. The origin of the name 'Cam' is *Camach Brighdi* or *Bhríde* (Brigid's crooked plain) and an early monastery of nuns in the area was referred to by the same name (Gwynn and Hadcock 1970, 375). Local tradition records that Brigid's mother was a native of the area, thus establishing the link with the saint (Kissane 2017, 150). The later medieval parish church is located on the NE-facing slope of Cam Hill and the present remains seem to have been constructed on the site of an earlier church. The parish church seems to have had its origins in the early medieval period, owing to the remains of a large ecclesiastical enclosure measuring *c*.150m in diameter, the modern graveyard sitting within this enclosure. *Nósa Ua Maine* and O'Donovan record that the Coarb of *Camach Brighdi* was one of the seven principal coarbs of the Uí Maine and that this Coarb had the privilege of baptizing members of this group, indicative of a traditional link between the Uí Maine elites and this foundation (*Nósa*, 537; *Tribes*, 77–9). Brideswell – *Tobar Bhríde* (St Brigid's Well), immediately to the east, is the site of an attested annual fair, traditionally held on the last Sunday of the summer, despite the veneration of St Brigid on the 1st of February, corresponding with the beginning of spring and *Imbolc*. The fair of Brideswell was held from at least as early as the first years of the seventeenth century (MacNeill 2008, 633–4) and an annual pattern day survives for Brideswell to the present day on the last Sunday in July. These dates match with the routine celebration of *Lughnasa*, the celebration of the harvest, indicating that the pattern day, and the fair that preceded it, may be of considerable antiquity, far earlier than the seventeenth century and likely in existence during later medieval times.

The closest church to Lough Croan is 5km to the north-west. This is the later medieval parish church of Tisrara – *Tigh Srathra* (house of the straddle) at Carrowntemple. It is believed to be an early medieval foundation, owing in part to the presence of *tempul* (Lat. *templum*) in the place-name (Ó Cróinín 2013, 37; Ó hAisibéil 2018, 168). There was a tradition up to recent times of waking high-ranking corpses at this place overnight, before continuing the journey from Tír Maine to Clonmacnoise to be interred, a custom inferred by the parish name (*OS Letters, Rosc.*, 8; Whelan 2018, 87). The presence of a number of grave memorials in remembrance of wealthy eighteenth-century O'Kelly/Kelly deceased, as well as an O'Kelly coat of arms carved in stone in the graveyard, indicate that Tisrara remained an important traditional Ó Cellaig burial place into the early modern and modern periods (Timoney, M.B., pers. comm.).

Service kindred landholdings at Lough Croan
The Uí Dubhagáin learned kindred, who were employed as *ollamh* by the Ó Cellaig lords in the fourteenth century, are also visible at Lough Croan. Prior to the grant to

them of their landholdings surrounding Callow Lough, in the townlands of Cartrondoogan and Ballydoogan particularly (FitzPatrick 2015b, 168, 188; 2016, 204), they also had a residence at *Culdaire* (*Cúl doire*) – Coolderry townland, located immediately to the north of Carrowntemple (*Reg. Clon.*, 456). Coolderry contains the remains of a substantial ringfort, the only identifiable evidence of past settlement in the townland. The *Registry of Clonmacnoise* states that the Uí Dubhagáin were keepers of the records of the church of Clonmacnoise, a role they may have acquired as a result of associations that the family originally had with the Monastery of St Enda on the Aran Islands, an ecclesiastical dependency of Clonmacnoise (Kehnel 1997, 214). It is clear, therefore, that the Uí Dubhagáin supplied members of their family to roles in both the secular and ecclesiastical locales of Ó Cellaig territory during the later medieval period. The presence of the Uí Dubhagáin at Coolderry, so close to the later medieval parish church and early medieval ecclesiastical site at Carrowntemple, may demonstrate a link between the family and this church. A number of the Uí Dubhagáin held important positions within the church from the twelfth century through to the fifteenth century at least, in particular one Marianus Ó Dubhagáin, a parish priest at nearby Cam (Kehnel 1997, 214–15). Taken together, this illustrates a much earlier established relationship between the Uí Dubhagáin and their secular Ó Cellaig patrons, prior to the mid-fourteenth century when the well-known Seán Mór Ó Dubhagáin was *saoi sheancadha ocus ollam* to the Uí Chellaig (*AU*; *AFM*).

Lough Croan in the literary sources
Lough Croan as a locale is mentioned in a variety of medieval historical sources. Alongside this, a small number of literary references survive and these are worthy of inspection as they indicate that it was an important place from an early period. The ninth-century Patrician hagiography *Vita tripartita Sancti Patricii* records 'Loch Cróine' very early in its Connacht sequence (*Vita tripartita*, 85–7). *Acallam na Senórach*, the most important of the Fenian Cycle tales, reinforces the lake's elite credentials. An episode in the narrative, the first meeting of Patrick with Muiredach Mór, king of Connacht, takes place at Lough Croan (*Acallam*, 33). Patrick performs his most powerful miracle here, raising Áed, the king's son, back to life following his collapse and death after a game of 'hurling' (ibid., 38). Cathal Crobhdearg Ó Conchobair commissioned this saga, and it has been suggested that he also constructed a royal centre on the southern shore of Lough Croan in the early thirteenth century (Connon 2014, 53). The construction of this Ó Conchobair royal centre, which may have taken the form of a *crannóg* such as Edward's Island, as well as his likely establishment of the Cistercian house at nearby *Disert Briole*, bolsters the argument that the main branch of the Uí Chellaig were forced away from this part of Tír Maine, consistent with the arrival of the Clann Uadach in the immediate area in the twelfth century.

Plate 5.3 'Fair Hill' viewed from the north. The stone cross shaft is located close to the summit of this natural hillock, possibly sited in the same location as the previously recorded standing stone (author's photograph).

Tullyneeny – Tulaigh an Aonaigh – *an assembly site at Lough Croan*
Tullyneeny (*Tulaigh an Aonaigh*) is located 2.5km due south of Lough Croan. This toponym has been tentatively translated as 'the mound/hill of the assembly' (Curley 2022, 206). In Old Irish *tulach/tilach* implies a 'hill of assembly', with a number of instances surviving for the use of this term in describing assembly venues in Gaelic society (FitzPatrick 2004, 30–1). Within the adjacent Gortaphuill townland is the landmark which gives the locality its name, known as 'Fair Hill', 74m OD, and which is topped today by a stone cross shaft, recorded by the ASI as a wayside cross. The 1st Edition OS 25-Inch map records a standing stone at this location in the late nineteenth century, which is no longer extant (Pl. 5.3).

Fair Hill is surrounded by a slightly elevated plateau, measuring *c.*720m², and the summit affords clear views north to Lough Croan and a wide panorama over the wider

Lakeland elite settlement in later medieval Uí Maine

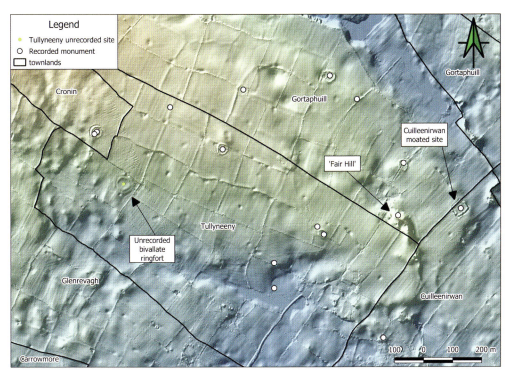

Figure 5.11 LiDAR DTM of the Tullyneeny landscape, indicating the unrecorded bivallate *ráth* in the western part of Tullyneeny townland (data source: OSi, courtesy of the Royal Irish Academy).

region. The archaeological remains on the plateau retain evidence of medieval settlement activity. There are fourteen monuments recorded in a 3km² area around Fair Hill. Six ringforts and a cashel are recorded, with associated features including premodern field systems. Aside from this, the creation of a DTM from the available LiDAR has identified a further ringfort. The slight remains visible in the topographical survey (at ITM 586764; 747418) represent a large bivallate *ráth*, with an internal space of 37m in diameter and surrounding embankments measuring *c*.8m on all sides. There is a trace of an entrance gap visible on the north-eastern side of the earthworks. These impressive dimensions are the largest of any of the ringforts within the indicated survey area and may represent the remains of a high-status medieval residence (Fig. 5.11).

Later medieval settlement activity is identifiable at Cuilleenirwan moated site, discussed earlier. It can be concluded that the moated site's location must have been informed somewhat by its closeness to Fair Hill, with its regular assemblies and the activities that presumably took place there in the medieval past.

Acallam na Senórach suggests that a mound or hill with a standing stone surmounting it lay somewhere in the vicinity of Lough Croan, reputedly marking the grave of a member of the Fianna (*Acallam*, 33–5). This shows that it was a known

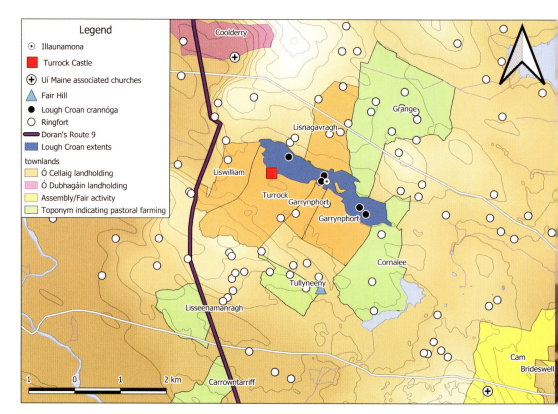

Figure 5.12 Summary of the Lough Croan case study, with principal locations outlined. Tullyneeny is shaded to represent both its assembly and pastoral farming associations.

place in the landscape, as well as creating a link to St Patrick, giving it a venerable quality. There is no evidence at any other location surrounding Lough Croan for either a standing stone in its current position or one recorded in any of the cartographic or antiquarian sources of the late nineteenth century, excepting the stone which once topped Fair Hill. The described episode refers to Patrick receiving homage from the nobles of Connacht in his nearby tent, an action not dissimilar to ceremonies that are known to have occurred at communal assemblies recorded from later medieval Ireland. With Fair Hill overlooking and providing commanding views over Lough Croan, this area should be viewed as a potential assembly venue for the later medieval Uí Chellaig lords. Location in respect to the lordly centre, landscape and environmental siting, and the toponymical and literary references, collectively suggest that Tullyneeny was a location for routine assembly and fair activity in later medieval Tír Maine (C.M. O'Sullivan 2004, 80; MacNeill 2008, 67; O'Flaherty 2014, 13; Kelly 2016b, 403; Curley 2022, 206). Finally, returning to the *Acallam*, the author is careful to describe the events, from the tribute provided to Patrick, through to the significance of

Lakeland elite settlement in later medieval Uí Maine

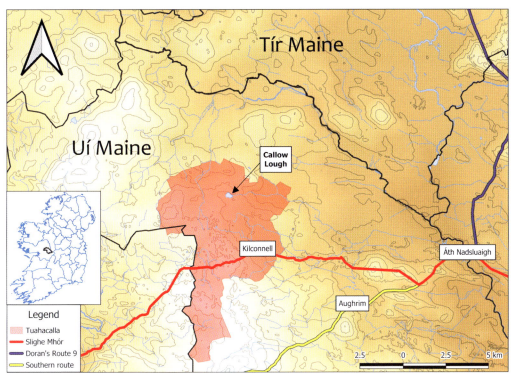

Figure 5.13 Location of Callow Lough within the *oireacht* of Tuahacalla – *Túath Caladh* in Uí Maine in modern east Galway. Boundaries of these territories in *c.*1400, defined after Nicholls (1969) and MacCotter (2014).

including acknowledgment of an antique funerary landmark in the region, with also a description of a game of 'hurling'. All three aspects preserve evidence of medieval Irish assembly practices, with the performance of games and horse-racing an important element (Gleeson 2015, 35). Combined, they may be pointing towards a key location within the Lough Croan landscape, identifiable at Tullyneeny, which was set aside for one of the key public roles of a medieval Gaelic king or lord.

CALLOW LOUGH, CO. GALWAY

The area surrounding Callow Lough, Co. Galway, presents itself as an important location within the Ó Cellaig lordship. This district retains evidence of the historical migration, contraction and subsequent expansion of the Uí Chellaig, with the zenith of their power beginning in the second half of the fourteenth century. Callow Lough and the settlement of Kilconnell are located within the *trícha cét* of Uí Maine, a territorial unit originally under the authority of the Soghain (MacCotter 2014, 207). From the twelfth century onwards, however, this territory came to be under the authority of the Uí Chellaig. By the mid-fourteenth century, Callow Lough was the focal point of the *oireacht* of *Túath Caladh* (*Nósa*, 546–7; Fig. 5.13).

The toponymy of the Callow Lough cenn áit

The area of particular interest here comprises a cluster of townlands surrounding Kilconnell and Callow Lough and again will be explored in a thematic fashion. The landscape character here is mixed, with areas of bogland dominating to the east approaching the River Suck, and the townland names, and their size, provide evidence for the former presence of tracts of land unsuitable for agriculture due to the dominance of woodland and wetland. It seems that the settlement activity is located between these more restrictive areas. The most significant names with settlement connotations include Callow – *An Caladh* (the landing place *or* ferry) and Pallas – *An Phailís*. There is also Ballyglass – *An Baile Glas* (the green settlement), and Doon Upper and Lower – *An Dún* (the fort). Doon Upper contains a number of archaeological monuments. The collection of monuments which gives the townland its name relates to a monument categorized as an enclosure known as Doon Fort, within which is the remains of a castle of unclassified form marked as Doon Castle on the 1st Edition OS 6-Inch map. Doon Castle may be the site referred to as *Done*, which was in the possession of 'Tege McMelaghlin Okelly' in 1574 (Nolan 1900–1, 120).

Place-names which incorporate a personal or familial name include Dundoogan – *Dún gCuagáin* (Coogan's fort), Lecarrowmactully – *Leithcheathrú Mhic Mhaoltuile* (the half-quarter of Mac Maoltuile), Ballynabanaba – *Baile na Banaba* (Banaba's settlement/townland) and Lisdonnellroe – *Lios Dónaill Rua* (Red Dónal's enclosure or fort) among others. It is also important to note the names of two adjacent townlands in the northern part of the study area, Ballydoogan – *Baile Uí Dhúgáin* (Ó Dubhagáin's settlement) and Cartrondoogan – *Cartrún Uí Dhúgáin* (Ó Dubhagáin's quarter). The Ó Dubhagáin landholdings in question have been identified with the hereditary Ó Dubhagáin poet historians referred to earlier (FitzPatrick 2015b, 168, 188; 2016, 204) and will be discussed more fully below.

The toponyms with religious associations focus on Kilconnell village and hinterland and are indicative of the lands owned and used by the medieval church. Kilconnell – *Cill Chonaill* (Conall's church) may refer to a Patrician-associated or sixth-century founder of the early medieval ecclesiastical site. St Conall of Drumcliff, Co. Clare, is regarded as the founder of this early church (Ó Riain 2016, 222). There is also an argument that St Conall's connection with Kilconnell is incorrect, rather the original religious establishment was founded by a female saint, one St Conainne (Mannion 2008, 12–13). Other names include Glebe (church lands used to support a parish priest), Abbeyfield, Monambraher – *Móin na mBráthar* (friars' bog), Hillswood – originally *Loch an Chléirigh Mór*, Loughaclerybeg – *Loch an Chléirigh Beag* (clergyman's lake[s]), and Gortadeegan – *Gort an Deagánaigh* (deacon's field). Two further names could be added to this grouping, another Cartrondoogan – *Ceathrú an*

Ghabhann (smith's quarter) and Loughaunbrean – *An Lochán Bréan* (the foul/stinking pool – possibly linked to tanning or blacksmithing also). These names may record the associated industrial activities which may have taken place near the religious house.

The final name of immediate note is Corraneena – *Corr an Aonaigh* (the round hill of the assembly), indicating the presence of an *óenach* or fair. The location of Corraneena within the Kilconnell area is interesting, due to its proximity to the centre of the settlement. A catalogue of evidence strengthens the case for the fair of Kilconnell being of considerable antiquity. In terms of communications, the area was well served by the *Slighe Mhór*. Geissel plots the most likely course of the *Slighe Mhór* and his section on Kilconnell follows a broadly similar route as that of the modern R348 (Geissel 2006, 93–5), historically the old main Galway road through Kilconnell village.

Callow Lough and Kilconnell in the historical sources
Kilconnell is centrally placed in relation to communication routes, but it does not loom large in the early historical sources. The first reliable reference comes in 1244, where we encounter 'Mac Domnall Mór of Kilconnell' (see Chapter 2), suggesting that he resided at a lordly centre somewhere in the immediate area. The next mention occurs in the fourteenth century and strongly suggests that the Uí Chellaig were re-establishing control over the *trícha cét* of Uí Maine at the expense of the declining Anglo-Norman interests in the region. This resurgence corresponds with the career of Uilliam Buide Ó Cellaig, lord of Uí Maine, and his son and successor, Maolsechlainn. In 1353 Uilliam Buide founded Kilconnell Franciscan Friary (*AFM*), while it is adjudged to be around this year that Uilliam also built the 'bawn of Callow' (*Tribes*, 74). Other sources seem to corroborate this re-establishment of an administrative and power base at or near Callow Lough. *Nósa Ua Maine* indicates that *Túath Caladh* was where local rents and taxes due to Ó Cellaig were collected (*Nósa*, 546–7), showing that it was a key administrative base within the lordship during the fourteenth century, at least.

Later sources indicate that Callow Lough and Kilconnell retained an importance to the Ó Cellaig wider dynastic family into the fifteenth and sixteenth centuries. In 1475, for example, we hear that 'The castle of Caladh was taken by Mac William of Clanrickard, and delivered up to the son of Melaghlin O'Kelly …' (*AFM*). This record refers to one Tadhg Ruadh Ó Cellaig 'of Callow', grandson of Uilliam Ó Cellaig (d. 1420). Tadhg Ruadh's father, Maolsechlainn (d. 1464), was a prominent patron of Kilconnell Friary during the second half of the fifteenth century and while neither Maolsechlainn nor Uilliam became lords of Uí Maine, it indicates that this more junior sept had the wealth and resources to undertake refurbishments to Kilconnell Friary. Moving into the sixteenth century, the annals associate Callow with prominent Ó Cellaig members in 1519 and 1593 (*AC*; *AFM*), while a series of fiants record the Uí Chellaig at Callow in the 1570s and 1580s (*Fiants* II, 209 [1593], 451 [3301], 675

Figure 5.14 Section of *Map of the province of Connaught* (1591) showing the barony of Kilconnell, Callow Lough, Kilconnell Abbey (Friary) and 'Annagh C. Mc Award' (TCD, MS 1209/68. Courtesy of the Board of Trinity College Dublin).

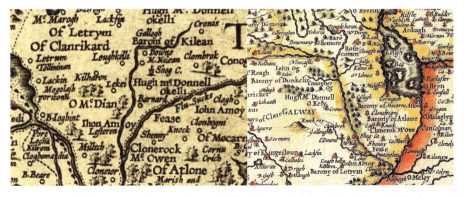

Figure 5.15 *Irlandiæ accvrata descriptio* (1606) (left) refers to the lake as 'Loughkelli'. *The theatre of the empire of Great Britaine: presenting an exact geography of the kingdom of England, Scotland, Ireland* … (right) records a stronghold at the site, and refers to it as 'Lough Kelly' (Library of Congress Geography and Map Division Washington, DC 20540–4650 US; Atlas.2.61.1, Cambridge University Library).

[4672]). The 1574 list of Galway castles and their owners confirms 'Callowgh' in the possession of 'W[ilia]m O Kelly of Callowgh' (Nolan 1900–1, 120). The final historical attestation to Callow Lough being a place of residence for the Uí Chellaig in the medieval period occurs in 1595, with Callow, likely referring to the castle, being removed from the possession of Feardorcha Ó Cellaig by a rival branch of the dynasty (*AFM*).

Lakeland elite settlement in later medieval Uí Maine

Figure 5.16 Orthographic image of Callow Lough and environs, Co. Galway, with the principal monuments labelled (image courtesy of Western Aerial Survey).

Callow Lough in the cartographic sources

Callow Lough is known by another name in the local area, 'Lough Acalla'. While this version of the place-name may simply correspond with the aforementioned Callow, it is possible that this is a corruption of another name given to the lake. Consulting the late sixteenth- and early seventeenth-century cartographic sources may provide a rationale for the alternative name. The 1591 *Map of the province of Connaught* illustrates the lake as well as the island at its centre, marking the site 'Callowgh C.' (Fig. 5.14). Boazio's 1606 map *Irlandiæ accvrata descriptio* refers to the lake as 'Loughkelli'. Speed's very early seventeenth-century map, *The theatre of the empire of Great Britaine: presenting an exact geography of the kingdom of England, Scotland, Ireland …*, records a stronghold at the site, and refers to it as 'Lough Kelly' (Fig. 5.15). The Lough may have been referred to in Irish as *Loch Ó Cellaig*, a name which over time became anglicized and shortened, resulting in the modern Lough Acalla.

The archaeology of the Callow Lough cenn áit

The historical, cartographical and place-name evidence suggests that Callow Lough was an important Ó Cellaig lordly centre. What are the archaeological remains associated with the lough and its vicinity? (Fig. 5.16).

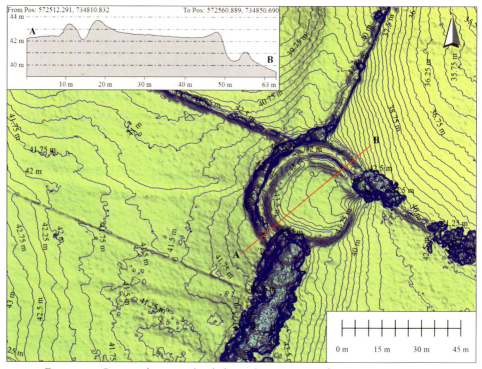

Figure 5.17 Contoured topographical plan and cross-section of Lisnagry Fort. Note the sub-rectangular annex appending Lisnagry Fort to the south-west, possibly a livestock corral (data source: Western Aerial Survey).

The archaeological remains in Callow townland are nearly exclusively of general medieval date. They come in the form of an unclassified castle, Callow Castle (Alcock, de hÓra and Gosling 1999, 398), adjacent to the southern lake shore and a substantial *crannóg* in the centre of the lake (ibid., 30). Three ringforts and an enclosure complete the record (ibid., 64), portraying a long continuity of settlement. The adjacent townland to the north, Lisdonnellroe, contains one bivallate ringfort, Lisnagry – *Lios na g-croidh*, 'the fort of the cattle/wealth', on the 1st Edition OS 6-Inch map, and one enclosure, Lisnacourty – *Lios na Cúirte* 'the fort of the court' (ibid., 131; 205; Fig. 5.16). Aerial photography of the area suggests an additional, heavily degraded earthwork monument, *c.*45m in external diameter, located 100m directly to the west of Lisnacourty (E 572271; N 734593). It appears as a nearly circular cropmark on certain of the aerial databases only, suggesting a deterioration of the site through time. Should this be a ringfort, which it probably was, it would have been a substantial example.

This discrete complex of monuments, coupled with the outlined names, indicate a landscape associated with lordship and wealth. It is possible that Lisdonnellroe – *Lios*

Dónaill Rua (Red Dónal's fort) may refer to the thirteenth-century king of Uí Maine, Domnall Mór Ó Cellaig, who was operating in the *trícha cét* during that time and died peacefully at Aughrim in 1224 (Nicholls 1969, 41). If either Lisnagry or Lisnacourty served as a residence of Domnall Mór, the bivallate site of Lisnagry would be the more likely choice because of its size and complexity (Fig. 5.17).

The DEM also highlights a number of low-relief features in the vicinity of Lisnacourty, possibly pre-modern earthen field boundaries, radiating out to the west and east away from the site. The orthophotograph of the district immediately surrounding Callow Lough reveals further linear features that do not conform to the modern field boundaries, suggesting a relative complexity of land division around the *cenn áit*, all hinting at an organized, productive agricultural landscape during later medieval times (Fig. 5.16).

Callow Lough crannóg

Inspecting the archaeological remains further, two monuments stand out as identifiable parts of a later medieval Gaelic lordly landscape. First, there is the *crannóg*, roughly circular in shape and measuring 30m in diameter, which is the most prominent feature on the lake and is of stone construction (Pl. 5.4; Fig. 5.18). A dry-stone revetment comprised of large square stones defines the perimeter of the site (Pl. 5.5a). A substantial dump of stone and earth forms the island, with parts of the *crannóg* surviving to 2m in height above the present waterline. Its morphology would categorize it as a high-cairn *crannóg*, suggesting that the final phases of occupation were later medieval in date. Considering the range of historical references surviving for the area, and the clear evidence from across Ireland for *crannóga* being occupied up to *c.*1600 (see Chapter 4), it is highly likely that this *crannóg* was part of an Ó Cellaig *cenn áit*.

The remains of a small sub-rectangular building, constructed of unmortared stone, are located centrally on the *crannóg* platform. This structure has internal dimensions of *c.*4m north-south and *c.*5m east-west. Its walls are 0.88m in width and survive to an average height of 1.3m. Access into the structure is provided by a 0.5m gap in the western end of the south wall. This was likely a simple roofed structure, perhaps a hut. However, given the relatively large size of the *crannóg*, the island must have supported a more complex structure or structures when occupied that do not survive above ground today to inspect, because they were probably constructed of wood. A stone-built jetty survives on the eastern side of the *crannóg*, much like the remains found at Rindoon, Co. Roscommon, which facilitated access onto the island (Curley 2021b, 20–1).

Despite the lack of historical attestation for this island, it must have been a central part of this Ó Cellaig *cenn áit*, particularly prior to the construction of the castle on the southern lakeshore. As such, evidence from historical accounts (*Topographia*, 37),

Plate 5.4 The high-cairn *crannóg* located in the centre of Callow Lough, viewed from the south-east. The trees hide the dry-stonewalled structure at its centre (author's photograph).

Plate 5.5 [a] Large stones marking the perimeter around the Callow Lough *crannóg*, on its southern side. [b] Noost or jetty features on the eastern side of the *crannóg* (author's photographs).

Lakeland elite settlement in later medieval Uí Maine

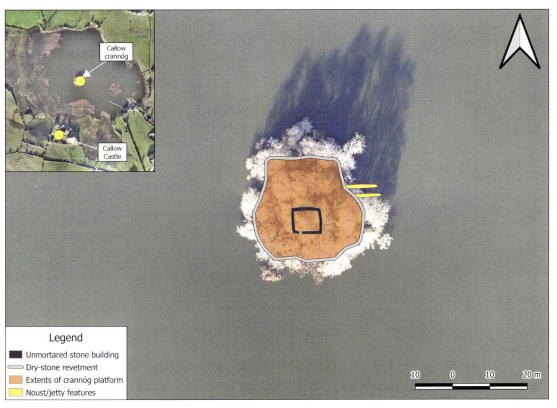

Figure 5.18 Plan of Callow Lough *crannóg*, with its unmortared stone building south of the centre of the *crannóg* platform, and the jetty features (data source: Western Aerial Survey).

and from the examination of similar sites elsewhere, indicate that the *crannóg* would have acted as an administrative centre, defended residence, guest accommodation and a location for feasting for the island dwellers, as well as a legitimizer of their antique origins in the area (see O'Conor 2018, 164–6). There is the possibility that this *crannóg* continued to serve a prominent role in the Callow landscape up until the end of the later medieval period, judging by the care taken to include the lake and the artificial island itself in the aforementioned cartographic sources.

A site possibly linked to the *crannóg* by function is the group of monuments located 200m to the south at the lake shore. We have already seen that the pairing of *crannóg* and fortified dry-land agricultural and administrative centre was a routine arrangement in these contexts, with notable examples seen at Lough Melvin, Co. Leitrim, and Lough Cé, Co. Roscommon (Curley 2021b, 22). However, it must be noted that some dry-land sites associated with *crannóga* consisted of completely undefended sites (O'Conor and Fredengren 2019, 95).

Figure 5.19 Flood mapping of Callow Lough, based on survey work undertaken by the OPW (image Source: GeoHive, OSi 2017).

The bódhún *of Callow*

If the *crannóg* at Callow was paired to a dry-land site, where was it located and what form did this site take? In order to understand this, the fourteenth-century mention of the construction or reconstruction of the 'bawn' of Callow could prove helpful. In terms of candidates for this *bódhún*, place-name evidence perhaps points in the direction of Lisnagry. However, Lisnagry is not in Callow townland, lessening the likelihood of it being the location in question. The alternative, and more likely location, is at or near the site of the later Callow Castle. The lake, and the modern water levels on the lake, are dependent on the ever-growing banks of vegetation that dominate on the shoreline and the lake itself. However, inspection of the southern shore of the lake strongly indicates that Callow Castle was once located on what was a small peninsula or inland promontory jutting out into the lake. This is best visualized through the flood mapping surveys conducted by the Office of Public Works, which indicate that large areas of what are now turlough zones approaching the lake shore are susceptible to flooding (Fig. 5.19). Corroborating evidence for the larger extents of the lake's area can be inferred from aerial photography captured during dry periods. In these circumstances, the algae formations in the lake, once dry, take on a scorched appearance, as the algal mats lay out over the turlough beds, thus indicating a former high water mark.

Lakeland elite settlement in later medieval Uí Maine

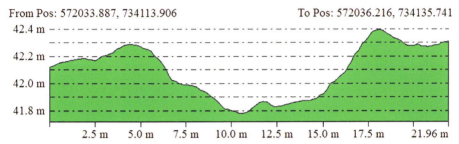

Figure 5.20 Cross-section of the wet ditch across the promontory at Callow Lough, and the location of the cross-section. The left-hand side of the cross-section corresponds with the southern end of the line (data courtesy of Western Aerial Survey).

Armed with this evidence, medieval settlement at Callow Lough can be better understood. The southern lake shore retains the promontory upon which Callow Castle is located, as well as a small spit of land immediately to its west that seems to have been of artificial or partially artificial construction. These two tracts of land combine to create a sheltered harbour to the west of the castle, showing this shoreline to be more complex than previously thought. It must be this area that gives us the name *An Caladh* (Callow – the landing place/ferry), indicating that this was a defined access point out on to this small lake and its *crannóg*.

The photographic and topographical data acquired for the lake and its hinterland has also led to the identification of a strong candidate for the *bódhún* of Callow. First, the detail captured in the orthophotograph is particularly beneficial in inspecting the southern lake shore. This shore seems to have been artificially modified in order to shape the promontory into a defensible site. The topographical data has uncovered a substantial earthen feature 97m to the south of the castle remains. This earthwork is

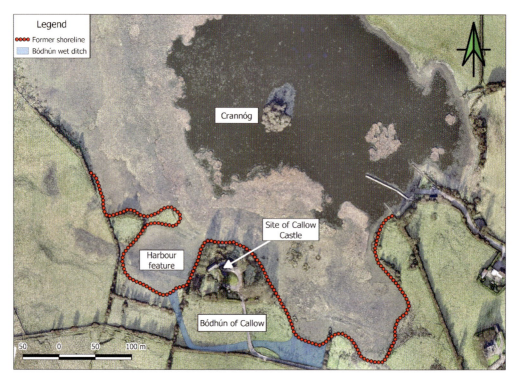

Figure 5.21 Composite orthophotograph and DEM image of the southern shore of Callow Lough, outlining the principal features of the Ó Cellaig lordly centre: *crannóg*, *bódhún*, harbour and site of the later castle (data source: Western Aerial Survey).

best preserved to the east of the laneway providing access to the modern dwelling on the promontory, and would have demarcated the zone from the rest of the surrounding area. It survives as a silted-up ditch, measuring 8–9m in width, with low earthen banks surviving on both its interior and exterior (see Fig. 5.20 for location and size). The DEM traces the ditch to the west of the laneway and connecting the two sides of the ditch together provides a full length for the feature of 200m from west to east, enclosing the entire space north of the ditch to an area measuring $c.14,820m^2$ in size. A cross-section of the ditch, utilizing the DEM data, gives an indication of the scale of the feature on the eastern side of the laneway, where it is best preserved. It survives as a wide (*c.* 12.5m total distance between banks) but shallow (*c.*60cm deep) feature, with its slight appearance likely the result of infilling and the silting up of the ditch over time.

The width of this ditch rules out the possibility that it was constructed for some form of drainage action. This earthwork represents the remains of a defensive wet ditch which was fed by the waters of Callow Lough. As such, it must be part of the physical remains of the *bódhún* at Callow, constructed or rebuilt in 1353, functioning in part as the *crannóg*'s dry-land service site (Fig. 5.21). Given the area enclosed by this *bódhún*, it is possible that a small number of houses were once located within, alongside the elite residence, providing accommodation for those who served the Ó Cellaig lord here on a daily basis. Its size would also have provided the space to safely house the lord's cattle herds in the area in times of trouble.

A modern private lane provides access between the existing farmstead (the site of Callow Castle) and the L17423. Both roads are extant on the 1st Edition OS 6-Inch map. Despite the absence of any earlier detailed cartographic sources for the area, it would appear that this modern lane may broadly follow the old formal route of approach to the castle, as well as what preceded it. Faint traces survive on the orthophotograph, DEM and on the ground for a slightly raised earthen feature immediately to the west of the modern lane (Fig. 5.20), all of which which may represent the remains of an entrance causeway across the *bódhún*'s ditch and onto the promontory.

Callow Castle
Callow Castle is marked in the 1st Edition OS 6-Inch map as being located in a modern farmyard, labelled Callow Lodge, located on the southern lakeshore, at the northern tip of the *bódhún*. Historical references survive for a castle at Callow Lough in the possession of members of sept branches of the Ó Cellaig dynasty in the late fifteenth and late sixteenth centuries, the first in 1475. The castle remains are very fragmentary today, with only one section of castle wall surviving to a maximum height of *c.*6m and measuring 16m in length (Pl. 5.6). This section possesses a base batter, confirming it to be an external wall, while what was part of the interior retains evidence of a small lancet window and a recess for joist holes and ceiling timbers on the first floor. The southern section of this wall, which is devoid of recesses, may have been part of what was the curtain wall of a bawn which was built up against the castle proper. The castle remains do not contain any diagnostic features beyond this, but a series of modern farm buildings incorporate worked stone with punch-dressing, including a series of finely-tooled quoin stones which seem to have been robbed out from the castle (Pl. 5.7). The property owner describes the former presence of a masonry vaulted chamber within the footprint of what was the castle, which was dismantled in the twentieth century (Fig. 5.22).

As we have seen already, punch-dressed cut stones often indicate that a late medieval castle was likely once located at the site. The existence of punch-dressed stones in the modern farmyard buildings at Callow and the evidence for the great majority of the castle sites in the Irish countryside being the remains of tower houses suggests that Callow Castle was in fact originally a tower house also.

Furthermore, the description of what appears to have been a vault over the ground floor of the castle at Callow suggests that the remains were of a tower house, as this is a feature of tower houses, especially those built before the late sixteenth century

Figure 5.22 Plan of the extents of Callow Castle today. The fragmentary remains correspond with the masonry section [B]. The modern dwelling and farm buildings are marked in grey, and the *bódhún* of Callow is visible [A]. C = oval area where the property owner indicated the masonry vaulting was once located, now domestic sheds (data source: Western Aerial Survey).

(McNeill 1997, 201–2, 205). In this respect, it is noteworthy that the first historical reference to Callow Castle comes in 1475, indicating that the tower house was in existence by that date. A recent radiocarbon dating project, which dated surviving wicker twigs used in the construction of vaults and arches in Irish tower houses, produced some interesting results. While many tower houses sampled in the project seem to have been erected in the second half of the fifteenth and early sixteenth century, many others were constructed in the first half of the fifteenth century, in both Gaelic and Gaelicized Ireland. From the negative evidence from this project, there was little indication for the fourteenth-century construction of tower houses (Sherlock 2013; 2015, 88; 2017). This suggests the possibility that the tower house at Callow, on the shore opposite the earlier *crannóg*, was built sometime in the first half of the fifteenth century, or perhaps a decade or two after 1450, as elsewhere in Gaelic Ireland. Indeed, it is possible that this castle was initially constructed at a similar point in time to the programme of building works undertaken by Maolsechlainn Ó Cellaig on Kilconnell Friary, perhaps as early as the mid-fifteenth century when Callow was under

Lakeland elite settlement in later medieval Uí Maine

Plate 5.6 Interior view of the much modified castle wall at Callow Castle. The lancet window (centre of image) has been blocked up and turned into a grotto, and the first floor joist holes and ceiling recess is evident above it (author's photograph).

Plate 5.7 One example of the finely tooled punch-dressing to be found incorporated into the fabric of the modern farm buildings on the site of Callow Castle (author's photograph).

the authority of a more junior sept of the Uí Maine lordship. The wet ditch of the *bódhún* across the promontory in Callow is likely to have continued its defensive purpose after the construction of the tower house. To repurpose the ditch in this manner is not surprising and parallels for the reuse of existing earthworks to create a bawn for one's tower house or castle is seen in a number of instances throughout late medieval Ireland (O'Keeffe 2015, 291).

The cultural landscape of the Callow Lough cenn áit
The toponymical, historical, cartographical and archaeological evidence has established Callow Lough as a focal point of Ó Cellaig authority from at least the mid-fourteenth century. The cultural landscape which surrounds Callow Lough adds to our understanding of how this *cenn áit* operated in the later medieval period.

Corraneena – Corr an Aonaigh, *a place of assembly attached to Callow Lough*
Presumably the location where taxation was levied and tribute was provided to the Uí Maine lord corresponded with settlement of Kilconnell and the seasonal gathering place where the communities of the rural hinterland assembled at the social focal point in *Túath Caladh*. In the name of Corraneena (*Corr an Aonaigh* – the rounded hill of the assembly) we likely have the medieval venue of assembly attached to the Callow Lough *cenn áit* and this location may have corresponded with the statement that, 'The (*túath*) district of Caladh (Callow) holds the stewardship of both petty rent and great exaction' (*Nósa*, 546–7). Evidence for an early origin for *óenach* activity at Kilconnell can be traced to the medieval period. Hagiographical and folkloric sources concerning local saints Kerrill and Connell refer to a rivalry between these two supposed sixth-century missionaries. The rivalry resulted in a pair of curses being cast between the two figures, with the more important curse for our purposes stating, 'May there be blood shed on every fair day in Kilconnell' (Mannion 2004, 59–60). Mannion has argued that this story is likely to date to a developing rivalry between the two religious houses of Kilconnell and Clonkeenkerrill during the fifteenth century (ibid., 61). Indirectly, this reference enables us to posit that Kilconnell was a recognized location of fair activity at least as far back as the later medieval period. However, the survival of the townland name, and its associations with a natural prominence (*Corr* – round hill) often found as the focal point of early medieval assembly landscapes, could indicate that the fair at Kilconnell had its origins in the early medieval period as an *óenach*. There is a 1616 record of a grant for a fair on the feast of St James at Kilconnell. This suggests a possible reaffirmation of a long-standing association with a seasonal fair in late July (Cunningham 2018, 130) and must correlate with the earlier hagiographical reference. The date of the feast day, close to the date of the festival of *Lughnasa*, means that the saint's day of the 25th of July may have been adopted in order to Christianize the gathering, hinting at the antiquity of the fair.

Modern cartographic sources indicate that Corraneena is located immediately to the south of, as well as incorporating, the western end of Kilconnell village. The northeast corner of Corraneena is shown in the 1st Edition OS 6-Inch map to retain an open space marked as 'Fair Green', one which is now largely built over. The 'Fair Green' indicates that the fair was still celebrated here into the early nineteenth century. An annual horse fair has also taken place into the twenty-first century. Circumstantial evidence for this location being suitable for assembly activity is seen by its closeness to the *Slighe Mhór*, which passed directly through Kilconnell. In summary, this suggests that Corraneena was the location of a later medieval fair, which may have had origins consistent with the concept of the early medieval *óenach*. With such a wealth of material extant for both Kilconnell Friary and Callow Lough, it confirms this entire landscape to be a key centre of activity for the later medieval Uí Chellaig, with the convention of a seasonal assembly central to that.

Service kindred landholdings at Callow Lough
The fourteenth-century rights tract *Nósa Ua Maine* is valuable in identifying the hereditary service kindreds attached to the Ó Cellaig lords. Some studies have been undertaken into the identification of the landholdings of service kindreds of later medieval Gaelic lordships, particularly through toponymical analyses (Hughes 1994–5). Research into the archaeologies of these landholdings has more recently been pioneered by FitzPatrick (FitzPatrick 2016; 2018). *Nósa Ua Maine* records a series of offices accorded to minor families in Uí Maine and Tír Maine. However, a degree of caution must be exercised when evaluating whether these offices realistically functioned at all times. It has been suggested that only important dynasties like the Uí Chonchobair kings of Connacht were able to realistically provide even rudimentary administrative offices for their territory in the thirteenth century (Ní Mhaonaigh 2000, 380–1; Nicholls 2003, 44). It is only from the fourteenth century that there is definite evidence for service kindreds in the Ó Cellaig lordship.

At least three hereditary office-holding families can be identified from *Nósa Ua Maine* around Callow Lough (*Nósa*, 548–9). The first are the Uí Dubhagáin, who were hereditary poet historians to the Uí Chellaig. Their presence at Lough Croan has been established. Sean Mór Ó Dubhagáin, who died in 1372, the author of several important literary and poetic works, was of this family (Carney 2008, 690; Simms 2018b, 424–5). Other members to serve as poet historians to the Uí Chellaig included Risteard and Maghnus? 'Cam Cluana' Ó Dubhagáin, who died in 1379 and 1394 respectively (*ACl.*; *AFM*; *MIA*; Ó Muraíle 2023, 12). As mentioned previously, the townlands of Ballydoogan and Cartondoogan, 3km to the north of Callow, seem to represent later medieval landholdings of these hereditary poet historians. Their closeness to the Callow lordly centre is telling and not without parallel. FitzPatrick notes the proximity of service kindreds' landholdings to their lords' residence

Figure 5.23 Lisfineel Fort (left) on the 1st Edition OS 6-inch map. Lisfineel Fort (right) from the Digital Globe aerial source (images courtesy of OSi).

throughout Gaelic Ireland (for instance, FitzPatrick 2018, 173–87) and this is replicated at Callow Lough. The Uí Dubhagáin remained here into the seventeenth century. 'Donell O Dugan' is described as being 'of Lisfenelle' in 1617 (*Cal. Pat. Rolls*, 356). The 1st Edition OS 6-Inch map labels a ringfort (Alcock, de hÓra and Gosling, 45) in Ballydoogan as 'Lisfineel Fort'. This very large ringfort, 39m in internal diameter and defined by as many as four earthen banks separated by three ditches, can still be seen today (Fig. 5.23). This site may have served as a principal residence of the Uí Dubhagáin during the later medieval period prior to the seventeenth century.

The second *Nósa Ua Maine* kindred linked to the Uí Chellaig lords are the Uí Longorgáin harpers of *Baile na Banabadh* (ang. Ballynabanaba). Ballynabanaba is located 2km to the east of Callow Lough. The Uí Shideacháin horn-players of *Lis na Cornairead* are also mentioned in the latter source as being linked to the Ó Cellaig lords (*Nósa*, 548–9). *Lis na Cornairead* (the fort of the horn-blowers[1]/cupbearers) (Ó hAisibéil, L., pers. comm.) may have been located in Ballynabanaba (Fletcher 2001, 195). The site of at least one univallate ringfort, *c.*29m in internal diameter, and a tower house of at least three storeys, which has evidence within it for ogee-headed windows of late fourteenth-century to mid sixteenth-century date, occurs in the townland, and may have been a residence of the Uí Máelalaid historians during the late medieval period (Alcock, de hÓra and Gosling 1999, 47, 396; *Tribes*, 177). An enclosure is also recorded on the inventory and seems to be the eroded remains of a ringfort, *c.*28m in internal diameter (ibid., 226). In all, this evidence suggests that three of the key offices relating to public recitation and performance, feasting, music, entertainment and related activities were all centred close to Callow, the Ó Cellaig lords' administrative and power base in the area.

It is possible to add two more landholdings of hereditary service kindreds to the Callow landscape. Just under 3km north-west of Callow Lough lies Annagh townland,

---

[1] One stokagh – *stocaire* – 'horn-blower' is recorded in association with the Uí Chellaig in a fiant for the year 1583, one 'Teig McDonogh of Colenegir' (*Fiants* II, 584 [4170]). This role is regarded as having been synonymous with hunting, war and feasting (FitzPatrick 2018, 184).

Lakeland elite settlement in later medieval Uí Maine 147

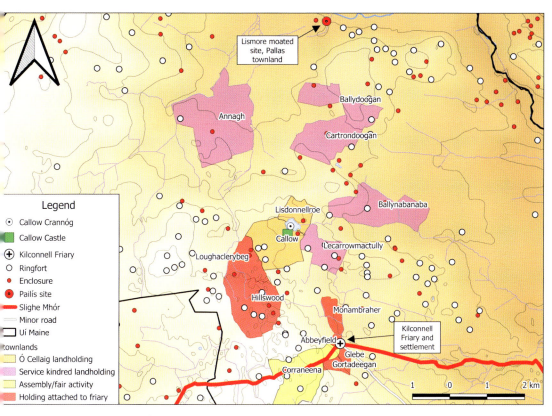

Figure 5.24 Some of the townland names surrounding Kilconnell and Callow Lough, and my interpretation.

recorded as one of the locations of residence for the *Meic an Bhaird* [Mac Ward] family of poets, a kindred recorded as serving the Uí Chellaig as early as 1356 (*AC*; *ACl.*). A poem, included in the fourteenth-century *Leabhar Ua Maine*, beginning *Cruas connacht clanna sogain* [The rigorous Connacht family of the Sogan], locates a branch of this family at Annagh (MacAlister 1941, 77–8/22–3). Furthermore, one Hugh McWarde is recorded in possession of a castle at Annagh in 1574 (Nolan 1900–1, 120). Browne's 1591 map corroborates the Meic an Bhaird presence adjacent to Callow Lough, with Annagh marked 'Annagh C. Mc Award', referencing a castle (Fig. 5.14). Annagh contains a univallate ringfort, *c.*31m in internal diameter. The grass-covered remains of a rectangular 'house site', possibly the base of a tower house, survives in its interior, measuring 8m east/west by 7.3m north/south (Alcock, de hÓra and Gosling 1999, 34). An oval enclosure, probably the remains of a ringfort, the internal measurements of which were 50m north-west/south-east by 40m north-east/south-west, once existed *c.*100m north of Annagh House (ibid., 166). Either of these sites may be the archaeological remnants of one of the Mac an Bhaird residences and also be the site of the historically attested castle.

Finally, the townland name of Lecarrowmactully – *Leithcheathrú Mhic Mhaoltuile* (the half-quarter of Mac Maoltuile) is likely to represent another learned kindred in the area, located directly to the east of Callow. The Mac Mhaoltuile/Ó Maoltuile [Mac Tullys] were a prominent Connacht family of hereditary physicians (Sheehan 2019, 22). Physicians often resided close to the chief's residence, with their landholdings often named after them (FitzPatrick 2015, 175; 2018, 170–1; 2023, 30). The Mac Maoltuile were prominent physicians to the Uí Chonchobair lords of Machaire Connacht, and a Mac Tully was present at Cathal Crobhdearg's inauguration *c.*1201 (O'Daly and O'Donovan 1853, 346–7). The Mac Mhaoltuile served as 'kern' *ceatharnaigh* (foot-soldiers) to the Uí Chellaig, according to fiants from the late sixteenth century (*Fiants* II, 209 [1593], III, 106 [5435]). The surname is noted by Egan in respect of nearby Kilcloony parish during the late medieval period, alongside the Mac Aodhagáin and Mac Céile lineages, and he raises the possibility that these learned kindreds may have been located here to collectively deliver a wider educational role to the Ó Cellaig lordship at that time (Egan 1960, 44–5). Sheehan highlights the routine presence of landholdings associated with medical families being strategically located close to road and riverine communication networks. These landholdings were carefully chosen to enable the physician to access patrons and patients beyond their own locales (Sheehan 2019, 24–5), meaning that Lecarrowmactully might have been chosen due to its closeness to the *Slighe Mhór*. The townland contains the remains of four ringforts and an enclosure (Alcock, de hÓra and Gosling 1999, 129, 204). The most prominent is delimited by two banks and one intervening ditch, measuring *c.*30m in internal diameter. It possesses a probable entrance to its east/north-east, with the internal bank having a dry-stone facing (ibid., 129). This may have been a residence of the Mac Maoltuile physicians.

Kilconnell Franciscan Friary
Kilconnell Friary is important to explore, in that it serves as a display of the increase in power and wealth exercised by the Ó Cellaig lords from the mid-fourteenth century onwards. Other scholars have engaged in more detailed and expansive study of Kilconnell Friary (Biggar 1900–1; 1902; 1903–4; Jennings 1944; McDermott 2012; Smith 2014b). However, a number of the surviving elements at, and surrounding, the friary need to be discussed due to their connection with the Uí Chellaig and will be summarized here. The Cambridge University Collection of Aerial Photography (CUCAP) includes a series of oblique aerial photographs of Kilconnell Friary taken in 1963 and 1969. These show the survival of a matrix of field systems surrounding the religious foundation (Pl. 5.8) and may represent something of the economic activities that supported the friary. In theory, a Franciscan or Dominican friary was not supposed to own land, in the way that, for example, a Cistercian monastery could possess thousands of acres. Yet, it has been shown that small farms of perhaps thirty to fifty acres may have been worked in the vicinity of these friaries in later medieval

Lakeland elite settlement in later medieval Uí Maine

Plate 5.8 Oblique aerial photographs of Kilconnell Friary and infields: (left) CUCAP no.: AHM033, date: 1963-06-30. (right) West of Kilconnell Friary. CUCAP no.: AYN065, date: 1969-07-10 (images courtesy of CUCAP).

Ireland. Such holdings would have been farmed by these friaries to provide their basic food requirements and none of this produce was sold for profit (O'Conor and Shanahan 2013, 13–15). It is possible that these field systems may be the remnants of such an attached farm. Alternatively, these fields could have been farmed by a lay population living adjacent to the friary and who, as the place-name evidence suggests, delivered industrial processes for the settlement, the Franciscans, and the secular lords at Callow Lough. The discovery of a horizontal mill bedstone of Galway granite immediately east of the friary in the townland of Crummagh in the 1960s suggests the former presence of a possibly medieval horizontal watermill as part of the wider friary complex at Kilconnell also. This survival provides further hints of the economic underpinning of this impressive establishment. The millstone is today located within the grounds of the Aughrim Heritage Park in that village.

The tombs of the friary reflect elite, probably secular patronage, not least the well-known 'flamboyant' tomb at Kilconnell, complete with its carved continental religious figures, including St James, perhaps indicating that the benefactor went on pilgrimage to Santiago de Compostela (M. Fitzpatrick 2010, 14; Moss 2018, 480–1; Nugent 2020, 296). As Franciscans and Dominicans were supposed to live austere lives and to take a vow of poverty, the richly decorated tomb is much more likely to mark the resting place of a lay lord, presumably an Ó Cellaig. The position of a canopied fourteenth or fifteenth-century tomb on the north wall of the chancel (Smith 2014a) (Pl. 5.9) occupies a routine location for the founder's tomb in later medieval monastic

Plate 5.9 Fourteenth- or fifteenth-century canopied tomb in the north wall of the friary chancel, with the mid-seventeenth-century Ó Mainnin grave slab located at its foot (author's photograph).

and friary church architecture and although the benefactor is unidentified, I have speculated elsewhere that this is the final resting place of a prominent, perhaps founding, member of the Ó Cellaig elite (Curley 2019, 18; 2021, 25). An Ó Mainnin grave slab is located at the foot of this tomb (Mannion 2015, 21–3), with the implication that the historically attested role of the Uí Mainnin of Soghain as one of the principal military vassals of the Uí Chellaig may be why a prominent member of that family was interred there (see *Nósa*, 241–3; *AT, s.a.* 1135; *AC, s.a.* 1377; *Fiants* II, 524 [3793], 584 [4170], 670 [4652], III, 106 [5438]; Curley 2021b, 26–7).

The continued use of Kilconnell Friary as an Ó Cellaig place of burial can be seen in the fifteenth and sixteenth centuries with the burial of at least Uilliam Ó Cellaig (1420) and Feardorcha Ó Cellaig (died after 1611), both lords of Uí Maine (Byrne 2011, 227). The collection of Ó Cellaig commissioned religious items is extensive and includes a fourteenth-century silver ciborium 'with a remonstrance in ye topp of wch

Lakeland elite settlement in later medieval Uí Maine

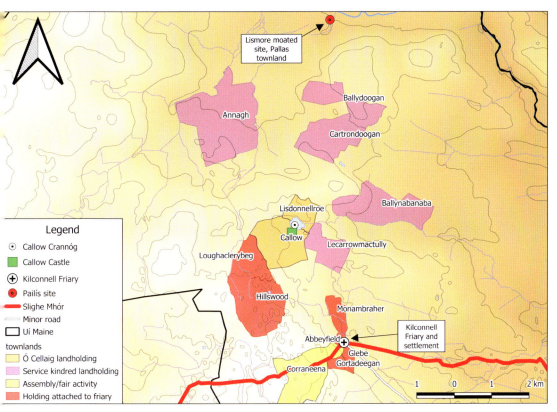

Figure 5.25 Summary of the Callow Lough and Kilconnell case study, with principal locations outlined, including Lismore moated site.

inscription M'Donagh Minagh Ychalle' (Jennings 1944, 68); a silver chalice inscribed 'Willelmi y Kelly' dated 1409; a ciborium inscribed 'Malachiae Kelly' dated 1480; a silver chalice in remembrance of Capt. Hugh Kelly of 'Bellaghforen' dated 1685; and a chalice, vestments and Mass book provided by William Kelly of Turrock (ibid., 66, 68). The *Mac Donnchad Muimnech Ó Cellaig* ciborium and the likely fourteenth-century tomb niche put paid to the erroneous dating of the friary to the fifteenth century (Curley 2021b, 27). A review of the Ó Cellaig patronage at Kilconnell is completed by acknowledging that the mid- and late fifteenth-century programme of building at the friary, as well as the introduction of Observant reform, both commissioned by Maolsechlainn Ó Cellaig (Smith 2014b), demonstrate just how important this religious foundation was to the lords of Uí Maine throughout the later medieval period.

The source material confirms that a highly organized and dynamic Gaelic lordly centre once existed at Callow Lough. The physical environment, as parsed through the place-names and the present-day landscape, indicate that this elite centre was located in a fertile agricultural landscape situated between zones of wetland and woodland. The connectivity of this *cenn áit*, and possibly part of the reason why it was sited where it was, can be partially explained by its closeness to the main east-west overland routeway in medieval Ireland, the *Slighe Mhór*, which passed through Kilconnell. This must have had a role to play in the convening of the annual assembly and fair in Kilconnell, a gathering that can be considered to be of considerable antiquity.

The earliest reference to Ó Cellaig settlement at Kilconnell is in 1244, which may have actually been located at Callow Lough. This *cenn áit* seems to have reached its zenith as a place of importance to the Uí Chellaig from the second half of the fourteenth century onwards, during which time the ecclesiastical hub of the district, the Franciscan friary, was established and extensively patronized. This is also the period during which the secular focal point of the landscape, Callow Lough, was either established or possibly re-established from a thirteenth-century or earlier origin. Prominent service kindreds of the newly ascendant Ó Cellaig lords acquired landholdings in the region, effectively creating a ring of minor families around the lake itself. This small lake and its immediate surrounds retain a medieval archaeology indicative, by comparison with other Gaelic territories, of high-status settlement and organization. The possible pairing of the substantial high-cairn *crannóg* with an undefended dry-land service site on the shore to its south, one with a sheltered harbour beside it, continued to be lived in by branches of the Uí Chellaig until the late sixteenth century (Fig. 5.22). The evidence at present suggests that a substantial promontory-fort like enclosure was built enclosing the dry-land service site in 1353 by Uilliam Buide Ó Cellaig. This upgrading of the site at Callow Lough was accompanied by the foundation of arguably one of the finest late medieval friaries in Connacht at nearby Kilconnell (Leask 1960, III, 167–8). At a later stage, probably in the first half of the fifteenth century based on analogy with elsewhere, but apparently before 1475, a tower house was built within the mid-fourteenth-century promontory fort or *bódhún*. Presumably this tower house was surrounded by agricultural and administrative buildings of timber or post-and-wattle (Cairns 1987, 24; O'Conor 1998, 33). If the tower house marked the site of the earlier dry-land service site associated with the *crannóg*, timber buildings associated with farming and local administration existed here before the building of the tower house and the earlier mid-fourteenth-century *bódhún*.

Cartographers took care in the late sixteenth and early seventeenth century to depict the *crannóg* and Callow Lough on maps. This suggests it continued to be occupied in some way and served a prominent role in the Callow landscape right up to the end of the later medieval period, long after the tower house was built and became the main Ó Cellaig residence here. O'Conor has argued that the continued occupation of *crannóga* beyond the early medieval period right down to just beyond 1600 was not due to an innate conservatism in later medieval Gaelic Ireland. Instead, he suggested that one of the cultural practices of Gaelic society during that period was the deliberate use by the elite of anachronisms and references to the past in order to provide political power and social prestige in the present. In the current context, he argued that one of the functions of *crannóga* during the later medieval period was for them to act as living 'theatres' for a display of lordly power that concentrated on referencing the past, particularly the ancestral past (O'Conor 2018, 151–66). Logue (2018, 288–92) has shown that while Hugh O'Neill, earl of Tyrone, built a tower house at his *cenn áit* of Dungannon with the most modern internal features then in use in the English Pale, he also maintained an earlier *crannóg* and used it to entertain and feast his vassal Gaelic lords in the traditional Irish manner as *Ó Néill Mór*, making this a clear example of an immensely powerful Elizabethan lord, albeit of native origin, using the past and its physical trappings to reinforce his position at a local level in Ulster. It is possible that the *crannóg* on Callow Lough continued to function in a politically and socially important way like this, despite the tower house on the lake's shore acting as the main Ó Cellaig residence and administrative centre in the area from the early fifteenth century onwards.

BALLAGHDACKER LOUGH, CO. GALWAY

The final elite settlement in this section concerns a lake located close to another Ó Cellaig lordly centre at Athleague, which will be dealt with separately in Chapter 6. Ballaghdacker – *Baile Locha Deacair* (the settlement of the lake of Deacair), also known as Hollygrove Lake, has an approximate area of 20.2ha and is located close to the traditional northern boundary of Tír Maine. By the fifteenth century, the area formed part of the *oireacht* of *Túath Átha Liaig* (Fig. 5.26). Ballaghdacker Lough was the setting for the kidnap, imprisonment and murder of Áed Ó Conchobair, king of Connacht, at the hand of the Uí Chellaig in 1356 and a location of presumed Ó Cellaig-facilitated safe refuge for Maol Ruanaidh Mac Diarmada, newly installed lord of Maigh Luirg, in 1393. The archaeological remains coupled with the historical references point to it having been an Ó Cellaig *cenn áit* in the fourteenth and fifteenth centuries.

The toponymy and history of Ballaghdacker Lough
Ballaghdacker Lough and its shoreline are spread across the three townlands of Easterfield or Cornacask to the north, Hollygrove to the south and Ballaghdacker to the east. Farranykelly – *Farann Uí Chellaig* (Ó Cellaig's land) is a townland immediately to the north of Cornacask, plainly a statement of Ó Cellaig landownership in what was a contested border area, while *Corr na Cásca* – lit. Easter hill, may point to the location having been associated with Easter festivities and fair activity during the medieval period. The wider environment surrounding the lake is interesting, as land immediately to the west and south is dominated by large tracts of bogland and wooded areas, meaning that any settlement that surrounded the lake would have benefitted

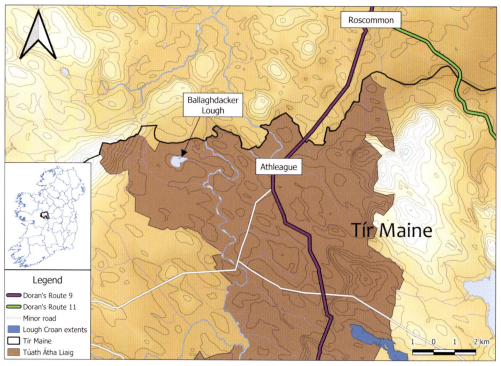

Figure 5.26 Location of Ballaghdacker Lough in the *oireacht* of Túath Átha Liaig. Boundaries of these territories in *c.*1400, defined after Nicholls (1969) and MacCotter (2014).

considerably from the natural defensibility that the landscape provided. Ballaghdacker Lough retains two *crannóga*, Sally Island and Stony Island (Alcock, de hÓra and Gosling 1999, 31, 29). Aside from the fourteenth-century entries, Ballaghdacker Lough is also recorded in fifteenth-century sources. *Leabhar Ua Maine* provides an entry for the year 1424, referring to *Móinín na hAibhle Léithe* at *Loch an Dúin* – 'the little bogland of the grey spark or thunderbolt' at 'the lake of the fortress' (Ó Muraíle, N., pers. comm.). This has been interpreted as being at or near Ballaghdacker Lough (Nicholls 1969, 52). The use of *liath* – grey, in the place-name is also seen at an adjacent townland, Monasternalea or Abbeygrey – *Mainistir na Liath* (Abbeygrey or Abbey of the grey men/monks – the Grey Friars was an alternative name for the Franciscans in medieval Europe) (Ó Clabaigh 2012, 119). This could be a descriptor used to characterize a feature or features in this landscape at large, or it could relate to the fact that the lands of Monasternalea were attached to an unidentified monastery or friary. Monasternalea possesses the remains of a large ecclesiastical enclosure and graveyard (Alcock, de hÓra and Gosling 1999, 324), as well as a bullaun stone, and this collection of seemingly early medieval archaeological remains are located to the south-west of the lake. Gwynn and Hadcock suggested an identification of Monasternalea with a 1574 record to a list of monasteries still in existence in Galway, under the name of *Kilmore-ne-togher*, but could not assign it to a religious order (Gwynn and Hadcock 1970, 363). It is possible that this site was in some way connected to the Franciscans or more likely the Cistercians during the later medieval period, albeit having its origins in early medieval times (Ó Clabaigh, C., pers. comm.). The second element in the place-name is *Loch an Dúin* – 'the lake of the fortress'. With two *crannóga* on Ballaghdacker Lough, it is probable that one or both of these sites are the physical remains described as fortified in the fifteenth-century *Leabhar Ua Maine*.

Analysis of the early fifteenth-century *Leabhar Breac* has yielded an identification not just of the scribe of this manuscript, Murchad Ó Cuindlis (Ó Concheanainn 1973, 67), but information contained in a memorandum in the *Leabhar Breac* also identifies the landholdings of the Ó Cuindlis learned family. FitzPatrick has recently provided a brief description of the learned kindred estate of the Ó Cuindlis at Ballaghdacker (FitzPatrick 2023, 85–6), which will be expanded upon here. The Ó Cuindlis landholdings were consistent with *Inisfarannan* (now Stony Island *crannóg*), part of Ballaghdacker townland, *Corrbachalla* (Curraghbaghla townland) and *Cluain Canann* (Clooncannon townland) (ibid., 66). *Cluain Canann* translates as 'the meadow of the *cana*'. The *cana/cano* was a junior grade of poet that in the early medieval period had an honour price of seven *séts*, the equivalent of three and a half milch cows (Kelly 2016b, 87). Given the presence of the Ó Cuindlis in this district, it may not be coincidental that the place-name retains an element associated with learned kindreds.

The archaeology of the Ballaghdacker Lough cenn áit

The historical evidence clarifies that the Ó Cuindlis resided at Ballaghdacker Lough in the later medieval period, while contemporaneously the Ó Cellaig lords utilized Athleague and Ballaghdacker Lough as part of their *cenn áit* in this area. The archaeology on and around the lake seems to be concentrated along its eastern range. Aside from the two *crannóga* on the lake, in Cornacask there is a subcircular univallate ringfort with internal dimensions of 36.8m east/west by 24.2m north/south, located 50m north-east of the lake (Alcock, de hÓra and Gosling 1999, 99; Fig. 5.29). To the east, in Coolaspaddaun townland, there are the ruined remains of a church and graveyard, known in the cartographic sources as Carrigeen church (ibid., 305). I commissioned an aerial survey over Ballaghdacker Lough and the resulting DEM has uncovered a possible additional archaeological site, located 240m to the east of the recorded ringfort. It appears on the DEM (E 578949; N 757957) as a circular earthen feature, possibly a degraded univallate ringfort, with a diameter of *c.*45m (Fig. 5.27).

Attention was drawn to Ballaghdacker by virtue of the 1356 and 1393 references to the location, the reference to *Inisfarannan* in the *Leabhar Breac* memorandum, as well as the settlement activity implied by the place-name itself. *Baile Locha Deacair* suggests that the townland was a focal point for habitation in the medieval past. However, aside from the *crannóg*, no recorded archaeological evidence survives that can be equated

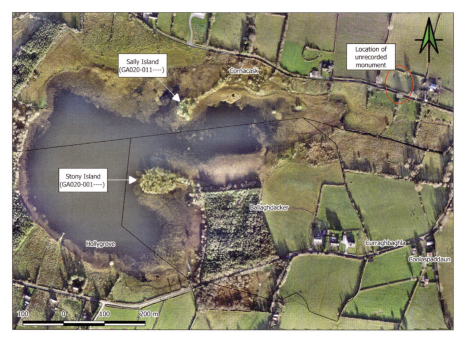

Figure 5.27 Orthophotograph of Ballaghdacker Lough and its environs, Co. Galway. Cornacask ringfort is located to the north-east of the lake (data courtesy of Western Aerial Survey).

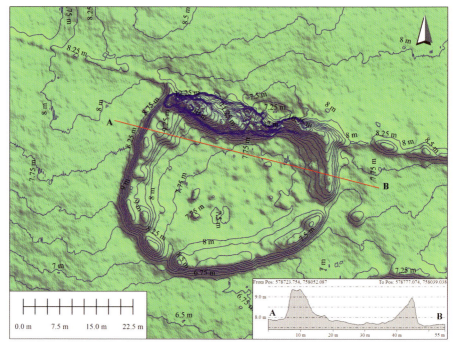

Figure 5.28 Contoured topographical plan and cross-section of Cornacask ringfort, a possible dry-land site linked to the *crannóg* of Sally Island, located 320m to its south-west (data source: Western Aerial Survey).

Lakeland elite settlement in later medieval Uí Maine

Figure 5.29 The possible moated site on the eastern shore of Ballaghdacker Lough. The proposed field boundary and the curved feature are visible to north and west (aerial image: Geohive; Topographical data courtesy of Western Aerial Survey).

with the place-name. The 1st Edition OS 6-Inch map is the only source to confirm settlement in the townland where it does not occur today, with a cluster of houses marked on the edge of what was effectively the turlough lands approaching the lakeshore as it was in the nineteenth century. Much of this area is today composed of planted commercial forestry (Fig. 5.27), which may hide the remnants of any dry-land site connected with the nearby *crannóg* of Stony Island.

The levelled moated site at Ballaghdacker Lough
Careful study of the OSi aerial data on GeoHive reveals a rectangular cropmark that bears comparison to the morphology of a moated site. The sub-rectangular feature measures *c.* 57m east/west by *c.* 33m north/south, with a possible entrance located on its eastern side. It appears to possess an external ditch and a corresponding internal bank, visible as contrasting darker and lighter colouration evident in the aerial photograph. It is surrounded by a linear feature to its north, likely the remnants of a field boundary, as well as a faint curved element to its west. This may mark the former shoreline of the lake, but it is possible that it is evidence that the moated site was created out of an earlier ringfort (O'Conor and Finan 2018, 116–19, 123–4). Due to what seems to be the repeated ploughing of the field, the site (ITM 578703; 757736)

Plate 5.10 Stony Island, as viewed from the eastern shore of Ballaghdacker Lough. The *crannóg* itself is heavily overgrown, but the southern edge of it is visible to the left of this image (author's photograph).

is barely discernible on the DEM (Fig. 5.29). The presence of a potential moated site 320m to the east of an historically attested *crannóg* at Ballaghdacker Lough indicates a more complex history of settlement than had previously been known.

However, in some respects it is unsurprising that there is evidence for a moated site at such a close remove from the *crannóg*. As noted, dry-land service sites, either undefended or in the form of ringforts or moated sites, housing agricultural and administrative buildings (and possibly some domestic ones, such as halls), were associated with many *crannóga*. Presumably this levelled moated site functioned as the dry-land service site associated with Stony Island *crannóg*.

Inisfarannan – Stony Island *crannóg*
Stony Island *crannóg* is today accessible thanks to a modern timber jetty linking it to the shoreline of the lake creating an assumption that the *crannóg* may always have been accessible via a causeway. However, the nineteenth-century cartographic sources, particularly the OS 25-Inch and Cassini maps, indicate that Stony Island was once surrounded by water, with no evidence of overland access. The earliest available cartographic source to depict Ballaghdacker Lough was Richard Griffith's early

Lakeland elite settlement in later medieval Uí Maine

Figure 5.30 Plan of Stony Island *crannóg* and levelled possible moated site, both located within Ballaghdacker townland (image courtesy of Western Aerial Survey).

nineteenth-century Bog Commission Maps (Griffith 1809–14). This depicts a large island, disconnected from the shore and situated in the centre of the lake (Fig. 6.13), as well as a substantial peninsular feature jutting into what appears to be wetland. Stony Island is represented by the peninsular feature, due to its location and also that at the time of Griffith's recording the lake levels had receded significantly enough due to drainage actions to expose the shallower lakebed to the eastern side of the lake. This is certainly not how Ballaghdacker Lough presents itself today (Pl. 5.10).

The *crannóg* is oval-shaped and measures 90m east/west by 60m north/south. Given its size, the largest example of a *crannóg* in the study area, it is possible that the artificial construction is based upon a natural rocky core, like the *crannóg* on Inchiquin Lough, Co. Clare and the Rock of Lough Cé (O'Conor, Brady, Connon and Fidalgo Romo 2010, 21–2). The *crannóg* is heavily overgrown, but its interior is raised 2m above the present level of the lake (Fig. 5.30).

Yet, evidence of the construction of the *crannóg* is apparent with the large square boulders that retain the entirety of the island perimeter. The internal space is composed primarily of small stones and rubble, covered with a layer of earth. This combination of stone construction and raised interior would allow it to be described

Figure 5.31 Plan of Sally Island *crannóg*, with a potential dry-land service site 320m to the north-east. Both located within Cornacask townland on the northern shore of Ballaghdacker Lough (image courtesy of Western Aerial Survey).

as a high-cairn *crannóg*, like the example on Callow Lough, suggesting that the final phases of occupation on it were later medieval in date, as indeed the historical and literary evidence also suggests.

Loch an Dúin – *Sally Island* crannóg

Sally Island *crannóg* is located some 170m to the north of Stony Island (Pl. 5.11). The *crannóg* platform is 40m in diameter above the water level, with an inner raised platform located centrally on the site that measures 28m in diameter. The platform survives to a maximum height of *c.*1.75m over the present surface of the lake, indicating it to be a high-cairn *crannóg*. The platform area, and the island more generally, retains significant quantities of large stones on its surface, which may be the remnants of now ruined, stone-built structures, or part of the fabric of the *crannóg* construction. The *crannóg* is connected to the shore by a very definite artificial causeway. The causeway measures *c.*78m from where it leaves the northern shoreline,

Lakeland elite settlement in later medieval Uí Maine

Plate 5.11 Sally Island, centre of image, as viewed from the north-western perimeter of Stony Island (author's photograph).

until it reaches Sally Island, with an average width of *c*.6–7m. It is demarcated by a low berm on either side, serving to keep the lake waters at bay (Fig. 5.31). Sally Island's morphology, causeway and the relative complexity of the site would strongly indicate that this monument was constructed or at least modified and reoccupied during the later medieval period, corresponding with the historical entries associating the lake with the Uí Chellaig.

Sally Island may therefore be the physical remains of the Ó Cellaig residence on the lake known as *Loch an Dúin*. It is possible that the subcircular ringfort, located 320m to the north-east, served as a dry-land service site connected to the *crannóg*, as an administrative and agricultural centre linked to the elite residence.

The cultural landscape of Ballaghdacker Lough
It is now apparent that the Uí Chellaig utilized this lakeland environment as one of their lordly centres in Tír Maine, particularly in the fourteenth and fifteenth centuries. While evidence for the cultural landscape surrounding this lacustrine *cenn áit* is not as strong as the previous sections discussed in this chapter, the presence of a prominent learned kindred landholding on this lake is noteworthy.

Service kindred landholdings at Ballaghdacker Lough

The most likely location for the Ó Cuindlis residence corresponds with Stony Island *crannóg*, the physical manifestation of *Inisfarannan*, particularly as neither Curraghbaghla nor Clooncannon possess any recorded archaeology. Resultantly, Ballaghdacker Lough served as a focal point for a learned kindred landholding, as well as acting as part of an Ó Cellaig *cenn áit*. Parallels for the contemporaneous occupation of more than one *crannóg* in a lakeland setting in later medieval Gaelic Ireland is seen at Ardakillin Lough, Co. Roscommon, in the fourteenth and fifteenth centuries, while Bartlett depicts two *crannóga* occupied simultaneously in Co. Monaghan in *c.*1602 (Bartlett 1602; Brady and O'Conor 2005, 134). There is even a possibility that this also occurred at Lough Croan, as outlined above.

The Ó Cuindlis seem to have had strong links with the Mac Aodhagáin legal lineage, a prominent family of *brehon* lawyers who provided services to a number of later medieval Irish lords, including the Uí Chonchobair (O'Daly and O'Donovan 1853, 346–7). The Meic Aodhagáin were originally a family of Soghain origin, and *Nósa Ua Maine* records 'Clann Aedhagain' as being a tributary family of the Uí Chellaig (*Nósa*, 533), until they became *ollamhain* or chief legal family to the Uí Maine lords (Breatnach 1983, 63–4). There is a suggestion for a Mac Aodhagáin landholding in Tír Maine, consistent with the townland name Lissyegan – *Lios Mhic/Uí Aogáin* (Meic Aodhagáin's fort). The argument for Lissyegan being a landholding of the Meic Aodhagáin is strengthened by its closeness, 3.5km distant to the north-east, from the Ó Cellaig settlement of Ahascragh – *Áth Eascrach Cuan*, a place associated with Donnchad Muimnech Ó Cellaig, king of Uí Maine. Lissyegan (Hodson) townland possesses the degraded remains of two ringforts.

Murchad Ó Cuindlis scribed the *Leabhar Ruadh Muimhneach*, which does not survive (Walsh 1947, 252), and the *Leabhar Breac*, a manuscript which we know was in the keeping of the Meic Aodhagáin from at least as early as the sixteenth century at their legal school of *Dún Daighre* (Duniry, Co. Galway), while also being scribed for a time close to another Mac Aodhagáin school at *Cluain Leathan* (possibly Ballymacegan or Kiltyroe) near Lorrha, Co. Tipperary (Ó Concheanainn 1973, 65; Fletcher 2001, 53). The Mac Aodhagáin maintained another legal school at Park (Park West/East), Co. Galway (Costello 1940), 19km west of Ballaghdacker Lough, meaning that the two learned families could have maintained regular contact. Later in the century (1449), one Cornelius Ó Cuindlis was transferred by the papal instruction of Nicholas V from the bishopric of Emly to become bishop of Clonfert (*Clonfert*, 90–1) and in 1453 Cornelius was instructed by the same Pope to licence the foundation of three to four new Franciscan friaries in the province of Tuam. Ryan pointed out that the diocese of Clonfert led the early fifteenth-century Observant reform movement in the religious orders (Ryan 2013, 67–8) and this was undertaken with the support or active involvement of the Uí Chellaig lords of the area (Smith 2014b). Given that

Lakeland elite settlement in later medieval Uí Maine

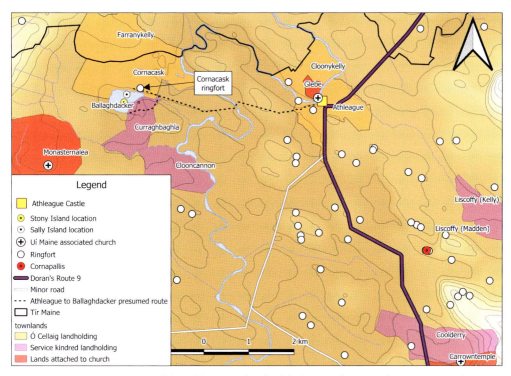

Figure 5.32 Summary of the Athleague and Ballaghdacker Lough case study, with principal locations outlined, including Cornapallis *páilís* site, discussed earlier.

Kilconnell Friary looms so large as a statement of Ó Cellaig wealth and authority in this period, it is likely that these lords would also have had a role in this revival in the orders in their region more generally.

The Ó Cuindlis do not seem to have any visibly identifiable connections with the Uí Chellaig lords in the early fifteenth century, but they were plainly a prominent player in the secular and ecclesiastical spheres within the area. However, this does not discount the fact that this prominent learned family resided and operated in close quarters to the Ó Cellaig *cenn áiteanna* at Ballaghdacker Lough and Athleague and were likely pressed in to the service of these lords in the process. These duties may be similar to that provided by the Ó Doibhlin service family at their landholding surrounding *Loch na Craoibhe* (Stewartstown Lough, Co. Tyrone). The Ó Doibhlin landholding included a *crannóg* on the lake and there is evidence to suggest that their Ó Neill lords liked to reside at *crannóg* sites, such as *An Chraobh*, to claim hospitality from their service families during the winter period (Logue and Ó Doibhlin 2020, 165–9). The presumed Ó Cuindlis residence at Stony Island indicates that activity on Ballaghdacker Lough was shared between this learned kindred and the Ó Cellaig lords. It is therefore safe to suggest that the other *crannóg* on the lake, Sally Island, must be identifiable with the 1356 and 1393 annalistic entries, as well as the site known in *Leabhar Ua Maine* as *Loch an Dúin*.

* * *

What is clear from these lacustrine lordly centres is that, despite the lack of previous research into elite later medieval settlement in the study area, the evidence from a multitude of sources strongly indicates that the Uí Maine lords actively located themselves in these settings, despite the fact that there are so few lakes to be found in their territory. The *crannóg*, as a settlement form, served as a routine focal point of these lordly centres, showing that these artificial islands are not a monument type exclusive to the early medieval period, but, as demonstrated, continued to be used into the late medieval period, with evidence to support this to be found in all three locations. The three *cenn áiteanna* of this chapter share some similarities in their organization. In every case, service kindreds associated with the Uí Chellaig were to be found relatively close to the lordly centre, while in the case of Callow Lough the landholdings of the learned families encircled the *cenn áit*. Despite the perceived remoteness of the three locations, all were served by recognized later medieval routeways, and in two cases, the focal point was close to, but at a slight remove from, a centre of general settlement and presumed trade. Religious foundations are also to be found within these landscapes, to serve the spiritual needs of the elite and general population of the area.

In terms of the physical manifestation of these *cenn áiteanna*, it is notable that there is no evidence at any of these sites for pre-tower house castles, corroborating the argument borne out earlier. Instead, elite residence in the pre-tower house period corresponded with the *crannóg*, coupled with a dry-land site, routinely in the form of a ringfort, moated site or, in the case of Callow Lough, a *bódhún*. Routinely the only monument type to be found in the landholdings of the learned families is the ringfort, albeit in the case of the Ó Cuindlis, their place of residence was probably the substantial *Inisfarannan crannóg*. This hints that some, if not all, of these ringfort settlement sites, traditionally regarded as a monument of early medieval date, continued to be occupied into the later medieval period, as the excavations at Loughbown and Mackney in the study area also show. The continuity of elite habitation in these three locations, from the high medieval period to the late medieval period, is demonstrated by the evidence for the Ó Cellaig building tower houses at Lough Croan (Turrock Castle), Callow Lough (Callow Castle) and Ballaghdacker Lough (nearby Athleague Castle), showing that these places retained an importance to the Uí Chellaig as lordly centres throughout the entire period. Finally, this chapter has highlighted the place of Uilliam Buide Ó Cellaig in the fortunes of the later medieval Ó Cellaig lordship of Uí Maine; his impact is seen, both historically and archaeologically, at all three lordly centres.

CHAPTER SIX

Riverine elite settlement in later medieval Uí Maine

Uí Chellaig elites sited their lordly centres at watery locations. We have seen this in Chapter 5, but the pattern continues here with what can be broadly defined as elite settlement along rivers as the focus. Certainly, the location of *cenn áiteanna* on the navigable waterways of the lordship has a more immediately practical purpose than what could be seen at the lacustrine sites. In this chapter, three Ó Cellaig *cenn áiteanna*, at Athlone, Galey Bay, and Athleague, Co. Roscommon, will be outlined and their character interpreted.

AN Ó CELLAIG *CENN ÁIT* AT ATHLONE

Chronologically speaking, the first identifiable Ó Cellaig lordly centre discussed in this chapter is to be found at Athlone. While Athlone has served as a principal location within wider medieval politics from at least as early as the establishment by Toirrdelbach Mór Ó Conchobair of a wooden bridge and *caistél* fortification there in the early twelfth century (*AFM, s.a.* 1120, 1129; Sherlock 2016, 4–5), he was not the first to recognize the value of this ford across the River Shannon. Archaeological evidence from Athlone and its vicinity record settlement at and near the ford from at least as far back as the Neolithic period, as well as a significant Bronze Age artefactual assemblage. Five decorated early Christian grave slabs, dating from the mid-eighth to the tenth centuries, also suggest an undocumented early ecclesiastical site on the river's eastern bank (Murtagh 2000, 8–11; Sherlock 2016, 3–5).

There is also an early claim for an Ó Cellaig stronghold here, one which precedes the Ó Conchobair control over the ford. An eleventh-century poem, attributed to Muirchertach Mac Líacc, for Tadg Mór Ó Cellaig, king of Uí Maine (d. 1014), entitled *Samhoin so, sodham go Tadg* [This Samhain, I go to Tadg], indicates that Tadg Mór had a residence at Athlone (Meyer 1912, 222–3; Ó Raghallaigh, C., pers. comm.). The poem also implies that travel to Athlone was undertaken by riverine transport, meaning that in this case Ó Cellaig's residence there is likely to have been close to the ford (ibid.). The poem suggests that Tadg Mór, the powerful eleventh-century king of Uí Maine and ally of Brian Boru, controlled the ford of Athlone and possessed a strategically positioned stronghold at this point of the River Shannon. The site for such a stronghold may have remained fixed through time, meaning that this fortification, whatever form it took, was later modified by Toirrdelbach Ó Conchobair

Plate 6.1 Athlone Castle on the western bank of the River Shannon (author's photograph).

in the twelfth century. Despite there being no surviving visible evidence to support this claim, some have argued that these pre-Norman, twelfth-century *caislen*, *caistél* and *caisdeoil* sites were motte and bailey castles (Barry 2007; O'Keeffe 2019). However, using evidence from fieldwork, radiocarbon dates and the historical sources, it has been argued that while sites such as Athlone were admittedly much more substantial than previous structures, they may have obtained their architectural form from a fusion of the native ringfort, *crannóg* and, in particular, the cashel tradition (Naessens and O'Conor 2012; Sherlock 2016, 19).

Moving into the later medieval period, an early fourteenth-century poem, *Uasal an síol Síol Ceallaigh* [The Uí Cheallaigh are a noble family], written by Seán Mór Ó Dubhagáin in praise of another Tadg Ó Cellaig (r. 1315–16), refers to him as the 'lord of Athlone' (Hoyne 2023, 297). Progressing into the fifteenth century, one example of the continued increase in power of the Uí Chellaig at the geographical limits of their territory culminated in their capture of Athlone Castle, first in 1433 for a short period (*AC*), followed by a presumed capture and occupation of the castle in 1455 (*AFM*). The Uí Chellaig were likely still in possession of Athlone Castle in 1490, when it was finally recovered by the Dillons (*AFM*; Murtagh 2000, 27; Sherlock 2016, 19). Despite this thirty-five year occupation, there is no available evidence to suggest that they made any substantial changes or modifications to the stronghold (Sherlock 2016, 37, 44). This is a trend observed at a number of Anglo-Norman castles captured by Gaelic Irish lords from the later fourteenth century and occupied by them down to the later sixteenth and seventeenth century (O'Conor 2007, 199–201; Murphy and O'Conor 2008, 26–8; Logue 2016).

In conclusion, the available evidence suggests that the possible Ó Cellaig residence at Athlone in the eleventh and early twelfth century was some sort of quite defensive-looking ringfort or cashel, a fortification possibly rebuilt and modified by Toirrdelbach Ó Conchobair in 1129. If the Uí Chellaig occupied Athlone for a period in the early fourteenth century, they would have resided in Athlone Castle when there. The castle at that stage and the accommodation then on offer within it would have consisted of an early thirteenth-century polygonal-shaped great tower set within an inner or upper ward. This was defined by a polygonal-shaped masonry-built curtain wall of similar date, with square or rectangular towers along its length. A lower or outer ward, replete with a twin-towered gatehouse, was added to the upper ward in the late thirteenth century. It is felt that timber residential and administrative buildings lay within this outer ward (Sherlock 2016, 33–7). Control of the Shannon and its famous ford must have been one of the reasons why the Uí Chellaig lords tried to control Athlone at times (ibid., 3). Certainly there is archaeological and historical evidence from across medieval Europe indicating that local princes and lords placed their fortified residences and castles beside rivers and fords to control and take economic advantage of the trade that took place along these waterways (Aarts 2016). There are references in the surviving sources and some field evidence for the Anglo-Normans using the Shannon in the vicinity of Athlone for both military and economic reasons (O'Conor and Naessens 2016a; Sherlock 2016, 15–18). The Uí Chellaig must have recognized the economic potential of the ford of the Shannon at Athlone from at least the eleventh century and this is one of the main reasons why they placed a residence here and tried again to control the settlement in the fourteenth and fifteenth centuries.

GALEY, CO. ROSCOMMON

The Ó Cellaig settlement activity in the area between Athlone and Roscommon town spells out a different story from the point of view of the lordship, in that the identifiable Ó Cellaig activity in this area does not seem to be as pronounced or as early as what has been identified at places such as Lough Croan, Kilconnell and, as we will see, Aughrim. Galey Bay, sited on the Shannon system on Lough Ree, is nevertheless an important location for the Ó Cellaig lordship from at least as early as the mid-fourteenth century and remained as such into the post-medieval period. Galey is considered a *cenn áit* of the Uí Chellaig in part because of its historical associations with the fourteenth-century Uilliam Buide Ó Cellaig. However, this is not the first allusion to this lordly centre in the historical record.

Plate 6.2 Galey, Co. Roscommon. The tower house remains and earthworks located on the small peninsula jutting out into Galey Bay, viewed from the south-west (image courtesy of Western Aerial Survey).

Galey Bay is a small sheltered bay on the north-western shore of Lough Ree, framed by Cruit Point to its north, and the north-eastern corner of Kilmore townland to its south (Pl. 6.2). Galey is located 3.6km south of the River Hind and is served immediately to its west by the modern N61, the effective descendant of Route 11 in the area. This is the north-eastern corner of Tír Maine, one of a number of Ó Cellaig lordly centres that were located within the *oireacht* known as 'O Murry & McEdmonds Eraght called the Heyny' (*Compossicion*, 168; Fig. 6.1). In the late medieval period, this region south of the Hind was *de jure* split between the MacEdmond branch of the Uí Chellaig and the Uí Mhuiredaig (O'Murry) dynasty (Connon, A., pers. comm.). The inquisition of Aodh Ó Cellaig, last lord of Uí Maine,

Riverine elite settlement in later medieval Uí Maine

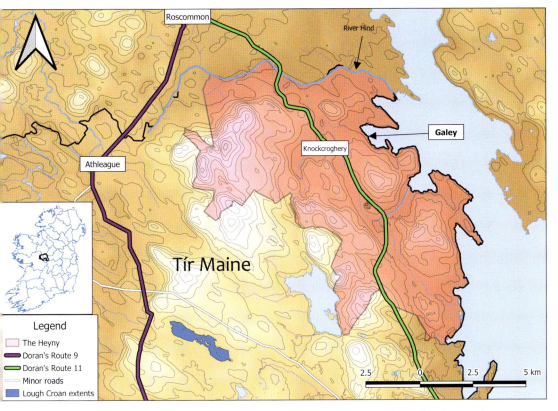

Figure 6.1 The principal locations to be discussed in the Galey Bay section, located in the *oireacht* of 'the Heyny' within Tír Maine. Boundaries of these territories in *c.*1400, defined after Nicholls (1969) and MacCotter (2014).

found that he was in possession of lands in the Heyny which by right belonged to the Uí Mhuiredaig, however, in what was probably much like the situation with the Uí Fhallamháin of Clann Uadach, the Ó Cellaig were the *de facto* lords of the entire *oireacht* at this time and probably for a considerable period before this also (Nicholls 2003, 41).

As has been outlined, large tracts of the wider region surrounding Galey Bay, particularly to the south, were dominated by the *Feadha* of Athlone, a now mostly lost woodland, except for areas along the shore of Lough Ree itself, which characterized much of this region in the later medieval past.

Galey in the historical and literary sources
Galey first appears on the historical record in 1156, when Ruaidrí Ó Conchobair, king of Connacht, used *Blean-Gaille* (Galey) and Rindoon as harbours for his fleet on Lough Ree (*AFM*). Galey's use as a harbour is unsurprising, due to the sheltered nature

of the bay and its closeness to Route 11, linking Athlone to Roscommon. The importance of Galey Bay, and presumably any stronghold that was located there in the later medieval period, was particularly seen by its proximity to Roscommon town, where in the sixteenth century there is evidence to suggest that goods and people were routinely transported into and out of Roscommon via Galey Bay into Lough Ree and thence into the Shannon system (Cronin 1980, 117; Loeber 2015, 137). The 1156 reference also demonstrates the importance of Rindoon as a harbour. It has been argued that a pre-Norman Ó Conchobhair fortification, possibly a sort of oval-shaped ditched enclosure defended by a timber palisade, overlooked this harbour (O'Conor and Shanahan 2018, 9–11). Clearly, with one of his established royal centres outside of his patrimonial lands of Machaire Connacht located at Athlone and possibly another one at Rindoon in Tír Maine, the ability to travel through the region to the west of Lough Ree and along the Shannon system unimpeded was of considerable importance to Ruaidrí Ó Conchobair. At this point Tír Maine was fully in the control of these Ó Conchobair overlords as part of their wider kingdom.

Galey is next encountered in the historical sources in the sixteenth century. *Gallee* – Galey is recorded in 1573 as one of the castles in the possession of Hugh (Aodh), the Ó Cellaig chief (Nicholls (transcribed) 1573, 2019) and features in the *Compossicion Booke of Conought* as the place of residence of Teige McOwen Ó Cellaig and Colloo McConnor (*Compossicion*, 167). These are the last historical references to Galey in Ó Cellaig possession. Aside from this, *Crích Gáille* by Lough Ree is mentioned in the Middle Irish tale *Buile Suibhne*. *Baile na Gaille* is referred to in the prose tract of the possibly twelfth-century *Sochar Mic Diarmada agus a chloinne* (Ní Shéaghdha 1963, 164; for date Simms 2009, 96–7), while a late sixteenth-century Scottish praise poem, *Dual ollamh do thriall le toisg* [It is customary for a poet to travel on a diplomatic mission], refers to Galey as a place of importance in late medieval Gaelic Ireland (O'Keeffe (trans.) 1913, 118–21; McLeod 2007, 178). Furthermore, I will now argue that the location described in a mid-fourteenth-century poem, *Filidh Éreann Go Haointeach*, describes also this lordly centre.

Filidh Éreann Go Haointeach: *Reconstructing a* cenn áit *through literary sources*
The first annalistic record of Uilliam Buide Ó Cellaig as lord of Uí Maine is in 1351, with his hosting, with his son Maolsechlainn, of the famous gathering known as 'Invitation Christmas' (*AC*). This is described as a general invitation to all the poetic classes in Ireland. The event is immortalized by a praise poem written by Gofraidh Fionn Ó Dálaigh entitled *Filidh Éreann Go Haointeach* in honour of Uilliam Buide (Knott (trans. and ed.) 1911). Key information from this poem helps us to better understand the mid-fourteenth-century *cenn áit* at Galey. The value that this poem can provide in reconstructing the past environment has parallels with multidisciplinary approaches elsewhere (Simms 2001; Finan and O'Conor 2002).

Location of Fionngháille

The location of this festivity in the poem is recorded as *Fionngháille*. This place-name has caused confusion, with some suggesting it to be Galey, Co. Roscommon (O'Donovan 1843, 104–5; Kerrigan 1996, 103–4), and others suggesting it to be near Gallagh, or corresponding with Lismore moated site, Pallas townland, both Co. Galway (Kelly 1853–7, 54; FitzPatrick 2016, 204; 2023, 147–8). The place-name evidence, however, strongly suggests that *Fionngháille* is represented by Galey rather than Gallagh or Lismore.[1] While this evidence is persuasive enough to rule out Lismore or Gallagh as the location of *Fionngháille*, the description of the event in *Filidh Éreann go haointeach* leaves one in little doubt as to its whereabouts. The approach to the fort is as described as coming over a 'ridge of the bright-furrowed slope' (*FÉGH*, 61), which is consistent with the physical environment and place-name survivals directly to the west of Galey and surrounding the modern village of Knockcroghery, which would also have served as a line of approach to Galey from the nearest routeway. Directly north-east of Knockcroghery, in Creggan townland, the elevation climbs to 59m OD, by contrast to the elevation recorded at Galey, 1.5km distant to the east, with a reduction of elevation to 38m OD. Conversely, Pallas townland contains a substantial zone of extremely flat bogland to its south and west and has no local high points or elevations which match the poem's description.

Another indicator of location is provided in a section which repeatedly refers to the presence of a lake adjacent to the residence, described as *Loch na nÉigeas* (*FÉGH*, 61). The literal translation is the 'lake of the scholars/poets', which, considering the event that is being described, would strongly suggest that the poet is using his licence to link the event with the physical environment, perhaps even that the poets attending this winter feast arrived by water transport. Such winter travel would have depended to a much greater extent on waterways and relatively easy accessibility than on the unpredictability of overland routes, discounting the more remote setting of Lismore

---

[1] Eleanor Knott was right to identify the '*dúna[dh] flatha Fionngháille*' (mentioned in line 110 of the poem *Filidh Éireann go haointeach*) with the castle of *Gáille*, anglicized 'Galey', on Lough Ree (near Knockcroghery), and right to reject D.H. Kelly's identification of it with the castle of *Gallach*, Castle Blakeney, Co. Galway. This is clear from the different inflexions of *Gáille* and *Gallach*. The former is an 'io'-stem, with genitive singular *gáille* (as in '*dúna[dh] flatha Fionngháille*' in the poem), whereas the latter is an 'o'-stem, with genitive singular *gallaigh*: we have an example of this in the entry in *AFM*, s.a. 1511, in the obituary for Maoileachlainn Ó Ceallaigh, who is said there to have been the builder of the castle of *Gallach* (as well as the castles of Monivea and Garbally): '... fear lás a ndearnadh caislen gallaigh an garbhdhoire 7 Muine an Meadha.' / 'It was he who erected the castles of Gallach, Garbh-dhoire, and Muine-an-Mheadha.' Thus, in *AFM*, volume V, 1310 (Irish), and p. 1311 (O'Donovan's translation). O'Donovan, footnote m, refers one back to his footnote g at 1275, which reads: '*Gallach*, now Gallagh, otherwise Castle-Blakeney, a small town in the barony of Killian. A few fragments of this castle still remain on a green hill near Castleblakeny.' *Tribes*, 104–5, has a note on William Buide Ó Cellaig, holder of the great feast of 1351. *Inter alia*, he says there that Uilliam built Galey castle – but I don't know on what authority he stated this: 'He also built the castle of Gaille, now Galey castle, still standing on the margin of Lough Ree, near Knockcroghery, in the county of Roscommon, where, according to the poem just referred to, he entertained the Irish poets and other professor of art in 1351 (104–5).' Note provided by M. Ní Dhonnchadha.

moated site (for an alternative view, see FitzPatrick 2023, 148). Both Knott and O'Sullivan have suggested that *Loch na nÉigeas* is a cognate for Lough Ree (Knott (trans. and ed.) 1911, 50–1, 68; C.M. O'Sullivan 2004, 115). Tellingly, there is no evidence of a lake or turlough in the vicinity of Pallas. The detail in the poem is describing a very particular location and Galey is the place intended.

The archaeology of the Galey cenn áit
The elite focal point of this landscape corresponds with the earthen and masonry remains categorized as a ringwork or inland promontory fort, and the later tower house, both located on the boundary between Longnamuck townland – *Long na muc* (house of the pigs *or* ship of the pigs)[2] and Galey (Pl. 6.2). Galey is strategically placed in order to utilize the small natural peninsula that juts into this sheltered bay of Lough Ree. This setting is very defensible as a result, as it serves as a bottleneck to transport coming in and out of the bay. On the landward side, Galey benefits defensibly from the use of the lake as an obstacle to attack over its entire eastern range. Overland access to Galey is thus provided only via a now disappeared route which approaches from the south-west.

The pre-tower house cathair *at* Fionngháille
Turning to the fortification at Galey, the site can be separated into two distinct phases. There is pre-fifteenth-century archaeology at the site, followed by late medieval activity in the form of a tower house castle. The natural promontory retains the traces for what were once substantial earthwork remains, which have been heavily modified through time, but are still evident on the ground. Coastal promontory forts have received some study in Ireland and their main period of occupation has been traditionally regarded as occurring primarily in the Iron Age, with some early medieval activity also apparent. There has been little by way of excavation at any of these sites and when they have been investigated it is more routinely with an Iron Age research agenda in mind, albeit there is excavated evidence for some Irish examples having been occupied in the early medieval period, and perhaps later (Edwards 1990, 41–2; Breen 2005, 57). However, a number of scholars have now been able to demonstrate that some coastal and estuarine promontories were occupied and built upon in the later medieval period (Breen 2005, 57–62; O'Sullivan and Breen 2007, 169–71; Malcolm 2007, 197–201; Naessens 2018, 105). While in these instances it has proven difficult to conclusively associate these sites with members of the Gaelic Ó Súilleabháin Bhéara, Ó Dubhda, Ó Flaithbheartaigh and Ó Máille elite in their respective territories, Breen has theorized that the five possible promontory forts in Ballydonegan Bay, Co. Cork, may have been inhabited as the later medieval settlements of the O'Donegan sept within the Ó Súilleabháin Bhéara lordship. Malcolm has suggested that a series of Anglo-

---

2 This place-name possibly relates to the housing and riverine transportation of live pigs or cured pork, utilising the natural harbour.

Riverine elite settlement in later medieval Uí Maine

Plate 6.3 Clockwise from top left [a–d]: Remnants of outer wet ditch, looking north; Cobbled entranceway onto the summit of the earthworks; large boulders, having fallen from the inner bank into the accompanying ditch; ruined nineteenth-century boathouse, which utilized the course of the northern section of the inner wet ditch (author's photographs).

Norman promontory-sited castles identified in the Ó Dubhda lordship of Uí Fhiachrach Muaidhe (broadly north, west and central Co. Mayo) were originally the lordly centres of the Gaelic lords of the area, prior to their appropriation (Breen 2005, 61; Malcolm 2007, 196–7). Kingston has indicated that a number of the Antrim Mac Domhnaill late medieval lordly centres are also sited on coastal promontories (Kingston 2004, 196–8). In terms of inland promontory forts, FitzPatrick has highlighted the probable later medieval use of these monuments in lakeland settings in her reconstruction and discussion of the Ó Duibhgeannáin learned kindred landholdings who served the Meic Diarmada lords of Maigh Luirg at Lough Meelagh, Co. Roscommon (FitzPatrick 2015b, 173–4).

The layout of the earthworks on the promontory at Galey consists of two broad ditches which surround the central prominence. These ditches are extant in the 1st Edition OS 6-Inch map. Both ditches have silted up over time, but parts of the inner ditch still survive to a depth of *c*.1.5m in places. The southern end of the outer ditch survives on the ground due south of the castle remains itself and is visible in the aerial photography. The northern end of the inner ditch has been modified to accommodate a late nineteenth-century brick-constructed boathouse which is now ruined. The modern cartographic sources record this boathouse, along with two other slipways close to the earthwork. One is consistent with the northern end of the outer ditch, while the second is located to the south of the earthworks. This second landing place is located within a relatively substantial open space (*c*.1,100m²) between the inner and outer ditches, which may have been large enough to accommodate a trading post connected with the lordly centre. Fieldwork undertaken with the assistance of a Royal Irish Academy research grant in 2023, consisting of a micro-topographical survey of the site and adjacent areas, and an Electrical Resistivity Tomography survey in two locations, corroborated the earlier observations. The survey results indicate that the outer ditch was as much as 7m wide, and the inner ditch as much as 8m wide along the survey line. A calculation of the ditch depths with the assistance of the ERT survey was less conclusive, owing to the nature of the soil composition. The latter survey does suggest distinctive low resistivity values in those discrete zones, which suggests that the overall depth of both ditches, when maintained, could have been as much as 2m (see Fig. 6.5). These two ditches were very likely wet ditches during the later medieval period. These would have been fed by the lake waters, adding significantly to the defensibility of the site (Pl. 6.3a; Fig. 6.2). The central prominence rises to a height of over 3m above the surrounding area and is *c*.43m in external dimensions east/west and *c*.52m north/south (Fig. 6.2). The internal dimensions of the raised platform measures *c*.28m east/west by *c*.37m north/south, while access to the interior is provided by a western-facing cobbled causewayed ramp, 5m in width, one which breaks the inner ditch and bank (Pl. 6.3b). The perimeter of this platform is defined by a much degraded bank, measuring 5.8m wide in places, with an internal height of *c*.0.45m and an external height of *c*.2m. This bank contains a substantial concentration of stone and a large quantity of disturbed stone has ended up in the inner ditch of the site (Pl. 6.3d). The survival of this perimeter bank is more complete on the southern side of the monument, including the survival of the lower courses of an outer dry-stone wall in places. South of the entrance ramp, the wall survives to a height of *c*.1m in places, with an average width of 1.5m to 2m from the west through to the south of the site, with the most substantial section of the surviving stone remains continuing for a length of 5m, located to the right of the entrance ramp.

To summarize the archaeological character of this site, it would have presented as a well-defended bivallate enclosure, surrounding a central natural promontory. This lakeland promontory fort was placed to provide commanding views over Galey Bay and the upper and middle sections of Lough Ree. A pair of substantial wet ditches, both of which may have had earthen banks although only one survives, guard the

Riverine elite settlement in later medieval Uí Maine

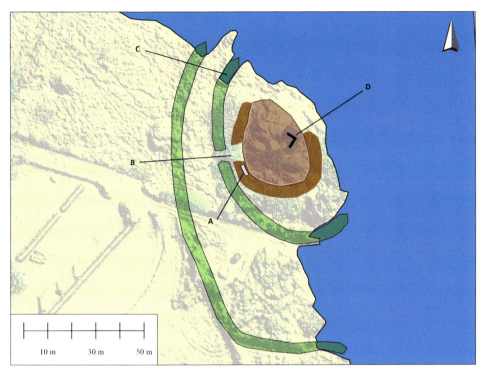

Figure 6.2 Plan of Galey promontory fort. The plan outlines the extents of the pair of silted up ditches which surround the natural promontory, in green, and the inner bank, in brown. A = Surviving section of dry-stone cashel wall; B = Cobbled causewayed ramp; C = Nineteenth-century boathouse constructed out of the northern end of the inner ditch; D = tower house remains (data courtesy of Western Aerial Survey).

approach to the platform. The outer bank is likely to have been topped with a timber fence or palisade, while there is evidence that the inner bank once had a substantial, but now degraded, dry-stone cashel wall surmounting it. Landward access was provided by a roadway which is now gone, but which retains some slight presence in aerial photographs. Water-bound access was presumably provided by one of the shallow areas located within the limits of the outer and inner ditches. The later boathouse may have replaced an earlier naust in the northern end of the inner ditch (Pl. 6.2; 6.3c), along with the slipways recorded in the cartographic sources for the northern and southern ends of these ditches.

Regarding the appearance of the structure that once stood on the platform, it is difficult to interpret. However, analysing *Filidh Éreann Go Haointeach* may help in understanding what topped the fortifications in the mid-fourteenth century. Ó Cellaig's residence at Galey is described in Irish variously as *dúnadh*, *brugh* and *chathrach* (*FÉGH*, 61, 63). The poem describes a fine stone and timber-constructed defended residence, but the nature of the source material gives little away concerning its exact shape. The description does, however, suggest that there are two parts to this *dúnadh*. First, there is the stone fortification that is prominent above the lake waters as it is approached from the west. Described as 'a capital letter of beauteous stone' – it may be describing a circular or oval-shaped structure, perhaps reminiscent of the letter 'O'. Ó Dálaigh describes what is located within the structure as a 'spacious' and 'domed' court of stone and timber. Such an account, particularly when highlighting the patron's hospitality, seems to refer to a substantial timber hall, with the stone mentioned perhaps manifesting archaeologically as dwarf walls that were constructed to serve as the foundations of the hall, in a partly timber, partly masonry constructed building (see O'Conor 1998, 63–6).

One critical piece of evidence that may assist in clarifying the nature of the construction comes from the word *chathrach*, used twice in the poem. *Cathrach* is the genitive singular of *cathair*, which has a number of translations, depending on the context. Through analysing its use in the poem, the most pertinent translation for our purposes is 'a circular dry-stone fort'. The evidence in support of the continued use, modification, and perhaps even construction of *cathair*/cashel strongholds as places of Gaelic elite residence in the later medieval period is strong. The poem refers to the joining of stone with timber on this construction, which indicates that the *cathair* wall possessed a timber superstructure which may have added to the site's defensibility at that time. The poem also describes the *cathair* having a lime-washed stone edifice. Lime-washing, which is more routinely understood to be a technique applied to castle walls, also seems to have been undertaken in some cases on cashels. For example, Cahermacnaghten cashel, Co. Clare, is referred to in a late sixteenth- or early seventeenth-century poem as the *aolta lios* or 'limewhite fort' (FitzPatrick 2009, 297), showing that the method is likely to have continued in use on *cathair*/cashel strongholds up to a relatively late date. Physical evidence for the *cathair* wall at Galey is likely to be consistent with the degraded remains of the stone-composed bank and dry-stone wall section that tops the earthworks, as well as the large quantity of loose stone found in the inner ditch, dislodged from their original location (Pl. 6.3d). It is possible that much of the dry-stonework of the *cathair* wall was robbed out in the recent past. Corroborating evidence for a more recent mass removal of stone from the site can be seen with the very fragmentary remains of the tower house itself, especially if the *cathair* wall served as a bawn for the later fortification. This conversion of earlier earthworks into a bawn enclosure is not an uncommon occurrence, with *cathair*, ringfort and natural topography used in various instances to act as bawn-type enclosures for later tower houses.

The description of the interior of the site suggests a timber and stone-constructed, elaborately decorated hall, domed in shape. This would suggest that the structure was possibly a large roundhouse. It is also possible that this was merely an artistic flourish and it may have taken the shape of a rectangular cruck-roofed hall, a construction

Riverine elite settlement in later medieval Uí Maine

Figure 6.3 Summary plan of the identified archaeological remains at Galey (image courtesy of Western Aerial Survey).

method common in later medieval Gaelic Ireland (O'Conor 1998, 97; Finan and O'Conor 2002; Donnelly and Sloan 2021, 5). Alternatively, this description of a circular building does have parallels with other later medieval dwellings found in the west of Ireland. There is an argument that the circular design is very stable in high winds and so their continued existence was to a certain extent determined by the local environment (O'Conor 2002a, 201–4; Gardiner and O'Conor 2017, 150). No material evidence of this hall survives. The construction of the tower house may well have destroyed this earlier structure and the disturbed nature of the earthwork summit makes it difficult to understand the remains on the interior.

In evaluating the archaeological remains in association with the literary evidence, it strongly points towards the former presence of a fine, lime-washed *cathair*-type defensive enclosure, which was placed on and utilized the peninsula jutting into Galey Bay. This was further surrounded by a pair of substantial, water-filled, defensive ditches, using the lake waters of Lough Ree on a smaller scale, but in much the same way as the wet ditch that was constructed across the peninsula at nearby Rindoon, to act as the south-eastern defended edge of the Anglo-Norman town and as a further defence for the castle, among other uses (O'Conor, Naessens and Sherlock 2015, 96–8). Access to the interior at Galey was provided by a causewayed, ramped entrance

Figure 6.4 Reconstruction of the Galey *cenn áit*, conjecturally as it would have appeared in the mid-fourteenth century, with *cathair* and newly-constructed feasting hall. This reconstruction is based on the surviving archaeological, architectural and literary evidence, and the present research (reconstruction by Uto Hogerzeil; image commissioned by this writer).

which cut the inner ditch and bank and presumably the outer ditch along its southwestern side. An entrance gateway into the *cathair* would be expected in this area. Upon entering the central prominence, the most dominant building, according to the poem, was a hall of stone and timber construction which was likely visible from the lake, as well as presumably some other service buildings (Figs. 6.3; 6.4). It is difficult to know when the *cathair* was constructed and it could conceivably have been in existence as far back as 1156, when Ruaidrí Ó Conchobair drew his ships and boats on the ice from Galey Bay to Rindoon. At this point it may have served as an Ó Conchobair stronghold on Lough Ree.

Riverine elite settlement in later medieval Uí Maine 179

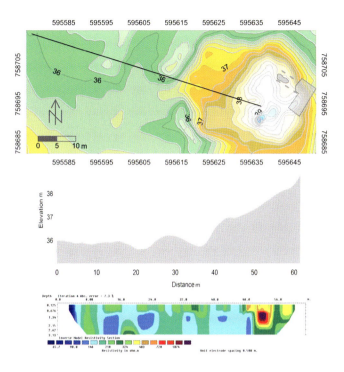

Figure 6.5 Topographical plan, Topographic profile, and Electrical Resistivity Tomography survey results at Galey (image courtesy of LGS; survey funded by Royal Irish Academy).

What is clear, however, is that it was both in use and, judging by the poetic record, carefully maintained and redeveloped by the mid-fourteenth century and the great Christmas feast in 1351. By this time, the *cathair* at Galey would have been old-fashioned and perhaps incorporated deliberate anachronisms in its appearance. This tactic may have been utilized by the Ó Cellaig lord in order to demonstrate his longstanding legacy and legitimacy at his *cenn áit* of Galey, and in Tír Maine more generally (O'Conor 2018, 164–5).

The tower house at Galey
Moving to the masonry remains, the sixteenth-century references to a castle at Galey must correspond with the remains of the castle that is sited on the north-eastern corner of the earthwork. These consist of the eastern corner of a tower house, currently surviving to its fourth floor. A number of features survive on the building, including a well-preserved garderobe built into the base-batter of the north-east facing wall. On the ground-floor level there is a section of a possibly vaulted ceiling, which, if so, suggests a construction date before the later sixteenth century (McNeill 1997, 213; Sweetman 2004, 269–73), as well as the possible remains of an entrance, facing south-

east. Well preserved loops survive at first-and second-floor levels, facing south-east, and there are also the possible remains of a window on the north-eastern wall. An intramural stairwell survives on the first floor providing access to the second floor and a probable access point to the third floor built into the north-east wall (Pl. 6.4; Fig. 6.6). Aside from this, there are collections of worked and punch-dressed stone found loose throughout the site, indicating that the tower house was probably constructed in the fifteenth or sixteenth century.

The topographical survey undertaken as part of the 2023 Royal Irish Academy-funded fieldwork was informative in terms of outlining the footprint of the tower house (Fig. 6.5). Using the rectangular area of higher elevation from the survey as the guide, the external dimensions of the tower house measured approximately 15.4m in length by 15m in width. The extant masonry remains possess a wall thicknesses of 2.7m, which can be presumed for the entire course of the, now lost, building. This suggests that the ground-floor internal area of Galey tower house may once have been as much as $c.156.85\text{m}^2$.

These impressive dimensions, when compared against the, admittedly few, available dimensions from other tower house remains within the study area, suggest that Galey Castle was likely a primary seat of the senior Ó Cellaig line at the time of its construction (Table 6.1). Both Loeber and Breen have theorized on this point, the latter author in respect of Dunboy Castle in his west Cork study area, and both concluded that the largeness of these residences may confirm that they were commissioned as chiefry castles (Loeber 2001, 305; Breen 2005, 74–5).

Table 6.1 Internal dimensions and area size of extant tower houses in the study area.

Site name	Internal length	Internal width	Ground floor internal area	Sept family
Galey	12.7m	12.35m	156.85m²	Ó Cellaig
Castlesampson	13.2m	10m	132m²	Mac Eochadha
Milltown	11m	8m	88m²	Ó Fallamháin
Garbally	7.1m	5.81m	41.25m²	Ó Cellaig
Scregg	7.85m	4.5m	35.33m²	Ó Cellaig

Given Galey's location on the Shannon, the commodity production and trade that is hinted from the place-names which surround the bay, and the historical attestations for Galey and its hinterland, would strengthen the argument that, at the time of its construction, the tower house at Galey was an Ó Cellaig chiefry castle, designed to demonstrate wealth, prosperity and legitimacy, while securing and capitalising on the

Riverine elite settlement in later medieval Uí Maine

Plate 6.4 Image of the internal remains in Galey tower house, viewed from the south-west. Note the vaulting in the centre foreground, the window and intramural stairway in the right foreground. Access to the third floor, and joist holes for the third-floor platform is visible to the top of the image (author's photograph).

economic value which the castle's placement on Lough Ree would have provided. In so doing, it is evidence of an important riverine/lacustrine counterpart to the strategically-sited Gaelic coastal tower houses discussed by other scholars (for instance, Breen 2001, 422). A similar trend could be argued for from the tower houses of Co. Wexford, in that the five largest examples were associated with wealthy estates and, tellingly, all sited by navigable waterways (Colfer 2013, 163–4). Aodh Ó Cellaig, lord of Uí Maine, was the last recorded Gaelic owner of Galey Castle, which indicates that this tower house continued to be recognized as a chiefry castle into the late sixteenth century.

The overall evidence suggests that it was only from the early fifteenth century that Gaelic lords started to build tower houses in numbers (Cairns 1987, 9). The architectural, social and historical evidence, such as it is, suggests that Galey Castle probably dates to before *c*.1550, being built either in the fifteenth or first half of the sixteenth century.

Riverine elite settlement in later medieval Uí Maine

Figure 6.7 Reconstruction of late medieval Galey. The tower house is surrounded by the earlier *cathair* (cashel), serving as the castle bawn. This reconstruction is based on the surviving archaeological and architectural evidence and the present research (reconstruction by Uto Hogerzeil; image commissioned by Heritage Office, Roscommon County Council).

The tower house builders are likely to have continued to use the cashel enclosure as the bawn for the castle (O'Keeffe 2015, 291; Fig. 6.7). This is seen elsewhere, in the case of tower houses located within cashels with the O'Heyne tower house at Cahererillan, Co. Galway, but also Ballyganner South, Ballyshanny and Cahercloggaun tower houses, all Co. Clare (FitzPatrick 2009, 302). More than this, the Rock of Lough Cé, Co. Roscommon, saw the Meic Diarmada utilizing the natural island/ *crannóg*, as well as the earlier mortared cashel wall, as the effective bawn wall for the tower house there (O'Conor, Brady, Connon and Fidalgo-Romo 2010, 24–7). The siting of a tower house on a *crannóg* is also seen in the case of the MacClancy tower house on Lough Melvin, Co. Leitrim (McDermott and O'Conor 2015). The reuse of older earthworks as an effective tower house bawn is seen with the use of the ringfort platform as a protected bawn for the Ó Conchobair Ruadh tower house at Tulsk Fort, Co. Roscommon (Brady 2009, 22–3). The pattern continues with the evidence from

Figure 6.6 *(opposite)* Reconstruction of the tower house at Galey, based on the surviving architectural evidence, the present research, and on analogy with similar castles elsewhere (reconstruction by Uto Hogerzeil; image commissioned by Heritage Office, Roscommon County Council).

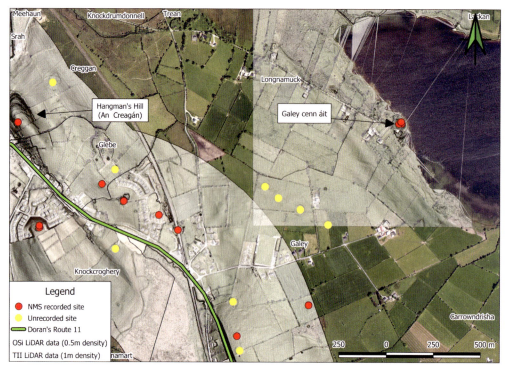

Figure 6.8 The merged OSi and TII LiDAR topographical datasets, highlighting the distribution of the unrecorded earthwork sites visible on the DTM (map source: Bing Maps, data courtesy of OSi and TII).

Caherdrinny, where the tower house was sited within a prehistoric concentric hilltop enclosure, and the O'Driscoll tower house sited on a promontory on Cape Clear Island, both Co. Cork. It is possible that in all these cases the tower house was located within these earlier earthworks partly with a view to displaying continuity with the past, and maintaining a legitimacy with the territories they controlled into the late medieval period. In the case of Galey Castle, it presents another instance of a tower house being constructed by a member of the Ó Cellaig elite at a long inhabited *cenn áit*. In every case, the tower house either replaced, or was incorporated into, the earlier elite residences, something which is also seen at Turrock Castle at Lough Croan, Callow Castle, and with the connected lordly centres of Ballaghdacker Lough and Athleague Castle.

The cultural landscape surrounding Galey
The archaeological evidence, coupled with the historical and literary references, have demonstrated that Galey was the focal point of a riverine elite landscape which retained its importance through the later medieval period. Further consultation of the available sources for this region can develop a fuller picture of the cultural landscape

Riverine elite settlement in later medieval Uí Maine 185

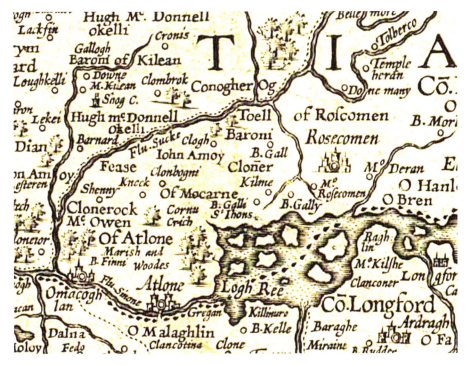

Figure 6.9 Boazio's *Irlandiæ accvrata descriptio* (1606) highlights a settlement near the western shore of Lough Ree as 'B. Gally' – *Baile na Gáile*, a settlement linked to the Galey *cenn áit* in the later medieval period (Library of Congress Geography and Map Division Washington, DC 20540–4650 US).

which surrounded the lordly centre. This section will outline the evidence for a settlement associated with the Galey *cenn áit*, a former route of approach to the lordly centre, as well as fleshing out the cultural landscape which existed around this centre, including the location of a prominent service kindred, a patronized religious house and a place of seasonal assembly in the Heyny *oireacht*.

Physical expression of Baile na Gáile
One of the complementary sources that can be brought to bear in this area is the combined topographical data acquired from OSi and TII. Inspecting the wider area around Galey has facilitated the identification of at least nine unrecorded circular or sub-rectangular earthworks ranging west from Galey, with survey data covering an incomplete *c.*5km² area incorporating the modern village of Knockcroghery back to Lough Ree (Fig. 6.8). Merging this with the recorded monuments in the same area raises the total number of earthworks to sixteen. The recorded monuments are nearly exclusively categorized as ringforts.

The location of these discovered enclosures is concentrated particularly to the south-east, but all are in the vicinity of the village of Knockcroghery, which is likely to be the physical representation of the settlement recorded in the Mac Diarmada rights tract as *Baile na Gaille* and marked in Boazio's 1606 map *Irlandiæ accvrata descriptio* as 'B. Gally', effectively a mutation of the Irish *Baile (na) Gáile* (the settlement of the creek). *Baile* is used to describe a village [*vicus*] or other nucleated settlement in early seventeenth-century Ireland (Fig. 6.9). Due to the growing evidence for the continued use of ringforts by the Gaelic Irish into the later medieval period, the loose clustering of these enclosures may not be coincidental and could point to a form of Gaelic settlement nucleation, which when coupled with the place-name survival, and the closeness to Route 11, points to the presumed survival of *Baile na Gáile* as a hamlet or village through the later medieval period and beyond.

Literary attestation to this settlement being extant in the mid-fourteenth century can be seen with a reference to a *baile* near the site of the feast (*FÉGH*, 59), albeit Knott's translation of *baile* as 'town' is oversimplified. The fourteenth-century reality would be more consistent with the translation of it being a place of settlement or habitation, not in the form of a town as we would conceive it in the present sense (Ó hAisibéil 2018, 177). Accepting this, it can be concluded that there was a viable settlement located in the vicinity of Galey, somewhere near the modern village of Knockcroghery, while remaining at a slight geographical remove from the *cenn áit*. Tower houses of the late medieval period, as well as presumably their antecedents as lordly centres in the thirteenth and fourteenth centuries, were undoubtedly the focal points of their communities (Barry 2006, 30). However, at Galey, Callow Lough, and Ballaghdacker Lough, the elite centre is seemingly consciously located at a slight geographical remove from any associated nucleus of general settlement. Barry has concluded that these elite residences served as a social focus of the community, as opposed to being a physical community hub (ibid., 28), creating a deliberate break between the elite and the general populous. While there exists cartographic and pictorial sources from the sixteenth century and beyond depicting small clusters of huts surrounding late medieval tower houses (Nicholls 2008, 404–6), from the evidence provided here at least, this more realistically represents the domiciles of those who provided direct, daily service to the lordly residence, rather than denoting the physical community hub associated with the *cenn áit*.

Accommodating the host
Filidh Éreann Go Haointeach also indicates that the throngs of learned classes and entertainers that attended Ó Cellaig's feast at Galey were housed on temporary streets, erected specifically for the event (*FÉGH*, 57, 59, 61). This was undoubtedly a major undertaking on the part of Ó Cellaig, with such an accommodation designed to display his wealth and generosity, but it is not necessarily without comparison. Simms notes that Aodh Mór Ó Neill may have adopted a similar approach in managing an event at his chief residence in the late fourteenth century (Simms 1978, 91). While it is nigh on impossible to identify the archaeological expression of such a transient event

Riverine elite settlement in later medieval Uí Maine

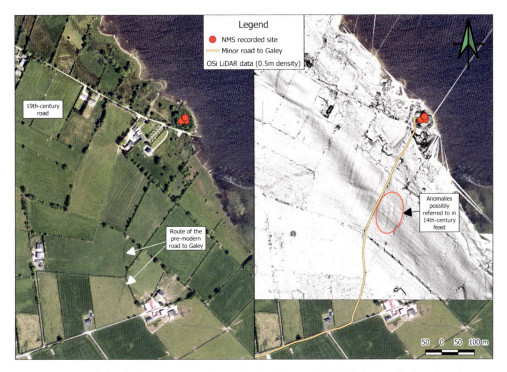

Figure 6.10 (left) The former approach to Galey. (right) LiDAR DTM shows a 'basket of eggs' arrangement to the east of the approach, possible evidence for what is described in stanzas 25–6 of *Filidh Éreann Go Haointeach* (data courtesy of OSi).

as this fourteenth-century feast, there are some subtle features visible in the DTM that may bear some relationship to the events described in the poem. These anomalous features follow the route of a now buried road and it could be speculated that these may be evidence of what is being described in stanzas 25–6:

> Such is the arrangement of them, ample roads between them; even as letters in their lines; in a crowded avenue.
>
> Each thread of road, bare, smooth, straight, firm within two threads of smooth, conical roofed houses (*FÉGH*, 59)

The modern road of approach to Galey was constructed at some point in the later nineteenth century, judging by its absence from the 1st Edition OS 6-inch map, but appearance on the later 25-inch map. The present road may have been constructed in order to provide access to the boathouse constructed adjacent to Galey in 1881 by the Crofton family of nearby Mote Park (Portrun 2019). Prior to the modern road, access to Galey was likely provided via a roadway that connects with Route 11 to the south of Knockcroghery. This route survives today in places as a local road as it initially branches off the N61, before transforming to grassland as it approaches Galey. Aerial photography of the area shows that the road can still be traced, visible as faint dark linear cropmarks, beneath the grass initially, before corresponding with a now established hedgerow. This road was still extant on the 1st Edition OS 6-Inch map. The anomalous features evident in the DTM to the immediate east of this hedgerow (*c.* 9m diameter each) may, very speculatively, correspond with the temporary habitations constructed for the feast (Fig. 6.10).

Ó Cellaig service kindreds and religious houses in the Heyny
The historical sources inform us that Seán Mór Ó Dubhagáin resided for the last seven years of his life at the hospital and religious house run by the Crutched Friars of St John the Baptist at Rindoon, *c.*5.5km from Galey (Breen 2009; O'Conor, Naessens and Sherlock 2015, 93), before passing away there in 1372 (*AU*; *AFM*). Historians have suggested that Ó Dubhagáin's importance to the Uí Chellaig was such that he either inspired, or actively originated and organized the feast at Galey in 1351 (Carney 2008, 690; Simms 2018b, 424). Considering the hereditary duties of his family as *ollamh seanchaí* to the Uí Chellaig lords, the fact that this prominent learned figure to the Ó Cellaig resided in his later years so close to one of their principal lordly centres is important to note.

In 1403, Conchobhar Anabaidh Ó Cellaig, lord of Uí Maine, died in *Loch Cróine* (*Ó CGF ii*, 67) and is also buried at St John the Baptist at Rindoon, where he had bestowed many benefits (*AC*; *ALC*). Younger sons of the senior Ó Cellaig line routinely supplied priors to this religious house, particularly in the mid-to-late fifteenth century (Genealogies 2011, 161). These references, coupled with other historical sources relating to the Anglo-Norman castle and town of Rindoon, confirm that by *c.*1320 the inhabitants of the town had deserted it and by the middle of that century the site had fallen into the hands of the Irish, most likely the Uí Chellaig, who were newly ascendant in Tír Maine. This change in circumstance may be consistent with the identified fifth archaeological phase of activity for the site, the so-called 'destruction phase' (O'Conor, Naessens and Sherlock 2015, 106; O'Conor and Shanahan 2018, 39). At the same time, the hospital continued to be supported and patronized by the Gaelic elite, particularly the Uí Chellaig lords, and they seem to have retained influence over this religious house until 1569 at least (Cronin 1980, 109).

Portrunny – Port Airchinnigh/Airchinneach, *an oireachtas assembly site for Galey*
Portrunny, *Port Airchinnigh* – the port of the *erenagh* (Connellan 1954, 55) is located on the western shore of Lough Ree, just to the south of the traditional limits of Tír Maine. The lacustrine/riverine characteristics of this assembly landscape are highly significant, coupled with its closeness to Galey, 1.5km to the south. The case for Portrunny being considered as a place of assembly in Tír Maine relates to two historical references, the first being an Ó Conchobair assembly in 1260 (*AC*) and the

Riverine elite settlement in later medieval Uí Maine

Plate 6.5 The ivy-covered remains of the medieval church at Portrunny (author's photograph).

second being an Ó Cellaig gathering documented in the early fifteenth century (*MacC*, s.a. 1406). Freeman, in his translation, mistakenly records the thirteenth-century assembly as occurring at Erenagh, Ballintober South barony, Co. Roscommon. However, it is referred to as being in Tír Maine. The alternative, and correct, location is revealed through an examination of the Irish. *Purt Airenaig* from the annalistic entry equates with *Port Airchinnigh/Airchinneach* (Portrunny townland, Kilmeane civil parish), as concluded by Revd Connellan (1954, 55). A bishop is mentioned in the entry, the bishop of Elphin, Máel Sechlainn or Milo Ó Conchobair, a junior member of the Síl Muiredaig dynasty, and five modern townlands in Kilmeane parish, including Portrunny, belonged to the aforementioned bishop (ibid.). Therefore, a seasonal assembly of the Uí Chonchobair took place at Portrunny in 1260, with the chosen venue indicative of their overlordship at this time over Tír Maine. The second attested use of Portrunny as a place of assembly occurred in 1406, with an assembly of the Uí Chellaig. Here, the annals refer to the assembly as an *oirechtus* (*MIA*). The *oireachtas* was a particular type of assembly activity in medieval Ireland. It was a habitual gathering of chiefs, their nobles and subjects for the purpose of conducting the business of the lordship. The *oireachtas* was usually convened at a fixed location in the lordship and corresponded primarily with dates in May – *Beltaine*, early August –

Plate 6.6 View east from medieval churchyard over Portrunny Bay, obscured by modern trees. This does, however, highlight the elevation and views that the church has over the bay at large (author's photograph).

Lughnasa, and November – *Samhain*, the time of the seasonal movement of cattle to and from summer pastures, and, in the case of *Lughnasa*, in order to mark the harvest (FitzPatrick 2004, 16; Swift 2017, 15).

Swift has recently argued that the historical entries relating to *oireachtas* gatherings should not be taken to indicate a specific type of assembly. Rather the terms used to describe these gatherings are outlining different functions undertaken as part of the overall event. Thus, an *oireachtas* was likely accompanied in reality by the provision of *cís agus cána/túarastla* (rent and tributes/stipends) and the other routine entertainments and activities that took place at the *óenach*. The *cís*, the rent or livestock/food render, came from the constituent communities within the overall lordship, while the transfer of goods (*cána/túarastla*) between lords was undertaken in order to create political alliances (Swift 2017, 11–17). These historical entries indicate that Portrunny was a place of *oireachtas* and general *óenach* gathering throughout the later medieval period. The initial thirteenth-century evidence links it to the Uí Chonchobair in their then expanded territory. The early fifteenth-century assembly was convened by the Uí Chellaig, who, as has been demonstrated, regained power over this region by the middle of the fourteenth century.

Portrunny Bay is a small, sheltered bay on the western shore of Lough Ree. The widest part of the bay measures *c.*430–500m from north to south and it is the next bay to the north of Galey. The water levels in the bay range from 60cm to an average depth of 6m (Portrun 2019). Portrunny is the only townland that presents with archaeological evidence that could be examined in relation to this area as a place of assembly. It possesses a small ecclesiastical complex including the remains of a church (Pl. 6.5), a house of indeterminate date, a holy well and a holy tree. The church site is located 170m from the shore itself, perched on a hill overlooking the bay (Pl. 6.6).

The holy well is dedicated to St Diarmuid of Inchcleraun, whose feast day was celebrated on 10 January (Ó Riain 2016, 263). Inchcleraun Island is located 3.3km east of the bay and is a large island with the remains of a substantial church complex on Lough Ree. Logistically this bay could well have served as a suitable natural harbour providing access between the religious community on the island and the mainland, perhaps resulting in the St Diarmuid connection.

The manifestation of this assembly is difficult to reconstruct. However, the physical setting of the gathering, approaching the relatively shallow Portrunny Bay, may have lent itself to ceremonial and commercial activity that incorporated the characteristics of the natural harbour. These large bodies of water are, in some instances, a part of *óenach* celebrations in medieval Ireland, perhaps even associated with livestock purification rituals (MacNeill 2008, 67; O'Flaherty 2014, 12). From a commercial perspective, the rent and tribute, in the form of livestock, provided to the lord at these gatherings may have been quickly traded, or processed into their resources at the postulated butchery and tanning complex indicated by the place-names of nearby Cornamart, Corboley, Curraghalaher and Longnamuck, with a view to trade or transportation utilizing the River Shannon and Lough Ree. An early fourteenth-century legal treatise by Giolla na Naomh Mac Aodhagáin refers to live cattle being traded from a boat and Kelly has theorized that, due to the provenance of the treatise being most likely in eastern Connacht, it may be describing trade on the River Shannon, thus highlighting the likely routine trade in both live cattle and their resources at sheltered bays such as Portrunny on Lough Ree (Kelly 2016a, 49; 2020, 169).

In appraising Portrunny as a site of assembly, its political and geographic characteristics must also be considered. This site is located very close to the boundary between Tír Maine and Machaire Connacht. Ó Riain highlights the societal value placed on the hosting of communal assemblies at territorial boundaries and even the logistical value of neighbouring communities using the gathering in order to trade, strengthen dynastic or familial ties, renew peace or wage war (Ó Riain 1972, 24; 1974, 67). FitzPatrick has also discussed the transition of assembly and inauguration practices in some cases away from prehistoric funerary monuments and to religious establishments (FitzPatrick 2003, 77; 2004, 174, 227, 229) and these characteristics are also readily apparent at Portrunny. To conclude, the historical evidence available

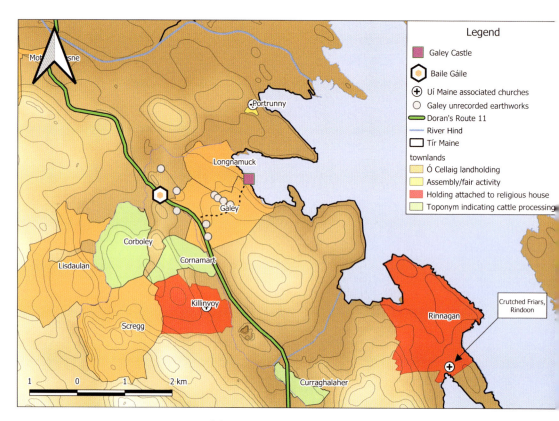

Figure 6.11 Summary of the Galey case study, with the principal locations outlined.

for Portrunny, coupled with its proximity to Galey and the topographical and the geopolitical character of the bay, provide a strong case for this site being an important *oireachtas* and *óenach* location for the later medieval Ó Cellaig lords, particularly as they returned to prominence in their ancestral *trícha cét*. The convention of a seasonal fair at Portrunny seems to have fallen out of use by the early seventeenth century, as the first patent issued to hold a fair at nearby Knockcroghery was granted to Colla O'Kelly during the reign of James I of England (Anon. 1853, 106).

This combination of lordly centre, semi-nucleated settlement, assembly place and patronized religious house, along with its centrality in relation to overland and riverine communication routes, presents Galey as a very prominent *cenn áit* for the Ó Cellaig elites, from the mid-fourteenth century through to the end of the medieval period and beyond. It is interesting to catalogue these various elements, which indicate that this *cenn áit* was ordered in what could be described as 'dispersed nucleation', in the sense that while this lordly centre is not tightly arranged geographically, many of the key features of later medieval lordship were to be found in the immediate hinterland around the focal point of Galey. The ordering of the elite landscape in this manner is

Riverine elite settlement in later medieval Uí Maine

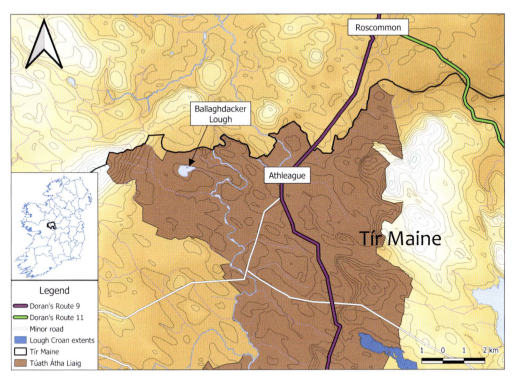

Figure 6.12 Location of Athleague in the *oireacht* of *Túath Átha Liaig*, close to the northern boundary of Tír Maine. Boundaries of these territories in *c.*1400, defined after Nicholls (1969) and MacCotter (2014).

not limited to Galey and this characteristic is also apparent at Lough Croan, Callow Lough and Ballaghdacker Lough/Athleague lordly centres. The possible reasons for this will be considered in Chapter 8.

ATHLEAGUE, CO. ROSCOMMON

The Athleague lordly centre has been identified as a location of interest, due to its presence on the historical record as a principal and highly-prized location within the Ó Cellaig lordship throughout the later medieval period. By the fifteenth century, Athleague was located within the *oireacht* of *Túath Átha Liaig*, close to the northern boundary of Tír Maine (Fig. 6.12). The defining physical feature in this area is the River Suck. Athleague (*Áth an liag* – ford of the stones) is located on one of a number of important fords along this river, around which settlement activity developed. Athleague served and continues to serve as one of a number of settlements located on the main Ballinasloe to Roscommon road, the effective descendant of Route 9, and as a bridging point between the southern and northern parts of the modern county. Exploring this riverine *cenn áit*, and the environment surrounding it, is key to understanding how this Gaelic lordship operated over the course of the whole period.

The natural environment and toponymy around Athleague
A series of fords punctuate the river in this area, chief among them Athleague, Ballyforan, *Áth Nadsluaigh* and the ford at Mount Talbot, formerly known as *Béal an átha* (the ford mouth), *Bhéal an Átha Uí Cheallaigh* (Ó Cellaig's ford mouth) and later *Cluain na gCloidhe* (the walled or ditched meadow) (Connolly 2014, 6, 9). The antecedent place-name of Mount Talbot, coupled with the townland names surrounding it, such as Cloonakilleg – *Cluain na coill' leaga* (lawn of the stony wood), Creeharmore – *Criathar mór* (great morass), among others, indicate a landscape characterized by woodland, in the form of the woods of Athleague, as well as bogland, and areas where travel was restricted, as the dominant aspect of this landscape. In general, the townlands become much larger immediately to the west of the River Suck in this region, by comparison with the townlands in the later medieval parishes of Taghboy and Tisrara, a clear indication of the more limited nature of these townlands in terms of being able to sustain populations in the district.

The limited nature of this area in terms of access and settlement as it extends west from the River Suck in the pre-modern period is strongly evident in the archaeological remains. Mapping the ringfort distribution indicates a general paucity of sites (Fig. 3.2), which is due to the vast expanses of bogland that dominate from Athleague in the north to Ahascragh and Ballinasloe to the south. It is likely, under these circumstances, that the modern route (N63) connecting Athleague to Mount Talbot, Ballygar, Newbridge, Mountbellew and onwards to central Galway, is actually a continuation of a long-established access route. The route has effectively chosen itself, as the higher value land facilitates easier transfer through an area that is characterized by these large areas of bog and woodland. The annual winter floods of the Suck Callows further limit the use of the area immediately adjacent to the river and this landscape is characterized by a series of small tributary rivers and streams such as the Shiven, Castlegar, Cloonlyon and Bunowen/Ahascragh Rivers that feed into the larger river. The centre of Athleague village is located where three townlands meet. These are named Athleague, Glebe (denoting land attached to a religious house) and Cloonykelly – *Cluain Uí Chellaig*, which indicates an Ó Cellaig landholding.

Historical background of later medieval Athleague
Athleague is the shortened form of the place-name *Áth Liag Maonagáin*, which refers to a St Maonagán of Athleague (Ó Riain 2016, 449). It is possible that the remains of the presumed later medieval parish church, located in Glebe, on the western bank of the River Suck adjacent to the bridge, had an early medieval precursor, which could be the foundation associated with Maonagáin. One of the earliest historical attestations

to Athleague is ecclesiastical in nature, and occurs in 1235. It tells us that 'The church of *an Druimne* at Athleague was burnt, with the charters and all the books of the Canons' (*AC*). This may be the reason why there is no surviving evidence on site of the early medieval ecclesiastical foundation, as it was plausibly built over in the aftermath of the fire. Athleague is recorded for a second time in the thirteenth century (1266), due to the death of a prominent prior of Roscommon and Athleague, Mael Isa Ó hAnainn (*AC*). This reference is used to attach the religious house to the order of Augustinian Canons and it seems to have ceased to exist by 1466 (Gwynn and Hadcock 1970, 158). A series of eighteenth- and nineteenth-century O'Kelly grave memorials, as well as the remains of a late medieval Ó Cellaig inscribed graveslab, indicate that the old parish church and graveyard at Athleague was an important traditional Ó Cellaig burial place in the area (Timoney, M.B., pers. comm.).

Moving later into the thirteenth century, Athleague was one of the districts in the King's Cantred of Tyrmany which was granted to an Anglo-Norman baron, Richard de Exeter, when he was given fifty librates[3] of land in 1280–1 within which he constructed a castle at Athleague (Walton 1980, 478–9). This castle is regarded as being destroyed by the Irish by 1284, after which de Exeter gave up custody of the royal castles of Roscommon and Rindoon (ibid.). The form and location of this castle is not known, however, the most likely position for it in the landscape is adjacent to the ford which gives Athleague its name. This is the first attested fortification at Athleague and this construction, if located where suggested, is possibly the first of a series of building phases to take place here. In 1337, Toirrdelbach Ó Conchobair, king of Connacht, built a stronghold or *foslongphort* at Athleague for defence against Edmund de Burgh (*AC*). However, later that year Toirrdelbach was defeated, wounded and taken prisoner by the Uí Chellaig, as well as having his horses and armour plundered and many of his men killed (*AC*). Perhaps this was in response to the construction at Athleague, which was located in the contested borderlands of Tír Maine. If so, these events may constitute further evidence of the grappling for control of Athleague that was taking place throughout the medieval period. From this point on, it can be concluded that Athleague was under the control of the Uí Chellaig.

Further evidence for the establishment of Athleague as an Ó Cellaig *cenn áit* survives for the late fourteenth century and the beginning of the fifteenth century. The late fourteenth-century praise poem, *Fa a urraidh labhras leac Theamhrach* [It is beneath a rightful ruler that the stone of Tara speaks], in praise of Maolsechlainn Ó Cellaig, refers to the Uí Chellaig as 'the fierce warriors of Athleague' (Ó Raghallaigh, C., pers. comm.). The Ó Cellaig genealogies in *Leabhar Ua Maine* record the death in 1410 of Tadhg Ó Cellaig, lord of Uí Maine, who died at *Áth Liag Maonagáin* (*Ó CGF ii*, 67). Tadhg presumably died in his own residence, located by the river ford. Two late

---

[3] A librate is defined as a unit of land with an annual value of one pound, with an area of 4 oxgangs of 13 acres each.

fifteenth-century entries highlight the continued presence of Ó Cellaig elite residence at Athleague. The *badhbhdhúin* of Athleague is described as being destroyed in 1487 (*AFM*), indicating that by this time there was an enclosing structure, which could have been constructed of stone or organic material around the stronghold. At this point, and through analogy with the presence of the fifteenth-century castle at Callow Lough, it can be argued that this bawn was part of a larger *cenn áit* complex at Athleague.

Athleague Castle is attested to in 1499, as part of a leadership struggle between branches of the Ó Cellaig family (*AFM*). The very end of the fifteenth century saw Athleague captured by Gearóid Mór Fitzgerald, earl of Kildare and justiciar of Ireland, and taken from the 'sons of William O'Kelly', who were sent west across the River Suck. It was recaptured by Mac William Burke in the same year and he delivered it up to a different branch of the dynasty, Maolsechlainn mac Tadhg mac Donnchadh Ó Cellaig of *Loch an Dúin*, the newly installed lord of Uí Maine. Sir Thomas le Strange was leasing Athleague Castle from Elizabeth I from as early as 1573 and it remained part of the le Strange possessions until at least 1596 (Nicholls (transcribed) 1573, 2019; *Compossicion*, 167; Cronin 1980, 110, 117). A fiant from 1578 records a pardon for 'Mellaghlen O Kellye, Wm. O Kellye, and Brien McRowrie, of Alieg' which indicated that the Uí Chellaig did not disappear from Athleague after le Strange's arrival (*Fiants* II, 438 [3221]). The fortified house extant on the site was possibly constructed by the earl of Clanricarde, who seems to have taken control of Athleague in *c.*1617 ('Clanricard letters', 167; Simington (ed.) 1949, 103). However, it is also possible that one of the le Strange owners of the estate could have constructed the fortified house in the very late sixteenth century or the early years of the seventeenth century.

The archaeology of the Athleague cenn áit
At the core of the Athleague lordly centre two elements of elite settlement are discernible from the historical record which can be ascribed to the Ó Cellaig. As we have seen, Athleague is historically attested as a lordly centre from the thirteenth century onwards, passing from Anglo-Norman hands through to Gaelic Ó Conchobhair, then Ó Cellaig hands, and finally English le Strange and Clanricarde control by the mid-seventeenth century. All of this building and habitation has left the focal point of activity, Athleague Castle, very much changed from its later medieval form (Pl. 6.7).

Athleague Castle
The surviving remains are that of a fortified house of likely very late sixteenth- or early seventeenth-century date. Fortified houses, a form of castle partly influenced by architectural principles linked to the Renaissance, date from the very late sixteenth century, with the last ones being built in the late 1640s (Craig 1982, 128–31; Sweetman 2000, 173–93; O'Conor 2007, 191; Lyttleton 2013, 108–60). The earliest example of a fortified house in Roscommon dates to *c.*1580 (Murphy and O'Conor

Riverine elite settlement in later medieval Uí Maine

Plate 6.7 Fortified house at Athleague Castle, Co. Roscommon (author's photograph).

2008, 29–35). The house stands as a rectangular three-storey structure with an attic, with internal dimensions of 15.3m north/south by 6.1m east/west, of which just the northern and southern gables survive complete. Rectangular towers, each of three storeys and an attic, with internal dimensions of 5.4m north/south by 5.1m east/west, are attached to the north-eastern and south-eastern angles with gables on the eastern and western walls, fireplaces on the western walls and windows on the other walls. This fortified house is described by Craig as both a U-plan building and a rectangle-plus-flankers building, with the architecture focused more on a pleasing aesthetic than defensive advantage (Craig 1976, 25; 1982, 128; Pl. 6.8).

While the masonry remains at Athleague hide much of its later medieval character, some traces do survive. The fortified house retains some punch-dressed building stones (Pl. 6.9). While punch-dressed stone does occur within a few fortified houses (Murphy and O'Conor 2008, 27), it is mostly associated with tower houses and friaries. This perhaps presents evidence for the recycling of stone and hints that the historically attested late fifteenth-century castle at Athleague was a tower house.

Recent remote sensing investigations undertaken immediately to the east of the castle remains has uncovered a complex arrangement of buried masonry structures, which appear to represent the former presence of an inner and outer bawn

Plate 6.8 Aerial image of the fortified house known as Athleague Castle. The two projecting towers flank a ruined rectangular building, which was located centrally, between the pair of chimney stacks (image courtesy of Carl Bryer).

surrounding the castle (Hall F., pers. comm.). This would have considerably altered the appearance of the site by comparison to how it survives today.

The bódhún *of Athleague*

The area surrounding the castle shows evidence of substantial earthworks, traces of which survive for inspection. Post-medieval and modern cartographic sources provide a better impression of what this site once possessed and record Athleague Castle as being surrounded by the redirected waters of the River Suck. The Strafford Survey map shows Athleague located at a loop on the river, with the castle and a mill sited on an island-type enclosure demarcated by both the Suck and a wet ditch (Fig. 6.13). To date, Murphy has been the only modern scholar to even remark on this substantial earthwork surrounding Athleague Castle (Murphy 2003, 46).

Riverine elite settlement in later medieval Uí Maine

Plate 6.9 Punch-dressed stone from within the fortified house of Athleague Castle, towards top centre of image. This was one of two such pieces incorporated into a first-floor fireplace in the north-western tower of the castle (author's photograph).

The wet ditch surrounding the castle has now silted up extensively, but traces survive in the form of a narrow drain, which broadly follows the same course of the earlier earthworks. However, the Bog Commission map of the district (Griffths 1809–14; Fig. 6.14) and the later OS 25-Inch and Cassini 6-Inch maps (Fig. 6.15 [a–b]) all indicate the survival of this wet ditch into the nineteenth century, with the latter two sources showing it in greater detail. Both of the more modern maps mark out an area of $c.21,950m^2$ that is demarcated by this ditch. The only point of access on to this 'island' was located close to the eastern end of the bridge across the River Suck. The measurements from these maps indicate that the ditch measured $c.8m–9m$ in width along most of its course and the ditch in the north-eastern corner seems to be cut to create a flanking defensive feature (Fig. 6.15; Pl. 6.10), making it a very substantial and complex earthwork with defensive functions, much more than what would be required just for a race to serve a mill complex.

This wet ditch therefore appears to have served either a contemporaneous dual role of defensive ditch and millrace for the occupants and lords of the castle, or possibly the ditch was constructed initially for the purpose of protection, with the secondary

Figure 6.13 Athleague Castle in its wider landscape setting, taken from the Strafford Survey map c.1636. Note the presence of an 'island' on the River Suck at Athleague (courtesy of the National Archives of Ireland: http://downsurvey.tcd.ie/down-survey-maps.php#c=Roscommon, accessed 16/11/2023).

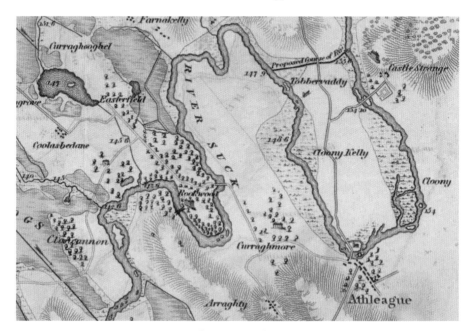

Figure 6.14 Bogs Commission map of the district of Athleague. Note the siting of Athleague Castle within a moated 'island' on the River Suck (Griffiths 1809–14).

Riverine elite settlement in later medieval Uí Maine

Plate 6.10 The silted up remnants of the flanking defensive section of the *bódhún* ditch during high water levels as it flows into the more recently cut drain (left of image). The degraded remains of an internal bank are also faintly visible, which would have been more substantial, and continued over the course of the *bódhún* ditch (author's photograph).

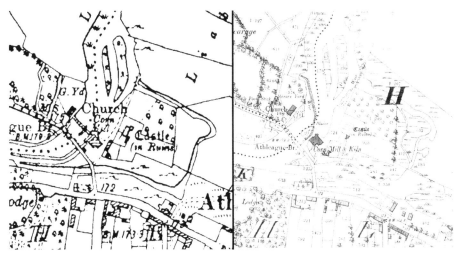

Figure 6.15 The wet ditch at Athleague Castle, as per the Cassini 6-inch [a] and Historic 25-inch [b] maps. The ditch was cut to accommodate flanking defence on the north-eastern side of the earthwork, providing cover over the earlier overland route north through the region.

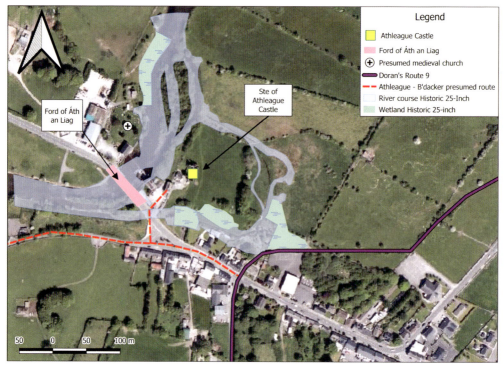

Figure 6.16 *Bódhún* of Athleague, after the OS Historic 25-inch map. Note the pre-modern routeway (Route 9) through the settlement of Athleague, consistent with the archaeological remains of a road-road/trackway at (RO041-048009-).

role of millrace occurring later in its history (Fig. 6.16). That being the case, it is possible that this earthwork was of some antiquity.

The presence of this wet ditch surrounding what was the focal point of lordly settlement at Athleague throughout the later medieval and post-medieval periods suggests this earthwork is the physical manifestation of the historically attested fifteenth-century *badhbhdhúin* (*bódhún*) of Athleague. Comparing it with the evidence of a wet ditch demarcating the promontory at Callow (Fig. 5.20), also described as a *bódhún*, enables us to theorize on what the archaeological character of these *bódhún* might have been more generally in later medieval Ireland. It is possible that their main use was as a very large enclosure (much larger than a normal castle courtyard or bawn) attached to and associated with the Gaelic lordly residence, the primary role of which was to contain and protect the chief's large herds of cattle from raiding. The areas that are enclosed at both Callow (*c.* 14,820m^2) and Athleague (*c.* 21,950m^2) would enable the sheltering of substantial herds, which we know were both a major economic generator and an important status symbol among these Gaelic lords. It is important to note that the 1st Edition OS 25-Inch map records a 'Fair Green' 220m to the east of

Riverine elite settlement in later medieval Uí Maine

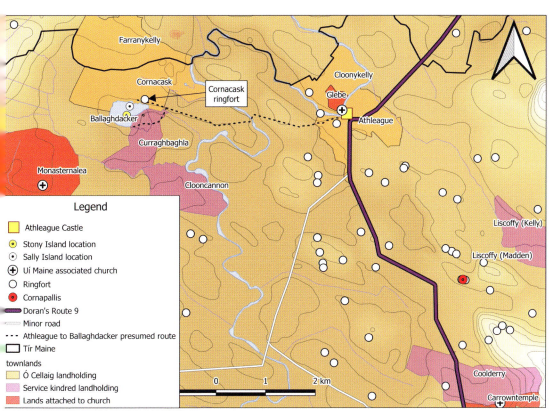

Figure 6.17 Summary of the Athleague and Ballaghdacker Lough case study, with principal locations outlined.

the *bódhún* earthwork at Athleague and the earl of Clanricarde was granted a patent to (re)establish two fairs at Athleague in 1635, possibly indicating that Athleague was the location for a bi-annual fair of long standing (Anon. 1853, 105, 143).

***

While one would expect that the intersection between navigable waterways and overland communication routes would provide the prime location around which later medieval settlement would take place, in the case of the Ó Cellaig lordship, this has never previously been satisfactorily addressed by research. What can be concluded from this chapter is that the river fords of this study area, as well as the sheltered bay at Galey and its closeness to a nearby terrestrial routeway, possess a number of attributes that make them particularly suitable as the physical community hubs of Uí Maine. In some instances they developed as a means of exploiting the natural communication and trade routes provided by the river (see McAlister 2019, 90–159). They also seem to have developed close to, or at, the intersection between overland routes and waterways, often at a fording place along the river, and this brought with it economic potential and presumably the ability to exact tariffs also (ibid., 109–21). The elite settlement forms found at these riverine *cenn áiteanna* again indicate that Ó Cellaig lordly centres remained relatively fixed through time, possibly through a combination of environmental determinism and the symbolism inherent in a multigenerational presence within the landscape. At Athlone, and earlier at *Dún Leodha/Áth Nadsluaigh*, the elusive form and location of the mid-twelfth-century *caistél* were discussed, along with what came before and after. At Galey, a natural promontory into Lough Ree was modified to greatly increase its defensibility and the focal point of the site in the fourteenth century, at least, was a substantial dry-stone built *cathair*/cashel enclosure. This cashel was reused as the effective bawn for a fifteenth- or early sixteenth-century tower house, replicating the trend of tower houses being constructed at identifiable earlier Ó Cellaig lordly centres, something that also occurs at Athleague. Once more, I have found the archaeological expression for the *bódhún*, and with two morphologically similar examples now extant, at Athleague and at Callow, it is possible to suggest that this earthwork should be considered as a monument type of its own and worthy of exploration in its own right. There is now also a growing body of evidence to suggest that there may have been a distinction created between the physical settlement focal point of the population at large and the space occupied by elite residence within the lordship. This separation of the public from the private with regard to the *cenn áiteanna* of the Ó Cellaig lords is an intriguing discovery and the reasons for this will be theorized at greater length in Chapter 8.

CHAPTER SEVEN

Elite settlement sited on major roadways in later medieval Uí Maine

The siting of elite Ó Cellaig settlement in close vicinity to major terrestrial routes, at first, seems obvious and that these would have been routine locations to find important lordly centres. Thus far, however, the areas under inspection have indicated that access to major roadways was only one of a number of factors involved in the siting of a lordly centre and in many cases it was of secondary importance. Nevertheless, in this chapter focus will turn to the *cenn áiteanna* which were sited on roadways, through analysing three locales – Aughrim, Co. Galway, the elite settlement sites of the expanded fifteenth- and sixteenth-century Ó Cellaig lordship in central Galway, and, briefly, Lisdaulan, Co. Roscommon. In doing so, I will treat with the locations which seem to have been primarily chosen as Ó Cellaig lordly centres because of the economic value provided by proximity to an overland communication route.

AUGHRIM, CO. GALWAY

Aughrim village is traditionally regarded as an important part of the Uí Maine landscape. An indenture from 1589 refers to the place as *Agherrymymany* (Aughrim Uí Maine) (Curtis 1935, 137) and this is also seen with a 1602 historical reference (*AFM*). The village name-stone proudly refers to the location as *Eachdruim Uí Cheallaigh*. The place was elevated to national importance due to its inextricable links to the events of 22 July 1691, the Battle of Aughrim during the Williamite War. However, the origins of this settlement seem to be closely tied to the fortunes of the later medieval Uí Chellaig kings and, later, the lords of Uí Maine. Aughrim was the focal point of an *oireacht* known in the *Compossicion* as 'Toehavreny', Tuahavriana – *Túath an Bhrenaidh*, located within the *trícha cét* of Uí Maine (*Compossicion*, 169; Nicholls 1969, section 42; Fig. 7.1).

Historical background of Aughrim
Aughrim – *Eachroim* (horse ridge) is located 7.4km to the south-west of Ballinasloe. Nearby is the early medieval church site of Kilcommadan – *Cill Chumadáin* (Comadán's church), and the coarb of Comadán of Kilcommadan is regarded as one

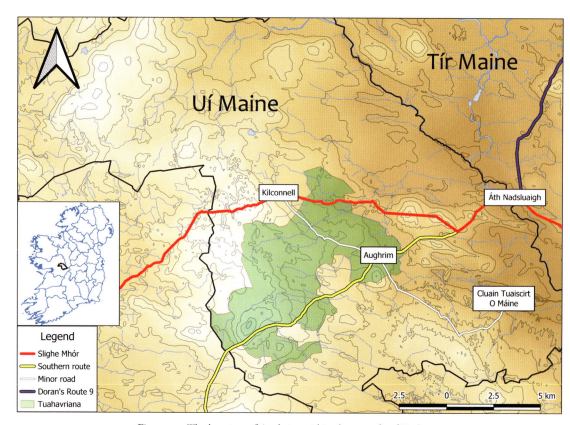

Figure 7.1 The location of Aughrim within the *oireacht* of Tuahavriana.

of the seven principal coarbs of Uí Maine (*Nósa*, 538). St Comadán has a well named for him locally and a fair day on 14 October (Ó Riain 2016, 215). The settlement of Aughrim is likely to be of some antiquity. One of the earliest references to Aughrim occurs with the murder of Bishop Máel Dúin in the early ninth century. At this point Aughrim was a Clonmacnoise-dependent ecclesiastical establishment west of the River Suck (Byrne 2004, 252). It is clear, therefore, that Aughrim was the site of a religious foundation from at least as early as the latter century and it most likely developed in part due to its proximity to the routeway that passed through this landscape. In fact, Aughrim seems to have grown up around a crossroads. The east-west route discussed earlier, referred to as the 'Southern Route', seems to have been crossed by a route running south from Kilconnell, thus connecting it with the *Slighe Mhór*. This is identifiable with the modern L3413, while the local road heading south from Aughrim, through Kilcommadan, on to the crossroads of Callaghan's Loughs, 5.9km distant, is likely to be a route of long standing also, providing eventual access on further east to the religious foundation of Cluain Tuaiscirt O Máine (Fig. 7.1).

Elite settlement sited on major roadways in later medieval Uí Maine

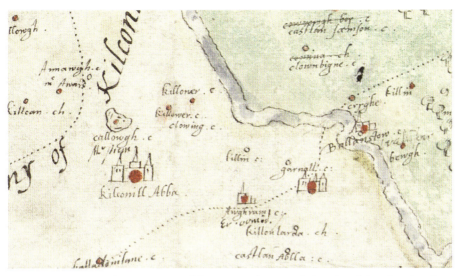

Figure 7.2 Section of Browne's *Map of the province of Connaught* (1591) with 'Awghram' in the centre of the image (copyright The Board of Trinity College Dublin, 2011).

Uí Chellaig links with Aughrim are firmly established by the early thirteenth century, with the death of Domnall Mór Ó Cellaig, king of Uí Maine. Domnall Mór died in 1224 'in his own bed' at *Eachdruim* (Nicholls 1969, 41). This is the first reference to Aughrim as a place of residence for an Ó Cellaig king. The continued Ó Cellaig presence in the vicinity of Aughrim is seen beyond the lifetime of Domnall Mór Ó Cellaig. As noted, 'Mac Domnall Mhór Ó Cellaig of Kilconnell' – Conchobhair Ó Cellaig – is referred to on a list of the kings summoned by Henry III in 1244 on his expedition against Scotland. This indicates that the Ó Cellaig elite remained in power in the *trícha cét* until the middle of the thirteenth century (*Foedera*, 150). The year for the Ó Cellaig loss of control at Aughrim may be consistent with the details of the provisioning of an English army led by the justiciar John Fitz Geoffrey in 1249, at *Athtruim in Connacht*, the description of which implies a substantial force in the area (*CIRCLE, Henry III*, 4). Authority over this area transferred from Gaelic Irish hands into Anglo-Norman as the thirteenth century progressed and the Ó Cellaig interactions with Aughrim amounted to their attempts to create obstacles to the de la Rochelle and Butler settlement there, and in the with the cantred of Omany, during the early years of the fourteenth century. The next historical reference to Aughrim is from the late sixteenth century. Ceallach Ó Cellaig, lord of Uí Maine, was in possession of 'Achrim' Castle in 1574 (Nolan 1900–1, 120), while his son Feardorcha seems to have resided here also (*Acts Privy Council*, xvii, 233–5). Aughrim Castle is also marked on the 1591 Browne map of Connacht (Fig. 7.2). The Aughrim *cenn áit* is likely to correspond with the present castle remains located in the village today.

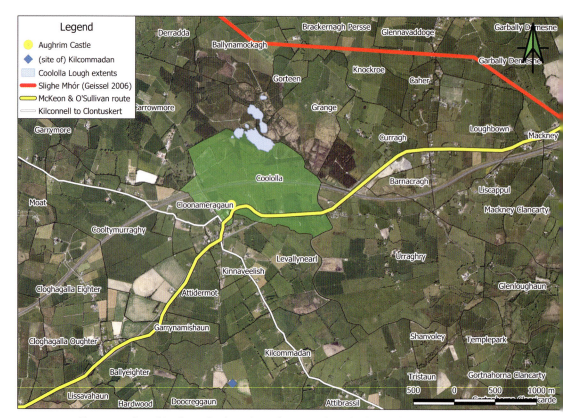

Figure 7.3 Site of Aughrim Castle in the wider east Galway landscape (base image: Bing Maps).

The Ó Cellaig cenn áit at Aughrim

The remains of the site known as Aughrim Castle (Alcock, de hÓra and Gosling 1999, 405) are located in Coololla townland immediately north north-east of the modern village. The castle site is described in the ASI database as an 'Anglo-Norman masonry castle' and is located at 58m OD, sited on ground broadly level with the surrounding area. It seems, therefore, that the site of this castle was not chosen for its commanding position. Possibly more important to the choice of location is what the 1st Edition OS 6-Inch map records as an older loop of the now R446 road that once passed directly through the settlement and in doing so passed immediately south of the fortification. The surrounding area, particularly to the south of the castle, is for the most part characterized by well-drained grassland, very suitable for agriculture. One exception to this is a zone of wetland and woodland, located 1km north of the site, where the nineteenth-century cartographic sources records a now largely drained lake known as Coololla Lough, which would have been unsuitable for settlement or farming activity,

Elite settlement sited on major roadways in later medieval Uí Maine

Plate 7.1 Aughrim Castle, Co. Galway (author's photograph).

but provided a sufficient physical deterrent to any attacking force from attempting an approach from the north-east. The wider landscape setting around Aughrim suggests that it developed as a place of importance not by its defensibility, rather from its attributes as a hub for trade, traffic and settlement within the landscape, being located at the junction of a number of regionally and locally important roadways (Fig. 7.3).

The earliest attested Ó Cellaig settlement at Aughrim isn't immediately identifiable in the archaeological record. If the residence of Domhnall Mór was located on the same site as Aughrim Castle, there are no features of this construction available for us to inspect today, as no above ground remains are visible in the vicinity of the later fortification. If one was to theorize how his residence might have looked, there are some examples in the immediate area, particularly at Loughbown I and Mackney, which provide clues. On comparison with these sites, Domhnall Mhór's residence in the 1220s may have been some form of cashel or ringfort. Analogy with the possible appropriation of a pre-existing Gaelic elite residence in Connacht and the construction of an Anglo-Norman castle can be seen with a series of sites identified in the Ó Dubhda lordship of Uí Fhiachrach Muaidhe (Malcolm 2007, 196–205).

The above ground remains at Aughrim Castle are primarily of an earthen character, coupled with some fragmentary masonry sections. These are located in the south-west

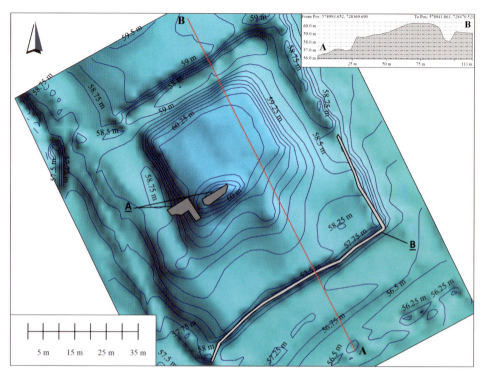

Figure 7.4 Contoured topographical plan and cross-section of the site of Aughrim Castle. The fragmentary masonry remains [A] correspond with that visible in Pl. 7.1. [B] indicates the outer enclosure where it is best preserved to the east and south of the site. Part of this enclosure ditch contains sections of mortared masonry (LiDAR data courtesy of TII).

corner of a rectangular elevated platform measuring *c.*35m on its long axis, *c.*24m on its short axis. This inner ward seems to have been the focal point of the site, and stands about 4m higher than the surrounding area. The masonry remains consist of the corner of an ivy-covered tower-like structure, surviving to first-floor level only, as well as a low section of wall, located immediately to the east of the tower. The two components are separated by a partially cobbled area, measuring 3.5m in width (Pl. 7.1; 7.3; Fig. 7.4). This suggests an entranceway guarded by a flanking tower providing access into the elevated rectangular platform.

To the south of this inner ward is a smaller raised area, *c.*27m long by *c.*16m wide. The masonry remains are located at the intersection between these two platforms. These central earthworks are surrounded by a large area of elevated ground, one measuring 74–5m in length on all axes. This outer ward is surrounded particularly to the north and south by a substantial ditch (maximum height 1.7m). Parts of the eastern section of this ditch are reveted with mortared masonry (Fig. 7.4; Pl. 7.2).

The surviving masonry remains are, however, much reduced from even the late seventeenth century. A miniature pictorial record survives of the castle, viewed from

Elite settlement sited on major roadways in later medieval Uí Maine 211

Plate 7.2 Outer enclosure ditch surrounding Aughrim Castle. Remains of mortared masonry in the eastern section of the enclosure ditch (author's photograph).

the south, as it stood at the time of the Battle of Aughrim in 1691. Sketched by Lieutenant Colonel Jacob Richards (Fig. 7.6), who served in the Williamite Army during the War of the Two Kings, Aughrim Castle is presented as a stronghold placed upon a raised earthen platform or low natural prominence. Located upon this elevated area was what appears to have been a stone curtain wall with two corner towers. A much higher third tower, of at least three, if not four, storeys, appears to be located within the enclosure. The surviving masonry remains on site today may correspond with the tower located on the left corner of the curtain wall as illustrated by Richards (Pl. 7.3).

In order to better understand the physical remains alongside the pictorial evidence, it was decided to complement the topographical plan with a Magnetic Gradiometry survey. This was conducted on a series of four 20m x 20m grids across sections of all three areas defined by the topographical plan. One of the major limiting factors in collecting a strong dataset from the Aughrim Castle site is the presence of a modern metal railing that surrounds a large memorial cross located within the inner ward (see Pl. 7.1). This object disturbed the dataset in this section of the survey area, as seen with the large contrasting black and white anomalies in the northern half of the survey image (Fig. 7.7).

Figure 7.5 Schematic plan of Aughrim Castle and an interpretation of the elevation data (LiDAR data courtesy of TII).

Despite this, there are a number of conclusions that can be made from the survey and applied to the site. Working in a possible reverse chronology, the red circles in Figure 7.7b correspond with what is likely to be dropped metal objects. Given that Aughrim Castle is a known battle site in the theatre of war in 1691, the uncovered features are likely to correspond to these events. The two hashed anomalies outlined conform to subtle features located to the south of the inner ward. The circular anomaly in the north-east of the survey measures 10m in external diameter and the linear itself has a thickness of c.1.7m. This may be the remains of a cylindrical corner tower located on the south-eastern corner of the inner ward. This anomaly, coupled with the surviving masonry remains on the south-western corner of the inner ward, may be the remains of a pair of non-identical corner towers, as illustrated by Richards. By contrast with the possible circular corner tower on the south-eastern corner, the masonry remains on the south-western end of the inner ward is likely to be a square, or sub-rectangular, corner tower, located adjacent to the cobbled entranceway into the inner ward. A rectangular anomaly was also uncovered through the survey, located in front of the inner ward entrance on the smaller raised area. It measures 13m on its long axis and 9m on its short axis. Due to its location in relation to the entranceway, this anomaly

Plate 7.3 Presumed entrance into the inner ward of Aughrim Castle, located between the degraded remains of a rectangular corner tower (left) and curtain wall (right) (author's photograph).

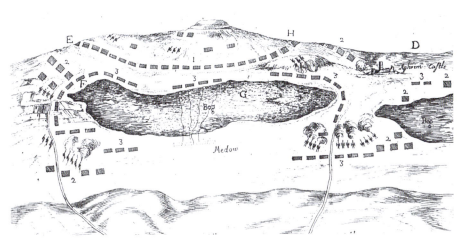

Figure 7.6 The Battle of Aughrim, illustrated by Jacob Richards, *c.*1691, with Aughrim Castle in the top right-hand corner (image courtesy of Dr Padraig Lenihan, University of Galway).

Figure 7.7 Magnetic Gradiometry survey at Aughrim Castle. Survey area 40m x 40m. Left [a] illustrates the survey and its position in relation to the surviving masonry remains. Right [b] provides an interpretation of the results (base image: Bing Maps).

could be the remains of a barbican gatehouse, constructed to provide additional protection to the castle entrance. More than this, a subtle circular anomaly, *c.*15m in diameter, marked by the white broken line in the south-eastern corner of the survey, appears to underserve the more substantial earthen remains on the site. It is difficult to say what this may represent, but it is worthy of further inspection. Finally, the partial survey of the inner ward is magnetically noisy and although the anomalies present no discernible pattern, they may represent the sub-surface remains of the tower illustrated in Richards' depiction of the Battle of Aughrim.

Combining the topographical plan with the results of the Magnetic Gradiometry survey enables a better understanding of the plan of Aughrim Castle. The topographical plan divides the site into three distinct areas, the outer ward, inner ward and the smaller platform immediately to the south of the inner ward. Access onto the site is difficult to deduce, however the proximity of the roadway to the south of the site implies that access to the castle precincts was facilitated via this road. Access into the inner ward is more concrete in its identification. This was likely located where the faced-off break in the masonry occurs between the south-western corner tower and the

Elite settlement sited on major roadways in later medieval Uí Maine 215

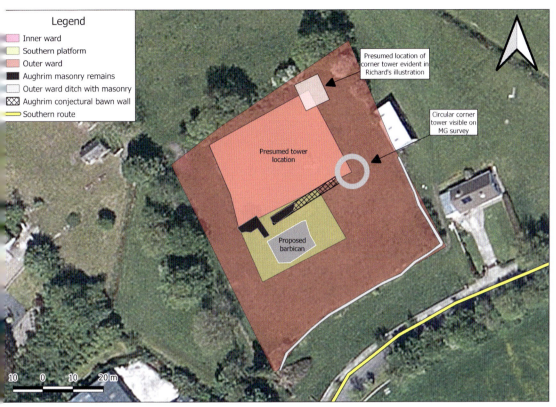

Figure 7.8 Summary interpretation of the remains at Aughrim Castle, based on the topographical plan, Magnetic Gradiometry survey, and late seventeenth-century illustration (base image: Bing Maps).

foundational remains of the curtain wall. The Magnetic Gradiometry survey provides evidence for what is likely to be a corner tower on the south-eastern corner of the curtain wall, as well as a rectangular structure, possibly a barbican gatehouse, located to the south of the inner ward (Fig. 7.7). Consultation of Richards' plan of the Battle of Aughrim seems to indicate that this curtain wall served to defend a tower which was located on the interior. No evidence survives from either survey that could be used to confirm a preceding phase or phases of construction at this site, which could be considered against the historical attestations for Richard de la Rochelle's thirteenth-century Anglo-Norman manor.

Richards' drawing shows a curtain wall with two flanking towers, possibly at its south-west and south-east angles. While rectangular flanking towers on curtain walls did exist on Anglo-Norman castles, as at Sligo Castle, being built in a phase dated to *c.*1310 (O'Conor 2002c, 189–90), curtain towers are normally round or D-shaped across western Europe during Anglo-Norman times from the late twelfth century into the fourteenth century (e.g., King 1988, 77, 92–3, 121). The appearance in Richards' drawing of the curtain wall suggests something later. There are hints of another tower at the back of the drawing, possibly the north-east corner tower. This suggests that there was a tower at each corner of the inner ward. If this is a tower house bawn, its plan is similar to that of Barryscourt Castle, Co. Cork (Sweetman 2000, 160; Pollock 2004, 162–3). Indeed, the thirteenth-century Cahir Castle in Co. Tipperary had two wards or bawns added to it in the fifteenth and sixteenth centuries (Sweetman 2000, 124). More locally, both Aughnanure and Fiddaun castles in Co. Galway have two wards or bawns surrounding the tower house (ibid., 166–9). Therefore, the combination of pictorial, LiDAR and field evidence suggests a very complex late medieval castle, probably of tower house form.

After the presumed reclamation post 1315 of Aughrim by the Uí Chellaig from the Butler lords, it is possible that the castle might have been reoccupied, but not greatly modified or added to. Parallels for this approach in Gaelic-occupied fortifications in fourteenth-century Connacht are seen with a lack of evidence for modification to sites such as Ballintober Castle (Ó Conchobair) (Loeber 2019, 18), Roscommon Castle (Ó Conchobair), Rindoon (Ó Conchobair and Ó Cellaig) and Athlone (Ó Cellaig), among others. Admittedly, though, societal and cultural practices among the Gaelic elite in this period did not advocate heavy modification of their newly acquired or reacquired fortifications, a trend that could also be suggested for Aughrim Castle. This aside, it is likely that from some point in the fifteenth or sixteenth centuries, the site of Aughrim Castle, as it survives in the pictorial and topographical remains, was constructed by a branch of the Uí Chellaig into a stronghold of tower house and bawn form. Given the site's centrality in the area and the absence of comparable remains in the immediate hinterland, it is quite likely that the site of Aughrim Castle was a fixed location of elite residence throughout the medieval period. This is something that can, however, only be confirmed through excavation. Conversely, what can be confirmed, is that the designation of the castle as an 'Anglo-Norman masonry castle' is misplaced and should be rectified on the ASI database.

THE FIFTEENTH- AND SIXTEENTH-CENTURY ELITE SETTLEMENT SITES OF THE WIDER Ó CELLAIG LORDSHIP

As has been elicited from the historical background, as well as certain elements discussed above, the area over which the Uí Chellaig lords presided did not remain fixed through time. By the latter end of the early medieval period their Uí Maine ancestors primarily operated out of Tír Maine. With the growing supremacy of the Uí Conchobhair dynasts over Tír Maine, and further afield, in the eleventh and twelfth centuries, the Uí Chellaig elite were eventually forced to migrate and subjugate the *trícha cét* of Sogain. This territory quickly became synonymous with the Uí Chellaig, with the resultant name change to Uí Maine. By the mid-thirteenth century, their power over this area was reduced by Anglo-Norman interests in Uí Maine, leading to an eventual return into Tír Maine, presumably beneath, and subject to, the Uí Conchobhair. But, by the mid-fourteenth century Ó Cellaig ambitions were on the rise once more, due in no small part to the power vacuum provided by the internal disputes among the Uí Conchobhair (Nicholls 2003, 170–5). At this time the authority of the Uí Chellaig began to expand beyond what was their traditional sphere of influence in, firstly, Tír Maine and then Uí Maine. Owing to the limitations of the natural boundary of the River Shannon and Lough Ree, territorial ambitions never realistically looked to the east. To the south, the powerful *Clann Ricaird* Burkes were not the most suitable opponents to aim their efforts at either. To the north, the Uí Conchobhair, although wounded and inward-looking, were still too powerful to be a suitable target either. With this in mind, the most fruitful locations into which the Uí Chellaig could attempt to expand their influence was over the area immediately to the west.

Ó Cellaig ambitions in Clantayg
Immediately to the west of Uí Maine was a region known variously in the pre-Norman period as Clann Taidg and Uí Diarmata (MacCotter 2014, 135). During the period under inspection, the lords of this area were the Anglo-Norman de Bermingham lords of Athenry, with the Gaelic Ó Mainnin lords also operating within the region, particularly in the area around their *oireacht* of 'Eraght O Mannyn' (*Compossicion*, 169), with its principal *cenn áit* of *Mionlach Ó Mainnín* – Menlough, Killoscobe civil parish, Co. Galway. This landscape is of mixed agricultural value, with the area dominated by large zones of wetland and woodland, interspersed by zones of fertile farmland. These landscape attributes are reflected in the large numbers of *cluain*, *doire*, *enach*, *coill* and similar names recorded among the place-names of the region (Joyce 1910, 233–6; 461–2; 491–3; 501–5). The principal *capita* of secular and ecclesiastical power in this area during the later medieval period were the de Bermingham town of Athenry and the twelfth-century, Gaelic-established, Cistercian foundation of Abbeyknockmoy (*Mainistir Chnoc Muaidhe*). While Abbeyknockmoy was founded by Cathal Crobhdearg Ó Conchobair in *c*.1190, by 1295 prominent members of the senior Ó Cellaig line were retiring and being laid to rest at the abbey (*AC*). Actions such as this, in the late thirteenth century, may indicate that the Uí Chellaig lords were attempting to compete with and emulate their more powerful neighbours through patronizing Abbeyknockmoy.

The first indication that the Uí Maine lords sought to expand their control outside their traditionally held boundaries is seen in the 1320s or 1330s, when Diarmaid mac Gilbert Ó Cellaig, lord of Uí Maine, hanged the Ó Mainnin chief of *Soghain*, after which he seized Ó Mainnin's 'castle' and estate of Clogher (*Tribes*, 107). The reference to 'Clogher' is regarded as Killaclogher, Monivea civil parish, Co. Galway (Mannion 2004, 38). Moving into the late fourteenth century, Uilliam Buide Ó Cellaig defeated the de Berminghams (Clann Mac Feorais) in 1372 (*AFM*). This clash is evidence of sustained incursions by the Uí Chellaig in Clantayg, in the area close to Athenry (Nicholls 1969, 47). The emergence of the Uí Chellaig as the dominant force in Clantayg seems to have been cemented by the early fifteenth century, considering that Tiaquin is described as the place of residence and death for Maolsechlainn Ó Cellaig, lord of Uí Maine, in 1401 (*Ó CGF*, 67). Tiaquin is also the site of an early Anglo-Norman castle (*AC, s.a.* 1266). The Uí Chellaig successfully established Tiaquin as a permanent powerbase by the early fifteenth century, a development that is corroborated by the evidence that one of Maolsechlainn's sons, Donnchadh Ó Cellaig, lord of Uí Maine, resided at Tiaquin during his reign (r. 1420–4) (*Tribes*, 118). This preference continues into the middle of the century, when the location is again referred to in relation to Ó Cellaig activities in 1461 (*AC*). *Teaqwyn* (Tiaquin) Castle is described as being in the possession of 'Melaghlin Okelly' in 1574 (Nolan 1900–1, 122).

The cenn áit *at Tiaquin*
This collection of historical evidence and archaeological remains indicates that the cantred of Clantayg was a key acquisition of the Uí Chellaig in the fifteenth century. Their principal headquarters were located at Tiaquin and Tiaquin Demesne retains evidence of what could have been a continuity of settlement activity through the fifteenth and sixteenth centuries. Four enclosures survive in the townland. The largest of these measures 44.5m east/west by 31.5m north/south (Fig. 7.9). It survives in only fair condition, with a bank and external ditch, and utilizes the height of its placement on the summit of a natural hillock to add significantly to its defensibility to the southwest. It is unclear if this was a settlement site used into the later medieval period, but its dimensions, relative defensibility and location within Tiaquin Demesne all increase the likelihood that this site was in use during the latter period. This may have been the residence of Maolsechlainn mac Uilliam Buide Ó Cellaig. Maolsechlainn is described in the original Irish as dying in 1401 *ina longphort féin*. O'Conor has referred to the use of the term *longphort* in the annalistic record, a term which seems to be used to describe a dry-land stronghold of cashel, ringfort or moated site morphology (O'Conor 1998, 85), something which, in this case, could also be argued for one of the monuments in Tiaquin Demesne.

The fifteenth century may also be the period during which the castle (Alcock, de hÓra and Gosling 1999, 417) was constructed. Categorized as a castle of unclassified form, due to the very fragmentary remains that survive of the site, Tiaquin Castle survives today as a rectangular platform standing *c.*1m above the surrounding ground level and measuring 24m by 10m, with some visible masonry rubble on the site. Despite the lack of diagnostic remains, it is possible, based on analogy with a number of other sites similarly categorized as castles of unclassified form encountered through the present research, that Tiaquin Castle may also have been a tower house.

Elite settlement sited on major roadways in later medieval Uí Maine

Figure 7.9 Aerial image and cross-section of the largest enclosure recorded for Tiaquin Demesne (image Source: GeoHive, OSi 2017).

Alternatively, it is conceivable that the thirteenth-century Anglo-Norman castle attested for Tiaquin was located at this site. In this light, Holland has demonstrated that quite a number of the thirteenth-century castles built east of Lough Corrib in Co. Galway were hall houses, with notable examples at Dunmore and Moylough (Holland 1997, 165–9). The hall house was often turned into a tower house in the late medieval period, when taken over by Gaelic lords. Vaults were routinely inserted over the first floor, as well as a ground-floor doorway. Occasionally, a third floor was also added. Sweetman noted that a series of Anglo-Norman hall houses in east Galway were modified and given tower house features during the late medieval period (Sweetman 2000, 92–3). This also happened at Shrule Castle in Co. Mayo (ibid., 97) and at Temple House Castle, Co. Sligo, in the fifteenth century, when the castle was under the control of the Uí Eadhra of Luighne (O'Conor and Naessens 2016b). It is therefore quite possible that the castle remains at Tiaquin once took the form of a tower house or remodelled hall house, during which time it would have conceivably served as one of the residences of Donnchadh Ó Cellaig, as well as the late sixteenth-century Maolsechlainn Ó Cellaig.

Plate 7.4 The early fifteenth-century tomb in the presbytery of Abbeyknockmoy (image courtesy of Martin A. Timoney).

Abbeyknockmoy and Ó Cellaig patronage
Indications of the Ó Cellaig supremacy in this area can be seen in a number of ways. In 1408, the death is recorded of Maurice Mac an Bhaird of *Cuil-an-úrtain*, described as the *ollamh* of the Uí Chellaig of Uí Maine (*AFM*; *ALC*). Cooloorta townland is located 4.5km to the east-north-east of Abbeyknockmoy and 10km to the north of Tiaquin (Ó Macháin 2023, 260). The location of the landholding of the Mac an Bhaird *ollamh* so close to a fifteenth-century Ó Cellaig *cenn áit* at Tiaquin highlights the intention to establish a permanent foothold in the area, as well as the level of security felt by the expansionist Uí Chellaig at that time. More than this, it is another instance of the trend of placing service kindred landholdings in the immediate surrounds of the *cenn áit* (FitzPatrick 2018, 173–87).

The Ó Cellaig patronage of Abbeyknockmoy is most readily seen with the building of the early fifteenth-century tomb to Maolsechlainn Ó Cellaig, lord of Uí Maine, and

Plate 7.5 Depiction of the 'Three Living and Three Dead Kings', Abbeyknockmoy (image source: History of Art Teaching Collection, Digital Image Collection, Trinity College Dublin).

his wife Fionola, with the tomb even worthy of an annalistic entry (*MacC, s.a.* 1402[1]). It was built into the north wall of the presbytery, in the location normally reserved for the founder's tomb (Pl. 7.4). Moss has indicated that while the tomb displays a devotion to John the Baptist that became current in fourteenth-century Ireland, it also exhibits deliberate anachronisms, which has been interpreted as the Uí Chellaig elite using material culture to confirm their rights to authority over this contested part of their now expanded territory (Moss 2015a, 204). This adoption of deliberate anachronisms is not limited to the tomb, in that the contemporaneous production of *Leabhar Ua Maine* is similarly antiquated in its style (ibid.). Of course, these archaisms have been shown to also be apparent in the settlement forms chosen by the Uí Chellaig, perhaps utilized in order to demonstrate long-standing legitimacy in being able to claim authority over Uí Maine and Tír Maine (O'Conor 2018, 164–5).

Further evidence of elite patronage, possibly also commissioned by Maolsechlainn Ó Cellaig, comes in the form of the now fragmentary wall paintings that once prominently adorned both the tomb surrounds as well as the areas immediately adjacent to the east. Above the tomb is a Crucifixion scene, while there is also a depiction elsewhere of a French morality tale, the 'Three Living and Three Dead Kings' (Pl. 7.5; Morton 2004, 342–6; Moss 2015a, 204).

Abbeyknockmoy's prominent place within this development of a *cenn áit* in the expanded lordship is not to be underestimated either. From the late fourteenth century onwards, the secular lords of Uí Maine, as well as the younger Ó Cellaig sons who went into the religious orders, heavily patronized the foundation (Smith 2014a), using their position to exercise authority over what must have been a wealthy resource in their expanded lordship. Abbeyknockmoy, and the nearby prominence of Knockroe [Glennaveel townland], were until recently the location for an annual pilgrimage and fair on 21 August, the day after St Bernard's Day. This is Bernard of Clairvaux, founder of the Cistercian order, yet it is quite likely that this date was chosen as a convenient new date for the pilgrimage in this area, due to its closeness to the traditional assembly of *Lughnasa*. MacNeill points out that this pilgrimage up Knockroe hill was part of a wider festivity centred on the settlement and religious lands of Abbeyknockmoy. These came in the form of a well-known and attended livestock fair and an early seventeenth-century royal charter survives which granted, or, more likely, regranted, permission to hold the annual fair at Abbeyknockmoy (MacNeill 2008, 128–31).

The tower houses of sixteenth-century Ó Cellaig Country
The historical background seems to indicate that the late fifteenth century was generally a period of decline among the Uí Chellaig, during which weakened and distant familial lines fought over the position of lord of Uí Maine. In spite of this

---

[1] Note the *Miscellaneous Irish Annals* are out by one year in this entry. All other sources record Maolsechlainn Ó Cellaig's death for the year 1401.

Elite settlement sited on major roadways in later medieval Uí Maine

Plate 7.6 Barnaderg Castle, Co. Galway, sixteenth-century tower house of the Uí Chellaig (author's photograph).

supposed discord, by 1504 Maolsechlainn Ó Cellaig, lord of Uí Maine, had constructed three castles, located at Garbally (*Garbh dhoire*), Monivea (*Muine an mheadha*) and Gallagh (*Gallach*), Co. Galway (*AFM*). These fortifications were recorded as being demolished by Ulick Fionn Burke of Clann Ricaird in the same year, but in and of themselves they indicate the wealth and resources still being utilized by the Uí Chellaig lords in this area at the beginning of the sixteenth century. Two further tower houses are located in the area and are claimed to have been constructed by the Uí Chellaig. These are Barnaderg Castle (Pl. 7.6) and Mullaghmore Castle. These are recorded in the 1574 list compiled for the Lord Deputy, Sir Henry Sidney, with *Bearnegarik* (Barnaderg) in the possession of 'Edmund Mc Melaghlin [O'Kelly]', and *Molloghmore* (Mullaghmore) in the possession of 'Tege Mc Wm Okelly' (Nolan 1900–1, 122).

The most westerly of the Maolsechlainn Ó Cellaig castles is Monivea. The site of Monivea Castle (Alcock, de hÓra and Gosling 1999, 415) is located in Monivea

Plate 7.7 Monivea Castle, Co. Galway, viewed from the north (image courtesy of Martin Curley).

Demesne, where the tower house structure was incorporated into a later country house, meaning that little is discernible from what survives. What remains today is a much-altered rectangular tower of three to four storeys, with external dimensions of 12.5m long by 9.5m wide, while the interior is now inaccessible (Pl. 7.7). One early, two light, flat-headed window survives on the east wall, but the remainder of the features appear to be of eighteenth- and nineteenth-century date.

Garbally is another castle of tower house form (ibid., 409; Pl. 7.9). Located in Garbally townland, it is the most centrally located of these three strongholds built by Maolsechlainn. The tower house does not have any evidence for a surrounding bawn, but it may be possible that the south-eastern limits of the small field that the castle is sited in today could conform to an older boundary around the site, perhaps the remnants of a bawn enclosure (Fig. 7.10).

The north-eastern wall and the adjoining sections of the north-western and south-eastern walls survive to the second floor, with the interior exposed (Pl. 7.8). The original pointed arch doorway survives at the eastern end of the south-eastern wall (Pl. 7.9; Fig. 7.11) and is defended by a murder-hole as well as a possible gunloop, located within a niche on its southern side. A narrow defensive window survives on

Elite settlement sited on major roadways in later medieval Uí Maine

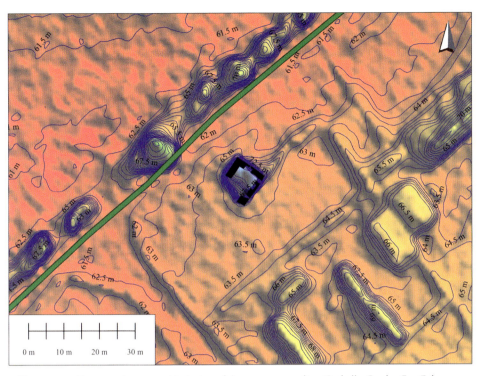

Figure 7.10 Contoured topographical plan of the area surrounding Garbally Castle, Co. Galway. The R339 regional road, marked in green, is likely the continuation of a long-established roadway through the region (data source: Bluesky Ltd).

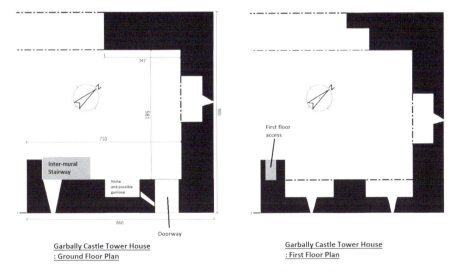

Figure 7.11 Plan of the surviving elements of the ground and first floors of Garbally Castle.

Plate 7.8 The remains of Garbally tower house, viewed from the south-west (author's photograph).

Plate 7.9 Original pointed doorway of Garbally Castle (author's photograph).

Plate 7.10 The two light ogee-headed window on the north-eastern wall, lighting the second floor, flanked by two narrow loops. Note a machicolation over this window, presumably accessed from the battlements on the castle roof (author's photograph).

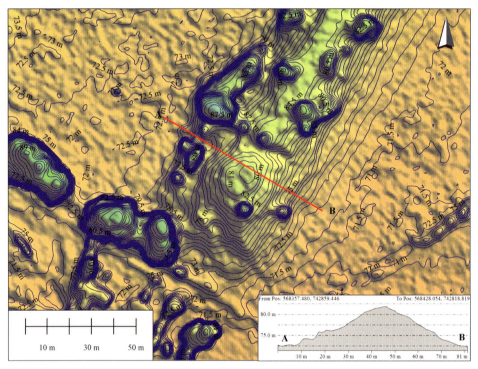

Figure 7.12 Contoured topographical plan and cross-section of the earthwork remains of Gallagh Castle, located as they are on the southern end of a small esker (data source: Bluesky Ltd).

Figure 7.13 Section of Browne's *Map of the province of Connaught* (1591) for the barony of Tiaquin. Gallagh Castle is located in the east of the barony. Garbally Castle is speculatively 'Garall', south of Mullaghmore Castle (Copyright The Board of Trinity College Dublin, 2011).

Plate 7.11 Site of Gallagh Castle, viewed from the south (author's photograph).

the north-eastern wall at ground-floor level and an intramural stairwell survives within the south-eastern wall, providing access to the first floor. A window opening is located in the stairwell. The first floor is more commodious, with evidence for four windows, but all are narrow slits, and one of these windows is ogee-headed (Plate 7.10). A wicker-centred, vaulted ceiling survives on this floor and the north-western wall retains evidence for an intramural stairwell which accessed the second floor. A two light ogee-headed window survives on the second floor, illuminating a large room. This was most likely the hall, due to its size and the fact that it was open to the roof, allowing for the use of a characteristic central hearth for feasting purposes (Sherlock 2011, 133; see Pl. 7.10). On the exterior of the surviving ogee-headed window on this floor there are the remains of a possible machicolation (Claffey 1983, 152–3; see Pl. 7.10; Fig. 7.11). Through its architectural remains, O'Keeffe dates Garbally Castle to the second half of the fifteenth century (O'Keeffe 2021, 193). Of the three tower houses, Garbally is the best surviving example.

The site of the third castle (Alcock, de hÓra and Gosling 1999, 409) is located outside of Castleblakeney village (*Gallach Uí Cheallaigh*), in Gallagh townland. No

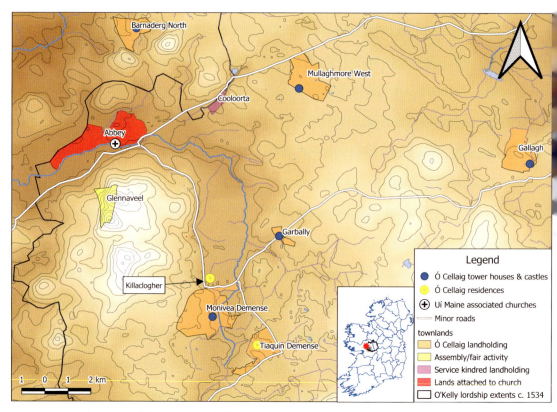

Figure 7.14 Summary of the Tiaquin and Abbeyknockmoy case study area, with the principal locations outlined.

masonry remains survive, yet based on analogy with the other 'unclassified castles' studied as part of this research, as well as the fact that the other 'Maolsechlainn' castles, particularly Garbally Castle, are of tower house form, it seems likely that Gallagh was also a tower house. What does survive is of earthwork form, with the visible remains comprised of what has been interpreted as a high flat-topped circular mound, measuring 15m in diameter and rising to a height of 8m. This has been described as motte-like in appearance and is retained with traces of a circular bank around the perimeter of the summit. More correctly, this castle was located at the summit at the southern end of a small esker, *c.*250m long, which runs broadly north/south (Pl. 7.11). A topographical plan of the site indicates that the 'circular' mound is actually more sub-rectangular in plan, *c.*30m on all axes, and is largely composed of rubble masonry. These characteristics are very faint, but the shape is reminiscent of a tower house and bawn arrangement. However, this can only be confirmed through further investigation (Fig. 7.12). Gallagh and possibly Garbally are marked on the 1591 Browne map (Fig. 7.13).

One of the main characteristics that connects these three castles is their siting. All three fortifications were constructed adjacent to a road running west from Caltra to Galway, now the R339. This communication routeway passes close to both Abbeyknockmoy to its north and Athenry to its south, while to the east of Caltra it connects to another regional road, the R358, which leads through Ahascragh and on to the important ford over the River Suck at *Áth Nadsluaigh*. Given the expanses of wetland that survive in this area to the present day, both north and south of these roads, it is likely that this is a route of considerable antiquity, through a landscape that would have been difficult to traverse. McAlister notes the siting of tower houses at roads and passes more generally in Ireland and the functions that this could supply to the castle builder. These range from the ability to hold off raiding parties and restricting access, through to their use as locations to toll travellers through the region (McAlister 2019, 154–7). Therefore, it is quite possible that Maolsechlainn's siting of these fortifications may have been as important as the constructions themselves, as he sought to keep communication, trade and revenue streams open between the traditional core of his lordship, closer to the River Suck and the secular and ecclesiastical foundations of Clantayg, and even further on to Galway. Given the relative immediacy with which Ulick Fionn Burke attacked these castles in 1504, it was plainly an attempt to limit the Ó Cellaig authority in this area. However, this demolition cannot have been complete, as demonstrated by the surviving archaeological remains, as well as the mention of *Moynvea* (Monivea) in the 1574 list (Nolan 1900–1, 122).

To conclude this section on the physical manifestation of the late medieval expansion of Ó Cellaig country, the range of historical evidence and archaeological remains enable us to consider the approach taken by these later medieval Gaelic lords in expanding their territory westward. Patronage and control of the important religious house and assembly site of Abbeyknockmoy certainly assisted the Uí Chellaig in retaining a stake in the area, even prior to their expansion into the cantred by force in the fourteenth and fifteenth centuries. The placement of the Mac an Bhaird *ollamh* within the district also signals the intent of the Uí Chellaig to ensure that one of their principal vassals were located near at hand. Thereafter, the construction and habitation of sites at Tiaquin, Monivea, Garbally, Gallagh, Barnaderg and Mullaghmore through to the late sixteenth century highlight the permanence of the Ó Cellaig association with the former de Bermingham and Uí Mainnin lands in the area, a district which produced a significant level of trade and wealth, as evidenced at Athenry and Abbeyknockmoy, and indeed nearby Galway, which the Uí Maine lords presumably sought to acquire and develop for their own economic benefit.

A LATE MEDIEVAL ROUTEWAY-SITED Ó CELLAIG CASTLE ELSEWHERE IN THE LORDSHIP

Lisdaulan Castle, Co. Roscommon

Lisdaulan was an Ó Cellaig centre at least during the sixteenth century, if not earlier (*Tribes*, 112–13). *Lis-dá-lon* is recorded in 1557, while *Lysdallon* is recorded as one of three castles in the possession of 'Hugh O Kelly', lord of Uí Maine, in 1573, the others being *Skrege* and *Gallee* (*ALC*; *Tribes*, 187; Nicholls (transcribed) 1573, 2019). Hugh Ó Cellaig of Lisdaulan is also mentioned in 1585, which indicates that Lisdaulan must have been his principal residence (*Compossicion*, 167, 172). However, it seems that an English garrison was billeted here during the 1590s (Cronin 1980, 116). A castle is marked at Lisdaulan on the 1591 Browne map of Connacht and the Strafford map of the 1630s and would have been sited just to the west of Route 11 linking Athlone to Roscommon.

Where was this late medieval Ó Cellaig residence within Lisdaulan townland? The most likely candidate for this is the site of a castle identified by the ASI at RO042-136001-. Very little survives of this castle today, except for the grass-covered remains of a sub-square raised area, measuring roughly 10m on all axes. This is surrounded by an irregularly shaped platform, which may or may not be the partial remains of a bawn-type feature. This is inconclusive and requires further investigation. Sandfield House lies 200m to the north-west of this site, built *c.*1710. A substantial number of late medieval punch-dressed quoins can be seen re-used in this house, including a series of stones which are finely tooled, and the remains of a two light ogee-headed window has been incorporated into an outbuilding adjacent to the latter house. These stones presumably came from the original castle. We know that both ogee-headed windows and punch-dressed stones are associated in a secular context with tower houses of mostly fifteenth- and sixteenth-century date (Leask 1941, 24, 75–124; McNeill 1997, 201–2; O'Conor and Williams 2015, 62–4). This strongly suggests that the late medieval Ó Cellaig residence at Lisdaulan was a tower house castle, built before *c.*1550, possibly in the fifteenth century.

***

As can be seen across this chapter, in certain instances the Ó Cellaig lord sought to site his lordly centres on or close to some of the principal overland routes of the wider territory. At Aughrim the *cenn áit* was of relative long-standing, despite being passed between a series of Gaelic and Anglo-Norman occupants from at least as early as the late twelfth century. It is likely that in this case the lordly centre was located in order to benefit from the traffic and revenue that passed to and from Ballinasloe, on to Loughrea and eventually Galway. The fragmentary surviving remains, coupled with the remote sensing survey and pictorial evidence, indicates that the site of Aughrim Castle was once a complex late medieval fortification, consisting of two wards, and an earlier rectangular masonry enclosure with at least two flanking towers. The entrance to this inner ward seems to have been guarded by a barbican gatehouse, while the focal point here is likely to have been a castle of tower house form. The later claim for authority over an extended territory was facilitated by the construction and occupation of fortifications along one of the routes from north-eastern Co. Galway through to the major medieval urban centres of the region, at Athenry and Galway itself. These fortifications are all likely to have been of tower house form, with the best surviving example located at Garbally, Co. Galway.

Lisdaulan Castle was located within what was the core of Ó Cellaig territory in the sixteenth century. The surviving archaeological remains indicate that the castle at Lisdaulan is likely to have been of tower house form. Lisdaulan was located in order to benefit from the overland road of Route 11 and there is evidence to suggest that it may have been linked to a watermill, which would have garnered wealth for the lord. The historical and cartographical evidence from two Ó Cellaig lordly centres, Athleague and Lisdaulan, appears to suggest that corn and corn milling were part of the economic underpinning of the lordship in the late medieval period. Yet, as castles of all dates were in some way agricultural centres, with land directly farmed from them, this should really come as no surprise. Most castles from the twelfth century through to the mid-seventeenth century would have had mills, usually watermills, nearby (O'Conor 1998, 26–35; 2004, 235–6; see Rynne 2004, 72–85; McAlister 2019, 78–80). This suggests that most Ó Cellaig castles and fortified sites of all dates would have had mills beside them as part of the agricultural complexes around these places. The evidence available from the fifteenth- and sixteenth-century Ó Cellaig lordship supports the same trend.

Finally, the surviving evidence presented in this chapter indicates that tower house castles were, yet again, the primary elite settlement form found at Ó Cellaig lordly centres in the late medieval period. This in and of itself highlights the previously low levels of recording of tower house sites within the study area, by comparison with the information gleaned from this research. Beyond this, though, the archaeological evidence for high levels of tower house building among the late medieval Uí Chellaig, as well as the physical evidence for patronage at religious foundations, indicate that this lordship remained wealthy and interested in displays of elite culture into the late medieval period, despite the conclusions which have been drawn to date on the Ó Cellaig lordship, based solely on the historical sources. As a result, the surviving archaeology presents a different picture on the state of the Uí Maine lordship in the fifteenth and sixteenth centuries than has traditionally been accepted, which is a significant conclusion to be able to make.

CHAPTER EIGHT

Understanding medieval Gaelic Ireland through the lens of the Ó Cellaig lordship

The information outlined over the preceding chapters has added considerably to our knowledge on the archaeology of the lordly centres in the later medieval Ó Cellaig lordship. This research can also provide insights into the character and development of later medieval Gaelic Irish society at an elite level more generally. This chapter will now address a number of these points. The aim of this work has been to identify and reconstruct the physical manifestation of the lordly centres of later medieval Uí Chellaig. In order to attempt this, it was necessary to adopt a multi-disciplinary approach, one which resulted in a detailed engagement with all available data in a democratic manner, to establish the fullest understanding of the past environment of the study area as possible, an approach advocated by a number of medieval archaeologists such as Geertz, Breen, Moreland and others. As such, this methodology required the examination of all available archaeological, historical, cartographic and literary evidence, from both Gaelic Irish and Anglo-Norman/English sources, in order to be able to identify these elite settlements on the ground. Thereafter, the locations were investigated in order to ascertain what was physically present at each of these places. What was revealed could be broadly divided chronologically into high medieval settlement forms, followed by the elite settlement archaeology of the late medieval Ó Cellaig lordship.

The elite settlement forms linked to the Uí Chellaig (and, of course, their vassal lords) for the high medieval period are *crannóga* and natural island fortresses; defended natural promontories; *bódhúin*; cashels and ringforts; and moated sites. The present study has uncovered continuity in the use of some of these settlement forms that goes beyond the high medieval era. In the late medieval period, the principal elite settlement form occupied by the Uí Chellaig was the tower house castle and the majority of these were constructed from the fifteenth century through to the middle of the sixteenth century. In many cases, however, these tower houses were constructed within Ó Cellaig *cenn áit* landscapes of long standing and the evidence suggests that the older settlement forms, particularly the *crannóg*, cashel and *bódhún*, were incorporated into the physical makeup of some late medieval Ó Cellaig lordly centres. The wealth and power of the lordship also seems to have increased during this period, as displayed through the construction of these tower houses, but also in the founding and remodelling of religious houses and their heavy patronage, among other displays of affluence.

THE HIGH MEDIEVAL ELITE SETTLEMENT FORMS OF THE UÍ CHELLAIG CRANNÓGA AND NATURAL ISLANDS

As outlined in Chapter 5, three lacustrine environments have presented themselves as Ó Cellaig *cenn áiteanna*. In all cases, *crannóga* and modified natural islands served as focal points for this settlement activity. Lough Croan retains evidence for at least five *crannóga* and modified natural islands and the extant artefactual assemblages from Edward's Island and the modified natural island of Illaunamona, coupled with a remote sensing investigation of the latter site, strongly argue for these two monuments having been occupied during the later medieval period. At Callow Lough, a substantial *crannóg* dominates the lake, with the remains of a sub-rectangular drystone-built house, as well as jetty features located on the eastern side of the island. Moreover, the Callow *crannóg* was deemed still sufficiently relevant to have been worthy of recording on Browne's 1591 map of Connacht. Ballaghdacker Lough is the location for two large *crannóga*, Stony Island (*Inisfarannan*), possibly formed out of a natural core, and Sally Island (*Loch an Dúin*), referenced in the historical sources for the fourteenth and fifteenth centuries. The morphology of Illaunamona, Callow *crannóg*, Stony Island and Sally Island all present with the attributes of high-cairn *crannóga* in the later phases of their construction, further evidence that they were modified and inhabited during the later medieval period (Fredengren 2002, 100–2, 272–6). The historical sources establish that all three of these lakes were frequented by the Ó Cellaig elite as lordly centres throughout the later medieval period, while the evidence from Ballaghdacker Lough suggests that the lake may have been in use contemporaneously as an Ó Cellaig residence as well as a residence for the Ó Cuindlis, a service kindred linked to the Ó Cellaig lord. As a result, I argue that one of the principal physical manifestations of Ó Cellaig lordly settlement in the period relates to the *crannóg*, as well as a natural island fortress, a conclusion which has not been identified prior to the present study.

How does this compare with the situation in Gaelic Ireland more generally? Beginning in modern Co. Roscommon, there are examples of *crannóga* and natural islands that were clearly inhabited during the later medieval period. For example, Ardakillin Lough, historically attested as a focal point of Ó Conchobhair lordship until at least the fifteenth century, bears all the hallmarks of a high-cairn *crannóg*, which seems to have been topped by a cashel-like wall (Brady and O'Conor 2005, 134; Shanahan 2008, 7–10). Further north, in what was once Maigh Luirg, the Mac Diarmada principal *cenn áit* at the Rock of Lough Cé is a fine example of where a natural lakeland feature was modified and added to, so as to develop a substantial occupation platform. A circular mortared stone-walled enclosure, which was cashel-like in form, occupied the western part of this island throughout the later medieval period. Other *crannóga* and island sites with evidence of continued use in north Roscommon into the sixteenth and seventeenth centuries include the Ó Conchobhair 'island' of Aghacarra on Cornacarta Lough, and the residence of the Mac Maghnusa lords of Tír Tuathail, identifiable with a *crannóg* on Lough Meelagh (O'Conor, Brady, Connon and Fidalgo-Romo 2010, 21–7; O'Conor 2018, 153–4).

On the Roscommon–Sligo border, Fredengren's research on Lough Gara has enabled the identification of features consistent with later medieval *crannóga*, an approach which has informed this investigation (Fredengren 2002, 273–4). Radiocarbon dates have been acquired from a series of *crannóga* in what is modern-day Co. Leitrim and show clear evidence for later medieval occupation and activity. This evidence is supported by historical references in the annals, which also show *crannóg* occupation in the Leitrim area right down to *c.*1600 (O'Conor and Fredengren 2019, 91). In central and western Co. Galway, Naessens has been able to demonstrate that both the pre- and post-expulsion periods in the high medieval history of the Uí Fhlaithbheartaigh lords of, first *Mag Seóla*, and latterly Iarchonnacht, are consistent with *cenn áiteanna* which manifested as *crannóga* and modified natural island fortresses (Naessens 2018). Naessens has also pointed out that the Uí Fhlaithbheartaigh deliberately selected a lacustrine location for their *cenn áit* in *Mag Seóla*, despite that landscape being largely devoid of lakes (ibid., 98). This is also the case in Uí Maine and Tír Maine, highlighting the importance ascribed by the Gaelic elite more generally to siting their lordly centres on or near water.

The evidence is not limited to Connacht, as the excavations of Island McHugh in Co. Tyrone, coupled with the research conducted in as geographically separate regions as Cos Fermanagh and Cork, can attest to the continued use of *crannóga* in later medieval Gaelic Ireland (Davies 1950; Foley and Williams 2006; Kelleher 2007; Bermingham, Moore, O'Keeffe and Gormley 2013; Bermingham 2014), as well as some of these places being the exclusive and private preserve of the Gaelic aristocracy. Indeed, the dating evidence from the Fermanagh *crannóga*, including Drumclay, clearly indicates the widespread occupation of these artificial and modified natural islands as defended residences during the whole later medieval period.

Promontory forts
A growing number of researchers have now demonstrated that some coastal and indeed inland promontories were occupied, and possibly even constructed upon, in the later medieval period, while the research undertaken by O'Conor at the early Anglo-Norman fortified promontory at Baginbun, Co. Wexford, is equally informative (O'Conor 2003, 17–31; FitzPatrick 2015b, 173–4). The current research has revealed two occupied inland promontory forts – at Callow Lough and Galey Bay. Both of these promontory forts are located in lakeland environments, with evidence that the occupants sought to manipulate the natural promontory jutting into the lake for defensive purposes. At Callow Lough, the peninsula was demarcated from the immediate hinterland by means of a substantial wet ditch (8m–9m wide) and associated banks. Micro-topographical data from here hints at the possibility of a

regulated access point, perhaps in the form of a gatehouse onto the promontory. This site is historically attested as a *bódhún* and will be discussed further presently. The promontory fort at Galey is of a similar archaeological expression. The small peninsula at Galey was modified to create a pair of wet ditches (7m (outer ditch) and 8m (inner ditch) wide) to separate the focal point of the peninsula from the surrounding area.

In both cases, the evidence suggests that earthen defences, probably in association with timber palisades, were the primary means by which these promontory forts were protected from landward attack. However, the identification of these features is an example of where there is an issue in typology at these locations, given that the ASI information is not satisfactory in attempting to summarize the archaeological remains on the ground. In the case of Galey, there is a modified natural promontory. But alongside this there is evidence for further earthen defences, as well as the degraded remains in the interior of the site of a cashel, not to mention the later insertion of a tower house on the central prominence. The complexity of remains at these sites needs to be recorded more fully than is presently the case, in order that important information relating to these places does not disappear over time. In summary, both promontory forts were located at historically attested Ó Cellaig lordly centres and this, coupled with the survival of these ditches, would argue for the later medieval construction and maintenance of these defensive elements, allowing them to be classifed as promontory forts.

The bódhún
The *bódhún* – 'cattle fort/cow-fortress' is a relatively amorphous monument type, in that the name is coined by its use in the later medieval historical sources alone. A deeper discussion into the origins of the *bódhún* as a specific feature of later medieval Gaelic Ireland has been outlined. I have highlighted two examples of this monument and its physical manifestation thus far. Both examples are found within the Ó Cellaig lordship, so any conclusions for other parts of the island of Ireland must be tempered by this restricted geographical discussion. However, a cursory search of the instances of 'bawn/*bábhún*' townland names on www.logainm.ie returns ten occurrences of the term by itself in the place-names record, not to mention the numerous examples that return with the use of bawn/*bábhún* as either a prefix or suffix to a longer name. Looking at the evidence on the ground from just two such sites suggests that the low-relief earthen remains in Bawnmore townland, near Geashill Castle, Co. Offaly, and the remains in Bawn townland, Killeshandra parish, Co. Cavan, may be physically similar to the *bódhúin* monuments of the Ó Cellaig lordship. As such, there must be many more examples of the *bódhún* waiting to be recorded in the Irish landscape.

There is a *bódhún* at Athleague, and another at Callow, and there is a morphological similarity apparent in both cases. Both are located in watery places and the 'cattle fort' is created by redirecting the surrounding lake or river waters into a defensive wet ditch as a means of delimiting a fortified zone. The wet ditch at Athleague measured 8m–9m in width, with faint traces of an internal bank. In both cases, the area contained by the ditch was in excess of 14,000m². Both of these *bódhúin* have a lordly residence located within their interior and access into the *bódhún* was carefully regulated at one point across the ditch, with additional defences, including flanking defences, presumably once standing all along the perimeter of the site.

The primary function of these very large earthen enclosures was likely to serve as the overnight protection for the lord's cattle and horse herds, when the *cenn áit*, or lordship at large, was believed to be under threat from a raid. Here, it must be noted that these fortifications could only have proven effective against small-scale attack and it is likely that in the case of larger-scale military incursions, the *bódhún* would have been of limited value. Instead, the natural landscape would have proven far more suitable and the historical sources indicate the frequent use by the Gaelic Irish of woodland and upland areas as places to protect their herds in time of attack (O'Conor 1998, 99–101). Suitable woodlands existed throughout the lordship that could have been utilized for this purpose (see Chapter 3). In peacetime, the *bódhúin* likely served as safe places to keep animals for a couple of days, until the available grass was consumed within it, and there was a ready supply of water available in both researched instances. It may have been a routine location for portioning out the lord's cattle for *cánal túarastla* (tribute) to other lords and for temporarily holding cattle as part of *cís* (rent/food stipend) from the constituent communities of the lordship. It could also have been used to gather animals to be slaughtered and butchered for the table and for the production of resources. Beyond these uses, it is possible that these large enclosed fortified zones served as mustering points and temporary accommodation for combatants and would have easily billeted a substantial troop of warriors, their horses, as well as the retinue of camp followers, such as women and horseboys, that would have been routine in the martial world of later medieval Connacht (O'Conor 2003, 26–8). Slight evidence for the possible use of the *bódhún* of Athleague in this manner comes with the 1337 construction by Toirrdelbach Ó Conchobair of what was described as a *foslongphort*, which can translate to 'fortified encampment' (*AC*; O'Conor 1998, 84).

Cashels and ringforts
Evidence for the continued use of ringforts and cashels as places of residence beyond the early medieval period has traditionally been a contentious issue in Irish archaeology. However, as has been demonstrated, there is a growing body of evidence in support of the continued occupation, and possibly even construction, of both of these monument types into the later medieval period. The Ó Cellaig lordship has never previously been surveyed in this regard, but the sheer numbers of these monument types in the area (ringforts = 767; enclosures = 258; cashels = 76), considered in association with the research undertaken on ringfort distributions and

densities in a Co. Meath case study area (Barrett and Graham 1975, 37–43), allow for the suggestion that it is highly likely that some of these monuments, located within what was a Gaelic-controlled region, continued to be inhabited throughout the later medieval period. Three developer-led excavations at Loughbown I and II, and at Mackney, all presented with evidence for later medieval occupation.

Two of the most prominent examples of cashels uncovered as part of this research have been the fragmentary remains of the historically attested *cathair* at Galey and the cashel uncovered on Illaunamona at Lough Croan. By the mid-fourteenth century, the *cathair* at Galey would have crowned the promontory fort, the likely focal point of the great Christmas feast described in *Filidh Éreann Go Haointeach*, while Illaunamona may have been where Conchobar Ó Cellaig, lord of Uí Maine, died in 1403. In both cases, these cashels seem to have served as the elite residence within their respective *cenn áiteanna*. In the immediate environs around these *cenn áiteanna*, additional ringforts seem to have played a role in the organization of the lordly centre. The *crannóga* of the lordship seem to have had dry-land service sites associated with them, some of which were ringforts. The proposed Illaunamona dry-land site is possibly the site of a ringfort at Garrynphort, with its intriguing place-name translation – chief house of the bank/landing place, while a univallate ringfort at Cornacask, immediately north of Ballaghdacker Lough, may have been linked to Sally Island *crannóg*. These dry-land sites would have served as the lord's public face and acted as the administrative and agricultural centres connected to these more private and exclusive lordly residences out on lakes.

A number of other ringforts within the immediate hinterland may have served as earlier or contemporaneous focal points within the landscape, but in the absence of historical information and excavation, the partial reliance on toponymical evidence means that the conclusions cannot be as certain. Examples include Liswilliam and Lisnagavragh, near the western and northern shores of Lough Croan respectively. At Lisnagavragh, the foundational remains of two rectangular stone houses within its interior may be the critical evidence for the continued occupation of this ringfort into the high or perhaps even late medieval period. The Callow Lough *cenn áit*, and specifically Lisdonnellroe townland, possesses the remains of two named ringforts, Lisnagry and Lisnacourty, and owing to their location and morphology, coupled with the seemingly early place-name survivals, this may indicate that they played a role at Callow Lough during the later medieval period also.

The case for the later medieval occupation of ringforts and cashels seems to be on much firmer ground when looking at the residences of the minor elites and the service kindreds. The historical attestation to the landholdings of both groupings, when identifiable and observed on the ground today, presents routinely with the case that the only settlement archaeology, and in some cases, the only archaeological monument of any type to be located in the townland, comes in the form of a ringfort or cashel.

This is apparent at the Ó Dubhagáin landholdings of Coolderry, Co. Roscommon, and Cartrondoogan and Ballydoogan, Co. Galway, with the latter townland containing the remains of a tri- or even quadrivallate ringfort, recorded in cartographic sources as 'Lisfineel', and still inhabited by a member of the Ó Dubhagáin sept into the early seventeenth century. Ringforts were also the primary medieval monument observed when investigating the landholdings of other service families associated with the Ó Cellaig, such as at Annagh (Mac an Bhaird poets), Ballynabanaba (Uí Longorgáin harpers and Uí Shideacháin horn-players), Lecarrowmactully (Mac Mhaoltuile physicians), Lissyegan (Mac Aodhagáin *brehon* kindred) and Liscoffy (Uí Chobhtaigh poets). A cashel serves as the principal settlement archaeology in Cornageeha townland, a landholding recorded in the 1574 State Paper list of 'castles' in Co. Roscommon as being in the possession of the Mac Dubhghaill, the hereditary captains of galloglass to the Ó Chellaig lords. It can be argued that many of the place-names which incorporate a service kindred family name, and thus a name that must have related to the granting of a landholding to a specific family, can be dated with relative confidence to the later medieval period. For instance, most traditional ecclesiastical kindreds, such as the Ó Dubhagáin, only seem to adopt surnames from the eleventh century onwards, while the use of *Mac* in family name formation also only appears from *c.*AD 1000 (Ó Murchadha 1999, 37–8). Finally, the minor elite *Clannmhaicne Eoghain* Uí Chellaig, the sept group who seem to have controlled the ford of the River Suck at modern-day Ballinasloe for much of the later medieval period, possessed historically attested strongholds in this area, which, based on the surviving remains in those townlands, suggest a ringfort morphology.

In the study area, it is the first occasion that these monument types have been demonstrated to have been inhabited during the later medieval period. There are parallels for the continued occupation of ringforts and cashels into the latter period to be found elsewhere on the island. One of the first researchers to highlight this later medieval milieu for these monuments was O'Conor, who theorized that the ringfort was not just a monument type in use during the early medieval period, instead demonstrating the need to consider the whole range of evidence on this issue, including cartographic, pictorial and distributional information, all of which point toward the continued use of ringforts as a viable settlement form beyond *c.* AD 1000 (O'Conor 1998, 89–94; 2004, 246–9). FitzPatrick states that the available evidence indicates that regional and local variations must be taken into account, which is contrary to the perceived archaeological norm that uniformly places these sites primarily in the early medieval period. FitzPatrick supports her argument through a re-evaluation of published and archived excavation reports of these sites, as well as more recent findings. These suggest that many Irish archaeologists need to change their views regarding the dating of these monuments and their use over time (FitzPatrick 2009, 277–83).

This latter argument has been supported more recently by the publication of the results of a series of developer-led excavations of ringforts, not least the Mackney and Loughbown sites, while the discovery of a diagnostic high medieval artefact in a stratified context, an Edwardian coin, among the assemblage excavated from a previously unidentified ringfort in Gortnacrannagh townland, Co. Roscommon, in advance of the N5 Bypass project construction (Channing, J., pers. comm.), only adds weight in favour of the later medieval occupation of ringforts. Indirect evidence for the continued use of ringforts can also be seen in the cases of a number of moated sites in north Roscommon. Finan and O'Conor have indicated that the moated site at Rockingham Demesne was built over a still occupied ringfort at some stage in the thirteenth century, while the moated sites at Carns and Cloonybeirne indicate to a greater or lesser degree that they were built over existing ringforts. This has led to the suggestion that in these instances the builders sought to remain in a location that had associations with the past, while wishing to embrace contemporary style fortifications (McNeary and Shanahan 2008, 191; 2012, 222–3; O'Conor and Finan 2018, 123).

There is also a growing body of evidence in support of the later medieval occupation of cashels. This monument type has presented with evidence for later medieval use from both wetland and dryland contexts, with morphological parallels to the two examples recognized over the course of the present study. O'Conor and Naessens have studied the morphology of a series of historically attested cashels on *crannóga* on some of the lakes of western Connacht, including Iniscremha Island and *Caislen na Circe* on Lough Corrib, Co. Galway, *Caislen na Caillighe* on Lough Mask, as well as the undocumented site at Garrison Island on Lough Cullen, both Co. Mayo. In all cases, the island fortification came in the form of a mortared stone enclosure of cashel form. To these sites can be added the cashel-like enclosure on the Rock of Lough Cé and the presumed cashel which once marked the perimeter of the high-cairn *crannóg* on Ardakillin Lough, both Co. Roscommon (Shanahan 2008, 9; Naessens and O'Conor 2012, 263–6). In the final two cases, these *crannóga*-sited cashels served as the focal points of historically attested, multi-generational, lordly centres in their respective regions. Naessens has also identified a number of cashels on *crannóga* and natural islands within the Uí Fhlaithbheartaigh lordship of Iarchonnacht that seem to present with evidence for high medieval, possibly high-status, occupation. The most substantial of these include two islands with cashel enclosures on Lough Skannive, Co. Galway, and an island cashel on Moher Lake, Co. Mayo, which may have been a high medieval Ó Máille *cenn áit* (Naessens 2018, 101–5).

The dryland-sited cashel, and evidence for their continued use into the later medieval period, presents with a number of investigated examples located within the Burren karst limestone landscape of Co. Clare and south Galway. Architectural and archaeological analysis of Cahermacnaughten, Cahermore and Caherahoagh indicates that they were all occupied into the late medieval period, as well as being modified or remodelled during this time (FitzPatrick 2009, 290–8). The excavations at Caherconnell, Co. Clare, have demonstrated through radio-carbon dating and the discovery of diagnostic artefacts that this cashel was *continuously* inhabited from possibly as early as the tenth century, right up until the seventeenth century (Comber and Hull 2008, 30–3; 2010, 157–9; Comber 2016; 2018a, 1–12; 2018b, 95–102). While these results are seen by some as anomalous instances of the continued occupation of these sites beyond their traditional date (O'Keeffe 2000, 24), FitzPatrick has convincingly argued that cashel occupation was commonplace in the Burren, at least among the minor Gaelic elite, into the late medieval and post-medieval periods (FitzPatrick 2009, 288). While it could be assumed that the enduring use of stone for the construction of settlement enclosures into the later medieval period is the result of the natural environment and the Burren's plentiful stone resources, the latter writer has suggested that this medieval and post-medieval built landscape is not unusual in terms of how later medieval Gaelic Irish society was organized. Rather the Burren likely serves as a showcase of what was a reality in the building traditions of the other west of Ireland Gaelic lordships, only that these, particularly stone, enclosures have degenerated in numbers through time (ibid., 285). While this degeneration also seems to be the case in the study area, there is also now good evidence for the continued occupation of cashels by the Ó Cellaig elite into the later medieval period.

None of the identified high medieval Ó Cellaig *cenn áiteanna* are of ringfort morphology. *Crannóga*, natural islands and inland promontory forts have thus far been demonstrated to have been the settlement forms chosen by the Ó Cellaig elite. Added to this, however, are the two dry-stone cashels located at Galey and Lough Croan. These cashels would have been notable by their appearance and their primarily dry-stone construction. The cashel as a monument type is not as numerous in the study area as the ringfort and this difference may have been a deliberate choice, one designed to distinguish the lordly residence in this area from the settlement environment at large. This may be the physical manifestation in the study area for the *ríglongphort* as seen in the hierarchy of social distinction shown through the choice of enclosed settlement forms recorded in a fourteenth-century battle-roll (*Caithréim Thoirdhealbhaigh*, 134; FitzPatrick 2009, 275). If this is the case, it shows that the high medieval Ó Cellaig elite favoured certain settlement forms over others in the pre-tower house period.

Moated sites
The final high medieval settlement form to be dealt with is the moated site. When the presumed example at Ballaghdacker is included, the total number of these monuments identified in this study area comes to nine. As outlined above, this monument type is traditionally regarded as a part of the wider Anglo-Norman manorial landscape, particularly in the south-east of the island, and associated with prosperous peasants and minor lords. There is a growing body of evidence indicating that moated sites were

also chosen as a place of residence by the elites of Gaelic-controlled regions in the late thirteenth and early fourteenth centuries (Graham 1988a, 22–3; O'Conor 1998, 87–8; 2001, 338–40; Finan and O'Conor 2002, 74–6; McNeary and Shanahan 2012, 211–12; Timoney 2021), an argument that could also be made for the study area.

The historical background showed that the cantreds of Omany (Uí Maine) and Tyrmany (Tír Maine) were the subject of speculative Anglo-Norman land grants during the thirteenth century. However, there is little evidence on the ground that the area was settled in any meaningful way outside of the Anglo-Norman towns established in eastern Connacht in this period. As a result, there is little to suggest that these moated sites were constructed as part of an attempt at developing an Anglo-Norman manor. Conversely, these examples seem to have been constructed relatively close to Ó Cellaig lordly centres, possibly as residences for undocumented service kindreds or related junior branches of the Uí Maine. Creeraun, Pallas and Cloonigny moated sites are all located within 9km of the Callow Lough *cenn áit*, while the Moat and Park moated sites are both less than 6km distant from the Aughrim *cenn áit*. Three are located within the extents of the Uí Fhallamháin territory of Clann Uadach (Cuilleenirwan, Bredagh and Coolnageer), a sept lineage of the Síl Muiredaig who were transplanted into Tír Maine during the twelfth century to control the resident Ó Cellaig lords. These three sites are situated close to the Ó Cellaig *cenn áit* of Lough Croan. It is possible that the Uí Fhallamháin chiefs adopted a construction trend that was similar to those then exhibited in central and north Roscommon, where a total of 53 moated sites are recorded. The majority of the latter sites were constructed within the Ó Conchobair *trícha cét* of Machaire Connacht and the *trícha cét* of their principal vassals, the Mac Diarmada of Maigh Luirg. It may be possible that the building practice among the Clann Uadach was undertaken in order to maintain a cultural link with their Ó Conchobair cousins.

Some of the Uí Maine moated sites are indirectly connected to the Ó Cellaig elites. Both Cloonigny and Coolnageer were later used as courtyards, effectively bawns, for historically attested castles of junior Ó Cellaig septs in the sixteenth century. Lismore moated site has been interpreted by FitzPatrick as a *pailís* hunting lodge and feasting hall associated with the Uí Chellaig and, due to its location, Lismore may have been connected with the Callow Lough *cenn áit* (FitzPatrick 2016, 204). Finally, the levelled moated site at Ballaghdacker may have served as the dry-land service site for Stony Island *crannóg*, a residence for the Ó Cuindlis family of historians. The Ó Cuindlis were important in learned circles in the fifteenth century, with their associations with the codices of *Leabhar Breac* and *Leabhar Ruadh Muimhneach* (Ó Concheanainn 1973, 65–7). That their landholdings and settlement archaeology correspond with a substantial *crannóg* on Ballaghdacker Lough, as well as a settlement form that was more in vogue among the Gaelic nobility and minor elites in the fourteenth century (O'Conor and Finan 2018, 122), could point to the status that this learned family enjoyed in this time and place. The use of moated sites as dry-land service sites to *crannóga* is also seen with the Rockingham Demesne moated site serving the Rock of Lough Cé, Co. Roscommon, and at Knockalough, on the southern shore of Cloonacleigha Lough, Co. Sligo (O'Conor 1998, 88; Finan 2018, 38–42).

In summary, this writer can demonstrate enough evidence from the moated sites of the study area to show that the majority were constructed by the Gaelic Irish. This conclusion is contrary to the evaluation provided by some medieval archaeologists, who consider them to be undocumented attempts at colonial settlement in these areas (O'Keeffe 2000, 77; 2001; 2018). These conclusions seem to derive from research on the dense distribution of moated sites in the east and south-east, to the general exclusion of those to the west of the Shannon. However, the weight of evidence from across the Gaelic north and west in medieval territories such as Machaire Connacht, Maigh Luirg, west Breifne and Fir Manach, as well as Lismore in Uí Maine, indicates that quite a number of moated sites in these areas were of Gaelic construction (see Chapter 4). Now, with a high degree of confidence, the moated sites of Uí Maine, Tír Maine and Clann Uadach can be added to that list.

The evidence for castles in high medieval Uí Maine
The traditional academic belief across Europe advocates that medieval elites constructed different types of castles to live in. Given the broad definition that can be applied to the defended residence known by that name, a whole range of monument types could conceivably be inspected with a view to hanging this title upon the surviving remains, including the settlement forms discussed in this chapter thus far. All of the monuments discussed are elite residences, as well as being the centres of estates and administration for the lordship, but they were not called castles by contemporaries, nor are they by modern scholars (De Meulemeester and O'Conor 2008, 324–5). Therefore, to refer to these elite residences as 'castles' does a disservice to the nuances of their construction, as well as the outlook of their builders and occupiers. Indeed, the settlement forms of the high medieval Ó Cellaig elite can be more correctly referred to as private, fortified residences as opposed to castles, with the distinction here relating to the physical remains as opposed to function, the key attribute which should define the monument. Therefore, it can be concluded that not all fortified private residences in this place and time can be defined as castles. Earlier in this work, the evidence for high medieval castles in the study area has been discussed, as well as the pitfalls inherent in this topic. Here, I will outline what evidence survives on the ground for castles of thirteenth- to mid-fourteenth-century date constructed by the Gaelic Irish and the Anglo-Normans prior to the advent of the tower house as the principal form of encastellation on the island.

Four definite monument classes dateable to the high medieval period, with one subclass, appear on the ASI database for the study area: Anglo-Norman masonry castle

[3], hall house [1], motte (motte and bailey) [3 rising to 4] and ringwork [2]. Additionally, some of the monuments that fall into the unclassified castle class may have been high medieval in date. However, one of the conclusions of this work is that the majority of these are, in fact, degraded castles of tower house form which belong to the late medieval period. The placement of these monuments in the aforementioned classes is not immutable. In the case of the Anglo-Norman masonry castle, three monuments comprise the record, one in Co. Roscommon, at the royal castle at Rindoon, and two in Co. Galway. The Galway examples, Ballinasloe Castle (see Curley 2021a, Appendix 4) and Aughrim Castle, survive on the ground as the fragmentary remains of late medieval castle and bawn complexes, devoid of any surface evidence for high medieval/Anglo-Norman period activity. These two sites are likely to have been occupied from the thirteenth century onwards, yet their classification as Anglo-Norman masonry castles is based purely on historical references, as opposed to the surviving archaeological remains.

One hall house is recorded, located within Park moated site, Co. Galway, and there is a possibility that this castle is perhaps a *caput* of a de la Rochelle or Butler manor attached to thirteenth-century Anglo-Norman Omany land grants (Holland 1994, 205–6; 1997, 162). This may be evidence for Anglo-Norman settlement beyond the manorial centres established at Aughrim and Ballinasloe, but this requires further investigation. A total of five earth and timber castles are recorded; three motte castles, two of which have associated baileys, and two ringwork castles. These earth and timber castles are seen as the physical manifestation of the first phases of Anglo-Norman settlement in the study area (Graham 1988a, 25–9) and their presence must relate to the speculative land grants in those two King's Cantreds of Omany and Tyrmany.

The south Roscommon motte and bailey castles are located at Cloonburren and Ballycreggan, both of which were sited close to the medieval routeways of the region, the *Slighe Mhór* and Route 11 respectively. A third motte is suggested by Dempsey for Castlesampson townland, however, the remains at Castlesampson can be more correctly interpreted as those of a degraded late medieval bawn and tower house complex attached to the Mac Eochadha of Magh Finn, situated near the summit of a natural gravel hillock, which is characteristic of the wider landscape of this part of south Roscommon. All three are deduced, despite the lack of historical documentation for any of the three sites, to have been constructed by Anglo-Norman lord Geoffrey de Constentin in the early 1210s (Graham 1988a, 25–6; Dempsey 2014, 22–5). The only later medieval reference for Cloonburren comes in 1226, when it is in use as a garrisoned fortress, presumably to guard the crossing of the River Shannon at nearby Clonmacnoise, then in the possession of Aedh Ó Conchobair, king of Connacht, and manned by mercenaries from Leinster (*ACl.*). This reference has been used to suggest that this motte and bailey castle was constructed by the Gaelic Irish (Graham 1988a, 25), but it is just as likely that it was merely occupied by the latter after a decline in

Anglo-Norman fortunes in the immediate area in the 1220s. In east Galway, a motte is recorded in Doon Upper (Alcock, de hÓra and Gosling 1999, 387). Again, this is undocumented and it could speculatively relate to the 1253 grant of Omany to Richard de la Rochelle, as motte castles were constructed throughout the thirteenth century (O'Conor 1998, 18). However, this site's morphology, coupled with its location, suggests that it is actually a raised ringfort, with the underlying natural ridge used as an aid in its construction (FitzPatrick 2023, 148–9).

The final high medieval castle monument type is the ringwork castle. Two examples are recorded, at Galey and Dundonnell, both Co. Roscommon. It has been demonstrated earlier that the remains at Galey more accurately correspond with that of an inland promontory fort, topped by a cashel, with the later addition of a tower house. The designation of the site as a ringwork castle must now, therefore, be rejected. The ringwork at Dundonnell, which seems to have been modified out of an earlier trivallate ringfort, has been argued elsewhere by this writer to be consistent with the historically attested 'Onagh Castle', a fortress constructed by the Anglo-Normans in 1236 'as a stronghold against the men of Connacht' (*AC*; Curley 2018, 139).

Having reviewed the surviving archaeological remains, the evidence for the construction and occupation of high medieval castles in the study area indicates three things. The available information leads to the conclusion that high medieval castles in this region were constructed exclusively, with the possible exception of Cloonburren, by the Anglo-Normans in their attempts to make good on a series of thirteenth-century speculative land grants within the cantreds of Tyrmany and Omany. These attempts at settlement, particularly outside of the towns, were largely unsuccessful, with the only possible archaeological evidence for a rural manor attached to the cantred of Omany located at Park. The lack of evidence for Anglo-Norman earthwork and masonry castles is contrary to the conclusions drawn by historians, which only consider the Anglo-Norman control of these areas largely on the strength of colonial administrative accounts. A similar issue was identified in terms of Anglo-Norman settlement in what is now Co. Leitrim as part of a review of the archaeological evidence for high medieval settlement in that county (O'Conor and Fredengren 2019, 83). Finally, there is no evidence either from archaeological remains or the historical record that the Uí Chellaig, or their vassal clans, constructed what contemporaries then and modern scholars now accept as castles during the high medieval period. Therefore, the settlement forms utilized by these Gaelic elites during the period from the twelfth to the later fourteenth century were not overly influenced by the Anglo-Normans. Instead, many of the settlement forms used by the Uí Chellaig and their vassal clans represent continuity from the early medieval period, with the exception of the moated site. Once more, this is contrary to some of the archaeological narratives being proposed for late pre-Norman and high medieval contexts in Ireland (O'Keeffe 1998; 2019; 2021, 30–59; O'Keeffe and MacCotter 2020).

Certainly, many of the aforementioned castles were occupied or reoccupied by the Uí Chellaig and their sept families during the late medieval period. Examples include the Ó Neachtain of the *Feadha* at Ballycreggan motte, the Mac Eochadha of Magh Finn at Dundonnell Castle and the Uí Chellaig themselves at Aughrim, but the overwhelming conclusion from the research is that the Gaelic Irish of this region did not construct or routinely inhabit the various monument types traditionally regarded as a castle during the high medieval period. It is worthwhile to consider the most up-to-date alternative view on this matter. The most recent publication to deal with the topic of castle building in later medieval Ireland has been *Ireland encastellated, AD 950–1550: insular castle-building in its European context* (O'Keeffe 2021). Early in the book, O'Keeffe makes clear his views regarding the origins of castles in Ireland, devoting a chapter to teasing out the terminology used to describe the private defended residences of tenth- to twelfth-century Ireland. O'Keeffe concluded that the range of elite settlement forms encountered, both in the literary and physical landscape, including the range of monument types outlined above – *crannóga*, cashels and ringforts – and on analogy with what he regards as continental parallels, can be regarded as castles (ibid., 30–59). However, O'Keeffe's analysis of the settlement forms of the Gaelic elite from just prior to the period under investigation here, as well as the continuity that has been identified through this research, seeks to place all of these settlement forms under the banner of 'castle'. Accepting this approach does not seem to acknowledge the nuances of later medieval Gaelic society, which will be discussed in greater detail below, while summarily accepting the concept of feudalism as having been adopted in Gaelic Irish society at about this time. Neither of these arguments have been proved satisfactorily by the latter writer or others and yet the acceptance of this approach has potential impacts on the future of research into later medieval Gaelic Ireland. Some of O'Keeffe's conclusions are based on a particular reading of the historical and landscape evidence for the *caistél* of *Dún Leodha*, which in and of itself serves to weaken the overall argument in my mind. In order to rebalance this debate, more critical research needs to be undertaken in this area of the discipline, in order to have questioning, and stronger evidence-based interpretations of the archaeology of later medieval Gaelic Ireland.

Gaelic settlement forms in the high medieval period
Having evaluated the high medieval settlement forms chosen by the Ó Cellaig, it is clear that there is little evidence for the Uí Maine elite building what contemporaries and modern scholars regard as castles, rather choosing residences which did not possess, in an immediately identifiable way at least, the complexity of defences comparable to the fortifications constructed by the Anglo-Normans during the same period. This conclusion is in keeping with the broader picture in high medieval Gaelic Ireland (MacNeill 1997, 157–64; O'Conor 1998, 75–7). The multidisciplinary methodology devised for this research sought to identify the later medieval lordly

centres of the Uí Chellaig, something never been systematically undertaken in the past. Suitable representative locations were identified and upon visiting the historically attested high medieval lordly centres, I did not find evidence for high medieval castles. Instead, evidence for *crannóga* and natural island fortresses, ringforts and cashels, *bódhúin*, promontory forts and moated sites was forthcoming in every case. We must now address the question as to why they chose to live in this manner?

There are practical as well as symbolic reasons explaining why they chose to live in this way. First, high medieval Gaelic society possessed a number of attributes that may have resulted in the routine preference among the Uí Chellaig to choose the elite settlement forms outlined above. This society was primarily clan or kin-based in its organization throughout the later medieval period and land or territory was owned by the sept group, as opposed to any single individual (Nicholls 2003, 8–9). Land was held at this group level and there is evidence throughout this era for periodic land redistribution and partible inheritance among the male members of a sept group, sometimes occurring on a very regular basis (O'Conor 1998, 97; Nicholls 2003, 64–73). This system of partible inheritance would have reduced an individual's desire to build complex fortifications on lands which might be transferred to another member of the sept later on.

Second, Gaelic lordly succession was not routinely transferred through primogeniture, rather the ascension to lordship was conferred, in theory at least, after an election of the most 'suitable' eligible candidate from within a four-generational kin group – the *derbfine*. In practice, this presented with countless examples in the annalistic record for succession disputes, bloodshed and ultimately, in many cases, the late medieval division of lordships between irreconcilable warring family factions (ibid., 27–30). The non-linear nature of lordly succession from within the Ó Cellaig senior line is seen with the transfer of power in a forty-two-year period beginning with the death of Donnchad Muimnech Ó Cellaig (r. 1295–1307). Three of Donnchad's nephews succeeded to the position after him, followed by Donnchad's own son Áed, then three more distant relations, prior to the ascension of Donnchad Muimnech's youngest attested son, Uilliam Buide Ó Cellaig, as lord of Uí Maine in *c.*1349.

Third, the most powerful and influential member of the sept was elected as the lord. In the case of the larger or expanding Gaelic territories, one of the ways in which these lords sought to state and restate their authority was by establishing or appropriating *cenn áiteanna* throughout their lordship and travelling between these over the course of the year. This meant that the lord was not in permanent residence at any one place and would have used this circuit as an opportunity to inspect the lordship (perhaps combined with a hunting season, see King 1988, 2), collect rent, demonstrate his status and reaffirm control, while he also expected to be accommodated by the communities which resided in different parts of the lordship. This has been identified as a characteristic of Gaelic royal and lordly lifestyles from the early medieval period onwards (Simms 2020, 69, 235). A peripatetic lifestyle of this kind is readily evident in the case of the later medieval Ó Néill lords of Tír Eoghain (Logue and Ó Doibhlin 2020, 167) and is similarly apparent, in particular, from the careers of Uilliam Buide Ó Cellaig and his son Maolsechlainn. Uilliam Buide was first encountered at his centre of Galey in 1351, before he established or re-established an Ó Cellaig *cenn áit* at Callow in 1353. Later in that decade, there was activity at his lordly centre at Ballaghdacker Lough. In the case of Ballaghdacker Lough, the Ó Cuindlis service kindred may have been tasked with attending to their Ó Cellaig lord on his travels to this part of the lordship. Toponymical and literary evidence also points to Uilliam Buide possibly having a residence at Lough Croan. His son Maolsechlainn presumably maintained the aforementioned lordly centres, but a late fourteenth-century praise poem suggests he also had a residence at Athleague, and the Ó Cellaig genealogies indicate that he died at his own residence at Tiaquin in 1401. All of these lordly centres continued to be used by members of the Uí Chellaig elite throughout the late medieval period, meaning that this practice also must have persisted, particularly as the Ó Cellaig lord sought to maintain authority over the lordship at its greatest extents from c.1400 onwards. This constantly-moving elite lifestyle probably did not cease in the late medieval period, with first Maolsechlainn Ó Cellaig constructing three castles, located at Garbally, Monivea and Gallagh, Co. Galway, before 1504, and then Aodh Ó Cellaig, last lord of Uí Maine, recorded in possession of three tower houses within his lordship in 1573.

Finally, and as has been demonstrated, one of the principal means by which these lords derived and stated their wealth was through the retention of large herds of cattle and horses. This predominantly pastoral economy among the elites meant that their wealth was moveable, not generally requiring protection through the construction of substantial defences, apart from that provided in a temporary capacity by the *bódhún*. In times of trouble, the lord's herds could be moved out of harms way, meaning that one of a Gaelic lord's primary commodities would be less vulnerable in times of attack, using the landscape as defence, as opposed to a fixed fortified location (O'Conor 1998, 100–1).

With these practical attributes of later medieval Gaelic Ireland taken into account, it helps to explain why the Uí Chellaig lords chose to construct and occupy settlement forms that were less substantial, not as defensible, and not requiring the same amount of resources to construct. The way in which this society was organized meant that there was an absence of security in lordly succession from father to son. The way that the territory was held by the kin group as opposed to the individual, the lifestyle espoused by many Gaelic lords to travel from *cenn áit* to *cenn áit* throughout the year, and the primacy of cattle as a form of currency and an expression of wealth, meant that the construction of complex castle-type fortifications was not favoured and was also possibly not a necessary or sensible commitment of resources in many cases.

In terms of the symbolic reasons for choosing to reside in these older settlement forms, it is becoming increasingly apparent that one of the major preoccupations of high medieval Gaelic lords concerned the display of power and authority through referencing the past. This was presumably undertaken to maintain or create a legacy and legitimacy of authority over the area under their control and could take many forms, including the commissioning of praise poems, design of tombs and production of manuscripts, as well as the holding of assemblies and inauguration ceremonies, even down to their personal presentation (Moss 2015a, 204; McGettigan 2016, 72–6; Simms 2018b, 424). Of course, for the purpose of this research, one of the ways in which this was achieved was through the place chosen to establish a lordly centre, as well as the incorporation of deliberate anachronisms into the settlement forms constructed and occupied by the lord. FitzPatrick has prosposed that 'pedigree of place' was an important consideration among the Gaelic elite. One manifestation of this relates to the venues chosen for seasonal assemblies and gatherings in later medieval Gaelic Ireland, and indeed places of inauguration. As FitzPatrick has demonstrated, these locations were often replete with prehistoric or early historic funerary and ritual monuments that retained an importance for those interacting with these landscapes beyond their perceived main period of use and into their 'afterlife' (FitzPatrick 2015a, 52, 55). The evidence of what appears to be multi-period activity, possibly originating in prehistory, at what became the Ó Cellaig inauguration mound at Cluain Tuaiscirt O Máine is an example of this 'pedigree of place' theory in action in the study area (Curley 2021a, Appendix 5). This may have had a role to play in the establishment of the early medieval monastic site, and the later Augustinian Priory of St Mary during the later medieval period, at Cluain Tuaiscirt O Máine. The remembrance of this ritual monument may also be at the heart of why Cluain Tuaiscirt O Máine became established as an Ó Cellaig venue of inauguration during the later medieval period.

In terms of the continued use of older settlement forms, the display of continuity within a landscape, and indeed within earlier monuments, seems to have held relevance for the Gaelic elite (FitzPatrick 2006, 70–2). FitzPatrick has highlighted this importance through the insertion of tower houses within three earlier cashels in the Burren landscape, at Cahercloggaun, Ballyshanny and Ballyganner South (FitzPatrick 2009, 302). Within the study area, a similar arrangement of late medieval castle being inserted within earlier Ó Cellaig elite centres is seen at Callow Lough, Galey and Athleague. More than this, the continuity of elite settlement at a particular location of importance throughout the entire later medieval period, and before, is demonstrable at Lough Croan, which may have originally been an elite centre of the *Delbna Nuadat* in the mid-eighth century, before being taken over by the Uí Maine and eventually their principal offshoot, the Uí Chellaig. The Ó Cellaig elite then continued to occupy this lacustrine landscape until 1573 at least.

The social value for the Gaelic elite continuing to use these older settlement forms is also demonstrable in the high medieval period. As has already been stated, when visiting high medieval Ó Cellaig lordly centres on the ground, there is no evidence for the construction of high medieval castles. As a result, the Ó Cellaig elite must have occupied, built within, and possibly even constructed, what are traditionally regarded as site types of an early medieval date as their places of residence. O'Conor has theorized that one of the reasons for this pattern relates to the Gaelic elite striving to construct deliberate anachronisms in their places of residence, as a demonstration of their lordly prowess, a social display designed to highlight their legitimate place within a landscape and a legacy tied to an ancient, heroic past (O'Conor 2018, 161–5). It is also possible to argue that these lordly residences, which did not present with the defensibility of castles, were chosen because of the importance placed by their owners in how their *cenn áit* was viewed as a statement of immutable authority within a lordship. This theatrical display of power would have come in the form of a lightly defended elite residence, such was the level of security felt by the lord, among their people, in their *cenn áit*. Parallels for this have been suggested for places such as Ardtornish and Finlaggan, lordly centres of the Lords of the Isles in western Scotland, and in the largely undefended Scandanavian royal centres of the same period, which are all notable by the deliberate choices in their location, construction and what their owners were attempting to display (Caldwell 2017, 142–3; Hansson 2020).

These constructed archaisms can be seen at many of the historically attested Ó Cellaig *cenn áiteanna*. In our three cases, these lordly centres possessed *crannóga* as their focal point, a monument type possessing a chronology that stretches the entire settlement history of Ireland, while at Galey, Uilliam Buide Ó Cellaig's mid-fourteenth-century *cenn áit* possessed an archaeological expression as a dry-stone walled cashel, again a monument traditionally regarded as being of early medieval date. In this instance, as well as in the case of the cashel uncovered on Illaunamona, it can be argued that these older settlement forms continued to be used by the Ó Cellaig elite into the later medieval period as a means of displaying an antique, archaic face to the world. Their northern neighbours, the Meic Diarmada and the Uí Conchobhair, chose to reside in a similar fashion, while simultaneously having the ability to fund the construction and patronage of up-to-date religious houses within their respective lordships (O'Conor 2018, 158–9). The parallel to this is seen with the Uí Chellaig constructing Kilconnell Friary in the mid-fourteenth century while residing at nearby Callow Lough where the principal high medieval settlement archaeology is a substantial *crannóg* and an historically attested *bódhún*. Similarly, when Uilliam Buide hosted the famous Christmas feast at his old-fashioned looking *cathair* at Galey, his *saoi sheancadha ocus ollam*, Seán Mór Ó Dubhagáin, would have been at his side. Seán Mór retired and died at the Ó Cellaig patronized hospital of the Crutched Friars of St John the Baptist at nearby Rindoon, a religious house rebuilt by the Uí Chellaig during the fifteenth century.

The foregoing aside, a point made by O'Conor in relation to this way of life must be highlighted here. Despite the attention placed on residing in these more old-fashioned elite settlement forms, Gaelic lords possessed the technical knowledge and resources to construct elaborate residences within these anachronistic settings. For this, O'Conor used the example of the large timber hall constructed within the Ó Conchobair moated site of Cloonfree. While the poetry sought to accentuate its deliberately old-fashioned looking feasting hall, its walls being built of post-and-wattle, and the heroic timeless nature of the activity that occurred within it, its description indicates that it possessed an entirely up-to-date, sophisticated cruck-roof system in order to support its heavy roof (Finan and O'Conor 2002, 81–2; O'Conor 2018, 166).

In the study area, there are two descriptions from 'house poems' associated with the Uí Chellaig worthy of consideration. Neither corresponded with upstanding remains, unfortunately, but the descriptions are illuminating. In the earlier of the two, *Táth aoinfhir ar iath Maineach*, great detail is applied to the building of a new 'court' by Uilliam Buide at an unidentified 'island' site, presumably a *crannóg* or natural island fortress at possibly Lough Croan or Callow Lough. This post and wattle feasting hall was described as a 'refined dwelling' that required the application of skilled craftsmen to construct it (*Táth aoinfhir*, q14–21). The building of this new 'court' on the island site represents a coupling of older settlement forms with the construction of up-to-date lordly accommodation. Similarly, in *Filidh Éreann Go Haointeach*, the focal point of Uilliam Buide's feast at Galey is a timber and stone-constructed, elaborately decorated hall, which seems to incorporate advanced building techniques and the employment of skilled carpenters and metalworkers. This feasting hall is located within a dry-stone-walled cashel, again showing the juxtaposition between the seemingly archaic cashel and the possibly old-fashioned looking, but first-rate elite residence within (*FÉGH*, 61, 63). Therefore, it can be safely concluded that, despite the narrative that the Gaelic Irish at this time were backward and poorer than their Anglo-Norman counterparts, the evidence presented here shows that the Ó Cellaig elite had the resources and technical knowledge to build complex defended settlements, but for practical, social and cultural reasons, a separate and different approach was advocated for in the case of these eastern Connacht lords.

Spatial organization in the later medieval Ó Cellaig lordly centres
One of the attributes noted as regards a number of the Ó Cellaig lordly centres was the way in which the elite environment was laid out spatially. These lordly centres served a number of purposes. They were the location of an elite defended residence, but they were also the administrative, agricultural, economic and trade centres for the lord's estate in that area. There were temporal as well as spiritual considerations to be satisfied. The high-status group would have required attendants in close proximity to serve the lord and his retinue on a day-to-day basis, while it is clear that learned

kindreds played an important role at these estates and were near at hand as a consequence. More than this, in all of the lordly centres investigated as part of this research, access to communication routes, both overland and riverine, was a common characteristic, while in the case of Callow Lough, Galey and Ballaghdacker Lough-Athleague, the lordly centre possessed some form of settlement nucleation of the wider community within the catchment area of the *cenn áit* itself. What is clear is that these lordly centres were the focal points within a wider cultural landscape which developed around the *cenn áit*. However, all of these traits, while being linked to the focal point of the elite landscape, the defended residence, were also positioned at a slight geographical remove from the core of the lordly centre.

This spatial organization is different from the high medieval Anglo-Norman lordly centres, where the catalogue of attributes described above would have been fulfilled by the establishment of a nucleated agricultural village or urban settlement adjacent to the elite residence. Historical evidence for this from the study area can be seen with the grants provided to Richard de la Rochelle to erect a castle, host markets, fairs and warrens, and establish a gallows at his manor of Aughrim and in the surrounding area in 1253 and 1258, while places such as Kilkenny, Dungarvan, Co. Waterford and Rindoon, Co. Roscommon, for instance, show the close spatial organization between the variety of roles expected at an Anglo-Norman lordly centre in a range of landscape contexts (see Bradley 2000; Ó Drisceoil 2020, 161–3; Pollock 2020, 197–208; O'Conor, Naessens and Sherlock 2015; O'Conor and Shanahan 2018; Shanahan and O'Conor 2020). Taking Rindoon as a case study, evidence survives for a hospital, town walls, a parish church, a number of houses aligned along a main street, a substantial harbour with a ship slipway, dock and jetty features, as well as the castle itself, and associated elite landscape features such as a fishpond, warren, windmill and possible deerpark (O'Conor and Shanahan 2018, 21–37).

These same roles also needed to be fulfilled at the lordly centres of the Gaelic elite. However, this profusion of amenities and economic features did not correspond with the establishment of towns in later medieval Gaelic Ireland, with a few notable exceptions (Nicholls 2003, 139–40; Simms 2018b, 421). The results of the excavations at the moated site in Rockingham Demesne in 2016, which uncovered a range of high medieval artefacts, as well as a large corn-drying kiln, has been attributed by Finan to the historical attestation of a *baile marcaid* (market) being constructed by the Meic Diarmada on the shores of Lough Cé in 1231 (*AC*; *ALC*; Finan 2020, 60–1). Finan is right to point out that this market is not likely to have constituted a later medieval urban settlement in Maigh Luirg, while also highlighting that these urban settlements seem to be absent from Gaelic Ireland more generally (Finan 2020, 63).

If we accept that the lordly centres of the study area were not accompanied by what modern observers would describe as towns or large villages, how did an Ó Cellaig lordly centre look in *c*.1350? The most suitable exemplars for this discussion are

Callow Lough, Galey, and Ballaghdacker Lough. In these instances, the *cenn áit* is located at a geographical remove from the presumed physical community hubs of Kilconnell, *Baile na Gáile* and Athleague respectively, all located on major roadways through eastern Connacht. The community hubs in these instances are located, on average, *c.*3km away from the *cenn áit*. Undoubtedly, the *cenn áit* would have had a small group of houses surrounding it. It is likely that the majority of these houses accommodated the day-to-day retainers to the lord's household and their families, in the form of householders, craftspeople, livestock herders and so on. Based on pictorial evidence from elsewhere, these houses are likely to have been similar to the 'creat', a circular or ovoid, one-room house, constructed of wattle and daub and covered with sods (O'Conor 1998, 95–6; 2002, 201–4). Aside from this accommodation, however, the community focus must have been consistent with the latter settlements. Using Barry's theory for where tower houses were placed in the landscape, the castle served as the social focus of the community, but not the physical one (Barry 2006, 28–30). The earlier elite residence seems to have operated in the same fashion. There are a number of valid suggestions as to why this divide was in place, including the additional security, exclusivity and privacy provided by maintaining this separation between the lord and the population of the settlement. While it is possible that all of these reasons had a role to play, one of the single-most important reasons for this space between the *cenn áit* and these 'dispersed' nucleated settlements relates back to the principal form of wealth accumulated by the later medieval Gaelic Irish, cattle. The overwhelming primacy of the pastoral economy to the Ó Cellaig elites may be at the heart of why the *cenn áit* was separated from the community hub, in the sense that the landholdings directly farmed by the lord would have encircled the *cenn áit*, meaning that this space was needed to feed and maintain the lord's substantial herds, something that may be elicited from Viscount Ramón de Perellós's account of Gaelic settlement practices among the Ó Neills in Tír Eoghain in 1397: 'Their dwellings are communal and most of them are set up near the oxen …' (Carpenter (ed.) 1988, 111). The place-names of Farranykelly – *Farann Uí Chellaig* (Ó Cellaig's land) at Ballaghdacker Lough, Cloonykelly – *Cluain Uí Chellaig* (Ó Cellaig's meadow) at Athleague, the ringfort name of Lisnagry – *Lios na g-croidh* (the fort of the cattle/wealth) at Callow Lough, and the *bódhúin* at these latter sites, along with the range of townland names referencing cattle surrounding Galey and Lough Croan, all point towards the immediate lands around these elite focal points being reserved for the maintenance of the lord's herds, the source of his wealth and status.

This observation can be extended to explain why some of the principal service kindreds identifiable as a part of the wider Ó Cellaig lordly centre also possessed landholdings that correspond broadly with modern townlands. These learned families received their lands in return for service to the lord and often held these roles through several generations. Certain services, such as those provided by physicians, poets and historians, were pivotal to the life of a Gaelic lord. As such, their holdings were often found in close proximity to the *cenn áit*. Conversely, in the case of military kindreds, their positioning in the landscape was also consistent with that role, as in the case of the Mac Dubhghaill galloglass kindred, who were strategically located at Ballygalda, effectively creating a 'soft border' at the edge of the territory (Curley and Timoney, 2024). Patrick has identified the Mac Domhnaill galloglass as being similarly placed in respect of the later medieval Ó Neill lords of Tír Eoghain in her research (Patrick 2022, 230–1).

One of the more routine means by which these service families received payment for their services was an immunity from paying *cís* (tribute), while gifts of horses, drinking goblets and herds of cattle and other livestock were routine (FitzPatrick 2018, 172; Simms 2018b, 423; 2020, 360, 366; Sheehan 2019, 23). Indeed, in certain cases, these learned and military families became large-scale farmers based on their patronage to a lord (Hughes 1994–5, 85–8). This means that the space granted by the lord to these families was provided in order that they could accumulate and maintain the wealth acquired through their services. One of the more striking examples of this accommodation of hereditary learned families at a lordly centre within the study area can be seen at Callow Lough, where the landholdings of five service kindreds to the Ó Cellaig lord have been identified across the northern and eastern sides of the lake itself.

In essence, the main difference between the Anglo-Norman manorial and urban settlements and those of the Gaelic Irish community, in this study area at least, relates to their spatial organization. Anglo-Norman settlements were clustered, with all of the key requirements of a lordly centre in close proximity to the elite residence. By contrast, the Ó Cellaig elite settlement landscape was organized in a manner possibly best described as 'dispersed nucleation', with all of the key requirements of the Gaelic lordly centre in geographical reach, within a couple of kilometres or so, and so more spread out. Perhaps security, particularly in a frontier setting, was high on the agenda when planning an Anglo-Norman lordly centre, while accommodation of the principal resource that drove the economy of later medieval Uí Maine, cattle, may have been the more important preoccupation in the development of an Ó Cellaig *cenn áit* and hinterland at that time. From a purely practical point of view, herds of cattle need a considerable amount of space within which to graze, as well as a regular and consistent water supply. It seems likely that these requirements played a significant role in the spatial organization of the Gaelic lordly centre and its constituent parts.

In discussing the nuanced spatial organization of the high medieval Ó Cellaig lordly centres, it has become apparent that one of the key, yet terribly underutilized, resources available to the archaeological researcher must be the place-name evidence that has survived to the present day. As has been stated, although undated, many of the townland divisions, in particular, and their accompanying names, can be dated to at least as early as the twelfth century, but it is possible that the townland system could date to the early medieval period or even earlier. It is safe to say that some of the key findings of this research would not have been uncovered, or the insights would have been severely limited, had the toponymical information which survives for the study area not been consulted and interpreted. In the absence of many of the socio-economic records, the place-name database, *logainm.ie*, is a means of gaining vital information for the reconstruction of the past environment and cultural landscape organization of later medieval Gaelic Ireland.

THE LATE MEDIEVAL SETTLEMENT LANDSCAPE

Tower house castles

Turning to the late medieval period, the principal elite settlement form to emerge in the Ó Cellaig lordship is the tower house castle. As has been outlined already, the tower house possesses a chronology that seems to really begin in the last decades of the fourteenth century and continue through to the 1640s (McNeill 1997, 202–5), with the vast majority, particularly the ones built by Gaelic lords, constructed in the fifteenth and sixteenth centuries. In terms of when the Uí Chellaig began building these castles, there is little clear information. The earliest potential tower house is the historically attested castle built by the *Clannmhaicne Eoghan* Uí Chellaig at *Áth na Stuaidhe* at Ballinasloe in 1406 (*MIA*), but only excavation will be able to conclusively state whether this castle was of tower house form. The next date for an Ó Cellaig tower house corresponds with a reference to a castle at Callow in the year 1475. In this instance, despite the fragmentary remains on site, it is highly likely that a tower house once stood here. As such, based on the presently available information, there is no evidence to suggest that tower houses were constructed by the Uí Chellaig prior to the beginning of the fifteenth century at least, which is in keeping with the information available from other Gaelic lordships. As for the origins of tower house-building in the Ó Cellaig lordship, we are on similarly unstable ground. There has been very little research to date into the reasons why the Gaelic elite began adopting the tower house as their settlement form of choice from around 1400. O'Conor has remarked that there is no available evidence to suggest that major changes occurred in military techniques or in how Gaelic society operated at this time, which may have necessitated the first widespread construction of castles during the later medieval period by the Gaelic Irish (O'Conor 1998, 102). Instead, one of the most reasoned arguments relating to this embracing of the tower house by the Gaelic Irish concerns the gradual cross-cultural exchange that took place over the decades and centuries since the Anglo-Normans first began to establish lordships in Ireland in the late twelfth century. By the fourteenth century, large parts of what was the Anglo-Norman colony had become Gaelicized, which saw the spread and adoption of a range of Irish customs, even down to the proclamation of their lords in a fashion in keeping with Gaelic inauguration practices (ibid., 103; FitzPatrick 2001; Simms 2018b, 426–9).

As stated, this exchange was cross-cultural in nature and aspects of Anglo-Norman culture were no doubt adopted by the Gaelic Irish also. Intermarriage between the two cultures is one of the most identifiable ways in which this contact was established, and ideas exchanged, and it is noteworthy that Gaelic women were married to Anglo-Norman men from the late twelfth and thirteenth centuries onwards. One notable early example is William *Gorm* de Lacy (1180–1233), son of Hugh de Lacy, lord of Meath, who married a daughter of Ruaidrí Ó Conchobair, high king of Ireland (Veach and Verstraten Veach 2013, 63–4). However, it is not until the second half of the fourteenth century that the Gaelic lords of what constitutes modern Roscommon, such as the Uí Chonchobair and the Meic Diarmada, began marrying women from the prominent Anglo-Norman families in the wider region.[1] From an Ó Cellaig perspective, Uilliam Buide (r. c.1349–81) and Maolsechlainn Ó Cellaig (r. 1381–1401) are the only attested lords of Uí Maine by c.1400 to have taken an Anglo-Norman wife. Uilliam Buide married a daughter of Seoinin *Búrc*, while Maolsechlainn married a daughter of one Báitéar a *Búrc*. There are other instances recorded in the annals and genealogies during this time for intermarriage between women from Ó Cellaig elite and minor elite families and men from Anglo-Norman families such as the *Búrc*, *Seoighe* (Joyce), Mac Jordan d'Exeter and *Mac Fheorais* (de Bermingham) (*AC, s.a.* 1356, 1419; *Ó CGF i*, 35, 48). Aside from intermarriage, opportunities for cross-cultural exchange would have occurred through marketplace and higher-level trade and economic contact, particularly in the Anglo-Norman towns located at the fringes of the lordship, as evidenced earlier through the presence of Anglo-Norman coinage at many of these sites. Another possible avenue for this interchange presented itself through the mustering of combatants for Anglo-Norman military expeditions to other regions and there are surviving records for the Uí Chellaig being summoned to fight for Henry III in Scotland in 1244, against the 'Irish of Meath' in 1289, and into the Leinster Mountains in late 1308. It is also worth noting that fosterage may have played a role in the development of pan-insular connections between Gaelic Irish and Anglo-Norman lords (Lennon 2005, 63). While there is no direct information on the Ó Cellaig in this respect, sobriquets such as Sinnach *Soghain*, Sitric *Teabthach* (of Tethba, modern Longford and north Westmeath) Tadhg *Tailltenn* (Teltown, Co. Meath) and Donnchad *Muimnech* (Munsterman) demonstrate that the Ó Cellaig elites must have entered into fosterage agreements with other native families during this time at the very least.

An indication of what must have been cross-cultural exchange is seen with the use of the Anglo-Norman first names, such as, Uilliam among the Ó Cellaig elite, the first

---

1 O'Conor, K., pers. comm., citing Charles Owen O'Conor Don, *The O'Conors of Connaught* (Dublin: Hodges, Figgis and Co., 1891), 140; Dermot MacDermot, *MacDermot of Moylurg* (Manorhamilton: Drumlin Publications, 1996), 90.

Uí Maine lord to be found with this name being Uilliam Buide Ó Cellaig. The most enduring physical manifestation of this cross-cultural exchange for late medieval Gaelic Ireland seems to come primarily in the form of the tower house (O'Conor 1998, 103–4; O'Keeffe 2000, 51–3). That it was built by both the Anglo-Normans and the Gaelic Irish indicates that a level of cultural uniformity had developed around this time. It is interesting to note the directness of cultural change that seems to occur upon the arrival of Anglo-Norman women into the lordly families of Gaelic Connacht and the fact that the generation that followed seemed to correspond with the adoption of the tower house as the elite settlement form of choice. In terms of the number of tower houses extant in the Ó Cellaig lordship, the ASI database records twenty. However, consultation of the database for the area records a total of forty-nine castles of unclassified form. Not all of the unclassified castles are dateable to the late medieval period, but a considerable number of them are referred to in the lists compiled of Galway and Roscommon castles and their owners in 1573–4 in advance of the *Compossicion of Conought* (Nolan 1900–1; Nicholls (transcribed) 1573, 2019). Judging by their presence in these lists, as well as annalistic entries, along with evidence from early modern and modern cartographic sources, it appears that most of these are the sites of late medieval Gaelic castles. This suggests an underrepresentation of the number of tower houses constructed and occupied in the area. There is a number of arguments to support this.

As has been outlined over the previous chapters, a number of the Ó Cellaig *cenn áiteanna* have castles of unclassified form located at them. In terms of the best way to approach the study of these castle sites, O'Conor and Williams have highlighted that it is only through the application of a multidisciplinary approach that a fuller understanding of late medieval castle studies in Ireland can be achieved, one which uses the combined evidence of all disciplines, sources and methods available, in order to give a clearer picture of how a particular castle developed through time. This is broadly the same methodology that this study has been based upon (O'Conor and Williams 2015, 64). Having applied the desk-based research to these sites, one of the principal means by which I could diagnose the likelihood of the former presence of a tower house at an Ó Cellaig lordly centre was through inspection of the surviving masonry, particularly investigation for the presence of punch-dressed stones and the remains of ogee-headed windows. Punch-dressed cut stones are seen in Ireland on buildings dating to the period from the last years of the fourteenth century through to *c.*1600, maybe a little later in parts of Connacht (McAfee 1997, 28). Punch-dressing is especially associated with late medieval tower houses and friaries (Leask 1941, 82; McNeill 1997, 202–3; O'Conor, Brady, Connon and Fidalgo-Romo 2010, 25; O'Conor and Williams 2015, 62–3; O'Conor and Fredengren 2019, 84). For their part, ogee-headed windows are also a feature of tower houses of mainly fifteenth- to mid-sixteenth-century date (Leask 1941, 24, 75–124; McNeill 1997, 201–2; O'Conor and Williams 2015, 62–4).

Medieval Gaelic Ireland and the Ó Cellaig lordship 259

When I inspected the remains at Turrock, Callow, Athleague, Mote Demesne and Lisdaulan, as well as what is recorded as an 'Anglo-Norman masonry castle' at both Aughrim and Ballinasloe, the physical evidence indicates that tower houses are likely to have once stood at all of these places. This adds seven tower houses to the study area, where the focus has been narrowed to the Ó Cellaig lordly centres specifically, as opposed to any other family groups. Using these seven sites as a representative sample, it can be argued that it is possible that most, if not all, of the castles of unclassified form in the study area could, in fact, be ruined tower houses, bringing the total number of castles of tower house form in this region to potentially as high as seventy-one, a huge increase on the twenty hitherto accepted.

The application of this methodology highlights how little archaeological research has been undertaken on the tower houses of the late medieval Ó Cellaig lordship and of Gaelic Ireland more generally to date (Barry 1993; 1996, 140; O'Conor 2001, 330–1; O'Conor and Williams 2015, 60–4). This lack of research has created an unfortunate ambiguity which revolves around the present physical state of the late medieval castles in south Roscommon and east Galway. For instance, the historically attested Ó Cellaig lordly castles at Lisdaulan, Callow, Athleague, Mote Demesne and Turrock, but also at Gallagh, Tiaquin, and Mullaghmore do not survive for inspection, while only partial remains survive for Galey, Aughrim, Barnaderg, Garbally and the *Clannmhaicne Eoghain* Ó Cellaig castle at Ballinasloe. However, in all cases, these monuments are likely to have been of tower house form. Arguably the only surviving late medieval lordly castle of the senior Ó Cellaig line still extant is at Monivea, Co. Galway, which was acquired by the French family in 1609 and that is very much altered from its late medieval phase. Beyond the Ó Cellaig themselves, it is clear that the lord of Uí Maine was not the only one to be able to afford a tower house in this period. Members of the cadet branches of the Uí Cellaig constructed them, as did members of vassal clans such as the Meic Eochadha of Magh Finn and the Uí Mainnin of Soghain, among others. More than this, prosperous members of traditional service kindreds, such as the Mac an Bhaird learned poetic family and the Mac Dubhghaill galloglass kindred, are recorded in possession of castles in these lists. These conceivably came in the form of tower houses. In modern Roscommon more generally, research by other scholars indicates that previously unrecognized tower houses were located at Ballinagare House (Uí Conchobair Donn), Tulsk Fort and possibly Strokestown, recorded in the State Paper List as *Beallnemolle* – Béal na mBuillí (both Uí Conchobair Ruadh), and on the Rock of Lough Cé (Meic Diarmada), showing that the lack of surviving above ground remains for tower houses extends into the eastern Connacht region more generally (Brady 2009, 22–3; O'Conor, Brady, Connon and Fidalgo-Romo 2010, 24–7; O'Conor and Williams 2015, 63–4; Nicholls (transcribed) 1573, 2019). Unfortunately, this lack of surviving remains in most cases has limited our understanding of the specifics of this settlement form among the Uí Chellaig during the final centuries of their authority in the region, leaving us, in most cases, with only the castle sites to inspect. While it is beyond the scope of this research, an important question to address with future study is the reason or reasons for the regional phenomenon of tower house removal.

How does this fit into the wider archaeological understanding of late medieval castle studies in Ireland? It is clear now that huge numbers of tower houses were constructed, particularly during the fifteenth and sixteenth century. Using archaeological, historical and cartographic sources, it has been plausibly argued that anything up to 7,000 tower houses were erected by the end of the sixteenth century (Barry 1996, 140; O'Conor 2008, 329–32; O'Conor and Williams 2015, 63–4). The evidence from Uí Maine helps corroborate this argument for much larger numbers of tower houses than has hitherto being argued by scholars from Leask to Sweetman. The very large numbers of tower houses constructed during this period, as opposed to the far fewer numbers erected in other eras, arguably made Ireland the most castellated part of Europe around the year 1600 – a fact that is not regularly acknowledged by scholars either inside or outside Ireland (Cairns 1987, 21; O'Conor 1998, 25; Barry 2008, 129; O'Conor 2023, 186). The evidence outlined above merely serves to confirm Barry's argument for far more of this castle type being built in late medieval Ireland than once thought when looking at the tower houses that once stood in the Ó Cellaig lordship. The decision by Loeber to provide a distribution map of the definite and possible tower houses within the Gaelic and Gaelicized lordships of late medieval Ireland using the information provided in the *Atlas of the Irish rural landscape* was open-minded in its approach (Aalen, Whelan and Stout (eds) 1997, 59, Fig. 67; Loeber 2001, 283; 2019, 9). The distribution map included the castles of unclassified form, presumably accepting that they must, by and large, represent degraded examples of tower houses on the ground, something which has been shown to be largely correct as regards the study area and contrasts with the very low numbers recorded by the ASI.

As regards the location of these Ó Cellaig tower houses, aside from the ones which seem to be sited close to the overland or riverine routeways as the main concern, all are to be found at lordly centres displaying a long duration of continuity of elite settlement through the later medieval period and, in some cases, before. As such, the adoption of the tower house as the settlement form of choice within these landscapes indicates that the Ó Cellaig elite sought to embrace the new trend in residence choice in late medieval Ireland, while being careful to retain a deliberate link with their lordly centres of long standing. As well as this, there is some evidence at these lordly centres for the continued importance, and indeed occupation, of the older settlement forms as a means of maintaining and enhancing this link with the past. For instance, Turrock Castle was constructed on the shore across from Edward's Island at Lough Croan. At Callow Lough, the tower house was constructed within the earlier *bódhún* and facing out onto the *crannóg* at the centre of that lake, which itself was worthy of depiction on

Browne's 1591 map, possibly indicative of its continued use into the late sixteenth century. At Athleague, the tower house was again constructed within a *bódhún* enclosure, while Galey Castle was located within a dry-stone walled cashel. Finally, Aughrim is a historically attested thirteenth-century Ó Cellaig lordly centre, where a branch of the dynasty also constructed and occupied a tower house at some point in the late medieval period. The location of these tower houses within and adjacent to these older settlement forms is important to note in terms of the elite mindset in and of itself, but it also greatly increases the likelihood that these *crannóga*, *bódhúin*, cashels and indeed promontory forts were still operational and important parts of a late medieval lordly centre, a narrative that is in keeping with the evidence available from other parts of Gaelic Ireland. In doing so, the lord may have been seeking to retain a physical link with the past at these places, in order to justify and restate his authority in the present (see Logue 2018).

The archaeological expression of wealth in the late medieval Ó Cellaig lordship
The history of late medieval Gaelic Ireland is a difficult topic to grapple with for the historian, given that the sources available for inspection are not as accessible, or as easy to interpret, as the traditional source material that has enabled the reconstruction of large parts of Anglo-Norman Ireland during the same period. The lack of socio-economic records is a case in point in relation to this imbalance in surviving documentation. As a result, many of the conclusions arrived at by historians in relation to this time and place in Ireland's history are coloured by these perceived difficulties with what they consider to be the primary information, that is, historical documentation alone. Some historians for this period still accept the type of conclusions drawn by Goddard Henry Orpen, who compared the Anglo-Norman arrival in Ireland in the late twelfth century with the civilizing effect that the Roman Empire had on Europe, highlighting the progress made and benefits provided by the Anglo-Normans to the island of Ireland and its society in the century and a half after 1169 (Orpen 2005, 560–87). The same historian, writing in the early twentieth century, letting his personal biases dominate his writing of history, bemoaned what he perceived to be a cultural regression in the years which followed the Gaelic Resurgence, which was 'distinguished by the recrudescence of Celtic tribalism and its spurious imitation by many of Anglo-Norman descent. The door was now finally closed on a century-and-a-half of remarkable progress, vigour, and comparative order, and two centuries of retrogression, stagnation, and comparative anarchy were about to be ushered in (ibid., 559). As noted above, few researchers have chosen to study the later medieval Ó Cellaig lordship, and when it has been studied, it has been primarily through the historical discipline. For the late medieval period, interpretation of the historical record has concluded that, somewhat in keeping with Orpen's stance, the Ó Cellaig lordship became consumed with internal dissension, developed a weak

central authority and, ultimately, stagnated and declined in terms of its power and influence (Nicholls 2003, 176–7; 2008, 425; Cosgrove 2008, 579). If this is the case, can this historical interpretation be identified in the archaeology?

The archaeological evidence from this period does not seem to corroborate the accepted historical narrative. If political decline can be measured through the physical expressions of lordship among these eastern Connacht lords, it seems that the opposite is, in fact, the case. As outlined above, tower houses were one of the principal lordly residences constructed by these late medieval lords, which indicates an interest in displaying modernity and affluence within their ancestral *cenn áiteanna* landscapes, and the scale of Galey Castle was certainly a demonstration of this prosperity and authority (Barry 1987, 168–98; Simms 2018b, 421). However, this is not the only way in which wealth and affluence was displayed by the Uí Chellaig at this time. This was a time when religious foundations were heavily patronized by the Ó Cellaig chiefs, with rebuilding works undertaken at Kilconnell Franciscan Friary, the Hospital of the Crutched Friars of St John the Baptist at Rindoon and the Augustinian Monastery of Cluain Tuaiscirt O Máine. It is also during this time that the architecturally-rich Ó Cellaig tomb was inserted and the wall paintings commissioned at Abbeyknockmoy, an important religious foundation within what was now an expanded territory under Ó Cellaig control. Furthermore, portable religious items, such as chalices, illustrated books and other religious objects commissioned by the Ó Cellaig for Kilconnell Friary continue this pattern of wealth display.

When considering books and manuscripts as artefacts, wealth is also demonstrable through the commissioning of *Leabhar Ua Maine*, the recording of *Nósa Ua Maine*, as well as the heavy patronage of praise poets during the fifteenth and sixteenth centuries. All are displays of the overt interest which these powerful and wealthy late medieval Gaelic lords took in patronizing the arts, while simultaneously cementing their legitimacy and documenting their legacy on the territories under their control. It is even possible to suggest that this interest in learning and the arts by the Uí Chellaig might have been a Gaelic Irish manifestation of the Renaissance ideas which were in vogue at the same time in continental Europe. Whether this is the case is immaterial for the present research. However, the information gleaned from the surviving archaeological remains of the late medieval Ó Cellaig lordship indicates that this territory was very wealthy and powerful during the fifteenth and sixteenth centuries, contradicting the accepted historical narrative, which relies on infrequent annalistic references to familial infighting and periodic divisions in the lordship in order to arrive at its conclusion. As a result, it can be stated with confidence that a reconstruction of the lordly centres and the cultural landscapes that surrounded them in the late medieval Ó Cellaig lordship is best achieved through application of the multidisciplinary approach. Here, toponymical and literary source material, coupled with the well-preserved, but sadly understudied and under-interpreted archaeological remains, can provide a well-rounded picture for this part of later medieval Gaelic Ireland, something which could not have been achieved through depending on the historical sources alone. The archaeological discipline in Ireland, particularly medieval archaeology, has increasingly valued the greater breadth of information available to the researcher of medieval Ireland. Unfortunately, the same approach does not seem to be recognized with parity in historical academia, which despite the merits of the research being undertaken, suffers from this singular approach (see, also O'Conor and Fredengren 2019, 80). Two recent publications which serve to illustrate the undervaluing of archaeology to the reconstruction of later medieval Ireland is seen with *The Cambridge history of Ireland, Volume I: 600–1550* (Smith (ed.) 2018), and *Gaelic Ulster in the Middle Ages* (Simms 2020), where the decision to largely marginalize the discipline of archaeology in both cases has distorted our understanding of this time and place. It is clear now that any future research into the character and organization of later medieval Gaelic Ireland must incorporate and interpret the vital information that can be gleaned from careful analysis of the archaeological remains of a given case study area in order to achieve a well-rounded reconstruction of the past environment and society.

THE LANDSCAPE AND ECONOMY OF THE LATER MEDIEVAL Ó CELLAIG LORDSHIP

The landscape of later medieval eastern Connacht, as reconstructed in Chapter 3, would have been very different to how it appears today. Cartographical, toponymical and historical information combined indicate that large areas of woodland once stood within the territory, particularly in what is now south Roscommon. Bogland was, and in much of the area still is, quite extensive, while the callowlands and floodplains of the Rivers Shannon, Suck and their tributaries contributed to zones that present with very little evidence of settlement in the later medieval period. Communication routes through this landscape were dictated by these diverse environmental conditions, with waterways presenting as an easier route of communication in some areas, by comparison to the meandering overland routes which developed in what is now eastern and central Galway in particular and which presumably required constant maintenance in order to keep them open.

Conversely, a lot of this region is underserved by very fertile soils, which meant that there was a considerable amount of agricultural land available to serve as the primary economic driver. One of the notable aspects of this research is that, perhaps unsurprisingly, the Ó Cellaig lordly centres were all located in the most productive agricultural areas of the territory. It is possible that there was a correlation between the territories held by vassal clans to the Uí Chellaig as opposed to the lords of Uí Maine themselves with a decline in terms of agricultural productivity in those former areas.

It has been demonstrated that a variety of resources were obtained from these diverse contexts, and the accumulation and distribution of these commodities would have served as the economic underpinning to the wealth displayed by the Uí Chellaig in the high and, particularly, the late medieval period. Certainly greater economic influence in the region would have provided the tools to establish greater political control, and this in turn assisted in the western expansion of the territory under their authority in the fifteenth century in Clann Taidg and Uí Diarmata. Indeed, this research has been able to reconstruct the changing extents of the territory under the authority of the Uí Chellaig and their Uí Maine ancestors from *c.* AD 800 through to *c.*1500, which highlights the amount of change in authority which occurred during that time, as well as providing a series of territorial maps which can be used to better understand the history and archaeology of the study area going forward.

***

This chapter has confirmed the settlement forms chosen by the Ó Cellaig elite, as found at their historically attested lordly centres, throughout the later medieval period. Broadly divided between high medieval and late medieval settlement forms, there is a distinct cultural trend which emerges in the Ó Cellaig lordship post *c.*1400, or perhaps a decade or two earlier, in the adoption of the tower house castle, a pattern which is matched in other Gaelic-controlled regions. Prior to this, however, this research highlights the long continuity of occupation of archaeological monuments that are traditionally accepted to belong to the early medieval period, in particular the *crannóg*, cashel and ringfort. Beyond these, evidence for Gaelic-constructed moated sites indicates what is likely to be the first real archaeological manifestation of cross-cultural exchange in a secular context between the Gaelic Irish and their Anglo-Norman counterparts in the region, perhaps influenced by building trends further away, in the Ó Conchobair *tricha cét* of Machaire Connacht. The final two high medieval elite settlement forms to be considered are largely unexplored in the archaeological discipline for later medieval Gaelic Ireland to date, and one of the major conclusions from this research is that the promontory fort and *bódhún* must be added to the list of site morphologies that need to be considered when studying the archaeology of Gaelic lordly centres into the future.

High medieval Anglo-Norman castles were found to be few on the ground, while Gaelic-constructed castles, or what contemporaries then, or modern scholars now, accept as castles, are absent entirely in the Ó Cellaig lordship. This indicates that Gaelic society was ordered and organized in a manner not conducive to the building of castles at this time, with the elite expressions of wealth and power occurring in different ways to that of the Anglo-Norman parts of Ireland in the high medieval period. How these Ó Cellaig lordly centres were organized geographically bolsters the earlier point, with the considerations and motives required from a Gaelic lord expressed on the landscape in a different way than by their Anglo-Norman counterparts. The evidence seems to suggest that 'dispersed nucleation' developed around Gaelic lordly centres due to a feeling of security in the landscape as well as the need to retain grazing lands around the *cenn áit* itself to maintain the lord's substantial livestock herds. By contrast, an Anglo-Norman lordly centre was clustered in a manorial or urban settlement expression, with the more pressing need for security in mind.

Moving to the late medieval period, a degree of homogeneousness begins to occur with how the Uí Chellaig elite chose to reside, as they adopted a trend seen throughout large parts of Gaelic Ireland in the form of the tower house. The origins of this emerging cultural uniformity between Gaelic Irish elite culture and Anglo-Norman culture are difficult to trace, but one of the clearest ways in which this may have occurred is intermarriage. The slight recording of tower houses on the ground, as distinct from other similar areas, has been addressed with regard to the need to inspect the large numbers of castles of unclassified form with a multidisciplinary methodology. This approach may enable the cataloguing of a number of sites which are perhaps listed too readily as being of unclassified form in the south Roscommon and east Galway region at present.

Finally, the vital, but underutilized role which archaeology can play in reconstructing the past environment of, in this case, later medieval Gaelic Ireland, is exemplified by the contrasting archaeological evidence which survives on the wealth and authority which the Ó Cellaig lords retained in their late medieval lordship, as distinct from what the traditional historical narratives have arrived at for the same time and place. Interpreting the broad range of available information using a multidisciplinary methodology, including the underutilized but very valuable place-name evidence, has allowed for a much richer and integrated understanding of the later medieval Ó Cellaig lordship to be presented. This, in turn, has a number of direct and indirect benefits for further research in this study area and in the study of later medieval Gaelic Ireland more generally.

A multidisciplinary methodology is the most suitable way through which to reconstruct different facets of the later medieval lordship of Uí Maine and this approach must be applied more generally to the study of the historic past. Indeed, I am concerned at the present state of affairs in historical studies in Ireland, which routinely sees many Irish historians shy away from the very valuable results and interpretations which have been arrived at by their colleagues working in the discipline of archaeology. It is plain to see that the only way to successfully reach an understanding of, in particular, later medieval Gaelic Ireland, is through a collaborative effort between disciplines. Until the need for such interdisciplinarity is accepted and adopted more fully, valuable interpretations and even vital information will be overlooked in our attempts to understand an entire period of our past.

The study has resulted in the emergence of a number of research questions which require further investigation, in time, in order to add to our understanding of the Ó Cellaig lordship specifically and later medieval Gaelic Ireland more generally. In terms of the geographical characteristics of this lordship, one of the first questions which deserves further research relates to the underexplored role which the important regional waterways of the Rivers Shannon and Suck played in the lives of the later medieval communities who lived within their catchments. This work would build on the important findings of Stark at Cloondadauv, Co. Galway, and of Hall on the castle sites of Lough Derg. Such study would be an important development in our understanding of the place which these rivers held in terms of communications, economically, recreationally, as well as symbolically, in this time and place, as well as considering the different types of watercraft employed for these purposes.

Another major question which needs to be answered by future research relates to the application of remote sensing investigations and a subsequent research excavation of a ringfort which is a historically attested residence of a member of the Ó Cellaig elite, vassal clan or service kindred family associated with the lords of Uí Maine. A number of potentially suitable targets could be considered for inspection, not least the ringforts at Lisnagavragh, Liswilliam, Garrynphort and Coolderry within the limits of the Lough Croan lordly centre, Lisnagry Fort in Lisdonnellroe townland and Lisfineel Fort in Ballydoogan townland in association with the Callow Lough lordly centre, or indeed the ringfort in Cornacask townland related to the Ballaghdacker Lough lordly centre. Furthermore, the site of the enclosure in Ashford townland may also be worth consideration with regard to the *Clannmhaicne Eoghain* minor Ó Cellaig lordly centre. An excavation of one or more of these sites would greatly enhance our understanding of ringfort occupation beyond the traditional dates ascribed to them, as well as informing us about the material culture and habitation practices of those strata of later medieval Gaelic society within the study area.

Based on the findings of the present research, it is clear that the promontory fort, as well as the newly-coined monument type known as the *bódhún*, had a significant role to play in the archaeologies of the *cenn áiteanna* of the later medieval Ó Cellaig lords. Adding the promontory forts of the study area to those sites already identified as being occupied by the Gaelic elite during the later medieval period indicates that the promontory fort, both inland and coastal, was a monument type and a geographical feature which was utilized beyond their perceived settlement dates. This also highlights the need to consider these locations when conducting research into the lordly centres of the later medieval Gaelic Irish elsewhere. The *bódhún* is another monument classification which researchers need to consider when exploring the physical appearance of these *cenn áiteanna*, as there are undoubtedly more examples to be uncovered through future research in many other parts of the island.

Something else which is worthy of further enquiry relates to the origins of, and reasons behind, the explosion in tower house building which occurred during the late medieval period. This would benefit from the skills of historical enquiry, in order to further clarify the theory proposed by Barry in 2008 and to better understand the cross-cultural contacts which resulted in this increased uniformity in elite residence construction which began at the very end of the fourteenth century, undertaken by both the Anglo-Norman and Gaelic Irish communities.

Further landscape and micro-landscape research is required into the lordly centres of the later medieval Gaelic elite, as well as their hinterlands, in order to identify if settlement patterns among the Gaelic Irish communities correspond with the 'dispersed nucleation' model proposed by the present writer. For instance, does this pattern of spatial organization which sees the *cenn áit* separated by a distance of *c.*3km from the communal hub bear any resemblance to the spatial organization in other Gaelic lordship. Are there any other reasons apparent to explain why this geographical separation was established, beyond what has been argued herein?

In keeping with the earlier point, the successful identification of Gaelic lordly centres in the field also opens up the opportunity to explore the lives and lifeways for those of lower status in the lordship. One way to do this would be through the identification of the *cenn áit* and then exploring their surroundings for lower status dwelling sites similar to the 'creat'-type houses discussed above. Remote sensing investigations and targeted excavation based on these findings would be the most suitable methodology through which to investigate these areas, with the overall intention of bringing the stories of the day-to-day retainers to the lord and their families to light. Pursuing these avenues of enquiry has the potential to greatly enrich our understanding of the wider Gaelic population during the later medieval period, an area of the research which, at present, requires a great deal of attention.

Bibliography

PRIMARY SOURCES

36th report of the deputy keeper of public records, Ireland. Anon. 1904. Dublin.
A calendar of Irish chancery letters, c.1244–1509. Crooks, P. (ed.) 2012. Dublin: Trinity College. https://chancery.tcd.ie/. Accessed 16/11/2023.
A calendar of papal registers relating to Clonfert diocese. Larkin, P. (ed.) 2016. Lettertec.
Acts of the privy council of England, vols I–XXXII. Dasent, J.R. (ed.) 1890–1907. London.
'A description of Ireland: AD 1618'. McInerney, L. (ed.) 2012. *The Other Clare*, vol. 37. 33–7.
Annals of Clonmacnoise, Ó Muraíle, N. (ed.) 2022. Dublin.
Annála Connacht: the annals of Connacht, AD 1224–1544. Freeman, A.D. (ed.) 1944; 1977. Dublin.
Annala rioghachta Eireann: Annals of the kingdom of Ireland, by the Four Masters, from the earliest period to the year 1616. O'Donovan, J. (ed.) 1856. Dublin.
The annals of Loch Cé, RS 54, 2 vols. Hennessy, W.M. (ed. and trans.) 1871; reprint 1939. London, Dublin.
'Annals of Tigernach'. Stokes, W. (ed.) 1895–7. *Revue Celtique* 16–18.
Annála Uladh, Annals of Ulster, 4 vols. Hennessy W.M. and MacCarthy, B. (eds) 1887–1901. Dublin.
'Bog Commission maps'. Griffiths, R. 1809–14. *Bord na Móna – Living History*. https://www.bordnamonalivinghistory.ie/maps/. Accessed 13/11/2023.
The book of Uí Maine, otherwise called 'The book of the O'Kellys', with introduction and indexes. MacAlister, R.A.S. (ed.) 1942. Dublin: Irish Manuscripts Commission.
Books of survey and distribution: being abstracts of various surveys and instruments of title, 1636–1703. vol. 1: County of Roscommon. Simington, R.C. (ed.) 1949. Dublin: Stationary Office.
Buile Shuibhne (The Frenzy of Suibhne). Being the adventures of Suibhne Geilt. A Middle Irish romance. O'Keeffe, J.G. (ed. and trans.) 1913. London: Irish Texts Society.
Caithréim Thoirdhealbhaigh. O'Grady S.H. (ed. and trans.) 1929. Dublin: Irish Texts Society.
Calendar of documents relating to Ireland, 1171–1307. 5 vols. Sweetman, H.S. (ed.) 1875–86. London.
Calendar of the justiciary rolls or proceedings in the court of the justiciar of Ireland, preserved in the Public Record Office of Ireland, 3 vols. Mills, J. and Griffiths, M.C. (eds) 1905–14. Dublin.
Calendar of Ormond deeds, 6 vols. Curtis, E. (ed.) 1932–43. Dublin.
Calendar of the state papers relating to Ireland, of the reigns of Henry VIII, Edward VI, Mary and Elizabeth, 5 vols. (1509–96). Hamilton, H.C. (ed.) 1860–90 (ed.). London: Longman, HMSO.
Calendar of the state papers relating to Ireland, of the reigns of Henry VIII, Edward VI, Mary and Elizabeth, 5 vols. (1596–1601). Atkinson, E.G. (ed.) 1893–1905. London: Longman, HMSO.
Cambridge University collection of aerial photographs. St Joseph, J.K.S. 1951. Cambridge: Committee for Aerial Photography, Cambridge University.

'Clanricard letters'. Cunningham, B. (ed.) 1996. *Journal of the Galway Archaeological and Historical Society*, vol. 48. 162–208.

Commissioners appointed to inquire into the state of the fairs and markets: Report. Anon. 1853. Dublin: HMSO.

The compossicion booke of Conought. Freeman, A.D. (ed.) 1936. Dublin.

Down Survey. Petty, W. (ed.) 1655–6. http://downsurvey.tcd.ie/down-survey-maps.php. Accessed 16/11/2023.

Fá urraidh labhras leac Theamhrach (MS RIA 626)

'Filidh Éreann go haointeach: William Ó Ceallaigh's Christmas feast to the poets of Ireland, AD 1351'. Knott, E. (ed. and trans.) 1911. *Ériu*, vol. 5. 50–69.

Gerald of Wales: The history and topography of Ireland. O'Meara, J. (ed.) 1982. London: Penguin Books.

Historic Environment Viewer. https://maps.archaeology.ie/HistoricEnvironment/. Accessed 16/11/2023.

Irish fiants of the Tudor sovereigns, 1521–1603, 4 vols. Nicholls, K.W. (ed.) 1994. Dublin: Éamonn de Búrca for Edmund Burke.

Irlandiæ accvrata descriptio. Boazio, B. c.1606. Antwerp: A. Ortelius.

Lebor na Cert: the Book of Rights. Dillon, M. 1962 (ed. and trans.). London: Irish Texts Society 46.

Map of the province of Connaught. Browne, J. 1591. *Map of the province of Connaught*, TCD, MS 1209/68.

Miscellaneous Irish annals (AD 1114–1437) Ó hInnse, S. (ed. and trans.) 1947. Dublin.

'Nósa Ua Maine: "The customs of the Uí Mhaine"'. Russell, P. (ed.) 2000. In Charles Edwards, T.M., Owen, M.E., and Russell, P. (eds), *The Welsh king and his court*, 527–51. Cardiff: University of Wales Press.

'O'Donnell's Kern'. In O'Grady, S. (ed. and trans.) 1892. *Silva gadelica (I–XXXI): a collection of tales in Irish with extracts illustrating persons and places*, 311–24. London: Williams and Norgate.

Ordnance Survey letters Galway: edited with an introduction by Michael Herity MRIA. Herity, M. (ed.) 2009. Dublin: Fourmasters Press.

Ordnance Survey letters Roscommon: edited with an introduction by Michael Herity MRIA. Herity, M. (ed.) 2010. Dublin: Fourmasters Press.

'Plan of Monaghan Fort'. in Bartlett, R. 1602. *Maps, drawings and plans by Richard Bartlett (Barthelet) and others, 1587–1625*.

'Roscommon castles and their owners 1573 [present writer's title]'. Nicholls, K. (transcribed), 2019. *SP 63/45/35(i)*.

Rymer's Foedera, vol. 1. Rymer, T. (ed.) 1739. London.

Tales of the elders of Ireland. Dooley, A. and Roe, H. (trans.) 1999. Oxford: Oxford University Press.

'Táth aoinfhir ar iath Maineach'. In Hoyne, M. (ed.) forthcoming. 'Uilliam Ó Ceallaigh, Gairm na Nollag 1351 agus stair eacnamaíoch fhilíocht na scol'.

The annals of Ulster. Mac Airt, S. and Mac Nioraill, G. (eds) 1983. Dublin.

The deeds of the Normans in Ireland: La geste des Engleis en Yrlande. Mullally, E. (ed.) 2019. Dublin: Four Courts Press.

'The history of the county of Galway – chapter XXXI'. Anon. 1892. *Tuam Herald*. Tuam, Co. Galway.

The manuscripts of Charles Haliday, Esq., of Dublin: Acts of the privy council of Ireland, 1556–1571. Haliday, C., Ussher, W., Gilbert, J.T. (eds) 1897. London: HMSO.

'The Ó Ceallaigh rulers of Uí Mhaine – a genealogical fragment, *c.*1400: part I'. Ó Muraíle, N. (ed.) 2008. *Journal of the Galway Archaeological and Historical Society*, vol. 60, 32–77.

'The Ó Ceallaigh rulers of Uí Mhaine – A genealogical fragment, *c.*1400: part II'. Ó Muraíle, N. (ed.) 2010. *Journal of the Galway Archaeological and Historical Society*, vol. 62, 51–77.

'The pilgrim from Catalonia/Aragon: Ramon de Perellós'. Carpenter, D. (ed.) 1988. in Haren, M., de Pontefarcy, Y. (eds), *The medieval pilgrimage to St Patrick's Purgatory: Lough Derg and the European tradition*, Enniskillen: Clogher Historical Society. 99–119.

'The Registry of Clonmacnoise; with notes and introductory remarks'. in O'Donovan, J. (ed.) 1857. *The Journal of the Kilkenny and South-East of Ireland Archaeological Society, new series*, vol. 1, no. 2, 444–60.

The theatre of the empire of Great Britaine: presenting an exact geography of the kingdoms of England, Scotland, Ireland … Speed, J. 1611–12. London.

The tribes and customs of Hy-Many, commonly called O'Kelly's Country, now first published from the Book of Lecan, a manuscript in the library of the Royal Irish Academy. O'Donovan, J. (ed.) 1843. Dublin: Irish Archaeological Society.

The tripartite Life of Patrick: with other documents relating to that saint, 2 vols. Stokes, W. (ed. and trans.) 1887. London.

Topographical poems by Seaán Mór Ó Dubhagáin and Giolla-Na Naomh Ó Huidhrín. Carney, J. (ed.) 1943. Dublin: Dublin Institute for Advanced Studies.

'Unpublished letters from Richard II in Ireland, 1394–5'. Curtis, E. (ed.) 1924–7. *Proceedings of the Royal Irish Academy*, vol. 37C, 276–303.

SECONDARY SOURCES

Aalen, F.H.A., Whelan, K., and Stout, M. (eds) 1997. *Atlas of the Irish rural landscape*. Cork: Cork University Press.

Ackermann, F. 1999. 'Airborne laser scanning – present status and future expectations'. *Journal of Photogrammetry & Remote Sensing*, vol. 54, 64–7.

Alcock, O., de hÓra, K., and Gosling, P. 1999. *Archaeological inventory of County Galway, volume II: North Galway*. Dublin: The Stationary Office.

Anderson, H., Scholkmann, B., and Svart Kristiansen, M. 2007. 'Medieval archaeology at the outset of the third millennium: research and teaching'. In Graham-Campbell, J., and Valor, M. (eds), *The archaeology of medieval Europe. volume I – eighth to twelfth centuries AD*. Aarhus: Aarhus University Press, 19–45.

Barrett, G., Graham, B.J. 1975. 'Some considerations concerning the dating and distribution of ring-forts in Ireland'. *Ulster Journal of Archaeology*, vol. 38, 33–47.

Barry, T.B. 1977. 'Medieval moated sites of south-east Ireland'. Oxford: PhD.

Barry, T.B. 1987. *The archaeology of medieval Ireland*. London: Methuen & Co. Ltd.

Barry, T.B. 1996. 'Rural settlement in Ireland in the Middle Ages: an overview'. *Ruralia*, vol. 1, 34–141.
Barry, T.B. 2006. 'Harold Leask's "single towers": Irish tower houses as part of larger settlement complexes'. In Ettel, P., Flambard Héricher, A.M., and McNeill, T.E. (eds), *Chateau Gaillard 22: Chateau et Peuplement Colloque de Voiron 2004*. Caen: Publications du CRAHM, 27–33.
Barry, T.B. 2007. 'The origins of Irish castles: a contribution to the debate'. In Manning, C. (ed.), *From ringforts to fortified houses: studies on castles and other monuments in honour of David Sweetman*. Dublin: Wordwell, 33–40.
Barry T.B. 2008. 'The study of Irish medieval castles: a bibliographic survey'. *Proceedings of the Royal Irish Academy*, vol. 108C, 115–36.
Bermingham, N. 2014. 'Drumclay crannog: a multi-generational crannog explored'. *Medieval Archaeology*, vol. 58, 376–82.
Bermingham, N., Moore, C., O'Keeffe, J., Gormley, M. 2013. 'Drumclay: a most surprising crannog'. *Archaeology Ireland*, vol. 27, 37–40.
Bhreathnach, E. 2014. *Ireland in the medieval world, AD 400–1000: landscape, kingship and religion*. Dublin: Four Courts Press.
Biggar, F.J. 1900–1. 'Killconnell Abbey'. *Journal of the Galway Archaeological and Historical Society*, vol. 1, 144–67.
Biggar, F.J. 1902. 'The Franciscan friary of Killconnell'. *Journal of the Galway Archaeological and Historical Society*, vol. 2, 3–20.
Biggar, F.J. 1903–4. 'Killconnell Abbey (continued from vol. II)'. *Journal of the Galway Archaeological and Historical Society*, vol. 3, 11–15.
Bolger, T. 2017. *Colonising a royal landscape: the history and archaeology of a medieval village at Mullamast, County Kildare*. Dublin: Transport Infrastructure Ireland.
Bower, N. 2009. 'Archaeological Excavation Report, Loughbown 1, Co. Galway'. *Eachtra Journal*, issue 2, 1–272.
Bower, N. 2014. 'Two ringforts in Loughbown: stockyard, souterrain, metalworking and cereal kilns'. In McKeon, J., and O'Sullivan, J. (eds), *The quiet landscape: archaeological investigations on the M6 Galway to Ballinasloe national road scheme*. Dublin: The National Roads Authority, 172–84.
Bradley, J. 2000. *Irish Historic Towns Atlas, no. 10, Kilkenny*. Dublin: Royal Irish Academy.
Brady, N. 2003. *Exploring Irish medieval landscapes: the Discovery Programme's Medieval Rural Settlement project, 2002–2008*. Dublin: Discovery Programme.
Brady, N. 2009. 'When mounds become castles: a case for the later usage of early medieval sites'. In Corlett, C., and Potterton, M. (eds), *Rural settlement in medieval Ireland in the light of recent archaeological excavations*. Dublin: Wordwell Books, 19–26.
Brady, N., and Gibson, P. 2005. 'The earthwork at Tulsk, Co. Roscommon: topographical and geophysical survey and preliminary excavation'. In *Discovery Programme Report 7: North Roscommon in the later medieval period: an introduction*. Dublin: Royal Irish Academy/Discovery Programme, 65–76.
Brady, N., and O'Conor, K. 2005. 'The later medieval usage of crannogs in Ireland'. *Ruralia*, 5, 127–36.

Breatnach, P.A. 1983. 'The chief's poet'. *Proceedings of the Royal Irish Academy*, vol. 83C, 37–79.

Breatnach, R.A. 1967. 'The Book of Uí Maine'. In *sine nomine* (ed.), *Great books of Ireland: Thomas Davis lectures*. Dublin, London: Clonmore & Reynolds; Burns & Oates, 77–89.

Breen, A. 2009. 'Ó Dubhagáin, Seoán Mór'. In McGuire, J., and Quinn, J. (eds), *Dictionary of Irish biography*. 9 vols, Cambridge: Cambridge University Press.

Breen, C. 2001. 'The maritime cultural landscape in medieval Gaelic Ireland'. In Duffy, P.J., Edwards, D., FitzPatrick, E. (eds), *Gaelic Ireland, c.1250–c.1650*, 418–36.

Breen, C. 2005. *The Gaelic lordship of the O'Sullivan Beare: a landscape cultural history*. Dublin: Four Courts Press.

Breen, C., and Raven, J. 2017. 'Maritime lordship in late-medieval Gaelic Ireland'. *Medieval Archaeology*, 61:1, 149–82.

Brown, E.A. 1974. 'The tyranny of a construct: feudalism and historians of medieval Europe'. *The American Historical Review*, 79, 1063–88.

Burke, D.G. *Burke's East Galway*. http://burkeseastgalway.com/. Accessed: 13/11/2023.

Byrne, F.J. 2004. *Irish kings and high-kings*. Dublin: Four Courts Press repr.

Byrne, F.J. 2008. 'Ireland and her neighbours, c.1014–1072'. In Ó Cróinín, D. (ed.), *A new history of Ireland I: prehistoric and early Ireland*. Oxford: Oxford University Press, 862–98.

Byrne, F.J. 2011. 'Later Gaelic kings and lords'. In Moody, T.W., Martin, F.X., and Byrne, F.J. (eds), *A new history of Ireland IX: maps, genealogies, lists. A companion to Irish history, Part II*. Oxford: Oxford University Press, 211–30.

Cairns, C.T. 1987. *Irish tower houses: a Co. Tipperary case study*. Athlone: Group for the Study of Irish Historic Settlement.

Caldwell, D.H. 2017. 'Galley-castles by land and sea'. In Martin, P. (ed.), *Island castles: a reassessment of the historic galley-castles of the Norse-Gaelic seaways*. Laxay: Islands Book Trust, 141–56.

Campbell, B.M.S. 2008. 'Benchmarking medieval economic development: England, Wales, Scotland, and Ireland, c.1290'. *The Economic History Review*, new series, vol. 61, no. 4, 896–945.

Campbell, E., FitzPatrick, E., and Horning, A. (eds), *Becoming and belonging in Ireland, AD c.1200–1600: essays in identity and cultural practice*. Cork: Cork University Press.

Carney, J. 2008. 'Literature in Irish, 1169–1534'. In Cosgrove, A. (ed.), *A new history of Ireland II: medieval Ireland, 1169–1534*. Oxford: Oxford University Press, 688–707.

Chevallier, C. 2019. 'What was the distribution of wealth in Ireland, c.1300?'. *History Ireland*, vol. 27, no. 4, 18–21.

Claffey, J.A. 1983. *History of Moylough-Mountbellew: Part I, from the earliest times to 1601*. Tuam: privately published.

Clyne, M. 2005. 'Archaeological excavations at Holy Trinity Abbey Lough Key, Co. Roscommon'. *Proceedings of the Royal Irish Academy*, vol. 105C, no. 2, 23–98.

Colfer, B. 2013. *Wexford castles: landscape, context and settlement*. Cork: Cork University Press.

Collins, J.F. 2016. 'Geology, soils and cattle production'. In O'Connell, M., Kelly, F., and McAdam, J.H. (eds), *Cattle in ancient and modern Ireland: farming practices, environment and economy*. Newcastle upon Tyne: Cambridge Scholars Publishing, 1–11.

Comber, M. 2016. 'The Irish cashel: enclosed settlement, fortified settlement or settled fortification?'. In Herold, H., and Christie, N. (eds), *Fortified settlements in early medieval Europe: defended communities of the 8th–10th centuries*. Oxford: Oxbow Books, 3–13.

Comber, M. 2018a. 'Central places in a rural archaeological landscape'. *Journal of the North Atlantic*, vol. 36, 1–12.

Comber, M. 2018b. 'The tale of items lost …: what objects tell us about the life of a medieval family at Caherconnell Cashel, Co. Clare'. In Fenwick, J. (ed.), *Lost and found III: rediscovering more of Ireland's past*. Dublin: Wordwell Books, 95–102.

Comber, M., and Hull, G. 2010. 'Excavations at Caherconnell Cashel, the Burren, Co. Clare: Implications for cashel chronology and Gaelic settlement'. *Proceedings of the Royal Irish Academy*, vol. 110C, 133–71.

Connellan, M. 1954. 'Port Airchinnigh-Airchinneach-Portrunny'. *The Irish Book Lover*, vol. 32, 55–6.

Connolly, Paul. 2014. *Mount Talbot – A journey through the ages*. Dublin: self-published.

Connolly, Philomena. 1982. 'An account of military expenditure in Leinster, 1308'. *Analecta Hibernia*, no. 30, 1–5.

Connolly, Philomena. 2002. *Medieval Record Sources*. Dublin: Four Courts Press.

Connon, A. 2014. 'The Roscommon locus of *Acallam na senórach* and some thoughts as to tempus and persona'. In Doyle, A., and Murray, K. (eds), *In dialogue with the Agallamh: essays in honour of Seán Ó Coileáin*. Dublin: Four Courts Press, 21–59.

Connon, A. forthcoming. 'The Ó Maoil Ruanaidh kingdoms of Crumthainn and Mag Luirg'.

Connon, A., and Shanahan, B. 2012. 'Creating borders in twelfth-century Ireland? Toirrdelbach Ua Conchobair's diversion of the River Suck'. In Ní Ghrádaigh, J., and O'Byrne, E. (eds), *The March in the islands of the medieval West*. Leiden: Koninklijke Brill, 139–70.

Cosgrove, A. 2008. 'Ireland beyond the Pale, 1399–1460'. In Cosgrove, A. (ed.), *A new history of Ireland II: medieval Ireland, 1169–1534*. Oxford: Oxford University Press, 569–90.

Costello, T.B. 1940. 'The ancient law school of Park, Co. Galway'. *Journal of the Galway Archaeological and Historical Society*, vol. 19, no. 1/2, 89–100.

Costello, E. 2020. *Transhumance and the making of Ireland's uplands, 1550–1900*. Woodbridge: Boydell Press.

Craig, M. 1976. *Classic Irish houses of the middle size*. London: Architectural Press.

Craig, M. 1982. *The architecture of Ireland from the earliest times to 1880*. London & Dublin: B.T. Batsford Limited.

Cronin, T. 1977. *The foundations of landlordism in the barony of Athlone, 1566–1666*. Unpublished MA dissertation, NUI Galway.

Cronin, T. 1980. 'The Elizabethan colony in Co. Roscommon'. In Murtagh, H. (ed.), *Irish midland studies: essays in commemoration of N.W. English*. Athlone: Old Athlone Society, 107–20.

Cunningham, B. 2018. *Medieval Irish pilgrims to Santiago de Compostela*. Dublin: Four Courts Press.

Curley, D. 2011. *A study of Dundonnell Castle, Co. Roscommon*. Unpublished MA dissertation, NUI Galway.

Curley, D. 2016. 'Dundonnell Castle, Co. Roscommon: a neglected and misunderstood monument in the Irish landscape'. *Roscommon Historical and Archaeological Society Journal*, vol. 13, 58–64.

Curley, D. 2018. 'Observations from remote sensing of the earthwork at Dundonnell Castle, Co. Roscommon'. In Farrell, R., O'Conor, K., and Potter, M. (eds), *Roscommon: history and society*. Dublin: Geography Publications, 133–56.

Curley, D. 2019. 'William Buide O'Kelly and the late medieval renaissance of the Uí Maine lordship'. *History Ireland*, vol. 27, no. 6, 16–19.

Curley, D.P. 2021a, *A multi-disciplinary study of lordly centres in the later medieval Uí Chellaig lordship of Uí Maine, c.1100-1600 AD*. Unpublished PhD dissertation, NUI, Galway.

Curley, D.P. 2021b, 'Le triúcha chéd in Chalaidh a máeraidecht idir mincís ⁊ mórthobach' – Multidisciplinary approaches to recovering an Ó Cellaig cenn áit in later medieval Uí Maine. *Eolas*, vol. 13, 2–42.

Curley, D.P. 2022, 'Reconstructing the Lough Croan cenn áit of the medieval Ó Cellaig lordship of Uí Maine', *Journal of the Royal Society of Antiquaries of Ireland*, 150, 201–24.

Curley, D.P. 2023, 'The medieval parish of Kilmeane in the historical and archaeological record'. In Timoney, M.B. (ed.), *Kilmeane, Co. Roscommon: the graveyard and the grave memorials*. Roscommon: Roscommon County Council, 261–6.

Curley, D.P., and Timoney, M.A. 2024. 'The River Suck-Hind tochailt – one event in the very active kingship of Toirrdelbach Ó Conchobair, king of Connacht and high king of Ireland, r. 1119–1156', *Medieval Archaeology*, vol. 68, no. 1, 72–101.

Curtis, E. 1932/3. 'Original documents relating to the Butler lordship of Achill, Burrishoole and Aughrim (1236–1640)'. *Journal of the Galway Archaeological and Historical Society*, vol. 15, no. 3/4, 121–8.

Curtis, E. 1935. 'Original documents relating to Aughrim, Burrishoole, and Aran'. *Journal of the Galway Archaeological and Historical Society*, vol. 16, no. 3/4, 134–9.

Davies, O. 1950. *Excavations at Island McHugh*. Belfast: Belfast Natural History and Philosophical Society.

De Meulemeester, J., and O'Conor, K. 2008. 'Fortifications'. In Graham-Campbell, J., and Valor, M. (eds), *The archaeology of medieval Europe, vol. I: eighth to twelfth centuries AD*. Aarhus: Aarhus University Press, 316–41.

Delaney, F. 2014. 'Ringfort with round-house, souterrain and cillín burials at Mackney'. In McKeon, J., and O'Sullivan, J. (eds), *The quiet landscape: archaeological investigations on the M6 Galway to Ballinasloe national road scheme*. Dublin: The National Roads Authority, 187–200.

Dempsey, K. 2014. *Recent revelations from thirteenth-century Roscommon: a report to Roscommon County Council*. Unpublished report.

Devane, C. 2013. 'The history of Kilbegly and its environs'. In Jackman, N., Moore, C., and Rynne, C. (eds), *The mill at Kilbegly: an archaeological investigation on the route of the M6 Ballinasloe to Athlone national road scheme*. Dublin: The National Roads Authority, 97–114.

Dolley, M., and Murphy, M.K. 1970. 'An early fourteenth-century coin hoard from the Co. Roscommon'. *The British Numismatic Journal*, vol. 39, 84–90.

Donnelly, C., Logue, P., and O'Neill, J. 2007. 'Timber castles and towers in sixteenth-century Ireland: some evidence from Ulster'. *Archaeology Ireland*, vol. 21, no. 2, 22–5.

Donnelly, C., and Sloan, B. 2021. 'Tullaghoge, Co. Tyrone'. *Archaeology Ireland*, Heritage Guide no. 93. Dublin: Wordwell Books.

Doran, L. 2004. 'Medieval communication routes through Longford and Roscommon and their associated settlements'. *Proceedings of the Royal Irish Academy*, vol. 104C, 57–80.

Doran, L., and Lyttleton, J. (eds) 2007. *Lordship in medieval Ireland: image and reality*. Dublin: Four Courts Press.

Dowdall, N. 1932. 'A description of the county of Longford, 1682'. *Journal of Ardagh and Clonmacnois Antiquarian Society*, vol. 1, no. 3, 25.

Downey, L., and Stuijts, I. 2013. 'Overview of historical Irish food products – A.T. Lucas (1960–2) revisited'. *Journal of Irish Archaeology*, vol. 22, 111–26.

Duffy, P.J., Edwards, D., and FitzPatrick, E. (eds) 2001. *Gaelic Ireland, c.1250–c.1650: land, lordship & settlement*. Dublin: Four Courts Press.

Duffy, S. 2014. *Brian Boru and the battle of Clontarf*. Dublin: Gill & Macmillan.

Edwards, N. 1990. *The archaeology of early medieval Ireland*. Pennsylvania: University of Pennsylvania Press.

Egan, P.K. 1960–1. 'An O'Kelly deed'. *Journal of the Galway Archaeological and Historical Society*, vol. 29, 78–82.

Egan, P.K., and Costello, M.A. 1958. 'Obligationes pro Annatis Diocesis Clonfertensis'. *Archivium Hibernicum*, vol. 21, 52–74.

Ellis, S. 1998. *Ireland in the age of the Tudors, 1447–1603: English expansion and the end of Gaelic rule*. London: Longman.

Etchingham, C. 2015. 'Skuldelev 2 and Viking-age ships and fleets in Ireland'. In Purcell, E., MacCotter, P., Nyhan, J., and Sheehan, J. (eds), *Clerics, kings and Vikings: essays on medieval Ireland in honour of Donnchadh Ó Corráin*, 79–90. Dublin: Four Courts Press.

Everett, N. 2014. *The woods of Ireland: a history, 700–1800*. Dublin: Four Courts Press.

Fanning, T. 1976. 'Excavations at Clontuskert Priory, Co. Galway'. *Proceedings of the Royal Irish Academy*, vol. 76, 97–169.

Finan, T. (ed.) 2010. *Medieval Lough Cé: history, archaeology and landscape*. Dublin: Four Courts Press.

Finan, T. 2010a. 'Introduction: Moylurg and Lough Cé in the later Middle Ages'. In Finan, T. (ed.), *Medieval Lough Cé: history, archaeology and landscape*. Dublin: Four Courts Press, 11–14.

Finan, T. 2014. 'Moated sites in County Roscommon, Ireland: a statistical approach'. *Chateau Gaillard 26: Etudes de Castellogie Medievale, Aarhus*. Caen: Publications du CRAHM, 177–80.

Finan, T. 2016. *Landscape and history on the medieval Irish frontier: the king's cantreds in the thirteenth century*. Turnhout, Belgium: Brepols.

Finan, T. 2018. 'Identity among the Mac Diarmada lords of Magh Luirg in the thirteenth century'. In Campbell, E., FitzPatrick, E., and Horning, A. (eds), *Becoming and belonging in Ireland, AD c.1200–1600: essays in identity and cultural practice*. Cork: Cork University Press, 28–44.

Finan, T. 2020. 'MacDermot's market at Lough Key: Gaelic Ireland's first "town"?'. In Corlett, C., and Potterton, M. (eds), *The town in medieval Ireland, in the light of recent archaeological excavations*. Dublin: Wordwell Books, 59–64.

Finan, T., and O'Conor, K. 2002. 'The moated site at Cloonfree, Co. Roscommon'. *Journal of the Galway Archaeological and Historical Society*, vol. 54, 72–87.

FitzPatrick, E. 2001. 'Assembly and inauguration places of the Burkes in late medieval Connacht'. In Duffy, P.J., Edwards, D., FitzPatrick, E. (eds), *Gaelic Ireland, c.1250–c.1650: land, lordship & settlement*. Dublin: Four Courts Press, 357–74.

FitzPatrick, E. 2003. 'Royal inauguration assembly and the church in medieval Ireland'. In *Political assemblies in the earlier Middle Ages: Studies in the Early Middle Ages 7*, Turnhout, Belgium: Brepols.

FitzPatrick, E. 2004. *Royal inauguration in Gaelic Ireland, c.1100–1600*. Woodbridge: Boydell Press.

FitzPatrick, E. 2006. 'The material world of the parish'. In FitzPatrick, E., and Gillespie, R. (eds), *The parish in medieval and early modern Ireland: community, territory and building*. Dublin: Four Courts Press.

FitzPatrick, E. 2009. 'Native enclosed settlement and the problem of the Irish "ring-fort"'. *Medieval Archaeology*, vol. 53, no. 1, 271–307.

FitzPatrick, E. 2012. 'Formaoil na Fiann: Hunting preserves and assembly places in Gaelic Ireland'. *Proceedings of the Harvard Celtic Colloquium*, vol. 32, 95–118.

FitzPatrick, E. 2015a. 'Assembly places and elite collective identities in medieval Ireland'. *Journal of the North Atlantic*, vol. 8, 52–68.

FitzPatrick, E. 2015b. 'Ollamh, biatach, comharba: lifeways of Gaelic learned families in medieval and early modern Ireland'. In Breatnach, L., Ó hUiginn, R., McManus, D., and Simms, K. (eds), *Proceedings of the XIV International Congress of Celtic Studies, Maynooth 2011*. Dublin: Dublin Institute of Advanced Studies, 165–89.

FitzPatrick, E. 2016. 'The last kings of Ireland: material expressions of Gaelic lordship, c.1300–1400 A.D'. In Buchanan, K., Dean, L.H.S., and Penman, M. (eds), *Medieval and early modern representations of authority in Scotland and the British Isles*. Abingdon: Routledge, 197–213.

FitzPatrick, E. 2018. 'Gaelic service kindreds and the landscape identity of lucht tighe'. In Campbell, E., FitzPatrick, E., and Horning, A. (eds), *Becoming and belonging in Ireland, AD 1200–1600: essays in identity and cultural practice*. Cork: Cork University Press, 167–88.

FitzPatrick, E. 2023. *Landscapes of the learned: placing Gaelic literati in Irish lordships, 1300–1600*. Oxford: Oxford University Press.

Fitzpatrick, M. 2010. 'Pilgrimage to Santiago de Compostela'. *Archaeology Ireland*, vol. 24, no. 4, 14–17.

Flanagan, M.T. 1997. 'Irish and Anglo-Norman warfare in twelfth-century Ireland'. In Bartlett, T., and Jeffery, K. (eds), *A military history of Ireland*. Cambridge: Cambridge University Press, 52–75.

Flanagan, M.T. 2008. 'High-kings with opposition, 1072–1166'. In Ó Cróinín, D. (ed.), *A new history of Ireland I: prehistoric and early Ireland*. Oxford: Oxford University Press, 899–933.

Fletcher, A. 2001. *Drama and the performing arts in pre-Cromwellian Ireland: a repertory of sources and documents from the earliest times until, c.1642*. Woodbridge: Boydell Press.

Foley, C., and Williams, B. 2006. 'The crannógs of County Fermanagh'. In Meek, M. (ed.), *The modern traveller to our past: festschrift in honour of Ann Hamlin*. Dublin: DPK, 53–64.

Fredengren, C. 2002. *Crannogs: a study of people's interaction with lakes, with particular reference to Lough Gara in the north-west of Ireland*. Dublin: Wordwell Books.

Fredengren, C., Kilfeather, A., and Stuijts, I. 2010. *Lough Kinale: studies of an Irish lake*. Discovery Programme Monograph 8. Dublin: Wordwell.

Gardiner, M., and O'Conor, K. 2017. 'The later medieval countryside lying beneath'. In Stanley, M., Swan, R., and O'Sullivan, A. (eds), *Stories of Ireland's past*. Dublin: Transport Infrastructure Ireland, 133–52.

Garton, T. 1981. 'A Romanesque doorway at Killaloe'. *Journal of the British Archaeological Association*, vol. 134, no. 1, 31–57.

Geertz, C. 1973. 'Thick description: towards an interpretive theory of culture'. In Geertz, C., *The interpretation of cultures*. New York: Basic Books, 3–30.

Geissel, H. 2006. *A road on the Long Ridge: in search of the ancient highway on the Esker Riada*. Newbridge, Co. Kildare: CRS Publications.

Giles, M. 2020. *Bog bodies: face to face with the past*. Manchester: Manchester University Press.

Glasscock, R. 2008. 'Land and people, *c.*1300'. In Cosgrove, A. (ed.), *A new history of Ireland II: medieval Ireland, 1169 –1534*. Oxford: Oxford University Press, 205–39.

Gleeson, P. 2015. 'Kingdoms, communities, and Óenaig: assembly practices in their northwest European context'. *Journal of the North Atlantic*, vol. 8, 33–51.

Goodwillie, R.N. 1992. *Turloughs over 10ha – vegetation survey and evaluation*. Unpublished report to NPWS.

Graham, B.J. 1988a. 'Medieval settlement in County Roscommon'. *Proceedings of the Royal Irish Academy*, vol. 88C, 19–38.

Graham, B.J. 1988b. 'Medieval timber and earthwork fortifications in western Ireland'. *Medieval Archaeology*, vol. 32, no. 1, 110–29.

Graham, B.J. 1990. 'Twelfth- and thirteenth-century earthwork fortifications in Ireland'. *The Irish Sword*, vol. 17, no. 69, 225–43.

Gwynn, A., and Hadcock, R.N. 1970. *Medieval religious houses: Ireland, with an appendix to early sites*. London: Longman.

Hall, F.J. 2016. *Castle siting and riverine engagement in the landscape of Lough Derg*. Unpublished MA dissertation, NUI Galway.

Hall, V.A., and Bunting, L. 2001. 'Tephra-dated pollen studies of medieval landscapes in the north of Ireland'. In Duffy, P.J., Edwards, D., FitzPatrick, E. (eds), *Gaelic Ireland, c.1250– c.1650: land, lordship & settlement*. Dublin: Four Courts Press, 207–22.

Hammond, M. 2019. *Personal names and naming practices in medieval and early modern Scotland*. Woodbridge: Boydell Press.

Hansson, M. 2020. 'Unfortified elite buildings in 13th-century Sweden'. *Chateau Gaillard*, vol. 29, 165–73.

Harbison, P. 2005. *A thousand years of church heritage in east Galway*. Dublin: Ashfield Press.

Hayes-McCoy, G.A. 1938. 'The early history of guns in Ireland'. *Journal of the Galway Archaeological and Historical Society*, vol. 18, no. 1/2, 43–65.
Hayes-McCoy, G.A. 1969; reprint 2009. *Irish battles: a military history of Ireland*. Belfast: Appletree Press.
Higham, R., and Barker, P. 1992. *Timber castles*. London: Batsford.
Holland, P. 1987–8. 'The Anglo-Normans in Co. Galway: the process of colonization'. *Journal of the Galway Archaeological and Historical Society*, vol. 41, 73–89.
Holland, P. 1994. 'Anglo-Norman Galway: rectangular earthworks and moated sites'. *Journal of the Galway Archaeological and Historical Society*, vol. 46, 203–11.
Holland, P. 1997. 'The Anglo-Norman landscape in County Galway, land-holdings, castles and settlements'. *Journal of the Galway Archaeological and Historical Society*, vol. 49, 159–93.
Hoyne, M. 2023. 'Classical modern Irish poems on the Í Cheallaigh within and without Leabhar Ua Maine'. In Boyle, E., and Ó hUiginn, R. (eds), *Book of Uí Mhaine: Codices Hibernenses Eximii – III*. Dublin: Royal Irish Academy, 274–301.
Hughes, A.J. 1994–5. 'Land acquisition by Gaelic bardic poets: insights from place-names and other sources'. *Ainm*, vol. 6, 74–102.
Jackman, N., and O'Keeffe, T. 2013. 'Conclusions'. In Jackman, N., Moore, C., and Rynne, C. (eds), *The mill at Kilbegly: an archaeological investigation on the route of the M6 Ballinasloe to Athlone national road scheme*. Dublin: The National Roads Authority, 149–52.
Jaski, B. 2013a. *Early Irish kingship and succession*. Dublin: Four Courts Press.
Jaski, B. 2013b. 'Medieval Irish genealogies and genetics'. In Duffy, S. (ed.), *Princes, prelates and poets in medieval Ireland: essays in honour of Katharine Simms*. Dublin: Four Courts Press, 3–17.
Jennings, B. 1944. 'The chalices and books of Kilconnell Abbey'. *Journal of the Galway Archaeological and Historical Society*, vol. 21, no. 1/2, 63–70.
Joyce, P.W. 1910. *The origin and history of Irish names of places*. London: Longmans.
Kehnel, A. 1997. *Clonmacnois: the church and lands of St Ciarán – change and continuity in an Irish monastic foundation (6th to 16th century)*. Munster: Lit Verslag.
Kelleher, J.V. 1971. 'Uí Maine in the annals and genealogies to 1225'. *Celtica*, vol. 9, 61–112.
Kelleher, C. 2007. 'The Gaelic O'Driscoll lords of Baltimore, Co. Cork'. In Doran, L., and Lyttleton, J. (eds), *Lordship in medieval Ireland: image and reality*. Dublin: Four Courts Press, 130–59.
Kelly, D.H. 1853–7. 'On an ancient terraced gravel hill near Castle Blakeney, County of Galway'. *Proceedings of the Royal Irish Academy*, vol. 6C, 49–54.
Kelly, F. 2016a. 'Cattle in ancient Ireland: early Irish legal aspects'. In O'Connell, M., Kelly, F., and McAdam, J.H. (eds), *Cattle in ancient and modern Ireland: farming practices, environment and economy*. Newcastle upon Tyne: Cambridge Scholars Publishing, 44–50.
Kelly, F. 2016b. *Early Irish farming: a study based mainly on the law-texts of the 7th and 8th centuries AD*. Dundalk: Dublin Institute for Advanced Studies.
Kelly, F. 2020. *The MacEgan legal treatise*. Dublin: Dublin Institute of Advanced Studies.
Kenny, M. 1983. 'The Drumercool Hoard: mints, moneyers and classes'. *Irish Numismatics*, no. 95, 169–75.

Kerrigan, J. 1996. 'Gailey Castle'. *Journal of the Roscommon Historical and Archaeological Society*, vol. 6, 103–4.

Kilfeather, A. 2010. 'A landscape of words: the place-names of Lough Kinale'. In Fredengren, C., Kilfeather, A., and Stuijts, I (eds), *Lough Kinale: studies of an Irish lake*. Dublin: Wordwell, 167–216.

King, D.J.C. 1988. *The castle in England and Wales: an interpretive history*. London: Croom Helm.

Kingston, S. 2004. *Ulster and the Isles in the fifteenth century: the lordship of Clann Domhnaill of Antrim*. Dublin: Four Courts Press.

Kissane, N. 2017. *Saint Brigid of Kildare: life, legend and cult*. Dublin: Four Courts Press.

Lanting, J.N., and Brindley, A.L. 1996. 'Irish logboats and their European context'. *The Journal of Irish Archaeology*, vol. 7, 85–95.

Leask, H. 1941. *Irish castles and castellated houses*. Dundalk: Tempest.

Leask, H. 1960. *Irish churches and monastic buildings, III: medieval Gothic, the last phases*. Dundalk: Dundalgan Press.

Lenihan, P. 2018. '"That much wasted country": wartime Roscommon, 1641–47'. In Farrell, R., O'Conor, K., and Potter, M. (eds), *Roscommon: history and society*. Dublin: Geography Publications, 259–78.

Lennon, C. 2005. *Sixteenth-century Ireland: the incomplete conquest*. Dublin: Gill & MacMillan.

Lewis, S. 1837. *A topographical dictionary of Ireland, comprising the several counties, cities, boroughs, corporate, market, and post towns, parishes and villages*. 2 vols, London: S. Lewis and Co.

Loeber, R. 2001. 'An architectural history of Gaelic castles and settlements, 1370–1600'. In Duffy, P.J., Edwards, D., FitzPatrick, E. (eds), *Gaelic Ireland, c.1250–c.1650: land, lordship & settlement*. Dublin: Four Courts Press, 271–314.

Loeber, R. 2015. 'Demesnes on the shores of Lough Ree and Lower Lough Erne from the sixteenth to the nineteenth centuries'. In Cunningham, B., and Murtagh, H. (eds), *Lough Ree: historic lakeland settlement*. Dublin: Four Courts Press, 131–62.

Loeber, R. 2019. 'An architectural history of Gaelic castles and settlements, 1370–1600'. In Loeber, R. *Irish houses and castles, 1400–1740*. Dublin: Four Courts Press, 1–34.

Logue, P. 2016. *A reinterpretation of the archaeology of the Nine Years' War in Ulster from a cultural perspective*. Unpublished PhD dissertation, Queen's University Belfast.

Logue, P. 2018. 'All things to all men: Aodh Ó Néill and the construction of identity'. In Campbell, E., FitzPatrick, E., and Horning, A. (eds), *Becoming and belonging in Ireland, AD 1200–1600: essays in identity and cultural practice*. Cork: Cork University Press, 269–92.

Logue, P., and Barkley, J. 2022. 'Excavations at Clontymullan Fort, a late medieval Gaelic moated site in County Fermanagh'. *Ulster Journal of Archaeology*, vol. 77, 81–100.

Logue, P., and Ó Doibhlin, D. 2020. 'Landscapes of hunting and assembly in the north of Ireland – three case-studies'. *The Journal of Irish Archaeology*, vol. 29, 159–75.

Logue, P., Devine, B., and Barkley, J. 2020. 'The meadow of Maolán's House'. *Archaeology Ireland*, vol. 34, no. 2, 23–6.

Lucas, A.T. 1970. 'Turf as a fuel in Ireland'. In McCourt, D., and Gailey, A. (eds), *Studies in folklife presented to Emrys Estyn Evans*. Belfast: Ulster Folk Museum, 172–202.

Lucas, A.T. 1985. 'Toghers or causeways: some evidence from archaeological, literary, historical and place-name sources'. *Proceedings of the Royal Irish Academy*, vol. 85C, 37–60.

Lucas, A.T. 1989. *Cattle in ancient Ireland*. Kilkenny: Boethius Press.

Lydon, J. 2003. *The lordship of Ireland in the Middle Ages*. Dublin: Four Courts Press.

Lydon, J. 2008a. 'The expansion and consolidation of the colony, 1215–54'. In Cosgrove, A. (ed.), *A new history of Ireland II: medieval Ireland, 1169–1534*. Oxford: Oxford University Press, 156–78.

Lydon, J. 2008b. 'A land of war'. In Cosgrove, A. (ed.), *A new history of Ireland II: medieval Ireland, 1169–1534*. Oxford: Oxford University Press, 240–74.

Lyttleton, J. 2013. *The Jacobean plantations in seventeenth-century Offaly: an archaeology of a changing world*. Dublin: Four Courts Press.

Mac Cuarta, B. 1987. 'Mathew De Renzy's letters on Irish affairs'. *Analecta Hibernica*, vol. 34, 109–82.

Mac Philib, S. 2000. 'Rush rafts in Ireland'. *Ulster Folklife*, vol. 46, 1–8.

Mac Shamhráin, A.S. 1991. 'Placenames as indicators of settlement'. *Archaeology Ireland*, vol. 5, no. 3, 19–21.

MacAlister, R.A.S. 1909. *The memorial slabs of Clonmacnoise: King's County*. Dublin: Dublin University Press.

MacAlister, R.A.S. (ed.) 1941. *The Book of Uí Maine, otherwise called 'The book of the O'Kelly's', with introduction and indexes*. Dublin: Irish Manuscripts Commission.

MacCotter, P. 2012. 'Drong and Dál as synonyms for Óenach'. *Peritia*, vols 22/23, 1–6.

MacCotter, P. 2014. *Medieval Ireland: territorial, political and economic divisions*. Dublin: Four Courts Press.

MacCotter, P. 2018. 'The M7 motorway historical landscape: studies in the history of Ormond'. *Tipperary Historical Journal*, 66–87.

MacDermot, D. 1996. *MacDermot of Moylurg*. Manorhamilton: Drumlin Publications.

MacDonald, A. 2003. 'The "cathedral", Temple Kelly and Temple Ciarán: notes from the annals'. In King, H. (ed.), *Clonmacnoise studies, vol. 2: seminar papers, 1998*. Dublin: Stationary Office, 125–35.

MacNeill, M. 2008. *The Festival of Lughnasa: a study of the survival of the Celtic festival of the beginning of harvest*. Dundalk: University College Dublin.

Malcolm, J. 2007. 'Castles and landscapes in Uí Fhiachrach Muaidhe, *c*.1235–*c*.1400'. In Doran, L., and Lyttleton, J. (eds), *Lordship in medieval Ireland: image and reality*. Dublin: Four Courts Press, 193–216.

Manning, C. 1997. 'The date of the round tower at Clonmacnoise'. *Archaeology Ireland*, vol. 11, no. 2, 12–13.

Mannion, J. 2004. *The life, legends and legacy of Saint Kerrill: a fifth-century east Galway evangelist*. Self-published.

Mannion, J. 2006. 'The Senchineoil and the Sogain: differentiating between the Pre-Celtic and early Celtic tribes of central east Galway'. *Journal of the Galway Archaeological and Historical Society*, vol. 58, 165–70.

Mannion, J. 2008. 'Tech Saxan: an Anglo-Saxon monastic settlement in early medieval east Galway'. *Journal of the Galway Archaeological and Historical Society*, vol. 60, 9–21.

Mannion, J. 2012. 'Elizabethan County Galway: the origin and evolution of an administrative unit of Tudor local government'. *Journal of the Galway Archaeological and Historical Society*, vol. 64, 64–89.

Mannion, J. 2014. '"In the shadow of a high-king": Tadg Mór Ua Cellaig and the battle of Clontarf'. *Sliabh Aughty Journal*, no. 15, 7–9.

Mannion, J. 2015. *Clann Uí Mhainnín: the Mannion clan historical trail – a guide to residential, ceremonial & burial sites*. Self-published.

Mannion, J. 2024. *Anglicizing Tudor Connacht: the expansion of English rule in the lordships of Clanrickard and Hy Many*. Dublin: Four Courts Press.

McAfee, P. 1997. *Irish stone walls*. Dublin: O'Brien Press.

McAlister, V.L. 2019. *The Irish tower house: society, economy and environment, c.1300–1650*. Manchester: Manchester University Press.

McCarthy, M., and Curley, D. 2018. 'Exploring the nature of the Fráoch saga: an examination of associations with the legendary warrior on Mag nAí'. *Emania*, vol. 24, 53–62.

McCormick, F. 2008. 'The decline of the cow: agricultural and settlement change in early medieval Ireland'. *Peritia*, vol. 20, 210–25.

McCracken, E. 1959. 'The woodlands of Ireland, *circa* 1600'. *Irish Historical Studies*, vol. 11, 271–96.

McCracken, E. 1971. *The Irish woods since Tudor times, their distribution and exploitation*. Plymouth: David & Charles Ltd.

McDermott, J.J., and O'Conor, K. 2015. 'Rosclogher Castle: a Gaelic lordship centre on Lough Melvin, Co. Leitrim'. *Journal of the Cumann Seanchais Bhreifne*, vol. 13, 470–97.

McDermott, Y. 2012. *Patronage and observance: the Franciscan and Dominican friaries in the Connacht lordships of Clann Uilliam Uachtair and Clann Uilliam Íochtair, 1350–1550*. Unpublished PhD dissertation, NUI Galway.

McDonald, K. 2022. *Living with the lake: the archaeology of lake settlement in Loughrea and the surrounding landscape*. Galway County Council & Heritage Council of Ireland.

McGettigan, D. 2016. *Richard II and the Irish kings*. Dublin: Four Courts Press.

McErlean, T. 1983. 'The Irish townland system of landscape organization'. In Reeves-Smyth, T., and Hammond, F. (eds), *Landscape archaeology in Ireland*. Dublin: BAR, 315–39.

McInerney, L. 2015. 'The Gallogass of Thomond: Gallóglaigh Thuadhmhumhain'. *North Munster Antiquarian Journal*, vol. 55, 21–45.

McKenzie, C.J., and Murphy, E.M. 2018. *Life and death in medieval Gaelic Ireland*. Dublin: Four Courts Press.

McKeon, J., and O'Sullivan, J. (eds), 2014. *The quiet landscape: archaeological investigations on the M6 Galway to Ballinasloe national road scheme*. Dublin: The National Roads Authority.

McLeod, W. 2007. 'Images of Scottish warriors in later Irish bardic poetry'. In Duffy, S. (ed.), *The world of the galloglass: kings, warlords and warriors in Ireland and Scotland, 1200–1600*. Dublin: Four Courts Press, 169–87.

McNeary, R., and Shanahan, B. 2008. 'Settlement and enclosure in a medieval Gaelic lordship: a case study from the territory of the O'Conors of north Roscommon'. *Landmarks and socio-economic systems: constructing of pre-industrial landscapes and their perception by contemporary societies*. Rennes: Presses Universitaires de Rennes, 187–97.

McNeary, R., and Shanahan, B. 2012. 'The March in Roscommon, 1170–1400: culture contact, continuity and change'. In Ní Ghrádaigh, J., and O'Byrne, E. (eds), *The March in the islands of the medieval West*. Leiden: Koninklijke Brill, 195–228.

McNeill, T. 1997. *Castles in Ireland: feudal power in a Gaelic world*. London: Routledge.

Meehan, R., and Parkes, M. 2014. *Karst, turloughs and eskers*. Roscommon County Council.

Meyer, K. (ed.) 1912. 'Mitteilungen aus irischen Handschriften: Die erste Ärzte Irlands'. *Zeitschrift für celtische Philologie*, vol. 8, 195–232.

Meyer, W. 2011. 'Castle archaeology – an introduction'. In Carver, M., and Klapste, J. (eds), *The archaeology of medieval Europe, vol II: twelfth to sixteenth centuries*. Aarhus: Aarhus University Press, 230–42.

Millett, B. 1986. 'Dioceses in Ireland up to the 15th century'. *Seanchas Ardmhacha: Journal of the Armagh Diocesan Historical Society*, vol. 12, no. 1, 1–42.

Mitchell, B. 2009. *A new genealogical atlas of Ireland*. 2nd edition. Dublin: Genealogical Publishing Company.

Mittelstraß, T. 2004. 'Die Rekonstruktion eines hölzernen Wohnturmes de 13. Jahrhunderts in Stabbauweise in Kanzach, Landkreis Biberach'. In Hofrichter, H. (ed.), *Holz in der Burgenarchitecktur*. Braubach, 117–24.

Molloy, J. 2009. *The parish of Clontuskert: glimpses into its past*. Ballinasloe: The Clontuskert Heritage Group.

Molloy, K., Feeser, I., and O'Connell, M. 2014. 'A pollen profile from Ballinphuill bog: vegetation and land-use history'. In McKeon, J., and O'Sullivan, J. (eds), *The quiet landscape: archaeological investigations on the M6 Galway to Ballinasloe national road scheme*. Dublin: Wordwell Books, 116–18.

Moore, A. 1978. 'MacKeoghs of Moyfinn (Part 2)'. *Old Athlone Society Journal*, vol. 2, no. 5, 56–70.

Moore, N., and Ó Cróinín, D. 2004. 'Ó Cobhthaigh family (per. 1415–1586), Gaelic poets'. In Harrison, B., and Matthew, H.C.G. (eds), *The Oxford dictionary of national biography*. 60 vols. Oxford: Oxford University Press.

Moreland, J. 2007. *Archaeology and text*. London: Gerald Duckworth & Co. Ltd.

Morton, K. 2002. 'A spectacular revelation: medieval wall paintings at Ardamullivan'. *Irish Arts Review Yearbook*, vol. 18, 104–13.

Morton, K. 2004. 'Irish medieval wall painting'. In *Medieval Ireland: the Barryscourt Lectures, I–X*. Kinsale: The Barryscourt Trust.

Morton, K. 2010. 'Illustrating history'. *Irish Arts Review*, vol. 27, no. 1, 96–101.

Moss, R. 2015a. 'Monuments of Christianity'. In Carpenter, A., and Moss, R. (eds), *Art and architecture of Ireland, volume I: medieval, c.400–c.1600*. Dublin: Royal Irish Academy, 121–233.

Moss, R. 2015b. 'Ua Conchobair (O'Conor)'. In Carpenter, A., and Moss, R. (eds), *Art and architecture of Ireland, volume I: medieval c.400–c.1600*. Dublin: Royal Irish Academy, 480–2.

Moss, R. 2018. 'Material culture'. In Smith, B. (ed.), *The Cambridge history of Ireland, volume I: 600–1550*. Cambridge: Cambridge University Press, 469–97.

Murphy, M. 2003. 'Roscommon Castle: underestimated in terms of location?' *Journal of the Galway Archaeological and Historical Society*, vol. 55, 38–49.

Murphy, M., and O'Conor, K. 2008. *Roscommon Castle: a visitor's guide*. Boyle: Roscommon County Council.

Murray, G. 2014. *The Cross of Cong: a masterpiece in medieval Irish art*. Newbridge, Kildare: Irish Academic Press.

Murtagh, H. 2000. *Athlone: history and settlement to 1800*. Athlone: Old Athlone Society.

Murtagh, H. 2015. 'Boating on Lough Ree'. In Cunningham, B., and Murtagh, H. (eds), *Lough Ree: historic lakeland settlement*. Dublin: Four Courts Press.

n. a. 2011. 'Genealogical tables'. In Moody, T.W., Martin, F.X., and Byrne, F.J. (eds), *A new history of Ireland, IX: maps, genealogies, lists – a companion to Irish history, Part II*. Oxford: Oxford University Press, 121–76.

Naessens, P. 2018. 'The Uí Fhlaithbheartaigh of Mag Seóla and Iarchonnacht: from inland kings to sea-lords'. In Campbell, E., FitzPatrick, E., and Horning, A. (eds), *Becoming and belonging in Ireland, AD 1200–1600: essays in identity and cultural practice*. Cork: Cork University Press, 88–107.

Naessens, P., and O'Conor, K. 2012. 'Pre-Norman fortification in eleventh- and twelfth-century Ireland'. In Ettel, P., Flambard Héricher, A.M., and O'Conor, K. (eds), *L'origine du château médiéval, actes du colloque de Rindern, Allemagne, volume 25*. Caen: Publications du CRAHM, Château Gaillard, Université de Caen, 259–68.

Ní Mhaonaigh, M. 2000. 'Nósa Ua Maine: fact or fiction?' In Charles-Edwards, T.M., Owen, M.E., and Russell, P. (eds), *The Welsh king and his court*. Cardiff: University of Wales Press, 362–81.

Ní Shéaghdha, N. 1963. 'The rights of Mac Diarmada'. *Celtica*, vol. 6, 156–72.

Nicholls, K.W. 1969. *Survey of Irish lordships: I Uí Maine and Síl Anmchadha*. Dublin: Irish Manuscripts Commission (unpublished).

Nicholls, K.W. 1972. 'A charter of William De Burgo'. *Analecta Hibernica*, no. 27, 120–2.

Nicholls, K.W. 1982. 'Anglo-French Ireland and after'. *Peritia*, vol. 1, 370–403.

Nicholls, K.W. 2001. 'Woodland cover in pre-modern Ireland'. In Duffy, P.J., Edwards, D., FitzPatrick, E. (eds), *Gaelic Ireland, c.1250–c.1650: land, lordship & settlement*. Dublin: Four Courts Press, 181–206.

Nicholls, K.W. 2003. *Gaelic and Gaelicized Ireland in the Middle Ages*. 2nd edition. Dublin: Lilliput Press.

Nicholls, K.W. 2007. 'Scottish mercenary kindreds in Ireland, 1250–1600'. In Duffy, S. (ed.), *The world of the galloglass: kings, warlords and warriors in Ireland and Scotland, 1200–1600*. Dublin: Four Courts Press, 86–105.

Nicholls, K.W. 2008. 'Gaelic society and economy in the high Middle Ages'. In Cosgrove, A. (ed.), *A new history of Ireland, volume II: medieval Ireland, 1169–1534*. Oxford: Oxford University Press, 397–438.

Nolan, J.P. 1900–1. 'Galway castles and owners in 1547'. *Journal of the Galway Archaeological and Historical Society*, vol. 1, 109–23.

Nugent, L. 2020. *Journeys of faith: stories of pilgrimage from medieval Ireland*. Dublin: Columba Books.

Ó Clabaigh, C. 2012. *The friars in Ireland, 1224–1540*. Dublin: Four Courts Press.

Ó Concheanainn, T. 1973. 'The scribe of the Leabhar Breac'. *Ériu*, vol. 24, 64–79.

Ó Corráin, D. 1972. *Ireland before the Normans*. Dublin: Gill and Macmillan.

Ó Cróinín, D. 2013. *Early medieval Ireland, 400–1200*. Abingdon: Routledge.
Ó Domhnaill, S. 1946. 'Warfare in sixteenth-century Ireland'. *Irish Historical Studies*, vol. 5, no. 17, 29–54.
Ó Drisceoil, C. 2020. '"Yet nothin is more certaine then death, nor more unncertaine, than the houre theireof": excavations in the chantry chapels of St Mary's Church, Kilkenny'. In Corlett, C., and Potterton, M. (eds), *The town in medieval Ireland, in the light of recent archaeological excavations*. Dublin: Wordwell Books, 161–84.
Ó hAisibéil, L. 2018. 'The place-names of Co. Roscommon'. In Farrell, R., O'Conor, K., and Potter, M. (eds), *Roscommon: history and society*. Dublin: Geography Publications, 157–90.
Ó hAodha, R. 2017. '"A very sufficient scholar"'. *History Ireland*, vol. 25, no. 6, 18–21.
Ó Lochlainn, C. 1940. 'Roadways in ancient Ireland'. In Ryan, J. (ed.), *Essays and studies presented to professor Eoin MacNeill on the occasion of his seventieth birthday, May 15th 1938*. Dublin: Three Candles, 465–74.
Ó Muraíle, N. 1989. 'Leabhar Ua Maine alias Leabhar Uí Dhubhagáin'. *Éigse*, vol. 23, 167–95.
Ó Muraíle, N. 2001. 'Settlement and place-names'. In Duffy, P.J., Edwards, D., and FitzPatrick, E. (eds), *Gaelic Ireland, c.1250–c.1650: land, lordship & settlement*. Dublin: Four Courts Press, 233–45.
Ó Murchadha, D. 1999. 'The formation of Gaelic surnames in Ireland: choosing the eponyms'. *Society for Name Studies in Britain and Ireland: Nomina*, vol. 22, 25–44.
Ó Riain, P. 1972. 'Boundary association in early Irish society'. *Studia Celtica*, vol. 7, 12–29.
Ó Riain, P. 1974. 'Battle-site and territorial extent in early Ireland'. *Zeitschrift für celtische Philologie*, vol. 33, 67–80.
Ó Riain, P. 2016. *A dictionary of Irish saints*. Dublin: Four Courts Press.
O'Brien, G. 2015. 'Island living: the modern story of life on the islands of Lough Ree'. In Cunningham, B., and Murtagh, H. (eds), *Lough Ree: historic lakeland settlement*. Dublin: Four Courts Press, 220–35.
O'Conor Don, C.O. 1891. *The O'Conors of Connaught*. Dublin: Hodges, Figgis and Co.
O'Conor, K.D. 1998. *The archaeology of medieval rural settlement in Ireland*. Dublin: Royal Irish Academy.
O'Conor, K.D. 2000. 'The ethnicity of Irish moated sites'. *Ruralia III*, 92–102.
O'Conor, K.D. 2001. 'The morphology of Gaelic lordly sites in north Connacht'. In Duffy, P.J., Edwards, D., and FitzPatrick, E. (eds), *Gaelic Ireland, c.1250–c.1650: land, lordship & settlement*. Dublin: Four Courts Press, 329–45.
O'Conor, K.D. 2002a. 'Housing in later medieval Gaelic Ireland'. *Ruralia IV*, 197–206.
O'Conor, K.D. 2002b. 'Motte castles in Ireland: permanent fortresses, residences and manorial centres'. *Chateau Gaillard*, vol. 20, 173–82.
O'Conor, K.D. 2002c. 'Sligo Castle'. In Timoney, M.A. (ed.), *A celebration of Sligo*. Carrick-on-Shannon: Sligo Field Club, 183–92.
O'Conor, K.D. 2003. 'A reinterpretation of the earthworks at Baginbun, Co. Wexford'. In Kenyon, J.R., and O'Conor, K.D. (eds), *The medieval castle in Ireland and Wales: essays in honour of Jeremy Knight*. Dublin: Four Courts Press, 17–31.
O'Conor, K.D. 2004. 'Medieval Rural Settlement in Munster'. In *Medieval Ireland: the Barryscourt Lectures I–X*. Kinsale: The Barryscourt Trust, 225–56.

O'Conor, K.D. 2005. 'Gaelic lordly settlement in 13th- and 14th-century Ireland'. In Holm, I., Innselset, S., and Óye, I. (eds), *Utmark: the Outfield as industry and ideology in the Iron Age and the Middle Ages*. Bergen: University of Bergen, 209–21.

O'Conor, K.D. 2007. 'English settlement and change in Roscommon during the late sixteenth and seventeenth centuries'. In Horning, A., Ó Baoill, R., Donnelly, C., and Logue, P. (eds), *The post-medieval archaeology of Ireland, 1550–1850*. Dublin: Wordwell Books, 189–204.

O'Conor, K.D. 2008. 'Castle studies in Ireland – the way forward'. *Chateau Gaillard*, vol. 23, 329–39.

O'Conor, K.D. 2015. 'Earth and timber fortifications'. In Carpenter, A., and Moss, R. (eds), *Art and architecture of Ireland, volume I: medieval, c.400–c.1600*. Dublin: Royal Irish Academy, 332–6.

O'Conor, K.D. 2018. '*Crannóga* in later medieval Ireland: continuity and change'. In Campbell, E., FitzPatrick, E., and Horning, A. (eds), *Becoming and belonging in Ireland, AD c.1200–1600: essays in identity and cultural practice*. Cork: Cork University Press, 148–66.

O'Conor, K.D. 2021. 'Settlement and place in Gaelic Ireland, 1100–1350'. *Eolas*, vol. 14, 44–72.

O'Conor, K.D. 2023. 'Moygara Castle through time'. In O'Conor, K.D. (ed.), *Moygara Castle and the O'Garas of Coolavin*. Dublin: Four Courts Press, 181–209.

O'Conor, K.D., Brady, N., Connon, A., and Fidalgo-Romo, C. 2010. 'The Rock of Lough Cé, Co. Roscommon'. In Finan, T. (ed.), *Medieval Lough Cé: history, archaeology and landscape*. Dublin: Four Courts Press, 15–40.

O'Conor, K.D., and Shanahan, B. 2013. *Roscommon Abbey: a visitor's guide*. Boyle: Roscommon County Council.

O'Conor, K.D., and Shanahan, B. 2018. *Rindoon Castle and deserted medieval town: a visitor's guide*. Boyle: Roscommon County Library.

O'Conor, K.D., and Fredengren, C. 2019. 'Medieval settlement in Leitrim, c.1169–c.1350'. In Kelly, L., and Scott, B. (eds), *Leitrim: history and society*. Dublin: Geography Publications, 79–101.

O'Conor, K.D., and Naessens, P. 2016a. 'The medieval harbour beside Rindoon Castle, Co. Roscommon, Ireland'. *Chateau Gaillard*, vol. 27, 237–42.

O'Conor, K.D., and Naessens, P. 2016b. 'Temple House: from Templar castle to New English mansion'. In Browne, M., and Ó Clabaigh, C. (eds), *Soldiers of Christ: the Knights Templar and the Knights Hospitaller in medieval Ireland*. Dublin: Four Courts Press, 124–50.

O'Conor, K.D., and Finan, T. 2018. 'Medieval settlement in north Roscommon, c.1200 AD–c.1350 AD'. In Farrell, R., O'Conor, K.D., and Potter, M. (eds), *Roscommon: history and society*. Dublin: Geography Publications, 105–32.

O'Conor, K.D., Naessens, P., and Sherlock, R. 2015. 'Rindoon Castle, Co. Roscommon: an Anglo-Norman fortress on the western shores of Lough Ree'. In Cunningham, B., and Murtagh, H. (eds), *Lough Ree: historic lakeland settlement*. Dublin: Four Courts Press, 83–109.

O'Conor, K.D., and Williams, J. 2015. 'Ballinagare Castle'. In Gibbons, L., and O'Conor, K.D. (eds), *Charles O'Conor of Ballinagare, 1710–91: life and works*. Dublin: Four Courts Press, 52–71.

O'Daly, J., and O'Donovan, J. 1853. 'Inauguration of Cathal Crobhdhearg O'Conor, king of Connaught'. *Transactions of the Kilkenny Archaeological Society*, vol. 2, no. 2, 335–47.

O'Flaherty, E. 2014. *Archaeological watermarks: turlough floodplains as communal spaces and places of assembly*. Online article (https://www.academia.edu/6115533. Accessed 13/11/2023)

O'Keeffe, P. 2001. *Ireland's principal roads: 123 AD–1608*. Dublin: National Roads Authority.

O'Keeffe, T. 1998. 'The fortifications of western Ireland, AD 1100–1300, and their interpretation'. *Journal of the Galway Archaeological and Historical Society*, vol. 50, 184–200.

O'Keeffe, T. 2000. *Medieval Ireland: an archaeology*. Stroud: Tempus Publishing Ltd.

O'Keeffe, T. 2001. 'Ethnicity and moated settlement in medieval Ireland: a review of current thinking'. *Annual Report of the Medieval Research Group*, vol. 15, 21–6.

O'Keeffe, T. 2015. *Medieval Irish buildings, 1100–1600*. Dublin: Four Courts Press.

O'Keeffe, T. 2018. 'Frontiers of the archaeological imagination: rethinking landscape and identity in thirteenth-century Roscommon, Ireland'. *Landscapes*, vol. 19, no. 1, 1–14.

O'Keeffe, T. 2019. 'Feudal power in a Gaelic world? Contextualizing the encastellation of pre-Norman Ireland'. *The Journal of Irish Archaeology*, vol. 28, 119–38.

O'Keeffe, T. 2021. *Ireland encastellated, AD 950–1550: Insular castle-building in its European context*. Dublin: Four Courts Press.

O'Keeffe, T., and MacCotter, P. 2020. 'Ireland's oldest stone castle'. *Archaeology Ireland*, vol. 34, no. 1, 14–18.

O'Mahoney, A. 2014. 'Clontuskert Augustinian Priory'. *Monastic Ireland*. http://monastic.ie/history/clontuskert-augustinian-priory/. Accessed: 13/11/2023.

O'Neill, T. 1987. *Merchants & mariners in medieval Ireland*. Dublin: Irish Academic Press.

Orpen, G.H. 1911; reprint 2005. *Ireland under the Normans*. Dublin: Four Courts Press.

O'Sullivan, A. 1998. *The archaeology of lake settlement in Ireland*. Dublin: Royal Irish Academy.

O'Sullivan, A. 2001. 'Crannogs in late medieval Gaelic Ireland, c.1350–c.1650'. In Duffy, P.J., Edwards, D., FitzPatrick, E. (eds), *Gaelic Ireland, c.1250–c.1650: land, lordship & settlement*. Dublin: Four Courts Press, 397–417.

O'Sullivan, A. 2009. 'Early medieval crannogs and imagined islands'. In Cooney, G., Becker, K., Coles, J., Ryan, M., and Sievers, S. (eds), *Relics of old decency: archaeological studies in later prehistory*. Dublin: Wordwell Books, 79–88.

O'Sullivan, A., and Breen, C. 2007. *Maritime Ireland: an archaeology of coastal communities*. Cheltenham: The History Press.

O'Sullivan, A., McCormick, F., Kerr, T.R., and Harney, L. 2014. *Early medieval Ireland, AD 400–1100: the evidence from archaeological excavations*. Dublin: Royal Irish Academy.

O'Sullivan, C.M. 2004. *Hospitality in medieval Ireland, 900–1500*. Dublin: Four Courts Press.

Overland, A., and O'Connell, M. 2013. 'Environment, flora and fauna'. In Jackman, N., Moore, C., and Rynne, C. (eds), *The mill at Kilbegly: an archaeological investigation on the route of the M6 Ballinasloe to Athlone national road scheme*. Dublin: Wordwell Books, 61–83.

Parkes, M., Meehan, R., and Préteseille, S. 2012. *The geological heritage of Roscommon: an audit of county geological sites in Roscommon*. Dublin: Irish Geological Heritage Programme.

Patrick, L. 2022. *Cultural landscapes of late medieval Gaelic Ulster*. Unpublished PhD dissertation, Queen's University Belfast.

Perros-Walton, H. 2013. 'Church reform in Connacht'. In Duffy, S. (ed.), *Princes, prelates and poets in medieval Ireland: essays in honour of Katharine Simms*. Dublin: Four Courts Press, 279–308.

Pollock, D. 2004. 'The bawn exposed: recent excavations at Barryscourt'. In *Medieval Ireland: the Barryscourt Lectures I–X*. Kinsale: The Barryscourt Trust, 145–76.

Pollock, D. 2020. 'The small walled town of Dungarvan, Co. Waterford'. In Corlett, C., and Potterton, M. (eds), *The town in medieval Ireland, in the light of recent archaeological excavations*. Dublin: Wordwell Books, 197–208.

Portrun Development Association. 2019. Galey Castle. http://www.portrun.ie/heritage/gailey-castle. Accessed: 13/11/2023.

Portrun Development Association. 2019. Portrunny Harbour. www.portrun.ie/heritage/harbour-heritage/. Accessed: 13/11/2023.

Read, C. 2010. 'Remembering where the bishop sat: exploring perceptions of the past at the Bishop's Seat, Kilteasheen, Co. Roscommon'. In Finan, T. (ed.), *Medieval Lough Cé: history, archaeology and landscape*. Dublin: Four Courts Press, 41–66.

Reynolds, S. 1994. *Fiefs and vassals: the medieval evidence reinterpreted*. Oxford: Oxford University Press.

Richter, M. 1988. *Medieval Ireland: the enduring tradition*. Dublin: Gill & Macmillan.

Ryan, S. 2013. 'The devotional landscape of medieval Irish cultural Catholicism *inter hibernicos et inter anglicos*, *c.*1200–*c.*1550'. In Rafferty, O.P. (ed.), *Irish Catholic identities*. Manchester: Manchester University Press, 62–74.

Rynne, E. 1966–71. 'Stone head from Curraghboy, Co. Roscommon'. *Journal of the Galway Archaeological and Historical Society*, vol. 32, 92–3.

Rynne, C. 2004. 'Technological change in Anglo-Norman Munster'. *Medieval Ireland: The Barryscourt Lectures I–X*, 65–96. Kinsale: The Barryscourt Trust.

Shanahan, B. 2008. 'Ardakillin royal centre. A report on recent fieldwork carried out by the Discovery Programme at the royal centre of Ardakillin, Co. Roscommon'. *Group for the Study of Irish Historic Settlement Newsletter*, no. 13, 7–13.

Shanahan, B., and O'Conor, K. 2020. 'Rindown, Co. Roscommon: recent investigations of the deserted medieval town'. In Corlett, C., and Potterton, M. (eds), *The town in medieval Ireland, in the light of recent archaeological excavations*. Dublin: Wordwell Books, 235–52.

Sheehan, Á. 2019. 'Locating the Gaelic medical families in Elizabethan Ireland'. In Cunningham, J. (ed.), *Early modern Ireland and the world of medicine: practitioners, collectors and contexts*. Manchester: Manchester University Press, 20–38.

Sherlock, R. 2011. 'The evolution of the Irish tower-house as a domestic space'. *Proceedings of the Royal Irish Academy*, vol. 111C, 115–40.

Sherlock, R. 2013. 'Using new techniques to date old castles'. *Archaeology Ireland*, vol. 27, no. 2, 19–23.

Sherlock, R. 2015. 'The spatial dynamic of the Irish tower house hall'. In McAlister, V., and Barry, T. (eds), *Space and settlement in medieval Ireland*. Dublin: Four Courts Press, 86–109.

Sherlock, R. 2016. *Athlone Castle*. Athlone: Westmeath County Council.

Simms, K. 1978. 'Guesting and feasting in Gaelic Ireland'. *The Journal of the Royal Society of Antiquaries of Ireland*, vol. 108, 67–100.

Simms, K. 1987; 2000. *From kings to warlords: the changing political structure of Gaelic Ireland in the later Middle Ages*. Woodbridge: Boydell Press.

Simms, K. 2001. 'Native sources for Gaelic settlement: the house poems'. In Duffy, P.J., Edwards, D., and FitzPatrick, E. (eds), *Gaelic Ireland, c.1250–c.1650: land, lordship & settlement*. Dublin: Four Courts Press, 246–70.

Simms, K. 2009. *Medieval Gaelic sources: Maynooth Research Guides for Irish Local History, no. 14*. Dublin: Four Courts Press.

Simms, K. 2015. 'The origins of the creaght: farming system or social unit?' In Murphy, M., and Stout, M. (eds), *Agriculture and settlement in Ireland*. Dublin: Four Courts Press, 101–18.

Simms, K. 2018a. 'The political recovery of Gaelic Ireland'. In Smith, B. (ed.), *The Cambridge history of Ireland, volume I: 600–1550*. Cambridge: Cambridge University Press, 272–99.

Simms, K. 2018b. 'Gaelic culture and society'. In Smith, B. (ed.), *The Cambridge history of Ireland, vol. I: 600–1550*. Cambridge: Cambridge University Press, 415–40.

Simms, K. 2020. *Gaelic Ulster in the Middle Ages*. Dublin: Four Courts Press.

Simms, K. (ed.) 2013. *Gaelic Ireland (c.600–c.1700): politics, culture and landscapes*. Dublin: Wordwell.

Simpson, L. 2004. 'Excavations on the southern side of the medieval town at Ship Street Little, Dublin'. In Duffy, S. (ed.), *Medieval Dublin, V*. Dublin: Four Courts Press, 9–51.

Smith, A. 1846. 'Journey to Connaught, April 1709'. *The miscellany of the Irish Archaeological Society, vol. 1*. Irish Archaeological Society, 161–78.

Smith, B. (ed.) 2018. *The Cambridge history of Ireland, vol. I: 600–1550*. Cambridge: Cambridge University Press.

Smith, K. 2014. 'Abbeyknockmoy Cistercian Abbey'. *Monastic Ireland*. http://monastic.ie/history/abbeyknockmoy_cistercian_abbey/. Accessed: 13/11/2023.

Smith, K. 2014. 'Kilconnell Franciscan Friary'. *Monastic Ireland*. http://monastic.ie/history/kilconnell-franciscan-friary/. Accessed: 13/11/2023.

Soderberg, J., and Immich, J.L. 2010. 'Animal contact: livestock approaches to understanding social boundaries in later medieval Roscommon'. In Finan, T. (ed.), *Medieval Lough Cé: history, archaeology and landscape*. Dublin: Four Courts Press, 97–118.

Stalley, R.A. 1978. 'William of Prene and the Royal Works in Ireland'. *Journal of the British Archaeological Association*, 3rd Series, vol. 41, 30–49.

Stalley, R. 1987. *The Cistercian monasteries of Ireland: an account of the history, art and architecture of the White Monks in Ireland from 1142–1540*. London and New Haven: Yale University Press.

Stark, E. 2012. *A landscape and architectural survey of Cloondadauv Castle, County Galway*. Unpublished MA dissertation, NUI Galway.

Stout, G. 2015. 'The Cistercian grange: a medieval farming system'. In Murphy, M., and Stout, M. (eds), *Agriculture and settlement in Ireland*. Dublin: Four Courts Press, 28–68.

Stout, M. 1997. *The Irish ringfort*. Dublin: Four Courts Press.

Stout, M. 2017. *Early medieval Ireland, 431–1169*. Dublin: Wordwell Books.

Sweetman, D. 2000. *The medieval castles of Ireland*. Woodbridge: Boydell Press.

Sweetman, D. 2004. 'The origin and development of the tower-house in Ireland'. *Medieval Ireland: the Barryscourt Lectures I–X*. Kinsale: The Barryscourt Trust, 257–88.

Swift, C. 2015. 'Follow the money: the financial resources of Diarmait Mac Murchada'. In Purcell, E., MacCotter, P., Nyhan, J., and Sheehan, J. (eds), *Clerics, kings and Vikings: essays on medieval Ireland in honour of Donnchadh Ó Corráin*. Dublin: Four Courts Press, 91–102.

Swift, C. 2017. 'An investigation of the word *oireachtas* in modern and medieval Ireland and its economic role in earlier periods'. *Studia Hibernica*, vol. 43, 1–24.

Timoney, M.A. 2021. 'Rathscanlan and Ballyara, ancestral place of the O'Hara Riabhach'. *Sligo Field Club Journal*, vol. 7, 77–100.

Valante, M.A. 2015. 'Fleets, forts and the geography of Toirdelbach Ua Conchobair's bid for the high-kingship'. In McAlister, V. and Barry, T. (eds), *Space and settlement in medieval Ireland*. Dublin: Four Courts Press, 48–63.

Veach, C., and Verstraten Veach, F. 2013. 'William Gorm de Lacy: "chiefest champion in these parts of Europe"'. In Duffy, S. (ed.), *Princes, prelates and poets in medieval Ireland: essays in honour of Katharine Simms*. Dublin: Four Courts Press, 63–84.

Verstaten, F. 2007. 'Images of Gaelic lordship in Ireland, c.1200–c.1400'. In Doran, L., and Lyttleton, J. (eds), *Lordship in medieval Ireland: image and reality*. Dublin: Four Courts Press, 47–74.

Wallace, A. and Maguire, F. 2021. *Final report on archaeological excavation at Society Street (Townparks), Ballinasloe, Co. Galway. Licence no. 20E0330, on behalf of SIAC Ltd*. Atlantic Archaeology.

Walsh, G. 2017. *Cattle breeds in Ireland: a history*. Taghmon: The Borie Press.

Walsh, P. 1936–7. 'Christian kings of Connacht'. *Journal of the Galway Archaeological and Historical Society*, vol. 17, 124–43.

Walsh, P. 1940–1. 'Connacht in the Book of Rights'. *Journal of the Galway Archaeological and Historical Society*, vol. 19, 1–15.

Walsh, P. 1947. 'The Book of Munster'. In Ó Lochlainn, C. (ed.), *Irish men of learning: studies by Father Paul Walsh*, Dublin: Three Candles.

Walton, H. 1980. *The English in Connacht, 1171–1333*. Unpublished PhD dissertation, Trinity College Dublin.

Watt, J.A. 2008. 'Gaelic polity and cultural identity'. In Cosgrove, A. (ed.), *A new history of Ireland II: medieval Ireland, 1169–1534*. Oxford: Oxford University Press, 314–51.

Whelan, K. 2018. *Religion, landscape and settlement in Ireland*. Dublin: Four Courts Press.

Index

Abbeyfield townland, Kilconnell parish, Co. Galway, 130
Abbeyknockmoy, Co. Galway, 27, 32, 53, 71, 73–4, 217, 220–2, 230–1, 262
Acallam na Senórach, 7, 125, 127, 128
Agherrymymany, see Aughrim
Aghacarra 'island', 236
Ahascragh, Co. Galway, 3, 27, 53, 162, 194, 231
Airgíalla [Oirghialla], Co. Armagh, 12, 93
Annagh townland and castle, Co. Galway, 132, 146–7, 240
Annagh House, Co. Galway, 147
arable agriculture, 43, 57, 60, 64–6
Ardakillin Lough, see Loch Cairgín
artefacts, 89–92, 115–7, 120, 123, 165, 235, 241–2, 253, 262
    bronze/copper alloy items, 116
Ashford townland, see Tuaim Sruthra
Áth Nadsluaigh, 24, 80–1, 83, 194, 204, 231; see also Ballinasloe
Athenry, Co. Galway 32, 36, 53, 58, 69, 101, 217–9, 231
    castle, 219
Athenry, 1st battle of (1249), 25
Athenry, 2nd battle of (1316), 28
Athleague, Co. Roscommon, 3, 30, 31, 33, 34, 35, 46, 48, 50–4, 65, 84, 102, 153, 155, 163, 164, 165, 184, 193–204, 233, 237, 238, 249, 250, 253, 254, 259, 261
    castle, 164, 184, 196–201
Athlone, Cos Roscommon & Westmeath, 3, 9, 22, 44–6, 50–1, 53, 67, 69, 78, 80, 93, 170, 204, 232
    castle, 23, 46, 66, 67, 84, 85, 166–7, 216
    Ó Cellaig *cenn áit*, 165–7
Aththrym, see Aughrim
Athtruim, see Aughrim
Aughnanure Castle, Co. Galway, 216

Aughrim, Co. Galway, 4, 21, 23, 27, 28, 36, 37, 49, 52, 53, 68, 83, 84, 89, 135, 149, 167, 205–16, 232, 243, 245, 247, 253, 259, 261
    castle, 84, 207–16, 233, 245
Aughrim, battle of (1691), 205, 211, 213–15
Augustinian Canons Regular, 9, 71, 72–3, 195, 250, 262

Badún of Rindoon, Co. Roscommon, 93
Badhún, see bódhún
Badhbhdhún, see bódhún
Baginbun, Co. Wexford, 236
Baile na Gáile, 51, 170, 185–6, 254, see also Knockcroghery
Ballaghdacker Lough [Hollygrove Lough], Co. Galway, 3, 31–2, 50, 91, 100, 108, 153–64, 184, 186, 193, 203, 235, 239, 242, 243, 249, 253, 254, 266
Ballinagare House, Co. Roscommon, 259
Ballinasloe, Co. Galway, 3, 9, 23, 24, 40, 41, 50, 52, 53, 64, 68, 77–80, 82, 83, 90, 193, 194, 205, 232, 240, 245, 256, 259
    castle, 245, 259
    horse fair, 64
Ballinphuill bog, Co. Galway, 43, 65
Ballintober Castle, Co. Roscommon, 216
Ballycreggan [*Carraig Uí Neachtain*], Co. Roscommon, 14, 245, 247
Ballydonegan Bay, Co. Cork, 172
Ballydoogan townland, Co. Galway, 125, 130, 145–6, 240, 266
Ballyeighter townland, Co. Galway, 68
Ballyforan, Co. Roscommon, 3, 53, 54, 194
Ballygalda [*Béal átha gallda*] townland, Co. Roscommon, 34, 52, 255
Ballyganner South tower house, Co. Clare, 183, 250

Ballygar, Co. Galway, 53, 194
Ballyglass townland, Co. Galway, 130
Ballyhanna, Co. Donegal, 70
Ballymoe, Co. Galway, 54
Ballynabanaba townland, Co. Galway, 130, 146, 240
Ballyshanny tower house, Co. Clare, 183, 250
Barnacullen townland, Co. Roscommon, 45
Barnaderg, *see Bhearna Dhearg*
Barnaderg Castle, 223, 231, 259
baronies
    Athlone, 1, 3, 15, 26, 48
    Clonmacnowen, Co. Galway, 1–2, 37
    Kilconnell, Co. Galway, 1, 36–7,
    Killian, Co. Galway, 1–2, 12, 15, 171n1
    Loughrea, Co. Galway, 12, 58,
    Moycarn, Co. Roscommon, 1, 16, 98n2
    Tiaquin, Co. Galway, 1, 2, 36, 228
Barryscourt Castle, Co. Cork, 216
Battle of the Conors (1180), 20
bawn enclosures, 66, 93, 104, 141, 144, 176, 183, 196–7, 202, 204, 216, 224, 230, 232, 237, 243, 245
Bawn townland, Killeshandra parish, Co. Cavan, 237
Bawnmore townland, Co. Offaly, 237
Béal na mBuillí – Strokestown, Co. Roscommon, 259
Bél Átha na nGarbhán, 35
Bellagad townland, Co. Galway, 46
Beltaine festival, 189
Bhéal an átha, *see* Mount Talbot
Bhéal an Átha Uí Cheallaigh, *see* Mount Talbot
Bhearna Dhearg [Barnaderg townland], Co. Galway, 24
Blean-Gaille, *see* Galey
boats and water-based transport, 52–4, 113, 115, 178
bódhún sites, 93–4, 107, 138–42, 144, 152, 164, 198–204, 234, 237–8, 249, 251, 260–1, 264, 266
bódhún of Ath – [Athlone], 93
bódhún of *Áth Buide* [Ballyboy, Co. Offaly], 93
bódhún of *Luimnech* [Limerick], 93

bog and peatland, 40–2
Bogganfin townland, Co. Roscommon, 46
Breaghmhuine [Brawney barony], Co. Westmeath, 58
Bredagh townland and moated site, Co. Roscommon, 96, 98–9, 243
Bréifne [broadly cantred of Breifne], 53, 94, 244
Brétach, the, 98, 98n2
Breuadh, *see* Bredagh
Brian Boru, 14–15, 165
Brideswell – *Tobar Bhríde*, Co. Roscommon, 2, 53, 124
Bristol, England, 67, 89
Bruce, Edward, 28
Buile Suibhne, 170
Bunowen/Ahascragh (river), 3, 194
Burke, Ulick Fionn (d. 1509), 35, 223, 231
Butler lordship, 27–8, 30, 37, 83–4, 207, 216
Butler, Edmund, 27
Butler, Theobald, 84

Caherahoagh cashel, Co. Clare, 241
Caherconnell cashel, Co. Clare, 89–90, 242
Cahercloggaun tower house, Co. Clare, 183, 250
Caherdrinny tower house, Co. Cork, 184
Cahererillan tower house, Co. Galway, 183
Cahermacnaghten cashel, Co. Clare, 176, 241
Cahermore cashel, Co. Clare, 241
Cahir Castle, Co. Tipperary, 216
Cairpre Crom, 17
caislen, 78, 80, 83, 166
    Caislen becc, 34
Caislen na Caillighe, Lough Mask, Co. Mayo, 78, 241
Caislen na Circe, Lough Corrib, Co. Galway, 78, 241
Caislen Suicin, 24, 83–4
caistél, 77–80, 82–3, 88, 106, 165–6, 204, 247
Caithréim Thoirdhealbhaigh, 6, 15, 28, 89, 242
Callaghan's Loughs, Co. Galway, 53, 206

Callow Castle, 134, 138–43, 164, 184,
Callow Lough [Lough Acalla], Co. Galway, 3, 31, 50, 91, 101, 102, 108, 125, 129–53, 160, 164, 184, 186, 193, 196, 202, 204, 235, 236, 237, 239, 243, 249, 250, 251, 252, 253, 254, 255, 256, 259, 260, 266
Callow *bódhún*, 31, 131, 138–9, 142
Callow Lodge, 141
Callow Lough *crannóg*, 135–7, 235
Caltragh burial ground, Coolnageer townland, Co. Roscommon, 116
Caltrapallis townland, Co. Galway, 100
Cam – *Camach Brighdi* [parish and medieval church], Co. Roscommon, 18, 96, 108, 117, 124–5
Cána/túarastla [tribute], 63, 190, 238
Cape Clear Island, Co. Cork, 184
Carboniferous Limestone, 1, 40, 46, 50, 60, 109, 118, 241
Carnagh townland, Co. Roscommon, 46
Carnfree, Co. Roscommon, 68
Carns moated site, Co. Roscommon, 241
Carrigeen church, Coolaspaddaun townland, Co. Galway, 155
Carrownderry townland, Co. Roscommon, 45
Carrowntarriff townland, Co. Roscommon, 59
Cartrondoogan [*Cartrún Uí Dhúgáin*] townland, Co. Galway, 125, 130, 240
Cartrondoogan [*Ceathrú an Ghabhainn*] townland, Co. Galway, 130–1
cashels, 35, 41, 78, 83, 86, 88–91, 93, 98, 100, 106, 120–1, 127, 166–7, 175–6, 183, 204, 209, 218, 234–5, 237–42, 246–8, 250–2, 261, 264
  on *crannóga*, 121, 241
  on promontory forts, 172–9
Castleblakeney, Co. Galway, 53, 171n1, 229
Castlegar (river), 3, 194
Castlenaughton, Co. Roscommon, 24
Castlesampson Castle, Co. Roscommon, 106, 180, 245
Castletown/Tullinadaly [*Tulach na dála*], Co. Galway, 14
cattle, *see* pastoral agriculture

cathair, *see* cashels
Ceallach mac Finnachta, 14
Cénel Coirpre Chruim, 12–3, 15, 17, 43, 91
cenn áit, 4, 17, 23, 25, 33, 36, 38, 56, 62, 66, 86, 92, 93–4, 98, 101, 103, 106, 109, 114, 123, 128, 130, 133, 135, 144, 151–3, 155, 161–5, 167, 170–2, 178–9, 184–6, 192, 194–6, 204, 205, 207, 208, 217–18, 220, 222, 232, 234–6, 238–9, 241–3, 248–9, 251, 253–5, 258, 262, 265–7
chiefry castles, 180–1
Cill Mhiadhan [Kilmeane], Co. Roscommon, 30, 189
cís [rent/food stipend], 55, 190, 238, 255
Cistercians, 27, 32, 63, 66, 71, 73, 125, 148, 155, 217, 222
Claenloch, battle of, 12
Clan Murtagh, sept branch of the Uí Chonchobair, 28
Clann Taidg and Uí Diarmata [broadly the cantred of Clantayg], 32, 101, 217–18, 231
Clann Chommáin, 12–14, 91
Clann Crimthann, 12–13, 15, 18, 91
Clann Ricaird lordship, *see* Mac Uilliam *Uachtar* de Burgh
Clann Somhairle, 34
Clann Uadach, 18–19, 64, 66, 98–9, 108, 117, 122–3, 125, 169, 243–4
Clannmhaicne Eoghain [Clonmacnowen], 23–4, 29, 32, 83, 240, 256, 259, 266
Clanricarde, earl of, 196, 203
Clare (river), 48
Clochar Mac Daimhin [Clogher], Co. Tyrone, 12
Clogher, Killaclogher townland, Co. Galway, 31, 32, 106, 217
Clonbrock Demesne townland, Co. Galway, 67, 100, 102
Clonfert, Co. Galway, 15
  diocese of, 19–20, 162
Clonkeenkerrill, Co. Galway, 144
Clonmacnoise, Co. Offaly, 15, 17, 24, 65, 124–5, 206, 245

Clonmacnowen, *see* Clannmhaicne Eoghain
Clontarf, battle of (1014), 14, 15
Clontuskert [*Cluain Tuaiscirt O Máine*], Co. Galway, 9, 53, 71, 72–3, 206, 250
Clontymullan moated site, Co. Fermanagh, 94
Cloonacleigha Lough, 244
Cloonakilleg townland, Co. Roscommon, 194
Cloonbigny Castle, Co. Roscommon, 106
Cloonburren, *see Cluain Buaráin*
Clooncannon townland, Co. Galway, 155, 162
Clooneen townland [*bealach an Cluainin*], Co. Roscommon, 52
Cloonfree moated site, Co. Roscommon, 75, 86, 94, 252
Cloonigny moated site, Co. Galway, 94, 99, 243
Cloonlyon (river), 3, 194
Cloonybeirne moated site, Co. Roscommon, 241
Cloonykelly townland, Co. Roscommon, 194, 254
Cluain Buaráin [Cloonburren townland?], Co. Roscommon, 24, 245–6
Cluain Cuill [Clonquill townland], Co. Galway, 24
Cluain Leathan [possibly Ballymacegan or Kiltyroe townlands], Co. Tipperary, 162
Cluain na gCloidhe, *see* Mount Talbot
Cnoc Gail [Knockhall townland?], Co. Roscommon, 20
Cogadh Gaedheal re Gallaibh, 15
coinage, 68–9, 89–90, 241, 257
Collooney, Co. Sligo, 78
Compossicion [Booke] of Connought, 32, 37, 38, 106, 170, 205, 258,
Coolagarry townland, Co. Roscommon, 16–17
Coolaspaddaun townland, Co. Galway, 155
Coolderry [*Culdaire*] townland, Co. Roscommon, 103, 125, 240, 266
Coolnageer townland and moated site, Co. Roscommon, 96, 99–100, 116, 243
Coololla townland, Co. Galway, 208
Cooloorta townland, Co. Galway, 220

Corboley townland, Co. Roscommon, 57, 60, 191,
Corca Achlann [*túath*], 27, 62
Corgarve townland, Co. Roscommon, 46
corn-drying kilns, 65, 89–90, 253
Cornacarta Lough, 236
Cornacask or Easterfield townland, Co. Galway, 153, 155–6, 160, 239, 266
Cornafulla townland, Co. Roscommon, 60
Cornageeha townland and cashel, Co. Roscommon, 34–5, 240
Cornalee townland, Co. Roscommon, 58
Cornamart townland, Co. Roscommon, 60, 191
Cornapallis townland, Co. Roscommon, 100, 102–4, 163
Cornaseer townland, Co. Roscommon, 45, 66
Corraclogh townland, Co. Roscommon, 46
Corramore townland, Co. Roscommon, 46
Corraneena townland, Co. Galway, 131, 144–5
crannóg settlements, 16–7, 75, 78–9, 82–3, 98, 106, 113–23, 125, 134–42, 152–3, 154–7, 158–64, 166, 183, 234–6, 239, 241–4, 247–8, 251–2, 260–1, 264
  high-cairn *crannóga*, 91–3, 120, 135–6, 152, 160, 235, 241
creach ríogh, 27
Creat, 254, 267
Creeharmore townland, Co. Roscommon, 194
Creeraun moated site, Co. Galway, 243
Creggan townland, Co. Roscommon, 171
Críoch Gáille, *see* Galey
Crofton family, 187
Cross of Cong, 18, 115
Cruas Connacht clanna sogain, 147
cruck-roof construction, 176, 252
Cruit Point, Co. Roscommon, 168
Crummagh townland, Co. Galway, 149
Cuil an úrtain, *see* Cooloorta
Cuilleenirwan townland and moated site, Co. Roscommon, 16, 95–8, 127, 243
cultural anachronisms, 63, 75, 153, 179, 222, 250–2,

Curraghalaher townland, Co. Roscommon, 46, 60, 191
Curraghbaghla townland, Co. Galway, 155, 162
Curry townland, Co. Roscommon, 46

Dál Cais, 14
Daire na gCapall, 20
de Bermingham [Clann Mac Feorais] lordship, 32, 100, 101, 217–8, 231, 257
de Burgh [Burke] lordship, 25, 28, 29, 32
de Burgh, Edmund *Albanach*, 30, 195
de Burgh, Richard, 1st Lord of Connacht (d. *c.*1242), 22–3
de Burgh, Richard, 2nd Earl of Ulster 'the Red Earl' (d. 1326), 28
de Burgh, Walter *Liath* (d. 1332), 29–30
de Burgh, William 'the Brown Earl' (d. 1333), 29
de Burgh, William *Liath* (d. 1324), 28, 63
de Constentin, Geoffrey, 24, 245
de Exeter, Richard, 195
de Geneville, Geoffrey, 46, 51
de la Rochelle [de Rupella] manor, 27, 207, 245
de la Rochelle, Philip, 84
de la Rochelle, Richard, 23, 25, 84, 215, 246, 253
de Lacy, Hugh, 257
de Lacy, William *Gorm*, 257
de Lezignan, Godfrey, 26
de Prene, William, 66
de Sandford, John, 27
deer, 67, 115, 253
Delbna Nuadat, 92, 250
Derbfhine, 14, 248
Derrineel townland, Co. Roscommon, 34, 46
Derrinlurg townland, Co. Roscommon, 51
Derryfada townland, Co. Roscommon, 48
Dillon family, 166,
Disert Briole [Dysart], Co. Roscommon, 125
'Dispersed nucleation', 192–3, 254–5, 265, 267
Dominican friaries, 148–9

Doon Upper and Lower [Doon Fort, Castle] townlands, Co. Galway, 130, 246
Doran's 'Route 9', 49–1, 52, 102, 109, 193
Doran's 'Route 11', 49, 51, 66, 168, 170, 186, 187, 232, 233, 245
Drum Clasaigh/Drum Drestan, Drum, Co. Roscommon, 12, 18
Drumclay *crannóg*, Co. Fermanagh, 92, 236
Drumercool townland, Co. Roscommon, 69
dry-land service sites, 113–14, 120, 137–8, 140, 152, 156–8, 160–1, 164, 218, 239, 243–4
Dublin government, 7, 111
Dual ollamh do thriall le toisg, 170
Dún Leodha [Dunlo], Co. Galway, 77–83, 88, 106, 204, 247
Dún na Mónadh, 24
Dunlo townland, Co. Galway, 77, 80
Dunamon, Co. Roscommon, 54, 84
Dunboy Castle, Co. Cork, 180
Dundonnell Castle, Co. Roscommon, 84–5, 246–7
Dundoogan townland, Co. Galway, 130
Dungannon, Co. Tyrone, 61, 153
Duniry, Co. Galway, 58, 162
Dunmore, Co. Galway, 78–9
  castle, 219
Durudh Mainnin, 98
Dysart, Co. Roscommon, 2, 3, 18, 48, 53, 54, 96, 99, 108, 117, 123

Eachdruim, *see* Aughrim
Earth Resistance surveying, 6, 118, 119, 121, 122
Easter religious festival, 153
Easterfield townland, *see* Cornacask
Ecclesiastical Taxation of Ireland (1302–6), 70–1
Edward I, King of England, 68, 89
Edward's Island *crannóg*, Lough Croan, Co. Roscommon, 114–16, 122, 125, 235, 260
Electrical Resistivity Tomography surveying, 6, 118, 121, 174, 179

Elizabeth I, queen of England, 38, 196
Emly, dioceses, 162
Erenagh townland, Co. Roscommon, 189

Fá urraidh labhras leac Theamhrach, 65, 195
Farranykelly townland, Co. Roscommon, 153, 254
fairs and markets, 4, 54–5, 58, 62, 64, 67, 84, 124, 128, 131, 144–5, 152–3, 192, 202–3, 206, 222, 253, 257
Fair Hill, Gortaphuill townland, Co. Roscommon, 95–6, 98, 126–8
Feacle townland, Co. Roscommon, 67
Feadha of Athlone, *see* woodland
Feamore townland, Co. Roscommon, 45
feasting halls, 75, 95, 97, 100–2, 104, 115, 137, 158, 176–178, 229, 243, 252
Feevagh townlands, Co. Roscommon, 48
Fenian Cycle, 7, 125, 127
Fermanagh *crannóga*, 92, 236
feudalism, 78, 82–3, 247
Fiddaun Castle, Co. Galway, 216
field systems, 59, 66, 127, 148–9,
Filidh Éreann Go Haointeach, 31, 65, 75, 86, 170–1, 175, 186–7, 239, 252
Fionngháille [Galey townland], Co. Roscommon, 31, 171–2
fishing and fish resources, 67–8,
Fitton, Edward, 36
Fitz Geoffrey, John, 23, 207
Fitzgerald, Gearóid Mór, earl of Kildare, 36, 196
Fohanagh [parish], Co. Galway, 100
fortified houses, 196–9
Foslongphort, 30, 195, 238
Fossakilly, Co. Sligo, 28
Franciscan order, 31, 71, 131, 148–9, 152, 154–5

Gaelic presence on Anglo-Norman military campaigns, 23, 25–8, 207, 257
Galey, Co. Roscommon, 31, 50, 60, 62, 65, 75, 86, 165, 167–72, 176–9, 184–8, 191–3, 203–4, 239, 242, 246, 249, 251–2, 253, 254, 259
castle, 86–7, 106, 179–84, 250, 261–2
promontory fort, 172–5, 236–7
Gallagh Castle, Co. Galway, 36, 37, 70, 171, 223, 228–30, 231, 249, 259,
Galloglass kindreds, 34, 71, 240, 255, 259
Galway granite, 149
Galway, town of, 3, 4, 36, 69, 231–3
Garbally Castle, Co. Galway, 35, 70, 106, 171n1, 180, 223–9, 230, 231, 233, 249, 259
Garrdha sites, 93
Garrison Island, Co. Mayo, 241
Garrynphort townland, Co. Roscommon, 113, 116, 119–20, 123, 239, 266
Geraldine Anglo-Norman magnates, 28
Glebe townland, Athleague, Co. Roscommon, 194
Glebe townland, Kilconnell, Co. Galway, 130
Glennanea townland, Co. Roscommon, 67
Gortadeegan townland, Co. Galway, 130
Gortnacrannagh townland, Co. Roscommon, 68–9, 241
Gothic architecture, 116
Gráinseach Chairn Bhuaileadh [Grange townland, Athlone barony], Co. Roscommon, 26, 59
Grange of O'Fallon, 66
Grey Friars [Franciscans], 154
Grey, Leonard, 36

hall house castles, 219, 245
harbour features, 53, 92, 113, 139–40, 152, 169–70, 172n2, 191, 253
Hen Domen motte and bailey castle, Powys, Wales, 83
Henry II, king of England, 58
Henry III, king of England, 21, 23, 25, 26, 74, 90, 207, 257
Henry VIII, king of England, 90
Heyny, *oireacht* of the, 32, 168–9, 185, 188
Hillswood townland, Co. Galway, 130
Hind (river), 2, 3, 30, 32, 50, 52, 102, 108, 168
hobelars, 63

Index

horse breeding and trade, 62–4
horizontal watermills, 65, 149
hunting, 67, 70, 100–4, 109, 146n1, 243, 248

Iarchonnacht, Co. Galway, 236, 241
Illaunnamona *crannóg*, Lough Croan, Co. Roscommon, 115–18, 120–3, 235, 239, 251
Imbolc festival, 124
inauguration, 22, 27–8, 55, 68, 73, 148, 191, 250, 257
Inchcleraun Island, Lough Ree, 191
Inchiquin Lough, Co. Clare, 159
Inchnagreeve *crannóg*, Lough Croan, Co. Roscommon, 115
Inchnagower *crannóg*, Lough Croan, Co. Roscommon, 115
Inchnaveague *crannóg*, Lough Croan, Co. Roscommon, 115
Indrechtach mac Muiredaig (d. 723), 12
Inis Locha Caoláin, 16
Inisfarannan [Stony Island *crannóg*], Ballaghdacker Lough, Co. Galway, 154–5, 157–63, 164, 235, 243
Island Mc Hugo, Loughrea Lake, Co. Galway, 91

James I, king of England, 192
jetty/naust features, 53, 135, 136–7, 158, 175, 235, 253
Johannes, sculptor, 72
John, king of England, 21–2

Kells, synod of, 19
Kelly, Capt. Hugh, of 'Bellaghforen', 151
Kellysgrove townland, *see Tuaim Cátraige*
Kern – *ceatharnaigh*, 71, 148
kidnapping, 20, 153
Kilbegly, Co. Roscommon, 43–4, 65
Kilbride [parish], Co. Roscommon, 18
Kilcloony [parish], Co. Galway, 148
Kilcommadan medieval church, Co. Galway, 205–6

Kilconnell, Co. Galway, 3, 4, 25, 31, 32, 34, 53, 65, 101, 129, 130–2, 142, 144–5, 147, 167, 206, 207, 254
    Kilconnell Franciscan Friary, 71–2, 148–52, 163, 251, 262
Kilglass townland, Co. Roscommon, 46
Killaclogher townland, Co. Galway, *see* Clogher
Killaloe, Co. Clare, 78
Killeglan townland, Co. Roscommon, 48, 78
Killeglan Karst Landscape, 48
Killinvoy townland, Co. Roscommon, 36,
Kilmeane townland, Co. Roscommon, 30
Kilmore townlands, Co. Roscommon, 45, 46, 168
Killosolan [parish], Co. Galway, 100
Kilteasheen, Co. Roscommon, 68
King's Cantreds, 22–3, 24, 25, 83–4, 195, 245
Kinsale, battle of (1601–2), 38
Knockadangan townland, Co. Roscommon, 48
Knockalough townland and moated site, Co. Roscommon, 244
Knockaunarainy townland, Co. Galway, 46
Knockcroghery, Co. Roscommon, 3, 51, 171, 171n1, 185, 186, 187, 192, *see also Baile na Gáile*
Knockdoe, battle of (1504), 35–6
Knockroe, Co. Galway, 2, 222

Lackan, Co. Sligo, 97
Le Strange, Thomas, 196
Leabhar Breac, 155, 162, 243
Leabhar Ruadh Muimhneach, 162, 243
Leabhar Ua Maine, 21, 23, 31, 72, 147, 154, 155, 164, 195, 222, 262
Lebor na Cert, 6, 12
Lecarrow, Co. Roscommon, 3
Lecarrowmactully townland, Co. Galway, 130, 148, 240
Leinster Mountains, 28, 257
Leitrim *crannóga*, 92, 137, 183, 236
Liathdruim, Co. Galway, 58
life expectancy, 70

Light Detection and Ranging (LiDAR), 6, 84, 95, 97, 110, 117, 118, 127, 184, 187, 210, 212, 216
lime-washing, 104, 176–7
Lis na Cornairead, Ballynabanaba townland?, Co. Galway, 146
Liscam townland, Co. Roscommon, 65
Liscoffy townland, Co. Roscommon, 103–4, 240
Lisdaulan, Co. Roscommon, 36–7, 64, 65, 205, 232, 233, 259
Lisdillure [*Lissadillure*], Co. Roscommon, 14
Lisdonnellroe townland, Co. Galway, 130, 134, 239, 266
Lisfineel Fort, Lisdonnellroe townland, Co. Galway, 146, 240, 266
Lismore moated site, *see* Pallas townland
Lisnacourty Fort, Lisdonnellroe townland, Co. Galway, 134–5, 239
Lisnagavragh townland and ringfort, Co. Roscommon, 109–11, 115, 239, 266
Lisnagirra townland, Co. Roscommon, 46
Lisnagry Fort, Callow Lough, Co. Galway, 134–5, 138, 239, 254, 266
Lisseenamanragh townland, Co. Roscommon, 59
Lissyegan townlands, Co. Galway, 162, 240
Liswilliam townland and ringfort, Co. Roscommon, 112–13, 239, 266
Loch an Chléirigh Mór, *see* Hillswood
Loch an Dúin [Sally Island *crannóg*], Ballaghdacker Lough, Co. Galway, 31, 154–6, 160–1, 163–4, 196, 235, 239
Loch Cairgín [Ardakillin Lough], Co. Roscommon, 78, 162, 235, 241
Loch na Craoibhe [Stewartstown Lough, Co. Tyrone], 163
Loch na nÉigeas, *see* Lough Ree
Longnamuck townland, Co. Roscommon, 172, 191
longphort sites, 25, 86, 89, 98, 218
lordly residences, *see* cenn áit
Lough Acalla, *see* Callow Lough
Lough Allen, 53

Lough Cé [Lough Key], Co. Roscommon, 68, 78, 137, 159, 183, 235, 241, 244, 253, 259
Lough Corrib, 78, 219, 241
Lough Croan, 3, 16, 26, 33, 36, 50, 51, 58–60, 62, 92, 96, 98, 102, 104, 108–29, 145, 162, 164, 167, 184, 188, 193, 235, 239, 242, 243, 249, 250, 252, 254, 260, 266
Lough Cullen, 241
Lough Derg, 53, 266
Lough Funshinagh, 3, 50
Lough Gara, 92, 236
Lough Kelly [Callow Lough], 132–3
Lough Loung, 53–4
Lough Mask, 78, 241
Lough Meelagh, 173, 236
Lough Melvin, 137, 183
Lough Ree, 3, 45, 50, 52–3, 58, 67, 167–72, 171–2, 171n1, 174, 177, 178, 181, 185, 188, 191, 204, 217
Lough Skannive, 241
Loughaclerybeg townland, Co. Galway, 130
Loughaunbrean townland, Co. Galway, 131
Loughbown I, Co. Galway, 58, 62, 65, 67, 68, 89, 91, 164, 209, 239, 241
Loughbown II, Co. Galway, 89, 91
Loughrea, Co. Galway, 52, 69, 232
Loughrea Lake, 91, 108
Lughnasa festival, 124, 144, 190, 222

Mac an Bhaird/Clann an Bhaird [Mac Ward], 31, 147, 220, 231, 240, 259
Mac an Bhaird, Maurice (d. 1408), 220
Mac Aodhagáin/Clann Aedhagáin [Mac Egan] brehons, 60, 148, 162, 191, 240
Mac Aodhagáin, Giolla na Naomh, 60, 191
Mac Branain, Conn, 27
Mac Céile [McHale] lineage, 148
Mac Diarmada [MacDermott] lordship, 8, 14, 31, 68, 153, 173, 183, 186, 235, 243, 251, 253, 257, 259
Mac Diarmada, Maol Ruanaidh, 31, 153
Mac Domhnaill [Mac Donnell] lordship/military kindred, 173, 255

Mac Dubhghaill/Clann Dubhghaill [Mac Dowell], 34, 240, 255, 259
Mac Eochadha [Mac Keogh], 98n2, 106, 180, 245, 247, 259
Mac Firbhisigh [Forbes] lineage, 97
Mac Jordan d'Exeter, 257
Mac Líacc, Muirchertach, 165
Mac Lochlainn, Niall mac Muirchertach, king of Ulster, 20
Mac Maghnusa [Mac Manus] lordship, 236
Mac Mathghamhna, Rudhraighe, 93,
Mac Maoltuile/Ó Maoltuile [Mac Tully], 130, 148, 240
Mac Uilliam *Íochtar* de Burgh [Mayo lordship], 29–30, 32, 35
Mac Uilliam *Uachtar* de Burgh [Clann Ricaird lordship], 29, 32, 34–6, 38, 131, 217, 223
MacClancy lordship, 183
Machaire Connacht/*Magh nAí* [broadly cantred of Moyhee], 3, 12, 16, 18, 23, 30, 50, 52, 92, 98, 108, 148, 170, 191, 243, 244, 264
Máel Dúin, bishop of Aughrim, 206
Máel Sechlainn Mór, king of Mide, 14–15
Mag Seóla, Co. Galway, 236
Mag Srúibe Gealáin [Roo townland], Co. Roscommon, 20
Magh Finn, *tuath* of, Co. Roscommon, 16, 48, 67, 98n2, 106, 245, 247, 259
Magh Rúscach [Rooskagh townland], Co. Roscommon, 24
Magh Seincheineoil, 12
Magnetic Gradiometry surveying, 6, 211, 214, 215
Magnetic Susceptibility surveying, 6, 118, 119, 122
Maguire lords of Fir Manach, 94
Maigh Luirg [broadly cantred of Moylurg], 8, 23, 31, 68–9, 92, 153, 173, 235, 243, 244
Maine Mór mac Eochaidh Ferdaghiall, 12
maor Ua Maine, 18
McConnor, Colloo, 170
McWarde, Hugh, 147

medical kindreds, 70, 148
Menlough, Co. Galway, 53, 217
metalworking and smithing, 66, 89, 119, 131, 149, 252
mills and milling, 26, 65, 112, 149, 198–9, 233
moated sites, 75, 82, 86, 94–101, 106, 127, 151, 157–9, 164, 171–2, 218, 234, 241–4, 245–6, 248, 252–3, 264
Moher Lake, 241
Monaghan *crannóga*, 162
Monambraher townland, Co. Galway, 130
Monasternalea/Abbeygrey [*Kilmore-ne-togher?*], Co. Galway, 154
Monivea Castle, Co. Galway, 35, 70, 106, 171n1, 223–4, 231, 249, 259
Mote Demesne and Park, Co. Roscommon, 187, 259
motte castles, 78–9, 81–2, 166, 230, 245–6
motte and bailey castles, 166, 245
Mount Talbot, Co. Galway, 38, 53, 67, 194
Mountbellew, Co. Galway, 194
Moydow Hill, Co. Roscommon, 2
Moylough Castle, Co. Galway, 219
Moylurg, *see* Maigh Luirg
Mullaghmore Castle, Co. Galway, 223, 228, 231, 259
Múscraige Tíre, Co. Tipperary, 19

Na Trí Túatha [broadly cantred of Trithweth], 18, 23, 27, 92
natural island settlements, 17, 91, 113, 115, 117, 119–21, 123, 183, 234–6, 241–2, 248, 252
Newbridge, Co. Galway, 53, 194
Nine Years War (1593–1603), 37–8
Nósa Ua Maine, 6, 13, 14, 63, 72, 98, 99, 124, 131, 145–6, 162, 262

Ó Briain [O'Brien] lordship, 28
Ó Cellaig [O'Kelly] lordship (throughout)
  religious patronage, 31, 71–5, 149, 151, 220–2, 231, 233–4, 251
Ó Cellaig, Áed* (d. 1134), 17
Ó Cellaig, Áed (d. early 14th century), 29

Ó Cellaig, Aodh (d. 1467), 35
Ó Cellaig, Aodh* (d. 1590), 36–7, 168, 170, 181, 232, 249
Ó Cellaig, Brian (d. 1393), 35
Ó Cellaig, Brian Óg of *Cluain na gCloidhe*, 38
Ó Cellaig, Ceallach*, 36, 207
Ó Cellaig, Conchobar* (d. 1130), 19
Ó Cellaig, Conchobar* (d. 1180), 17, 20
Ó Cellaig, Conchobar* (d. 1268), 24–6, 98, 207
Ó Cellaig, Conchobar* (d. 1318), 28
Ó Cellaig, Conchobar Anabaidh* (d. 1403), 33, 74, 122, 188
Ó Cellaig, Conor *na gCearrbhach* of Gallagh, 37
Ó Cellaig, Diarmaid* (d. *c.*1349), 31, 217
Ó Cellaig, Domhnall mac Aodh *na gCailleach*, 36
Ó Cellaig, Domnall Mór* (d. 1224), 21, 23–5, 38, 131, 135, 207
Ó Cellaig, Domnall* (d. 1295), 27
Ó Cellaig, Donatus, 72
Ó Cellaig, Donnchad* (d. 1074), 16
Ó Cellaig, Donnchad Muimnech* (d. 1307), 27, 151, 162, 248, 257
Ó Cellaig, Donnchadh mac Áed, 30
Ó Cellaig, Donnchadh* (d. 1424), 31–2, 34–5, 196, 218–9,
Ó Cellaig, Donnchadh* (d. *c.*1557), 36, 111, 114
Ó Cellag, Éamonn, 114
Ó Cellaig, Eoghan, 23
Ó Cellaig, Feardorcha* (d. post-1611), 37, 132, 150, 207
Ó Cellaig, Gilbert* (d. 1322), 27–9, 31, 217
Ó Cellaig, Lochlainn, 24
Ó Cellaig, Maine* (d. 1268), 26
Ó Cellaig, Maolsechlainn* (d. 1401), 31–34, 35, 65, 70, 74, 131, 170, 195, 218, 220, 222, 249, 257
Ó Cellaig, Maolsechlainn 'mac an Abba', 36
Ó Cellaig, Maolsechlainn mac Aodh* (d. 1511), 35–6, 70, 223–4, 230, 249

note: * = a King of Uí Maine.

Ó Cellaig, Maolsechlainn mac Tadhg*, 35, 196
Ó Cellaig, Maolsechlainn mac Uilliam Ruadh (d. 1464), 72, 131, 142, 151
Ó Cellaig, Murchad*, 14
Ó Cellaig, Odo (Aodh), 72
Ó Cellaig, Ruaidhrí* (d. 1339), 29–30
Ó Cellaig, Shane *na Maighe* of Clonmacnowen, 37, 94
Ó Cellaig, Tadg* (d. 1316), 27–8, 30, 166
Ó Cellaig, Tadg Mór* (d. 1014), 14–15, 165
Ó Cellaig, Tadhg Fionn, 24
Ó Cellaig, Tadhg mac William of Mullaghmore, 36, 37, 223
Ó Cellaig, Tadhg Óg* (d. 1340), 30–1
Ó Cellaig, Tadhg Ruadh* (d. 1410), 34, 131
Ó Cellaig Tadhg Tailltenn (d. 1180), 20, 257
Ó Cellaig, Teige McOwen, 170
Ó Cellaig, Uilliam Buide* (d. 1381), 30–2, 34, 58, 70, 71, 75, 86, 100, 104, 112, 122, 131, 152, 164, 167, 170, 171n1, 217, 218, 248, 249, 251, 252, 257–8
Ó Cellaig, Uilliam Ruadh* (d. 1420), 32, 34, 72, 131, 150
Ó Cobhtaigh [O'Coffey] poets, 103–4, 240
Ó Conchobair [O'Conor] lordship, 8, 12, 18–21, 24, 26, 28, 30–1, 38, 52, 74, 111, 145, 148, 162, 170, 196, 217, 235, 259
Ó Conchobair Donn lordship, 34, 259
Ó Conchobair Ruadh lordship, 34, 183, 259
Ó Conchobair, Áed mac Domnaill, 19
Ó Conchobair, Áed mac Feidlim (d. 1274), 27, 98
Ó Conchobair, Áed mac Eoghan (d. 1309), 94
Ó Conchobair, Áed (d. 1356), 31, 153
Ó Conchobair, Aedh (d. 1228), 22, 245
Ó Conchobair, Cathal, 30
Ó Conchobair, Cathal Carrach, 21
Ó Conchobair, Cathal Crobhdearg (d. 1224), 21–2, 73, 125, 148, 217
Ó Conchobair, Conchobar (d. 1144), 19
Ó Conchobair, Conchobar Maenmaige, 20
Ó Conchobair, Feidlim (d. 1265), 23, 25, 27
Ó Conchobair, Fedlimid (d. 1316), 28
Ó Conchobair, Máel Sechlainn [Milo], 189

Ó Conchobair, Ruaidrí, high-king (d. 1198), 19, 58, 169–70, 178, 257
Ó Conchobair, Ruaidrí (d. 1316), 28
Ó Conchobair, Toirrdelbach, (d. 1350), 30, 62, 195, 238
Ó Conchobair, Toirrdelbach Mór, high-king (d. 1156), 18–9, 52, 53–4, 77, 79, 165, 167
Ó Conchobair *Sligigh*, 111
Ó Cuindlis [Candless] learned kindred, 155, 162–4, 235, 243, 249
Ó Cuindlis, Cornelius, 162
Ó Cuindlis, Murchad, 155, 162
Ó Dálaigh, Gofraidh Fionn, 170, 176
Ó Doibhlin [Devlin] lineage, 163
Ó Donnagáin [O'Donegan] lineage, 172
Ó Drisceoil [O'Driscoll] lordship, 184
Ó Dubhagáin [O'Duggan] poet historians, 39, 103, 124–5, 130, 145–6, 240
    O'Dugan, Donell, 146
    Maghnus? *Cam Cluana*, 145
    Marianus, 125
    Risteard, 125
    Seán Mór, 10, 74, 125, 145, 166, 188, 251
Ó Dubhda [O'Dowd] lordship, 172–3, 209
Ó Duibgeannáin [O'Duignan], 173
Ó Eadhra [O'Hara] lordship, 219
Ó Fallamháin [O'Fallon], 18, 64, 66, 98, 111, 117, 123, 169, 180, 243
Ó Fallamháin, Ferchar (d. 1169), 18
Ó Flaithbheartaigh [O'Flaherty] lordship, 172, 236, 241
Ó hAnainn, Mael Isa, 195
Ó hEidin, Maél Ruanaid, 15
Ó Huidhrín, Giolla-Na-Naomh, 10
Ó Longorgáin [Longergan], harpers, 146, 240
Ó Madadháin [O'Madden] lordship, 11, 16, 19, 20, 32
Ó Máel Sechlainn, Donnchad, king of Mide, 98–9
Ó Máelbrigde, 98n2
Ó Máelalaid [O'Mullally], 14, 19, 146
Ó Máelruanaid/Muintir Máelruanaid [O'Mulrooney], 13, 18

Ó Máille [O'Malley] lordship, 172, 241
Ó Mainnin [O'Mannion] lordship, 21, 31, 98, 106, 150, 217, 231, 259
Ó Muiredaig [O'Murray/O'Murry], 33, 168–9
Ó Nechtain [O'Naughton], 13, 19, 247
Ó Néill [O'Neill] lords of Tír Eoghain, 249, 254–5
Ó Neill, Aodh Mór (d. 1364), 186
Ó Neill, Aodh [*Ó Néill Mór*], baron of Dungannon, earl of Tyrone (d. 1616), 61, 153
Ó Shideacháin, horn-players, 146, 240
Ó Súilleabháin Bhéara [O'Sullivan Beare] lordship, 49, 110, 172
O'Donnell, Red Hugh, 37, 38
O'Heyne lordship, 183
O'Kelly, Colla of Skrine, 38, 192
O'Kelly, Edmund mc Brene, 99
O'Kelly, Egnaham McDonell, 100
O'Kelly, Melaghlin, 218
O'Kelly, Tege McMelaghlin, 130
O'Kelly, Roger of Aghrane, 38
O'Kelly, William of Callowgh, 132
Observant Reform movement, 72, 151, 162
Óenach [*aonach*/*oireachtas*] assemblies, 54–6, 58, 61–2, 112, 126–9, 131, 144–5, 188–92
Óenach Maénmaige, battle of, 19, 21
ogee-headed windows, 146, 227, 229, 232, 258
Oireachtaí – eraghts [late-medieval territorial unit], 32–3, 108, 123, 129–30, 153–4, 168–9, 185, 193, 205, 217
Oireachtas gatherings, *see óenach*
Oirghialla, *see* Airgíalla
Omany, cantred of, 23, 30, 37, 83–84, 207, 243, 245–6, *see also* Uí Maine
Onagh Castle, 24, 84–5, 246
Ormond, earl of, 37
'Oscalli', 26, *see also* Ó Cellaig

pailís sites, 97, 100–1, 103–4, 107, 163, 243
Pallas townland and moated site, Fohanagh parish, Co. Galway, 94, 96, 100–4, 130, 171–2, 243

Park townlands, Clonbern parish, Co. Galway, 162
Park moated site, Killallaghtan parish, Co. Galway, 243, 245–6
pastoral agriculture, 56–62
    cattle raiding, 18–19, 27, 57–8, 93, 202, 231, 238
    cattle trade and markets, 61–2
    native cattle breeds, 56–7, 58
    resources from cattle, 56–8, 60, 62, 70
    sheep, 62
    size of cattle herds, 61
    transhumance, 57
'pedigree of place', 250
peripatetic lordly lifestyle, 249
Pinnocke, Michael, 111
plashing, 52
Poddle (river), 62,
Pollalaher townland, Co. Roscommon, 60
Pope Nicholas V, 162
population estimates, 70
Portrunny Bay, Co. Roscommon, 188–92
praise poetry, 7, 15, 31, 54, 65, 72, 86, 93, 94, 104, 166, 170, 195, 249, 250
prehistoric burial mounds, 12, 26, 98, 191, 250
promontory forts, 138–41, 144, 152, 172–5, 184, 202, 204, 236–7, 239, 242, 246, 248, 261, 264, 266
punch-dressed stone, 112, 141, 143, 180, 197, 199, 232, 258

ráth, *see* ringfort
Rath Breasail, synod of, 19
Rathconrath barony, Co. Westmeath, 103
Rathcroghan, Co. Roscommon, 12
Reed's Island, Loughrea Lake, Co. Galway, 91
Registry of Clonmacnoise, 24, 125
religious items, commissioned, 150–1
Renaissance, 196, 262
Richards, Lieutenant Colonel Jacob, 211–15
Ríglongphort, 242
Rindoon, Co. Roscommon, 6, 46, 53, 66, 69, 84, 85, 93, 135, 169–70, 177, 178, 188, 195, 216, 245, 253
    castle, 6, 46, 66, 84, 85, 188, 195, 216, 245, 253
    the Hospital of Crutched Friars, 9, 33, 71, 73, 74, 188, 251, 253, 262
ringforts, 26, 35, 58, 68, 78, 81, 83, 85–6, 88–91, 98–100, 103, 110, 112–3, 115, 120, 125, 127, 134, 146–7, 155, 157, 161, 164, 166, 176, 183, 194, 209, 218, 234, 238–42, 246–7, 248, 254, 264, 266
    bivallate, 85, 88, 89, 127, 134–5, 174
    quadrivallate, 240
    raised ringfort, 79, 81, 88, 246
    trivallate, 88, 240, 246
    univallate, 26, 88, 90, 98, 146, 147, 155, 239
ringwork castles, 81–2, 85, 172, 245–6
Rock of Lough Cé, Co. Roscommon, 68, 78, 159, 183, 235, 241, 244, 259
Rockingham Demesne, Co. Roscommon, 68, 86, 241, 244, 253
Roscommon,
    castle, 34, 66, 84, 85, 195, 216
    diocese of, 19–20
    English of, 27
    town, 2, 51, 52, 66, 69, 115, 167, 170

Safe Harbour, Rindoon, 53
Sally Island *crannóg*, *see* Loch an Dúin
Samhain festival, 15, 165, 190
Samhoin so, sodham go Tadg, 15, 165
Santiago de Compostela, 149
Scotland, 25, 26, 34, 170 207, 251, 257
Scregg townland, Co. Roscommon, 46, 180
Shannon (river), 3, 11, 17, 22, 46, 50, 52–4, 62, 67, 80, 83, 165–7, 170, 180, 191, 217, 244–5, 263
Shannonbridge, Co. Offaly, 3, 67
sheep and derived products, *see* pastoral agriculture
Shiven (river), 3, 194
Shrule Castle, Co. Mayo, 36, 219
Sidney, Henry, 223
Síl Anmchadha, 11, 16, 19, 20, 36
Síl Crimtaind Cáeil, 13,
Síl Muiredaig, 12, 13, 18, 117, 189, 243

Síol Ceallaigh Cladaigh, 24
Skeanamuck townland, Co. Roscommon, 67
Slighe Assail, 50–1
Slighe Mhór [*Eiscir Riada*], 50, 52, 131, 145, 148, 152, 206, 245
Sligo Castle, 111, 215
Sliocht Lochlainn, 24
Sochar Mic Diarmada agus a cloinne, 170
Soghan/Soghain, 12, 16, 19, 21, 31, 38, 91, 106, 129, 150, 162, 216–17, 257, 259
soil quality and agriculture, 40–2, 60, 65, 109
souterrains, 89, 90, 112–3
'Southern Route', 52, 206
St Bernard of Clairvaux, 222
St Brigid, 124
St Comadán, 205–6
St Conall of Drumcliff, 130
St Conainne, 130
St Diarmuid of Inchcleraun, 191
St Enda, 125
St Grellan, 12
St James, 144, 149
St John the Evangelist Church, Ballinasloe, Co. Galway, 80
St Kerrill, 144
St Maonagán of Athleague, 194–5
St Michael's Catholic Church, Ballinasloe, Co. Galway, 80
St Patrick, 125, 128
Stony Island *crannóg*, see Inisfarannan
Strokestown, Co. Roscommon, 18, 20, 259
Suck (river), 2, 3, 12, 23, 24, 35, 41, 47, 49, 50–4, 67, 80, 82–3, 130, 193–4, 196, 198–200, 206, 231, 240, 263, 266
    Suck Callows, 3, 50, 194
Suthkyn, see *Áth Nadsluaigh*, Ballinasloe, *Caislen Suicin*

Taghboy [parish], Co. Roscommon, 3, 33, 108, 123, 194
tanning and leather production, 46, 58, 60, 62, 66, 70, 131, 191
Táth aoinfhir ar iath Maineach, 54, 58, 75, 104, 122, 252

Taughmaconnell [parish], Co. Roscommon, 12, 16, 48, 51, 78, 98n2
Temple House Castle, Co. Sligo, 219
Temple Kelly, 17–18
Thomond, 28
Thomond, earl of, 37
Tiaquin [*Tigh Da Choinne*], Co. Galway, 32, 34, 53, 74, 218–20, 230, 231, 249, 259
Tibarny townland, Co. Roscommon, 51
Tír Ailello [broadly Tyrelele], 23
Tír Briúin na Sinna, *tuath* of, 18
Tír Fhiachrach [broadly cantred of Tyryethrachmoye], Co. Sligo, 97
Tír Fhiachrach bhfeadh [*Tirieghrachbothe*], see *Feadha* of Athlone
Tír Maine [broadly cantred of Tyrmany], 3, 11–12, 15–21, 23–7, 29–30, 32, 36, 38, 45, 50, 52, 55, 62, 66, 74, 88, 96, 98–102, 108–9, 117, 121, 124–5, 128, 145, 153, 161–2, 168–70, 179, 188–91, 193, 195, 216–17, 222, 236, 243–4
Tisrara – *Tigh Srathra* [parish and medieval church], Carrowntemple townland, Co. Roscommon, 3, 33, 100, 108, 124–5, 194
Tochar-choille-an-chairn [Togher and Culligharny townlands], Co. Roscommon, 50–1
tóchair [wooden causeways], 50, 51–2
tombs, decorated, 71, 74, 149–51, 220, 222, 250, 262,
tower house castles, 34, 65, 86–8, 93, 104–7, 111–12, 114–15, 141–4, 146, 152–3, 164, 168, 172, 176–7, 179–84, 186, 197, 204, 216, 218–19, 222–33, 234, 237, 244–6, 249–50, 254, 256, 258–62, 264–5, 267
    tower house door, 111, 219, 224, 227
trade, 52–3, 55, 58–9, 62–3, 66–7, 68–70, 109, 164, 167, 180, 191, 204, 209, 231, 252, 257
Triallam timcheall na Fodla, 10
Trícha cét, [definition], 11
Trícha Máenmaige [broadly cantred of Monewagh], 12, 14, 16, 19, 28

Trinity Island, Co. Roscommon, 68
Trithweth, *see Na Trí Túath*
Tuahavriana, *see Túath an Bhrenaidh*
Tuaim Cátraige [Kellysgrove townland], Co. Galway, 103
Tuaim Sruthra [Ashford townland], Co. Roscommon, 24, 266
Tuam, (arch)diocese of, 19, 74, 162
Túath an Bhrenaidh, Co. Galway, 205–6
Túath Átha Liaig, Co. Roscommon, 108, 123, 153–4, 193
Túath Caladh, Co. Galway, 129–31, 144
Tullyneeny townland, Co. Roscommon, 58, 112, 126–9
Tulsk, Co. Roscommon, 51
Tulsk Fort, Co. Roscommon, 183, 259
turf for fuel, 42
turloughs, 3, 26, 49–50, 52, 57, 108–9, 115, 117–18, 138, 157, 172,
Turrock House, Co. Roscommon, 110, 112, 114
Turrock townland and Castle, Co. Roscommon, 36, 110–2, 114–15, 119, 151, 164, 184, 259–60
Tyrmany, cantred of, 23–4, 26, 83, 195, 243, 245–6, *see also* Tír Maine

Uasal an síol Síol Ceallaigh, 166
Uí Briúin early medieval Connacht dynasty, 12
Uí Briúin Aí, 12, 13
Uí Chathail [Cahill], 13
Uí Fiachrach early medieval Connacht dynasty, 12
Uí Fhiachrach Aidne, 14–15
Uí Fhiachrach Muaidhe, 173, 209
Uí Maine [cantred of Omany] (throughout)
    Airthir Uí Maine, 35
    Early medieval history, 11–6
    Iarthair Uí Maine, 35
Uí Mhugróin [O'Moran?], 13

Vita tripartita Sancti Patricii, 125

War of the Two Kings, 211
wealth and its expression, 68–76
Wexford tower houses, 181
woodland, 42–9, 51, 57, 66, 102–3, 194, 238,
    Feadha [Faes] of Athlone, 14, 19, 30, 43–6, 47, 49, 51, 66, 169, 247
    woods of Athleague, 43, 45, 46, 49, 103, 194
    woods of *Bruigheol*, 43, 45, 48–9, 51
woodland resources, 66–7